# Upgrading and Fixing Macs and iMacs™ For Dummies™

CW00392633

## Keystrokes for a Freeze

When your Mac appears frozen, wait at least five to ten minutes before pressing any keys on the keyboard. You can, however, try to move the mouse; if the pointer moves, your Mac might be hung, not frozen. (See Chapter 20.) After the wait is over, try the following keystrokes, in order, until one works:

| Press . . . | In an Attempt to . . |
|---|---|
| Esc | Cancel the last command and continue working. |
| ⌘+. (Period) | Cancel the currently running task and continue working. |
| ⌘+S | Save your work and continue working. |
| ⌘+Q | Quit the program. In the Finder, attempt to restart or shut down immediately. |
| ⌘+Option+Esc | Perform a Force Quit. If a dialog box appears, click the Force Quit button. If the Finder appears, attempt to restart or shut down immediately |
| ⌘+Power | Force a quit to the Finder. If a dialog box appears, type **G F** and press Return. If the Finder appears, attempt to restart or shut down immediately. |
| Control+⌘+Power | Soft reset the Mac. You'll likely lose data, but it's the only option after a freeze. |
| Reset key or button | Hard reset the Mac. You'll likely lose data, but it's the only option if soft reset won't work. |

## Web Sites for Mac Parts

Here's a quick list of vendors that carry harder-to-find Mac parts and upgrades for older Macs.

| | | |
|---|---|---|
| MilagroMac | Logic boards, processor upgrades, replacement drives, power supplies, and networking | www.milagromac.com |
| MicroMac | Logic boards, processor upgrades, cache RAM, video upgrades, and reconditioned systems | www.micromac.com |
| Shreve Systems | Logic boards, processor upgrades, replacement drives, reconditioned systems, PCI and NuBus cards, and refurbished peripherals | www.shrevesystems.com |
| Pre-Owned Electronics | Processors, refurbish systems, peripherals, drives, and input devices | www.preowned.com |
| PowerOn | Processor cards, refurbished Macs, replacement drives, refurbished peripherals, PCI and NuBus cards, and mounting kits | www.poweron.com |
| MacResQ | Logic boards, refurbished Macs, replacements drives, refurbished peripherals, PCI and NuBus cards, communications slot cards, mounting kits, and bezels | www.macresq.com |
| MacWorks | Processor cards, power supplies, replacement drives, NuBus cards, communications slot cards, and mounting kits | www.macworks.com |
| Proline | Mounting kits and bezels (for internal and removable drives) | www.proline.com |

For Dummies®: Bestselling Book Series for Beginners

# Upgrading and Fixing Macs® and iMacs™ For Dummies®

Cheat Sheet

## Startup Commands

You may use a number of different keys and keyboard combinations to alter the way your Mac or iMac behaves as it starts up. These can be useful for troubleshooting and testing.

| Hold Down . . . | For This Duration | To . . . |
| --- | --- | --- |
| Shift | From the startup tone until the Welcome to Macintosh screen | Start up without extensions |
| ⌘+Option | Any time during the "parade of icons" startup (or as you insert a removable disk) until you see the Rebuild Desktop dialog box | Rebuild the desktop database file |
| Space | From the startup tone (or soon after it) until Extensions Manager appears | Change extension sets (or alter loading extensions) before the startup process begins |
| C | From the startup tone until the Welcome to Macintosh screen | Start up from internal CD-ROM (or DVD) drive |
| Option ("colorful" Macs only) | From the startup tone until the Startup Manager appears | Change the startup volume graphically |
| ⌘+Option+P+R | From the startup tone until the startup tone repeats at least twice | Zap PRAM |
| ⌘+Option+ Shift+Delete | From the startup tone until the Welcome to Macintosh screen | Skip the default startup disk |
| ⌘+Option+Shift+ Delete+*number key* | From the startup tone until the Welcome to Macintosh screen | Start up from the disk at the specified SCSI ID number |
| Mouse button (floppy-based Macs) | From the startup tone until the diskette ejects | Eject diskette at startup |
| Mouse button (slot-loading iMacs) | From the startup tone until the disc ejects | Eject disc at startup |

## Web Sites for Troubleshooting

| | |
| --- | --- |
| Apple Support | http://www.apple.com/support/ |
| Apple Software Updates | http://asu.info.apple.com/ |
| Apple Tech Info Library | http://til.info.apple.com/ |
| MacFixIt | http://www.macfixit.com/ |
| MacInTouch | http://www.macintouch.com |
| Mac-Upgrade (my site) | http://www.mac-upgrade.com/ |

For Dummies®: Bestselling Book Series for Beginners

TM

# BESTSELLING BOOK SERIES

## *References for the Rest of Us!*®

Are you intimidated and confused by computers? Do you find that traditional manuals are overloaded with technical details you'll never use? Do your friends and family always call you to fix simple problems on their PCs? Then the *...For Dummies*® computer book series from IDG Books Worldwide is for you.

*...For Dummies* books are written for those frustrated computer users who know they aren't really dumb but find that PC hardware, software, and indeed the unique vocabulary of computing make them feel helpless. *...For Dummies* books use a lighthearted approach, a down-to-earth style, and even cartoons and humorous icons to dispel computer novices' fears and build their confidence. Lighthearted but not lightweight, these books are a perfect survival guide for anyone forced to use a computer.

*"I like my copy so much I told friends; now they bought copies."*

— Irene C., Orwell, Ohio

*"Quick, concise, nontechnical, and humorous."*

— Jay A., Elburn, Illinois

*"Thanks, I needed this book. Now I can sleep at night."*

— Robin F., British Columbia, Canada

Already, millions of satisfied readers agree. They have made *...For Dummies* books the #1 introductory level computer book series and have written asking for more. So, if you're looking for the most fun and easy way to learn about computers, look to *...For Dummies* books to give you a helping hand.

1/99

# Upgrading & Fixing Macs® & iMacs™ FOR DUMMIES®

## by Todd Stauffer

IDG Books Worldwide, Inc.
An International Data Group Company

Foster City, CA ◆ Chicago, IL ◆ Indianapolis, IN ◆ New York, NY

**Upgrading & Fixing Macs® & iMacs™ For Dummies®**

Published by
**IDG Books Worldwide, Inc.**
An International Data Group Company
919 E. Hillsdale Blvd.
Suite 400
Foster City, CA 94404
www.idgbooks.com (IDG Books Worldwide Web site)
www.dummies.com (Dummies Press Web site)

Library of Congress Catalog Card No.: 99-69386

ISBN: 0-7645-0644-7

Printed in the United States of America

10 9 8 7 6 5 4 3 2 1

1B/RS/QU/QQ/IN

Distributed in the United States by IDG Books Worldwide, Inc.

Distributed by CDG Books Canada Inc. for Canada; by Transworld Publishers Limited in the United Kingdom; by IDG Norge Books for Norway; by IDG Sweden Books for Sweden; by IDG Books Australia Publishing Corporation Pty. Ltd. for Australia and New Zealand; by TransQuest Publishers Pte Ltd. for Singapore, Malaysia, Thailand, Indonesia, and Hong Kong; by Gotop Information Inc. for Taiwan; by ICG Muse, Inc. for Japan; by Intersoft for South Africa; by Eyrolles for France; by International Thomson Publishing for Germany, Austria and Switzerland; by Distribuidora Cuspide for Argentina; by LR International for Brazil; by Galileo Libros for Chile; by Ediciones ZETA S.C.R. Ltda. for Peru; by WS Computer Publishing Corporation, Inc., for the Philippines; by Contemporanea de Ediciones for Venezuela; by Express Computer Distributors for the Caribbean and West Indies; by Micronesia Media Distributor, Inc. for Micronesia; by Chips Computadoras S.A. de C.V. for Mexico; by Editorial Norma de Panama S.A. for Panama; by American Bookshops for Finland.

For general information on IDG Books Worldwide's books in the U.S., please call our Consumer Customer Service department at 800-762-2974. For reseller information, including discounts and premium sales, please call our Reseller Customer Service department at 800-434-3422.

For information on where to purchase IDG Books Worldwide's books outside the U.S., please contact our International Sales department at 317-596-5530 or fax 317-572-4002.

For consumer information on foreign language translations, please contact our Customer Service department at 1-800-434-3422, fax 317-572-4002, or e-mail rights@idgbooks.com.

For information on licensing foreign or domestic rights, please phone +1-650-653-7098.

For sales inquiries and special prices for bulk quantities, please contact our Order Services department at 800-434-3422 or write to the address above.

For information on using IDG Books Worldwide's books in the classroom or for ordering examination copies, please contact our Educational Sales department at 800-434-2086 or fax 317-572-4005.

For press review copies, author interviews, or other publicity information, please contact our Public Relations department at 650-653-7000 or fax 650-653-7500.

For authorization to photocopy items for corporate, personal, or educational use, please contact Copyright Clearance Center, 222 Rosewood Drive, Danvers, MA 01923, or fax 978-750-4470.

is a registered trademark under exclusive license to IDG Books Worldwide, Inc. from International Data Group, Inc.

# About the Author

**Todd Stauffer** is the author or co-author of more than twenty computer books, including *Macworld Mac Upgrade and Repair Bible*, *How to Do Everything with Your iMac,* and *Macworld Mac OS 9 Bible* (with Lon Poole). Todd is also the writer and co-host of Disk Doctors, an Emmy-awarded, nationally televised call-in show on computer upgrading and troubleshooting.

Todd is a contributing editor for MacCentral.com and publisher of Mac-Upgrade.com. He's written for MacAddict, Mac Home, MacTech, CMP Techweb, Publish magazine, and others. He'd give it all up in a heartbeat if Steven Spielberg or Ron Howard told him to come make coffee for their production meetings.

# ABOUT IDG BOOKS WORLDWIDE

Welcome to the world of IDG Books Worldwide.

IDG Books Worldwide, Inc., is a subsidiary of International Data Group, the world's largest publisher of computer-related information and the leading global provider of information services on information technology. IDG was founded more than 30 years ago by Patrick J. McGovern and now employs more than 9,000 people worldwide. IDG publishes more than 290 computer publications in over 75 countries. More than 90 million people read one or more IDG publications each month.

Launched in 1990, IDG Books Worldwide is today the #1 publisher of best-selling computer books in the United States. We are proud to have received eight awards from the Computer Press Association in recognition of editorial excellence and three from Computer Currents' First Annual Readers' Choice Awards. Our best-selling ...For Dummies® series has more than 50 million copies in print with translations in 31 languages. IDG Books Worldwide, through a joint venture with IDG's Hi-Tech Beijing, became the first U.S. publisher to publish a computer book in the People's Republic of China. In record time, IDG Books Worldwide has become the first choice for millions of readers around the world who want to learn how to better manage their businesses.

Our mission is simple: Every one of our books is designed to bring extra value and skill-building instructions to the reader. Our books are written by experts who understand and care about our readers. The knowledge base of our editorial staff comes from years of experience in publishing, education, and journalism — experience we use to produce books to carry us into the new millennium. In short, we care about books, so we attract the best people. We devote special attention to details such as audience, interior design, use of icons, and illustrations. And because we use an efficient process of authoring, editing, and desktop publishing our books electronically, we can spend more time ensuring superior content and less time on the technicalities of making books.

You can count on our commitment to deliver high-quality books at competitive prices on topics you want to read about. At IDG Books Worldwide, we continue in the IDG tradition of delivering quality for more than 30 years. You'll find no better book on a subject than one from IDG Books Worldwide.

John Kilcullen
Chairman and CEO
IDG Books Worldwide, Inc.

*Eighth Annual Computer Press Awards ≥ 1992*

*Ninth Annual Computer Press Awards ≥ 1993*

*Tenth Annual Computer Press Awards ≥ 1994*

*Eleventh Annual Computer Press Awards ≥ 1995*

IDG is the world's leading IT media, research and exposition company. Founded in 1964, IDG had 1997 revenues of $2.05 billion and has more than 9,000 employees worldwide. IDG offers the widest range of media options that reach IT buyers in 75 countries representing 95% of worldwide IT spending. IDG's diverse product and services portfolio spans six key areas including print publishing, online publishing, expositions and conferences, market research, education and training, and global marketing services. More than 90 million people read one or more of IDG's 290 magazines and newspapers, including IDG's leading global brands — Computerworld, PC World, Network World, Macworld and the Channel World family of publications. IDG Books Worldwide is one of the fastest-growing computer book publishers in the world, with more than 700 titles in 36 languages. The "...For Dummies®" series alone has more than 50 million copies in print. IDG offers online users the largest network of technology-specific Web sites around the world through IDG.net (http://www.idg.net), which comprises more than 225 targeted Web sites in 55 countries worldwide. International Data Corporation (IDC) is the world's largest provider of information technology data, analysis and consulting, with research centers in over 41 countries and more than 400 research analysts worldwide. IDG World Expo is a leading producer of more than 168 globally branded conferences and expositions in 35 countries including E3 (Electronic Entertainment Expo), Macworld Expo, ComNet, Windows World Expo, ICE (Internet Commerce Expo), Agenda, DEMO, and Spotlight. IDG's training subsidiary, ExecuTrain, is the world's largest computer training company, with more than 230 locations worldwide and 785 training courses. IDG Marketing Services helps industry-leading IT companies build international brand recognition by developing global integrated marketing programs via IDG's print, online and exposition products worldwide. Further information about the company can be found at www.idg.com.                                                                                      1/26/00

# Author's Acknowledgments

Most book projects require heartache, dedication, patience, and determination to see them through from conception to the crisply printed page. *Upgrading & Fixing Macs & iMacs For Dummies*, by contrast, was accomplished with little more than an occasional delivery from a local Vietnamese take-out place.

Hats off to Mike Roney, acquisitions editor, for championing the project in the face of stiff editorial opposition. Dangling his career from the Brooklyn Bridge with nothing but a smile on his face, he finally pushed this project through in direct opposition to, as it turns out, received wisdom and good taste.

Big thanks to project editor Susan Pink for helping to shape the whole project, keeping me on-task, vigorously seeking out better turns of phrase and, in a pinch, reminding me that the weather is worse where she is than it is where I am. Likewise, Dennis Cohen, technical editor to the stars, took a break from his higher profile commitments to squeeze in my little book, making it that much better for his effort.

I'd also like to thank David Rogelberg and the cast and crew down at Studio B, the only writers agency with a name that sounds more like an improv-comedy troupe.

And, as always, personal thanks to Donna Ladd, who, in consistently and constantly embracing the role of supporter and partner, couldn't even remember the name of this book 90 percent of the time. (I'm kidding! Thanks for the support and love.)

## Publisher's Acknowledgments

We're proud of this book; please register your comments through our IDG Books Worldwide Online Registration Form located at http://my2cents.dummies.com.

Some of the people who helped bring this book to market include the following:

*Acquisitions, Editorial, and Media Development*

**Project Editor:** Susan Pink

**Acquisitions Editor:** Mike Roney

**Proof Editor:** Teresa Artman

**Technical Editor:** Dennis Cohen

**Senior Editor, Freelance:** Constance Carlisle

**Media Development Manager:** Heather Heath Dismore

**Editorial Assistants:** Beth Parlon, Candace Nicholson

*Production*

**Project Coordinator:** E. Shawn Aylsworth

**Layout and Graphics:** Barry Offringa, Brian Torwelle

**Proofreader:** Laura Albert, Corey Bowen, Charles Spencer, York Production Services, Inc.

**Indexer:** York Production Services, Inc.

*Special Help:*
Karl Brandt, Angie Hunckler, Shelley Norris, Brent Savage

---

*General and Administrative*

**IDG Books Worldwide, Inc.:** John Kilcullen, CEO

**IDG Books Technology Publishing Group:** Richard Swadley, Senior Vice President and Publisher; Walter R. Bruce III, Vice President and Publisher; Joseph Wikert, Vice President and Publisher; Mary Bednarek, Vice President and Director, Product Development; Andy Cummings, Publishing Director, General User Group; Mary C. Corder, Editorial Director; Barry Pruett, Publishing Director

**IDG Books Consumer Publishing Group:** Roland Elgey, Senior Vice President and Publisher; Kathleen A. Welton, Vice President and Publisher; Kevin Thornton, Acquisitions Manager; Kristin A. Cocks, Editorial Director

**IDG Books Internet Publishing Group:** Brenda McLaughlin, Senior Vice President and Publisher; Sofia Marchant, Online Marketing Manager

**IDG Books Production for Branded Press:** Debbie Stailey, Director of Production; Cindy L. Phipps, Manager of Project Coordination, Production Proofreading, and Indexing; Tony Augsburger, Manager of Prepress, Reprints, and Systems; Laura Carpenter, Production Control Manager; Shelley Lea, Supervisor of Graphics and Design; Debbie J. Gates, Production Systems Specialist; Robert Springer, Supervisor of Proofreading; Kathie Schutte, Production Supervisor

**Dummies Packaging and Book Design:** Patty Page, Manager, Promotions Marketing

◆

The publisher would like to give special thanks to Patrick J. McGovern, without whom this book would not have been possible.

◆

# Contents at a Glance

# Cartoons at a Glance

## By Rich Tennant

page 7

page 49

page 195

page 305

page 347

**Fax:** 978-546-7747
**E-mail:** richtennant@the5thwave.com
**World Wide Web:** www.the5thwave.com

# Table of Contents

# Introduction

● ● ● ● ● ● ● ● ● ● ● ● ● ● ● ● ● ● ● ● ● ● ● ● ● ● ● ● ● ● ● ● ● ● ● ● ● ● ● ● ● ● ● ● ● ● ● ● ● ● ● ●

*W*hat if you could get a Mac that offers all the tools you need to be more productive and more creative? A Mac that performs the tasks you throw at it with speed, style, and grace? How would you like faster Web access, quicker application switching, and access to all those new whiz-bang devices in Mac catalogs?

And what if you could perform these improvements yourself and fit them into your budget?

You can, thanks to this book. (Try not to "Whoop!" too loudly in the book-store. You'll scare the people over in the Gardening section.) *Upgrading & Fixing Macs & iMacs For Dummies* helps you figure out how to get the most out of your current Mac. Your Mac is an investment, whether or not you use it for moneymaking enterprises. If you're educating, entertaining, or improving yourself, your family, or your organization with your Mac, it's worth your time to get the most out of it.

Even better, this book helps you get your Mac Guru merit badge, enabling you to troubleshoot problems and fix software and hardware issues that crop up with nearly any Mac model. If you're having a specific problem or if you're just fed up with some aspect of your Mac experience, check out this book. I bet you can find an easy answer — or the tools to discover the answer on your own — in these pages.

## About This Book

I've been dying to write a fun-to-read Mac upgrading and troubleshooting guide for years. Finally, IDG Books agreed. *Upgrading & Fixing Macs & iMacs For Dummies* is a simple guide to upgrading and troubleshooting any desktop Macintosh model, including the iMac. If your Mac is too slow, if it has trouble performing important tasks, or if you're just not getting everything out of the experience, you find the answer in here.

Note that the book has "Fixing Macs & iMacs" in the title. Don't let that intimidate you. Any fixing you do requires, at most, a screwdriver. (No sandblasters, voltmeters, or gas masks are required.) Most of the time, fixing your Mac means you're troubleshooting the software, altering an important setting, or rearranging and testing devices to make sure they're installed properly.

In this book, you get a comprehensive guide that takes you through what a *user* can do to get a Mac up and running again. If a component is truly broken and needs to be looked at by a professional, I'll let you know.

By the end of this book, you'll have a greater understanding of how to get the most out of your Mac by improving its speed and capabilities. You'll also know what to do in a crisis and how to get your Mac — and your data — back in service as quickly as possible.

# Conventions Used in This Book

Here are a few conventions I use in this book:

- ✔ When I refer to an item in a menu, I use something like File ⇨ Open, which means "Pull down the File menu and choose the Open command."

- ✔ New terms show up in *italics*. If it's a term that hasn't appeared in Webster's in the past ten years, I'll define, explain and, in most cases, make fun of it before moving on.

- ✔ For keyboard shortcuts, something like ⌘+Q means hold down the ⌘ key (the one with the little apple and pretzel on it), press the letter Q on the keyboard, and then release them at the same time. ⌘+Shift+Q means hold down the ⌘ and Shift keys while pressing the Q key and then release them all at once.

- ✔ Web addresses are shown in a special typeface, for example, www.mac-upgrade.com.

# What You're Not to Read

You can take two approaches to reading this book. First, you can read it from beginning to end to find out everything you can about how your Mac works, what upgrades you can perform inside and out, and how to troubleshoot. (Plus, if you read straight through, you'll understand the surprising plot twist in Chapter 17.)

Second, if you have a specific question or you encounter an immediate problem, you can head right to that chapter (or the Part of Tens) and start reading. Each chapter focuses on a different technology; some of them may be of no interest to you at this time. Read about the upgrades and fixes you need to perform right now, and then you can keep the book handy on a shelf and grab it when you want to explore a new technology.

I recommend that you read Chapter 21 as soon as you can, though, so you can implement your backup, virus checking, and maintenance strategy. Then skim the Part of Tens to familiarize yourself with common troubleshooting fixes and tools. Other than that, just read what you need to accomplish your upgrading and fixing goals.

# Foolish Assumptions

Although you might be a complete novice when it comes to upgrading or troubleshooting your Mac, I assume in this book that you know how to get around on a Mac's screen with the mouse and that you're familiar with the Mac's Finder. If you've never used a Mac (or if you've never used any computer), consider *Macs For Dummies, Mac OS 9 For Dummies,* or *Mac OS 9 Bible* (all published by IDG Books Worldwide, Inc.) as a companion to this text.

If you're already a Mac administrator or if you want to get inside a PowerBook, you'll find that *Macworld Mac Upgrade and Repair Bible* (published by IDG Books Worldwide, Inc.) is a complete reference for the intermediate Mac Guru. This book uses almost 1000 pages to explain how to upgrade and troubleshoot nearly every Mac, PowerBook, and Mac OS clone model.

I also assume you're using a Mac with Mac OS 9.*x* or earlier on your iMac, Power Macintosh, or earlier Mac. If you happen to have upgraded to Mac OS X, Apple's all-new, high-end operating system, you might want to use this book with another book that covers software troubleshooting with Mac OS X. (Extensions, drivers, and control panels are different in Mac OS X.)

# How This Book Is Organized

*Upgrading & Fixing Macs & iMacs For Dummies* is divided into five parts, numbered four through eight. (Just kidding.) The parts have a logical progression, taking you from the basic upgrading and fixing decision to advanced topics on getting inside your Mac or troubleshooting the System Folder. That said, each chapter is self-contained, so you can go directly to the topic that interests you.

## Part I, Pre-Med: Getting Started with Upgrades and Fixes

In Part I, you find the basics of making your upgrade or fixing decision. You get a Mac anatomy lesson, where you find out how Macs work and why they slow down. Then you determine what, exactly, is the problem with your Mac so that you can choose the right chapter for further upgrading or troubleshooting.

## Part II, The Clinic: Upgrading and Fixing on the Outside

A lot of upgrading and fixing can be accomplished on the outside of the Mac or iMac, without getting your hands dirty inside the machine. (Actually, it's not very dirty in there, although sometimes it's a touch dusty.) In Chapter 4, you see the different types of ports that Macs sport for external upgrading. In subsequent chapters, you use those ports to add new devices or update your old ones. (To troubleshoot a particular device, turn to the related chapter.)

## Part III, Advanced Surgery: Getting inside Your Mac

With most Mac models, it's pretty easy to pop the top. After you're inside, you can add some wonderful capabilities to your Mac, such as a faster processor, more storage, or perhaps most importantly, more RAM. You can also troubleshoot each of those items or spring into the slightly complex world of Mac networking. Part III ends with an in-depth look at everyone's favorite high-tech beach ball, including some secret internal upgrades to prolong the life of your iMac.

## Part IV, Internal Medicine and Maintenance

If you're a human (I guess I should have put this back in the "Foolish Assumptions" section), you know that check-ups, exercise, and good food can make you more productive, faster, and longer lasting. The same thing is true for Macs: A regular maintenance schedule keeps software sickness away. When something does hit — a bug, corruption, or a conflict — Part IV shows you the proper treatments.

## Part V, The Part of Tens

Some of the most important chapters in the book are chapters in the Part of Tens. Talk about action-packed — these chapters include some incredibly useful troubleshooting and upgrading tips sardined into as few words as possible. (You can't imagine how long I had to work on *that*.) Check out the top ten problems and how to fix them, the top ten tools in the Mac Guru's toolbox, and the top ten issues for the latest Macs — iMacs and Power Macintosh G3 and G4 machines.

# Icons Used in This Book

 You don't have to read these, but they usually help you do something quicker, more intelligently, or in a way that makes you look more like a glamorous international spy. (Which explains why I never have an easy time with customs officers.)

 When you see this icon, you know I'm telling you something important or reminding you of an issue already discussed. Just read these things and keep them in mind.

 Every once in a while, I geek out and decide to tell you something trivial you don't need to know about the arcana of Macintosh technology. If you're shooting for guru status, consider reading these; if not, ignore me as though I were a pesky little brother.

 The only time you *shouldn't* read these carefully is if your arm is on fire, in which case you should stop, drop, and roll. Otherwise, check out these for tips on keeping your Mac and yourself out of harm's way.

 This icon points the way to a Web-based resource that you can check out for further information.

# Where to Go from Here

The world of Mac upgrading and troubleshooting is always a moving target; let's keep the dialog going on the Internet. If you don't find the answer you need or you want a better explanation, visit www.mac-upgrade.com for general news, reviews, and tips. For errata and frequently asked questions regarding this book, visit www.mac-upgrade.com/dummies/. If you still don't get your question answered, or if you have a comment, kudos, a concern, or criticism, reach me directly at questions@mac-upgrade.com. If you require a response, note the timeframe in your message, such as **1 Week: Networking Question** or something similar. Thanks, and I hope to hear from you!

# Part I
# Pre-Med: Getting Started with Upgrades and Fixes

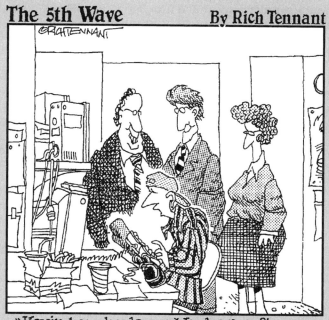

The 5th Wave — By Rich Tennant

"Kevin here heads our Windows software development team. Right now he's working on a spreadsheet program that's sort of a combination Lotus 1-2-3, - FrankenWolf."

# In this part . . .

Like any new endeavor — home improvement, artistic expression, tort reform — upgrading and trouble-shooting a Macintosh requires a little background information and thought. First, you need to understand what upgrading means and how it's accomplished. Then you need to think about the trade-offs of upgrading, consider the costs, and give yourself permission to improve your Mac. Next, you focus on a quick anatomy lesson that shows how a Mac's different components work — and work together — to make it compute the way it does. Finally, you begin early diagnostics to help you figure out whether your Mac is broken or just needs some tweaking and upgrading to run well.

# Chapter 1

# The Upgrade or Repair Decision

**D**eciding to upgrade your Macintosh might be the toughest decision you ever have to make. Oh, sure, there's the joining-the-Peace-Corps decision, the buying-season-tickets-to-the-opera decision, and the letting-your-child-get-a-learner's-permit decision — those are all toughies, too. But the decision to upgrade your existing Mac is probably the toughest if only because new Macs are very shiny, and at a crude, instinctual level, we all love shiny things.

Yet, sometimes you have to make due with things that are decidedly less shiny, like an older Mac. Not that there's a problem with that. As you'll see throughout this text, you can use plenty of nip-and-tuck solutions to improve the quality of life for your Macintosh, even if you're the sort of person who believes that beauty comes from within.

In this chapter, you look at the decision to upgrade (or fix) your Mac or iMac. First, you need to decide whether or not your Mac fits your needs and what it might take to make your Mac a bit more optimal. Then you see what you can realistically expect to upgrade or repair on your Mac. Finally, you see a few scenarios that help you in "knowin' what to throw away and knowin' what to keep."

Although it's certainly not a prerequisite for upgrading Macs, an intimate knowledge of Kenny Rogers's songs will help you find your moral compass in almost any situation.

# Is Your Mac Failing You?

You probably spent an absurd amount of money when you bought your Mac, but it fulfilled its responsibilities reasonably well. Over time, though, your Mac might have begun to slow down or show signs of aging. Or perhaps it simply fails to offer the same features and excitement of a new model. Hey, it happens to the best of us — you're having a mid-Mac crisis.

Actually, there are good reasons why Macs can seem as if they're not as useful as they once were. The most obvious is when something is broken and needs to be fixed. But let's begin by looking at some other factors that might be addressed with upgrades and fixes. Here are some speed bumps for aging Macs:

- ✔ **New System software arrives.** Every new version of the Mac OS (the software that gives your Mac it's unique personality through windows, menus, and buttons) tends to require more RAM and faster processors for the best computing. This happens because of new features for all or just because newer Macs need to be supported by the Mac OS.

- ✔ **New applications are demanding.** If you install the latest programs, games, and utilities, you'll find that they're more demanding than their predecessors. Packed with features, higher quality images, and usually plenty of add-ons, the latest applications can make a perfectly useful Mac seem to crawl compared to new models.

- ✔ **Disk space gets filled.** Crowded disk space is one of the more obvious signs that you're outgrowing your Mac. What some Mac users don't know, though, is that a full disk can also lead to a slower Mac and to problems with crashing and freezing. Fortunately, it's generally pretty easy to install new disks or come up with other solutions to increase a Mac's capability to store files, documents, and programs.

- ✔ **Capability envy.** Perhaps the most obvious reason to upgrade, though, is the fact that your Mac just doesn't seem to do what you need or want. Maybe you're in a three-legged race with the Joneses or maybe you're honestly trying to accomplish some work. In either case, an aging Mac might not offer the colorful bells and whistles of newer models. That doesn't necessarily mean you can't add them.

When evaluating your Mac's capabilities, the most important thing to remember is not necessarily the capabilities of the latest and greatest Macs. Instead, decide how capable your Mac needs to be so you can accomplish your goals.

But how do you figure that out? What you need is a good, solid rule to help you. Fortunately, I see one coming right now.

# The 75/25 rule

The 75/25 rule is simple. If you're on a budget, you should aim for a Macintosh system that performs 75 percent of the tasks you throw at it with aplomb and grace. The Mac should be capable of the other 25 percent of tasks, but they don't have to be the Mac's forte.

Obviously, it would be nice to have a Mac that could perform absolutely every task you toss at it with dignity under fire. But the cost for that sort of performance works out to something around five grand every six months per Mac; if that's your budget, forget about this book. Send me an email and I'll fly out personally to help you buy your new Macs (for a fat commission, obviously).

If your budget is a little closer to reality, the 75/25 rule kicks in. You should upgrade to the point that the majority of the tasks you perform do so in a pleasing way, even if you have to fiddle a bit to get the other tasks to work out.

For example, as a writer, I've found a number of things that are very important to the way I work, including a comfortable keyboard, a great monitor, and a very fast printer. Less important is a fancy image scanner (I work with images, but not too often) and a blazingly fast processor. When I'm working with text, I like everything to proceed smoothly because that's what I do 75 percent of the time. When I'm working with images, it's okay if I don't have the best or fastest equipment, because I don't do those things as often.

You'll find that the tasks that are important to you — and those that you perform repetitively — are worth any investment you make in them. Less frequent tasks can be accomplished with a little corner-cutting, if your budget requires.

# Mac's okay, you're okay

One of the most important steps to accepting the 75/25 rule, however, is giving yourself permission to upgrade. If you're an accountant type (and I consider anyone an accountant type who has his or her checking account balanced), what you'll want to see is a little money talk. I'm happy to oblige.

The first thing I'll do is encourage you to think of your Mac as an investment, especially if you use it to make a living. But even if you don't, you should consider your Mac an investment if you use it for personal finance, education, personal growth, artistic endeavors, or that most sacred of computer benefits, improving hand-eye coordination.

The question now becomes, how much is your time worth? If you're a professional, you might already know the answer. If you're a student or you work for a wage or a salary, you have to make your best guess. Let's pretend that your time is worth $20 an hour.

Now suppose that your computer wastes three hours of your time per week because it is too slow, isn't as capable as it needs to be, or makes you jump through some annoying hoops to get something accomplished. At $20 per hour, that's about $60 per week you're losing, or:

$60 x 52 weeks = $3120

which translates into about $3000 a year you're losing if you get a two-week vacation. In other words, you're losing three grand a year because of that silly Mac. Feel free to put this book down and go give your Mac a stern talking-to. I'll wait.

Seriously, you can look at this as an opportunity. Whatever amount of time your Mac is wasting for you, time is money and your Mac is probably worth a little investment to get things running more smoothly. As long as the amount of that investment doesn't outstrip the worth of the Mac (or the cost of a new Mac), the investment will be worth it. The next issue, then, is to consider what, exactly, is wrong with your Mac.

# *Your Mac Relationship-O-Meter*

Part of recognizing how to work on the investment you've already put into your relationship with your Mac is determining what about it gets on your nerves. You need to be honest with yourself and your Mac, even if you think this might be a little hurtful. No pain, no gain.

Here are a few questions to think about while you're considering what you might like to change about your current Mac:

- **What drives you crazy?** Is there anything that simply doesn't work well or works too slowly to make your computing a pleasurable experience? Being happy with the major tasks you perform on your Mac is an important part of evaluating its productivity. If something drives you crazy, you should change it, whether it's a modem, a printer, a screen, a keyboard, a disk, or the whole darn ball of wax.

- **Is anything harming you?** You have my personal permission, as your Macintosh relationship counselor, to toss out any part of your Mac that encourages bad posture, squinting, cramped hands, or other issues that could literally be harming your person. Any ergonomic issue is worth addressing with an upgrade.

- **What upgrades would encourage productivity?** As noted in that first bullet up there, you should be happy with your Mac if you intend to be productive with it. One thing that helps productivity is *speed*. I like to tell the story of the time I finally broke down and bought a fast laser printer after using a slower inkjet for a few years. Suddenly, I found I was actually getting to the FedEx drop-off on time, thus increasing both my happiness and my well being.

✔ **What upgrades would increase your capabilities?** Whether or not you do official work-type stuff with your Mac, adding an upgrade that increases its capabilities could mean more productivity, more job satisfaction, or more clients. In fact, you might be able to add a new bullet point to your resume or a new item on your menu of business services. Think how this could snowball into a promotion, a huge client, or maybe even one of those gravy-train accounts you've been hoping to get for years! Am I overstating things to say that adding a color printer, a digital camera, or a high-resolution scanner might just make you one of the wealthiest people on the planet?

Before you can fully make all these judgements about your Mac, you might need to know a little bit about yourself.

## Different people need different Macs

You might have decided that your Mac doesn't meet your needs and it's time to make some changes, whether that means fixes for your current Mac or a clean break and a new Mac. But what you might not be sure of is what your ideal Mac looks like. If you don't get to know yourself a little better, you might be destined to make the same mistakes over and over again.

In general, people fit a basic category that can help them determine what sort of computing capabilities are necessary for their productivity and happiness. To that end, here are some basic profiles:

✔ **Input/output people.** If you're a designer, writer, administrator, or professional, your focus with the computer is probably getting data into your Mac and spitting it back out. That means a good keyboard, monitor, and mouse or trackball, along with a great printer. You'll probably also want a decent scanner and a good Internet or network connection. And you'll want a removable drive for backing up and archiving your data.

✔ **Graphics people.** Designers, artists, and architects will have Macs with beefy graphics subsystems, meaning a great monitor, a powerful video expansion card, a lot of random access memory (RAM), and special input devices such as a scanner and a pen-based input tablet. The graphics professional also needs a high-end processor — maybe the fastest available — and a good printer for proofs, probably a color printer, even if it's a touch on the slow side. This system will also include a high-capacity removable disk drive for transferring large graphics files, a very high-speed Internet connection, or both.

✔ **Multimedia and video production people.** The video editor or hobbyist will need a special AV card or a FireWire connection for getting audio and video into the Mac. You'll also need a high-speed processor, a fast and large hard disk, and lots of RAM. The monitor isn't as important; ditto the printer, which doesn't have to be the highest quality. You might want a CD or DVD burner and a high-speed Internet connection if any of your produced work will be transferred that way.

✔ **Communications people.** For the executive, manager, telecommuter, small retailer, or salesperson, you need a connected computer. That means the Internet connection and, perhaps, portability of the system will be key. At the least, you need a good removable drive, a good printer, and a great fax solution, but the monitor, scanner, and processor can all be mid-range.

✔ **Home and games people.** Ironically, an edutainment (educational entertainment) or gaming-oriented computer can be a fairly powerful machine, especially if you're serious about the gaming graphics. That said though, a home machine is typically mid-range all the way around, allowing it to be flexible. A good (but not huge) monitor, a good-quality color printer, and a reasonably fast processor are all requisites. The entertainment system should probably have a fast CD-ROM or a DVD-ROM drive, as well as a good graphics expansion card and perhaps a fancy joystick.

Although you might not fit in any of these categories exactly (and if you do, maybe you should run and get your hair dyed to prove that you're not such a conformist), you can probably see where I'm going. To have fun getting things accomplished, it's important that you and your Mac are a good match.

## Need a new Mac?

Apple has made it easier for us to consider the benefits of buying a new computer by following their recent, more simplified product strategy. When you compare your Mac to a new Mac, you're pretty much looking at an iMac, a Power Macintosh, or a notebook computer (either an iBook or a PowerBook). If your Mac doesn't fair well, it might be time to get a new machine.

But how do you arrive at a verdict? Usually the most persuasive way is to add up the cost of the upgrades you're planning for your Mac, and then see whether the same or less money might bring you a full-featured, brand-new Macintosh. For instance, consider the cost of getting an aging Performa 6400 model up to the specifications of the median iMac model:

| | |
|---|---|
| Processor upgrade | $300 |
| RAM upgrade | $100 |
| Hard disk upgrade | $150 |
| Video card upgrade | $150 |
| Total | $700 |

Now at the time of this writing, it would cost about $700 to bring that Performa 6400, made in 1995, up to "modern" specs. That's actually not bad, although you still haven't updated the Performa to use USB or FireWire port peripherals, which the vast majority of new external upgrades support. You might also need to invest in a new modem, as well as an Ethernet card, to bring the Performa up to iMac specs.

Of course, some of these upgrades might not be of any use to you. Even more pertinent, the Performa supports technologies that the iMac doesn't — Apple Desktop Bus, SCSI, and traditional serial ports. If you have devices that require these types of ports, moving to the iMac will mean you have to give up those peripherals, perhaps buying replacements.

So, the decision to buy new is two-fold:

- ✔ **What are the relative costs?** Spec out the upgrades necessary for acceptable performance and see how the prices compare to a new Mac.

- ✔ **What do you lose in the bargain?** When you upgrade to Apple's sleeker, slimmer machines, are you actually losing capabilities? Macs in the past have come with SCSI ports, AV cards, support for two monitors, expansion slots, serial ports, and other technologies that you might have to pay to add to newer Macs. Don't forget to factor that in.

The bottom line is: As long as your Mac model is reasonably new and upgradable (some models are better than others), you can probably come up with enough upgrades to make it as powerful as you want. But it could cost you something, so do a little math before diving in.

# Am I Ready for This?

Just in case you've read these first few pages with your head swimming, let's switch gears quickly and make sure you're ready to upgrade and fix your Mac. It actually doesn't take much knowledge, wisdom, or coordination. The mere fact that *I'm* writing this book is a Technicolor testament to the utter lack of intelligence required to work with your Mac. You don't need to know computing or computers inside out to troubleshoot or upgrade your Mac.

For the most part, you'll probably fare better with some upgrading tasks if you're the sort of person who can hook a VCR up to a TV. You'll do better with other the troubleshooting tasks if you can program a VCR. In almost every case, though, the upgrades covered in this book are something that just about everyone can do, as long as you play by the rules and observe all traffic signs.

So what, exactly, are you going to have to do?

## *Upgrading versus fixing*

The first item to get out of the way is a discussion on the title of this book. Yes, you guessed correctly if you said that IDG Books pays me per title word — *Upgrading & Fixing Macs & iMacs For Dummies* is a doozie. That's part of what I need to talk about.

When I talk about upgrading and fixing a computer, what do I really mean? Well, I'm trying to address two basic issues: *underperformance* and *failure*. (Wow, this just got really depressing, didn't it?) All I mean is that and you'll be *upgrading* things that work but not all that well, and you'll be *fixing* things that aren't working at all.

There, that doesn't sound so bad.

*Fixing,* in this context, doesn't mean hooking things up to a voltmeter, pulling out the soldering iron, or duct taping anything. For the most part, fixing things means *troubleshooting* and performing the occasional first-aid tasks. I'll show you how to adjust your monitor, for instance, not how to crack open your monitor and stick metal into things until your teeth glow.

In fact, when you're *fixing* your Mac, you're really more likely to be working with the software that's installed on your Mac — the Mac OS and its various drivers and extensions — than you are to be poking around inside the Mac.

The *poking* comes when you're replacing or upgrading components. Sometimes you'll replace a component to "fix" it, although most of the time you'll be replacing components because you want to upgrade the Mac's capabilities.

Most important to remember is that, in many cases, upgrading or fixing Macs is very easy up to the moment it becomes *outrageously difficult*. At that moment, your best plan is to get thee to an authorized Apple repair shop. I'll try to point out instances that fit that category.

## *That thing you'll do*

So what sort of upgrades and fixes are you likely to be able to pull off yourself? There are a few basic categories of upgrades and fixes you'll want to make to help bring your Mac up to champion-level specifications. These categories include speeding up your Mac, improving productivity, and adding capabilities. Let's take a quick look-see at each.

Chapter 2 describes, in the greatest 15 or so pages ever written, the various components in a Mac and how they work together. If the items in the following lists confuse you, you might find the answers in Chapter 2. If you're confused as to why these lists appears in Chapter 1 when their explanations are in Chapter 2, you'll force me to admit that I'm paid also per cross-reference.

### Speed up your Mac

Most people think of speed when they think of upgrading, although speed isn't all there is to upgrading. Speed is *a lot* of what upgrading is about though, and many different components can be upgraded to help speed up your Mac:

- **Memory.** I've seen posters that read, "You can never be too thin or have too much RAM." Random access memory (RAM) is the single most important upgrade for a slow Mac. RAM allows applications more room in which to think, while allowing you to have more applications open at once. RAM also keeps your Mac from accessing the hard disk more often than it should, which is a prime reason that older Macs begin to slow down when used with newer Mac OS versions and applications. You can see how to upgrade RAM in Chapter 15.

- **Processor.** The central processing unit (CPU) is the brains of the operation. The slower the CPU, the slower the rest of your computer will be — even the printer, graphics, and input devices might seem slower if your CPU is overworked. Many, many Mac models have a direct processor upgrade solution, while others need a little more sleight of hand to be upgraded. I discuss this in depth in Chapter 16.

- **Hard drives.** Hard drives need to be fast and spacious. If too many files are filling up your current hard drive, that might be slowing down your Mac. Likewise, older drives are simply slower technology, with the savings passed on to you. Get a newer drive and, depending on your Mac model, you might see a nice little boost. Chapter 17 covers adding drives.

- **Modem.** I'll explain this later, but faster modems aren't really *faster*. (This will be great fodder for dinner parties; I'll offer the lowdown in Chapter 6.) But a newer, more capable modem can make your Internet surfing sessions and file downloading go quite a bit faster.

- **Networking.** Ethernet is faster than LocalTalk, which is faster than swapping Zip disks or floppies between your Macs. And AirPort is a fast wireless option, with Fast Ethernet at the head of the network-speed train. If you need to get files from one Mac to another, a network is the way to do it. Networking is covered in Chapter 18.

- **Video.** You can install special cards that speed up your Mac's capability to draw in two dimensions. I know, you're already thinking to yourself, "Where do I buy?" But wait. What would you say to 3-D acceleration? Are you kidding? 3-D and acceleration in the same sentence? It's a sale! I focus on video cards in Chapter 14.

- **Printing.** The latest printers are faster and cheaper than ever, with laser printers generally faster than inkjet printers and workgroup printers faster than basic lasers. If you need to print quickly, such upgrades await. Printing is covered in Chapter 10.

### Improve your quality

After you've sped up your Mac, you need to speed yourself up to be more productive, right? Sure . . . that's what I'd say if I was trying to sell Power Granola down at the local health-food store. But the real productivity might come from a combination of speed upgrades and upgrades that add quality to your Mac's current capabilities. For example:

- ✔ **Scanning.** A scanner gives you more capabilities when it comes to working with art, documents, or even text. With optical character recognition (OCR), you can scan documents into your computer and then translate them into text that you can edit in a word processor. Or scan documents for digital storage or fax transmission directly from your Mac. You can take a look at scanners in Chapter 8.

- ✔ **Printers and accessories.** A color printer might increase your productivity by keeping you away from the print house or the copy shop. Plus, different printers offer accessories such as envelope feeders, different formats, or even integrated capabilities (such as photocopying and scanning).

- ✔ **Input devices.** A new keyboard, a more comfortable mouse, or a pen-based input device can help you be more comfortable and productive, whether you're an artist or a regular Jane. Input gets a look in Chapter 5.

- ✔ **Backup and storage devices.** Put bluntly, the best way to be unproductive is to not back up your Mac. One day, it will crash. If you haven't backed up your data, your boss, significant other, or clients will likely "get unproductive" all over your backside. If I could, I'd put the word *backup* in every chapter of this book, or at least Chapters 11, 17, 20, 21, and 22.

- ✔ **Networking.** Talked to your co-workers recently? Well, you can avoid that even longer if you have a good solid network between your Macs. Productivity might go up significantly if you stay planted in your seat, getting up only occasionally to wash, forage, and perform a little Tai Chi.

### Do more with your Mac

Oh sure, you plan a vacation together every year, but are you and your Mac really learning and growing together? One of the great things about buying this book (not to mention buying additional copies, which make great gifts) is the opportunity to explore new vistas that your Mac can help you leap toward.

What I'm trying to say is that you can add new capabilities to your Mac and, ergo, to your arsenal of Things You Know:

✔ **Audio and video.** If you have a camcorder, you can edit your videos. If you have a *digital* camcorder, an idea, talent, $38,000 and a bevy of friends who are unknown actors, you can follow your dream. (Actually, you'd be following my dream.) Macs are used by professionals everywhere to create sounds, compose music, edit video, and jump through amazing hoops that compose that which we call *multimedia* Fade in on chapters 8 and 9.

✔ **CD and DVD.** If your Mac doesn't have a CD-ROM drive, you should consider upgrading just to survive — all new software comes on CD-ROM these days. But what about creating your own CDs? With special drives, you can create audio and data CDs for backup (there's that word again), archiving, or just talking with your Mac. Likewise, DVD offers you the opportunity to store even more data (on DVD-ROMs) or watch DVD movies on your Mac. See Chapter 11.

✔ **Do Windows.** Sure you bought a Mac for all that great Mac-ish stuff. But wouldn't you love to shop on the other aisles? With hardware or software upgrades, your Mac can run Microsoft Windows applications or even other operating systems such as DOS or Linux, if you like. Companies such as Connectix (www.connectix.com) and FWB (www.fwb.com) offer software *emulators* that make it possible to run Windows on your Mac. Or, in some cases, you can add an internal expansion card that actually puts a Pentium-class processor inside your Mac. If you're interested, converge with Chapter 14.

# Chapter 2

# How a Mac Works...
# or Doesn't Work

Clearly, most computer users don't care about getting inside a computer to see how it ticks. The fact that ever-simpler computers are becoming more popular these days suggests that plugging the computer in and making it work are the major concerns of most computer users.

But if you plan to do some upgrading or fixing, knowing how a computer works and why it does some of the things it does can help. After all, if you plan to hunt down the solution to a problem or a slowdown, you need to know what you're looking at. It's like in those action movies where they have fifteen seconds left to defuse the bomb. You'd be a lot happier in that situation if you knew what the green wire did *before* you cut it.

## Making It Tick: Subsystems

When you type a key, most of the time that character appears on-screen. When you choose a menu command or double-click a program's icon, your computer takes the appropriate action, and the desired effect is brought about. But how does all this happen? If you guessed "little squirrels inside the case," you're half right.

Any Mac is comprised of three different subsystems that interact with you and among themselves to make things happen. Here they are:

✔ **Processing.** Processing is the brains of the operation, bossing everything else around. This is where applications are stored, computations are made, and commands are carried out.

✔ **Input/output.** The input/output (or I/O, for short) subsystem includes everything that communicates with you, the human. That includes components where data is put into the computer (such as a scanner or keyboard) or taken out of the computer (such as a printer or monitor).

✔ **Storage.** This subsystem is equivalent to long-term memory — it's where files and documents are stored when you save them in applications. The computer's short-term memory is in the processing subsystem (so it can work with a particular set of calculations and data when it needs to), but the Mac's long-term memory is in the storage subsystem, which is comprised of hard disks and removable drives (Zip drives, CD-ROM drives, floppy drives, and so on). Ultimately, storage is the subsystem where the computer does an electronic equivalent of writing stuff down so that it doesn't forget.

How about an example of how these subsystems work? Suppose you're going to open a document in AppleWorks, the popular application that ships with many Macs (older Macs might have a similar application under its previous name, ClarisWorks). Here's how the subsystems work together to create the computing experience:

1. You begin by using the mouse (input/output) to double-click the AppleWorks icon in the Finder.

2. The Finder receives this command, creates an area in system memory for the application and determines how the application will be loaded (processing). AppleWorks is found on the hard disk (storage) and is copied into system memory and launched (processing).

3. You then choose the Open command with the mouse (input/output), and ClarisWorks responds with a dialog box (processing). The file you choose is loaded from the hard disk (storage), and then you edit it using the keyboard (input/output and processing).

4. Finally, you choose the Print command with the mouse (input/output). AppleWorks creates an image of your document suitable for printing (processing) and sends the image to the printer, which prints the document (input/output).

As you might well imagine, this narrative has been optioned by Hollywood and will soon appear as a major motion picture. Exciting, eh?

So, when you're trying to determine what needs to be fixed or updated, you might be able to begin by isolating a particular subsystem: processing, input/output, or storage. After you decide where the slowdown might be, you can consider which part of that subsystem is ripe for replacement. Let's take a look at each subsystem.

# Thinkin' Things: CPU and Memory

The first subsystem is the processing subsystem: the brain of your Mac. The processing subsystem has three components: the central processing unit (CPU), system memory (RAM), and cache memory.

## The CPU

At the heart of any computer is the central processing unit (CPU), which is ultimately responsible for processing all the data that the computer deals with. In your Mac, the CPU is a relatively small, square computer chip that sits directly on the logic board — the main circuit board in your Mac's computer. Figure 2-1 shows a CPU on its logic board.

Some CPUs aren't installed directly on the logic board; instead, they're on special pull-out circuit boards (called *daughtercards*) that make them easier for upgrading. I cover that in Chapter 16.

**Figure 2-1:** The CPU (under a metal heat sink, to dissipate heat) plugged into a Power Macintosh G3 logic board.

The CPU is the reasoning center of your Mac, allowing it to perform mathematical equations and work with data. If it makes you comfortable, think of the CPU as a digital abacus — data goes in, gets moved around, and comes back out.

Although many users tend to call their Mac's enclosure the *CPU,* as in "I'm going to install a new hard disk in my CPU, Bertha," the CPU is actually a small chip on the main circuit board. That small chip doesn't want hard drives installed inside it. Your Mac's enclosure is more properly called a *case,* or a *Mac,* as in "I just read this book that told me how to open my Mac's case and install a hard disk, Bertha."

Okay, so we've established what a CPU is. Let's move on to the types of CPUs and the speed of CPUs so you know how to comparison-shop when you're looking over the numbers.

### Speed is the thing

Remember in the musical *Grease* when all the guys get together and sing about their cars? That was a '50s thing. In the '00s, people sing about their CPU speeds.

The speed at which a particular CPU computes is governed by a quartz clock installed on the logic board or the CPU's own circuit board. This crystal oscillates at a given frequency, in megahertz, acting as a timing mechanism for the CPU. This gives the CPU a speed of sorts, which you can use for comparisons.

But the comparison holds up only when you're talking about processors that have the same capabilities. If you have a PowerPC 604 processor running at 200 MHz, for instance, it's faster than a PowerPC 604 running at 150 MHz. But a PowerPC 603 processor running at 250 MHz is slower at many tasks than either of those processors. That's because the 604 is more capable than the 603 at a given MHz level.

So, when you're comparing CPUs, make sure you're comparing not just the speed of the CPU but the type as well. What do I mean by *type*?

### Types of Mac CPUs

Over the lifetime of the Macintosh line (since 1984), two major CPU architectures have been used: the Motorola 680x0 series and the PowerPC series. These two chips are not compatible, which means separate programming code is required for each. Some clever maneuvering by Apple, however, made it possible for the Mac OS (as well as many computer applications) to run on both processors.

- ✔ **The Motorola 680x0 series.** These processors were used (in ever-increasing speeds and complexity) in the classic Mac models: the Mac II series, Centris, Quadra, and some early Performa models. Macs that use these chips are no longer supported by Mac OS 8.5 or higher.

✔ **The IBM/Motorola PowerPC series.** Starting in early 1994, Apple introduced a new line of CPUs — the PowerPC. Based on a more advanced architecture (called *RISC*, for *Reduced Instruction Set Computing*), these chips were able to run faster than the older Motorola series. Plus, Apple had been able to increase the speed of the processors exponentially. Original PowerPC processors ran at 60 MHz, but these days, processors are punching through 500 MHz and computational speeds once reserved for supercomputers.

The 680x0 series has the *x* in its name because it represents a number of different processors that were numbered slightly differently. The original Macs used the 68000 processor. Most Mac II models included a 68020 processor. Later, the 68030 and 68040 processors were introduced, each more powerful than the last.

The PowerPC series has also been through a few different iterations. Each new numbered series has made improvements on the former, in most cases including a boost in speed. Table 2-1 shows how the currently available PowerPC processors stack up.

| Table 2-1 | PowerPC Processors Used in Mac OS Computers | |
|---|---|---|
| *PowerPC Processor* | *Megahertz Range* | *Improvements* |
| 601 | 60–120 MHz | Original PowerPC chip |
| 603/603e | 75–300 MHz | Consumes less power, slightly faster than 601 |
| 604/604e | 120–350 MHz | Faster than 601, 603; 604e is low power |
| 750 (G3) | 233–500 MHz | Low power, faster than 601, 603, 604 |
| 7400 (G4) | 350 MHz and up | Faster than the G3, improved math and multimedia calculations |

As newer PowerPC processors have been introduced, each has been faster than the last at the same megahertz levels. This is because the chips are designed more efficiently and with newer technologies than older chips. For instance, the PowerPC 7400 chip includes something called the Velocity Engine, which allows it to compute some multimedia-related tasks (video drawing, graphics rendering) much more quickly than a PowerPC G3 processor.

So, taken together, a newer CPU with a higher clock rate makes for a speedier Mac in most cases. But the CPU isn't the only component in the processing subsystem.

## Mac's main memory

Sometimes it's convenient to think of computer memory as similar to human memory. (It's completely inaccurate, but convenient.) Humans have short-term and long-term memory. Short-term memory is used to remember things you're working on or thinking about in the present. Long-term memory is used to remember things that happened at some point in the past (such as your anniversary already happening or your phone bill coming due).

The Mac's equivalent to human short-term memory is its *main memory*. For instance, everything you see at any given time on your computer screen is in main memory — as is a good portion of the document you're working on in a word-processing program or the image you're viewing in your Web browser. So what is main memory? It's little silicon chips on a small circuit board plugged into your Mac's logic board. Those chips are called random access memory, or RAM. Using these chips, you can add more RAM to your Mac, thus giving it more system memory to work with.

Adding RAM can boost the speed of your Mac, sometimes significantly. When your Mac is low on available RAM (short-term memory), it has to access the hard disk (long-term memory) to retrieve data that it needs for processing. But accessing the hard disk is much slower than accessing RAM, so the entire operation slows down. The more RAM you have, the less this slowdown has to happen.

RAM is measured in *megabytes* (MB), which means, roughly, millions of bytes. A *byte* is the amount of computer memory necessary to store one text character, like the letter *t*. Millions of bytes, then, would represent millions of characters. The more RAM you have, the more capable your Mac is of managing complex and multiple computational tasks. It follows that the Mac will work more quickly and productively with more RAM.

In fact, it's a classic mistake made by novice computer users to call their hard drive *memory* and proceed to tell you something like "I have 3 gigabytes of memory left on my Mac." In this context, *memory* should refer to RAM, not your hard drive. Most modern Macs have between 32MB and 256MB of RAM, with some high-end Macs reaching 1GB of RAM or more. Hard drives tend to be much larger in capacity, and they're designed for long-term storage, not short-term memory like RAM.

As mentioned, RAM is usually a collection of chips, called DRAMs (dynamic random access memory), placed on a module that can then be easily installed in a RAM socket on the logic board of your Mac. The module, depending on the design supported by your Mac model, is either a single inline memory module (SIMM) or a dual inline memory module (DIMM), see Figure 2-2.

**Figure 2-2:**
Above, a
SIMM;
below, a
DIMM.

SIMMs were the standard for years, but now DIMMs have replaced them in popularity and are in nearly all Macs made in the past five years. Both module types are designed to make it easy to add to or upgrade the RAM in your Mac.

Nearly every Mac model has different RAM requirements — you'll want to check your manual carefully and see Chapter 15 for details. For the most part, though, this is the sort of upgrade that is easily handled by anyone with the deftness to manually rewind a cassette using a pinky finger.

## A little cache memory

Your Mac has memory all over the place. One of those types of RAM is *cache memory*, which is used to speed up the transfer of data from system RAM to the processor. In a way, cache memory is sort of like the town gossip — it takes the juiciest bit of data and transfers it very quickly to interested parties.

Remember that the more RAM you have, the faster your Mac is likely to be because it doesn't access the hard disk as frequently. Taken one step further, the more cache RAM you have (to a point), the faster your Mac is, because cache RAM is ultra-high-speed RAM that can move data more quickly than standard RAM. It's also expensive, which explains why your Mac isn't made with boatloads of the stuff.

Instead, cache RAM sits between main memory and the CPU, drawing out portions of data that are likely to be used often by the CPU. Then when the CPU has a request for data, it looks in cache RAM first. If it finds the data there, it's said to score a *hit*. That data is moved more quickly than if it were in main memory, thus speeding up the processor.

To add to the overall complication, cache memory has a few different types, or *levels:*

✔ **Level 1.** Level 1 cache is a small bit of memory — usually 8 to 32 kilobytes — that sits on the processor chip itself. The processor uses this memory to hold the very next instructions and data that will be needed.

✔ **Level 2.** Level 2 cache is a larger amount of very high-speed RAM — between 256 kilobytes and 2 megabytes — that acts as a buffer between the processor's on-board cache and the system's main RAM. Traditional Level 2 cache is a RAM module installed in a socket on the logic board.

✔ **Backside cache.** This is a special type of Level 2 cache that, instead of being in a socket on the logic board, is on the processor's card. In fact, both the processor and the cache are on their own separate memory bus, allowing them to transfer data at very high speeds — usually either one-half of the processor's clock speed or the same clock speed as the processor. (So, a 300-MHz processor might have a backside cache that runs at either 150 or 300 MHz, depending on the design and price.)

# Dear Diary: Storage

Your Mac can use a number of different devices to store files and documents for the long term. By default, all Macs (except the very earliest models) have internal hard drives, and all come with either a floppy drive, a CD-ROM drive, or both. The latest Mac models eschew floppy drives, but might include a DVD-ROM drive as standard.

In any case, this section takes a quick look at the basic drive types and the technologies involved.

## Hard drives

Hard disk drives are small metal boxes containing disks, or *platters*, that are covered in a special coating. A magnetized *head* — something like a magnetic version of a phonograph's needle — passes over the platter, reading and writing tiny bits of data and then sending those bits to the main system RAM, where it can then be processed by the CPU.

The first Mac hard drives held 5 to 20 megabytes of data. Since then, Macs have included drives in ever-increasing sizes, from 40MB and 80MB to 230MB, 500MB, and even 810MB. These days, almost any new hard drive runs in the gigabytes — thousands of megabytes. Figure 2-3 shows an internal hard drive mechanism.

**Figure 2-3:**
A typical
internal
hard drive;
this is an
IDE-type
drive.

For years nearly every Mac that had a hard drive relied on SCSI (Small Computer System Interface) technology. SCSI hard drives tend to be a bit quicker than the alternatives, and the SCSI bus in Macs offers a number of interesting expansion options. (You can add not only hard drives, for instance, but also scanners, CD-ROM drives, removable media drives, and other more specialized devices, too.)

In the past five years, most Macs have begun to include IDE (Integrated Drive Electronics) hard drives and internal interfaces instead of SCSI. IDE, a popular interface for Intel-compatible PCs, is a more inexpensive technology that offers good performance. Many Macs can still accept external SCSI devices (via a SCSI port built into those Macs), although the latest Power Macintosh G3 and G4 models feature FireWire, which can also be used for external hard drives, instead of SCSI.

The universal serial bus (USB) ports on an iMac or a newer Power Macintosh machine can be used for an external hard drive, even though they're a little slow for moving that much data. If you have an iMac that doesn't feature FireWire ports, for instance, USB is your best choice for an external drive.

Almost any modern hard drive designed for SCSI or IDE-based Macs will be fast enough for nearly any user. Plus, the faster the drive, the more capable it will be for projects that require large files, such as recording digital audio and video. If you expect to make professional-caliber QuickTime movies, for instance, you'll want a fast drive.

Here are the specific statistics to keep an eye on:

- ✔ **Seek time.** This is the average elapsed time, in milliseconds, that it takes the read/write head to find data on the spinning platter inside the drive. Seek times between 8 and 17 milliseconds are optimal.

- ✔ **RPM.** Revolutions per minute (RPM) represents the speed at which the drive's spindle (on which the platters are mounted) spins. Speeds of 4800 and 5400 RPM are typical; speeds of 7200 RPM or greater are generally considered ideal for demanding audio-visual tasks.

## Compact discs and DVD

CD-ROM drives have been standard-issue for all Power Macintosh models, with newer Power Macs and iMac DV models shipping with DVD-ROM drives. CD-ROM drives were optional in many Quadra, Centris, LCIII, and Performa models. As a result, CD-ROM drives are the standard for commercial software and Mac OS system software installations.

Did your Mac miss the revolution? You can add both external and internal CD-ROM drives to many systems. Most Macintosh-oriented CD-ROM drives use SCSI technology for connecting to the Mac, although USB and FireWire versions are available for Macs that lack SCSI.

DVD drives are CD-ROM-drive backward-compatible, which means you can insert a disc using either CD-ROM or DVD technology and have no trouble reading it with your Macintosh. If you have expectations of running games, watching commercial movies, or using multimedia educational (or reference) titles, a DVD drive would be a good upgrade.

### Create your own discs

You can also buy drives that allow you to create your own compact discs for music or data storage. Here's a look at the technologies:

- ✔ **Compact disc-recordable (CD-R).** These drives are capable of writing data to special CD-R media. The drives can only write data once, but CD-R discs are inexpensive, making this a great solution for backup, transferring files, or creating music compilations.

- ✔ **Compact disc-rewritable (CD-RW).** Today's writable CD drives generally support both CD-R and CD-RW. CD-RW media is more expensive, but in exchange you get the added ability to overwrite data you've previously saved to the CD.

- ✔ **Digital versatile disc-random access memory (DVD-RAM).** Want to create DVDs? They offer much more data storage than traditional CDs, but must be read by DVD-ROM and DVD-RAM drives. And if you like the idea of creating your own disc (which can hold many gigabytes of data), DVD-RAM drives can be added to most Macs.

### Disc speeds

For comparison purposes, CD-ROM and DVD-ROM drives offer two important statistics — throughput levels and seek times.

Drives measure *throughput* in kilobytes per second, but, in practical terms, this number is usually expressed as a multiple — for instance, a 4x, or 4-speed, drive has four times the data throughput rate of an audio CD player. Audio CD players transmit data at 150 kilobytes per second, so a 4x drive is capable of transmitting 600 kilobytes per second. In more recent years, the speed at which CD-ROMs are capable of transferring data has skyrocketed to 24x and beyond.

When you're shopping, you might also come across the seek time for a given drive. *Seek time* represents the amount of time (on average) that it takes the drive to find a particular bit of data on the disc. Times of 150 ms (milliseconds) or less are adequate.

## Removable media

A *removable drive* is any type that lets you swap disks or cartridges to increase the overall capacity for storage. These drives range from the floppy drive built into many Macs to cartridge drives (Zip, Jaz, Orb), which might be built in or optional. If your Mac lacks these capabilities, they can be added both internally (directly inside your Mac's case, if it supports another drive) or externally, through SCSI, USB, FireWire, or other ports.

Following are some of the more common types of removable drives and their typical uses:

- **Floppy drive.** Although the latest Mac models no longer include floppy drives, they were a standard for nearly fifteen years. Capacities have ranged from 400K to 1.4MB of data per disk. All Apple Macintosh floppy drives have an auto-eject feature (the disk ejects when you drag its icon to the Trash in the Mac OS Finder). Earlier Macs also feature auto-inject floppy drives, which pulled the diskette into the drive automatically. The high-density drives in most Mac models are called SuperDrives because, with the correct software (PC Exchange) loaded, these drives are capable of reading, writing, and formatting MS-DOS, ProDOS (Apple II), and similar formats. That makes it possible for you to stick a DOS-formatted diskette into your Mac, read data from it, write data to it, and return it to a colleague's Intel-compatible computer.

- **SuperDisk.** Not to be confused with SuperDrives, SuperDisk is a marketing name for the *LS120* standard, which is a standard that allows compatible drives to read both standard floppy disks and special 120MB disks. These drives became a popular alternative for Macs when the floppy-less iMac first shipped. They're available in internal and external models.

✔ **Syquest.** Syquest cartridge drives were a popular standard for Mac creative professionals in the late 1980s and early 1990s. The removable Syquest cartridges work a little like hard disk drives, with a drive head and a platter. Popular capacities are 44MB, 88MB, and 200MB and (the more recent) 105MB, 230MB, and 270MB Syquest cartridges. The Syquest, Inc. company has gone out of business, although you can still occasionally find cartridges and drives that use this standard.

✔ **Bernoulli.** This competing standard by Iomega was very similar to Syquest drives in form and function. Sizes ranged from 35MB to 150MB. Again, they're not used often, but you can find cartridges for existing drives.

✔ **Magneto-optical.** A popular format in the early 1990s, this drive technology was heralded as a laser-based replacement for many drive technologies because of its capability to reach higher into impressive storage capacities. Popularity waned for a while, but a recent surge and improved technology is making M-O popular again.

✔ **Zip and Jaz.** Iomega marketed the Zip drive as an inexpensive 100MB storage solution to supplant the floppy drive. Since then, millions have been sold, including many that are now preconfigured in Apple and clone Mac OS machines. An addition to the standard, Zip 250, speeds up the drives and more than doubles cartridge capacity to 250MB. The Jaz drive, Zip's older brother, is a 500MB to 2GB drive capable of hard drive speeds. Figure 2-4 shows a Zip drive.

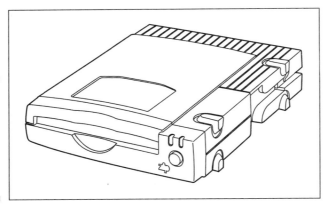

**Figure 2-4:**
The Zip drive comes in both external and internal versions.

# What Are You Doing, Dave?

What would a computer be if it didn't interact with humans? Probably less error prone. Be that as it may, we need input/output devices — our third subsystem — if Macs are going to be of much use.

# Plugging stuff into your Mac

In general, input/output (I/O) devices are external devices that hang off your computer's case, although some are installed inside your Mac's case (assuming it's healthy enough to survive surgery). Here are just a few of the fabulous ways you can hook up input/output devices:

✔ **Serial ports.** Many Macs have serial ports, which were standard until the arrival of the iMac and blue Power Macintosh G3. On most models, one of the ports is labeled with a picture of a phone and the other one features a small printer icon.

✔ **Universal serial bus (USB).** USB ports replaced serial ports on newer Mac models, offering higher speed connections, support for more devices and *hot pluggability,* which means you need to wear oven mitts when your touch the connectors. (Editor's Note: The term actually means you can plug devices in while the Mac is turned on.)

✔ **SCSI.** Many Mac models feature an external SCSI port, allowing you to hook up multiple SCSI devices by *daisy-chaining* them (hooking them to one another in a chain). SCSI devices include hard drives, CD and DVD drives, scanners, cameras, and other devices.

✔ **FireWire.** Mac models that don't offer an external SCSI port (with the exception of the early iMac models) offer FireWire ports. FireWire, like USB, is hot-pluggable, but it's also very fast, making it great for the stuff that SCSI is great for — hard drives, CD and DVD drives, and so on. FireWire is also popular for transferring video from digital camcorders to the Mac so that it can be edited.

✔ **ADB ports.** ADB, or Apple Desktop Bus, is a special port on many Macs used for a keyboard, a mouse, a graphics tablet, and as a power source for some other peripherals (such as some modems). ADB can also accept multiple daisy-chained devices. (Newer Macs use USB for these sorts of devices.)

✔ **Special ports.** Most Macs also feature a monitor port, a port for speakers, a line-in (microphone or audio device) port, and a telephone jack or an Ethernet networking port. All these are designed to accept particular types of peripherals to expand the Mac's capabilities.

✔ **Expansion cards.** Most non-iMac desktop Macs let you plug in circuit boards, called *expansion cards*, that add input/output capabilities to your Mac. Four major types of expansion cards exist: processor direct slot (PDS) cards, Nubus slot cards, PCI (Peripheral Component Interconnect) and AGP (Advanced Graphics Port) cards. Which type of card you get depends on the type of expansion slots your Mac offers.

## *Testing your I/O quotient*

So what sort of devices can be used for input and output? Instead of wracking your brain trying to invent different ways for computers to interact with the outside world, why don't I just tell you about some? It will be less painful for both of us:

- ✔ **Getting data into the computer.** Using keyboards, touchpads, trackballs, mice, joysticks, and graphics tablets, you can get all sorts of data into your computer.

- ✔ **Getting images and sound into the computer.** Using digital cameras, MIDI devices, audio/video input devices, and scanners, you can add images to your documents, file them away in databases, or use sound in your presentations. Power Macs and a few other models can even accept voice commands using special software and an Apple PlainTalk microphone. You even have a number of ways to get video from a VCR or camcorder into your Mac for editing.

- ✔ **Receiving visual results from the computer.** Monitors and printers are popular upgrades for serious Mac users. The more you sit in front of your computer (or the printed pages it spits out), the more you'll want a high-quality device.

- ✔ **Receiving audible results from the computer.** Using the Mac's built-in sound (on most models), you can hook up a stereo receiver or powered speakers to hear digitally generated sounds. You can also hook up MIDI devices on which your Mac can play songs. Or your Mac can speak selections of text using Apple's Text-to-Speech technology.

- ✔ **Communication between computers.** Macs can communicate with other Macs or other types of computers in a number of different ways. Using modems (*mo*dulate-*dem*odulate devices), your Mac can access other computers over phone lines. Using network connections, such as the Ethernet or LocalTalk ports on most Macs, you can move files between computers and print to distant printers. Using other devices with that Ethernet port — such as digital subscriber line (DSL), cable, or ISDN modems — you can get higher speed access to distant computers and the Internet.

- ✔ **Working with Microsoft Windows.** Exchanging files with Microsoft Windows users is pretty easy to do. The Mac OS supports Windows floppies and removable media, you can network your Mac to Windows machines, and you can exchange data over the Internet with pretty much any computer. But what if you need to run Microsoft Windows applications? You can do that, too, with special software called *emulation software* that lets you run Windows applications on your Mac. Or, if your Mac supports internal expansion cards, you can add a special PCI expansion card that puts an Intel-compatible processor in your Mac, letting you run Windows applications at full speed.

Experiencing input/output overload? (Isn't that what happened to the robot in *Lost in Space*?) Don't worry . . . we get to all these different types of communication. Right now, hum quietly to yourself and try to relax. You now know almost everything there is to know about Macs! (Actually, you just know everything *I* know about Macs. You might still want to brush up by talking to smarter people occasionally.)

# Chapter 3

# Diagnosis: Broken or Just Slow?

Do computers really slow down? After all, it doesn't seem to make sense. Most computer components are solid-state; radios and TVs don't seem to slow down, even if they have manual dials and little rabbit-ear antennas stuck together with aluminum foil and chewing gum. Do microwaves and dishwashers slow down?

And, yet, it's clear that an aging Mac can seem to slow down after a few years of use. Sometimes is has to do with Mac maintenance: you need to run file-management utilities (exercise) and go easy on the software upgrades (junk food) to keep your Mac in fighting shape. Eventually, though, the weight of new technologies and upgraded software capabilities might require you to consider a hardware upgrade to keep your Mac feeling younger.

And when you think about a hardware upgrade, you need to determine what, exactly, is slowing down. Today's secret word is *bottleneck* — traffic jams in your Mac that cause it to slow down for some reason. In this chapter, you examine those bottlenecks and see what you can do to get around them.

# Why Is My Mac Slowing Down?

Chances are, when you first got your Mac, it was pleasantly speedy. Windows popped open, documents poured out of your printer, and that spellchecker went humming from word to word to word to word in your word-processing program.

After a while, though, you might notice that your Mac is slower to wake from sleep, takes longer to get up and moving when you issue a command, or isn't as adept at talking to its peripherals — printing takes longer or your Internet connection seems slower. Your Mac, like the rest of us, is getting older.

Aside from the possibility that your Mac simply doesn't find the day-to-day very rewarding and needs a vacation (maybe I'm just projecting, here), there are two main reasons why it would slow down over time:

✔ **The Mac's storage subsystem needs maintenance or an overhaul.** (If you read Chapter 2, you can see that I'm already using that subsystem discussion from that chapter.) One major reason that a Mac will slow down over time is poor maintenance of the disks inside and attached to the Mac. First, it's important that any main hard disk have at least 10 to 15 percent of its space free for new files — this space is used by the operating system and applications for temporary files, memory swapping, and other tasks that affect day-to-day performance. Second, an unwatched disk becomes *fragmented* over time, making it more difficult for the Mac to open files in a timely manner. The result is a slowdown. Figure 3-1 shows an example of fragmentation in a disk doctor program.

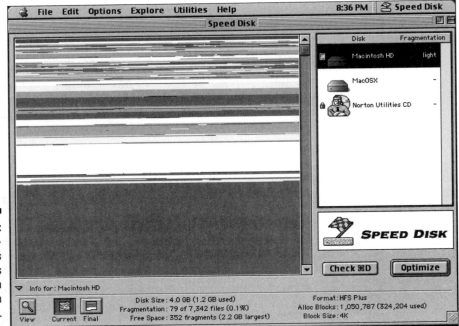

**Figure 3-1:** Fragmentation levels (light, in this example) in Norton Utilities.

✔ **You've added new software or you're performing more complex tasks.** This is the real reason most Macs seem to slow down. Whereas new Mac OS versions can sometimes actually speed things up a bit (especially for Power Macintoshes), often Apple adds new features and technologies that can slow down older computers when you update to a new OS version. Other applications can do the same thing by adding new features that become more and more power hungry. Microsoft Word 5.1, for instance, ran on most Mac II series computers with plenty of gusto. Mac Word 6.0, however, required even faster Quadra and Centris machines. Mac Word 98, taking things even further, doesn't run particularly speedily on anything below a second-generation (PowerPC 603- or 604-based) Power Macintosh.

So, it's all your fault. Sorry. (I'm willing to shoulder half the blame, but only if you bring snacks.) If you keep up with Mac maintenance and never upgrade your software, you shouldn't see too much of a slowdown. Some people compute happily that way for years.

Of course, most of us can't or don't want to compute that way — it's nice to run a new software version, play a new game, or upgrade to all the neat-o features Apple includes in the latest Mac OS versions. So, our only recourse is to ferret out those bottlenecks and figure out what upgrades and fixes will best get things rolling again.

## What is fragmentation?

Ideally, your Mac would write all data to the hard drive (and other storage media) sequentially, or *contiguously*, meaning it lays out the entire file on the disk in a nice, unbroken row. This makes it easier for the Mac to find a particular file when you ask for it. And contiguous files are more quickly loaded into main memory for use by your applications. When you first get a new Mac or a new storage disk, this is exactly what happens.

Over time, though, files get saved and deleted, saved and deleted, until the available space on a drive isn't in nice, neat rows anymore. Instead, the only spaces available are smaller spaces scattered all over the drive. When your Mac goes to write a file, it might need to use many of these little spaces to write down all the data in that file. The file has now become fragmented.

This slows the drive, because it has to jump around on its little platters finding the different parts of the file before it can load it into memory. It's like moving around on the tracks of an audio CD to get a few seconds of one song on one track, a few seconds of another song on another track, and so on. (Of course, the hard disk does all this in milliseconds, but those milliseconds add up after a while. Really.)

So, fragmentation is what those disk doctor programs attack, basically by picking up most of the files on the drive and rearranging them so that they're saved contiguously, leaving as much clear space as possible for new files. If you keep up with your fragmentation, you should get better performance out of your hard drive and hence your Mac.

## *Bottlenecks: Pouring it on thick*

I'm always surprised by how few people seem to know what I'm about to tell you about bottlenecks. I know *you* know it, but think of the ten to fifteen poor saps for whom you plan to purchase this book as a gift. Most of them don't know what I'm about to say.

If you have a bottle of ketchup, it will pour more quickly if you hold it at a 45-degree angle to the plate, rather than point straight down while violently slapping the bottom or vigorously shaking the bottle until you burst a blood vessel.

Why is this? Because of the neck of the bottle. If you hold the ketchup bottle at a 90-degree angle, all the ketchup in the larger base of the bottom will attempt to escape through the neck of the bottle at the same time. When it gets to the neck of the bottle, it clogs up and takes longer for *any* ketchup to reach your plate.

Computers work the *same way*. Tilt them at a 45-degree angle for maximum efficiency.

I'm kidding. But computer bottlenecks are the virtual equivalent of a ketchup bottle's neck. When you have a component that's computing data very quickly, and it tries to cram all that data through a slower component within your Mac, a bottleneck occurs. The data gets backed up, subsystems within the Mac get irritable and, in the end, you end up slapping the thing on its side just to try to get anything out of it at all.

For example, a common bottleneck for many Mac owners is not having enough RAM; without enough RAM, even a normally speedy Power Macintosh can slow way down. You might think your Mac doesn't process quickly enough or that its hard disk isn't fast enough. But the fact might be that your Mac lacks RAM. Without enough RAM, your Mac wastes time shuffling data around, even if the processor isn't being overtaxed (see Figure 3-2).

**Figure 3-2:**
The About
This
Computer
box on most
Macs
shows you
available
system
RAM.

So, what seems at first glance to be a slow processor or something wrong with the input/output subsystem might actually be a lack of RAM. (For instance, if your Mac is slow when displaying Web pages, the problem might be too little RAM instead of a slow processor or modem.) In most cases, a RAM upgrade is cheaper than a processor upgrade or a new Internet connection, so it's best to be on top of this bottleneck thing so that you don't waste money.

## Find that bottleneck!

Consider what's changed about your Mac since it started slowing down. This might be a good time to call forth the 75/25 rule I detailed in Chapter 1. What tasks are among your most important 75 percent? Have those tasks changed since you last remember your Mac being a speed demon? Maybe you're suddenly surfing the Internet more, you're printing more complex graphics, or you've developed an interest in video editing or high-end gaming.

If you've kept up with your hard drive maintenance, the slowdown is caused by a bottleneck. Let's look at some of the common ones and see if any ring true for your situation:

- ✔ **RAM.** RAM is the most common bottleneck in most Mac systems, and it's among the easiest upgrade. New programs almost always require more RAM than an earlier version, and this is absolutely true of the Mac OS. In Mac OS 9, for instance, the basic RAM requirement is 32MB, with 48 to 64MB the minimum for decent performance.

  Why are RAM numbers (and similar computer numbers) always 16, 32, 64 and so on? Because computers deal primarily in bits and bytes, most numbers related to that are multiples of 8. (A byte is 8 bits.) So, although it might be possible in some Macs to have 44MB of RAM, it's unlikely; you'll probably have 32, 64, 96, and so on.

- ✔ **Cache.** In many cases, a Mac's processor isn't being fully tasked, even if your Mac seems slow. The problem might be that the processor is waiting for data to arrive from main memory. When that's the case, cache RAM can certainly help because it speeds up the transactions between main RAM and the processor.

- ✔ **Processor.** Because new applications tend to be more complex, eventually they can become too much for a typical processor to handle. (There's also a self-fulfilling prophecy at work here. The faster the average processor in new computers, the more processor speed typical applications require, if only because it's easier for programmers to write applications less efficiently.) If you've had your Mac for a while and you're asking it to take on more complex calculations — image editing, 3-D, high-end gaming, sophisticated spreadsheet math, charts and graphs, and so on — the processor might need a boost.

- ✔ **Network.** If you're using an older technology for your network, the size of the files created by newer applications can begin to clog the slower speeds of old networking approaches. The faster your network technology, the more quickly you can share data with other users.

- ✔ **Modem.** If you use a modem to access the Internet, you might notice two bottlenecks. First, older modems transfer larger files more slowly and, the more seasoned a 'netter you are, the more likely your downloaded files will be large. Second, the more *often* you log on, the more you'll notice the *latency* of a modem connection — all that negotiation a modem has to go through just to create and maintain a connection. With a higher speed Internet solution, you'll clear the bottleneck on both fronts.

- ✔ **Video card.** A sophisticated graphics card not only adds colors and resolution to your monitor's capabilities but also takes on some of the hard work of rendering 3-D and other complex images on-screen. With its own RAM, processor, and sophisticated algorithms, a video card can make an entire Mac seem to speed up, even if the Mac's processor and system RAM don't change.

- ✔ **Hard drive.** When you run out of disk space on your main hard drive, you hamper your Mac's capability to use Virtual Memory and temporary files needed for best performance. Plus, if you begin to work with more complex files and technologies, some older hard drives can't keep up — they simple don't transfer data fast enough to keep up with tasks such as video editing, high-speed gaming, or even creating recordable CD-ROMs.

- ✔ **Printer.** Some printers (mostly, PostScript laser printers) have their own processors and RAM, thus freeing up a common bottleneck that occurs when a Mac tries to render a printing page while it performs other tasks. Likewise, aging printers aren't always designed for the most complex printing tasks, slowing down your entire Mac while they try to print graphics-heavy pages, for instance.

- ✔ **Port choice.** One of the more annoyingly complex problems you face with a Mac is choosing which port to use to connect devices. Internal drives and cards are fastest; traditional serial ports (the modem and printer ports on many Macs) are the slowest. The type of port connection used between peripherals and your Mac can create a dramatic bottleneck that slows things down.

You might encounter other bottlenecks, depending on how specialized the tasks are that you're trying to tackle. Overwhelmingly, though, those bottlenecks fall into two categories, again harkening back to Chapter 1: speed and quality. Which bottlenecks you're experiencing will dictate what you do to upgrade. You look at those in the diagnosis sections in the rest of this chapter.

# Diagnosis: Slow Computer

Grab your little black medical bag and take a trip into the world of the computer doctors. The key to any diagnosis is isolating the symptoms of your Mac's illness and seeing how they fit the possible causes.

Here, then, are some of the symptoms you might be encountering:

- **My Mac is slow when I have a lot of programs running at once.** Although a processor upgrade might help, the most important upgrade is RAM. The more main memory you have, the more programs you can run at once and the more quickly they'll all run, especially if you boost each application's individual memory partition, as discussed in Chapters 15 and 20.

- **My Mac is slow when I'm dealing with a two-dimensional graphics document.** If you're working with drawings or photos in PhotoShop or similar programs, the overwhelming need, again, is RAM. These high-level design programs demand a lot of RAM for the most efficient running. A close second in these cases is a fast processor, especially if your Mac is more than a few years old. You can also buy special video cards that speed up two-dimensional tasks, as discussed in Chapter 14.

- **My Mac is slow when I work with 3-D graphics, multimedia programs, and games.** RAM and a fast processor are priorities for anything involving three-dimensional computations. But the best results might be had by upgrading your graphics card to a newer 3-D accelerator, which has its own processor, RAM, and special driver software. This is especially true if your slow game or application supports the new graphics card.

- **My Mac is slow when I load and save documents.** RAM, the processor, and cache RAM can all contribute to what appears to be a slow hard drive. But the culprit might also be . . . a slow hard drive! This is especially true if you're trying to work with large (multi-megabyte) files. Upgrading to a new drive using advanced SCSI or FireWire technology might speed things up nicely; of course, you might also need a new interface card to give your Mac high-speed SCSI or FireWire capabilities.

- **My Mac is slow when I try to work with almost any document.** If your Mac is simply slow in general, especially while you're working in a document (as opposed to when you're printing, loading, or saving documents), it's possible that the applications you're using are taxing your Mac's processor, or that there isn't enough RAM available, or both. When most or all your applications are unbearably slow and you have plenty of RAM allocated, that's a good indication that a processor upgrade might be in order.

✓ **My Mac is slow when using a Web browser or America Online software.** If you have chronic slowdowns when accessing the Internet, this could be a processing or RAM issue. It's also possible that your Internet connection itself could be upgraded — you might go with a more capable modem, a cable modem, or a digital subscriber line connection to the Internet, if they're available in your area. (These are higher speed options that use Ethernet for the Internet connection.) If you have a modem connection, you should troubleshoot it first — it's always possible that you're not getting optimum connections with a perfectly capable modem.

✓ **My Mac is slow when I copy files over the network.** The latest software can go a long way to improving network copy operations, but the differences between LocalTalk connections and either Ethernet or AirPort wireless connections are very noticeable. If slow network copies are ruining your whole day, upgrade your network hardware.

✓ **My Mac is slow when it prints.** Most inkjet printers (and some personal laser printers) use the Mac's processor and RAM to create a printed image. In that case, upgrading your Mac's internals will speed up printing. With higher-end laser printers, the printer itself might need a RAM boost. If your printer is years old, though, technology has come a long way. You can get an inexpensive, high-speed (even color!) printer for a reasonable price.

✓ **My Power Macintosh is slow.** Macs that use the PowerPC processor run optimally with software designed to run on PowerPC machines, called *native* software. If you have older software (say, five or more years old), it might not run in native mode on your Power Mac, slowing things down quite a bit. (To a lesser extent, the same is true for classic Mac software that you're running on Mac OS X, as well as for software that hasn't been optimized for the Power Macintosh G4, if you have such a beast. See Chapter 25.) Most Power Macintosh models benefit greatly from both increased RAM and some form of cache RAM. Earlier Power Mac models didn't always include tons of cache RAM, so adding a cache memory module might be one way to speed things up.

# Diagnosis: Poor Quality

Upgrading and troubleshooting aren't always about boosting speed. Instead, other issues with your Mac might focus more on the quality of your computing experience.

Consider some common complaints about Macs and some of the steps you can take to remedy them. If any of these shoes fit, you might want to tie them on:

✔ **My monitor is difficult to look at.** It's possible that your monitor needs adjustment or servicing that you can accomplish on your own. Or you might need to take the monitor into the shop for a tweak or two — monitors do lose some of their quality with age, but adjustments can be made to get them back in fighting order. If your monitor is too small or doesn't offer everything you want or need, you might need to buy a new one.

✔ **My Mac doesn't display enough colors.** If you're creating and editing images, surfing the Web, or dealing with QuickTime movies or other multimedia, you might find that your monitor doesn't display enough colors. In many cases, you can upgrade the video card in your Mac to support more colors (thousands or millions instead of 256 colors, for instance), or you can add video RAM (VRAM) to your existing video circuitry.

✔ **I'd like more desktop space in which to work.** The video card or circuitry also dictates the resolution at which your monitor displays its desktop, assuming the monitor can support multiple resolutions. Therefore, if you upgrade your video card to support higher resolutions, you effectively get more space to work in. Likewise, you can add a video card and second monitor to most Macs, giving you extra space in which to work. As long as your Mac has available upgrade slots, it can likely support an additional monitor.

✔ **My print quality is low.** Newer printers have improved the resolution, colors, and speed at which they print. If your older printer looks too much like a computer printout (and not enough like a printed book), you can buy a new printer for better printing. A few upgrades are available to improve an existing printer, however, and you can also do some testing to get optimal printing from your current printer.

✔ **I want my inkjet to print in color.** Some Apple and Hewlett Packard printers shipped a few years ago offered color upgrade kits that added color-printing capability to the existing printer. In most cases, though, you need to buy a new printer to add color capability; fortunately, color printers are inexpensive.

✔ **I need Postscript quality output, but my printer isn't capable of it.** Ah, the world of Mac fonts. It's a jungle, but you can survive in the jungle if you know which bugs offer the most protein. Software workarounds and some hardware upgrades can give some printers PostScript capability. Or you can switch fonts around for the best printing quality on any printer.

✔ **I need to print more images on a page, but my laser printer can't do it.** If you have a PostScript laser printer, it needs enough RAM installed to print an entire page; the more complex the page, the more RAM needed. If your printer isn't printing an entire page, you might need to upgrade RAM or change some printer settings.

✔ **I hate my keyboard.** Macs tend to come with high-quality keyboards, but they're not tricked out like they could be. You can upgrade your keyboard using either ADB or USB, depending on the technology your Mac supports. You can even move the keyboard further away from the computer, if you'd like, or switch between different keyboards, or use one keyboard to control more than one computer.

✔ **I want a new mouse.** Mac OS 8.0 and higher has a capability called *contextual menus* that enables you to pop up a special menu of options when you hold down the Control key and click an item in the Finder (and in many applications). With a programmable mouse, you can use different buttons for the Control-click or for other keyboard-and-mouse-click combinations, as shown in Figure 3-3

✔ **I hate driving, flying, shooting with the keyboard.** Your Mac can be upgraded with gamepads, joysticks, steering wheels, airplane-simulator yokes, weapons control systems — even virtual golf clubs — that make gaming more fun and, perhaps, more realistic. Plus, many of these technologies can be adapted for use with regular applications to help those with physical disabilities.

✔ **I need to work with Intel-compatible PCs.** Macs have many compatibility options for talking to Intel-compatible PCs running DOS, Windows, or other operating systems. Macs with System 7.5 or higher can read and save files to DOS-formatted diskettes and removable disks; likewise, many Mac applications can open, close, and translate to PC formats. You can add the capability to *run* Windows or DOS software using an *emulator* — either software or hardware that actually runs Microsoft Windows on your Mac. And you can use many technologies — Ethernet, modems, and AirPort wireless connections — to transfer files between Macs and PCs.

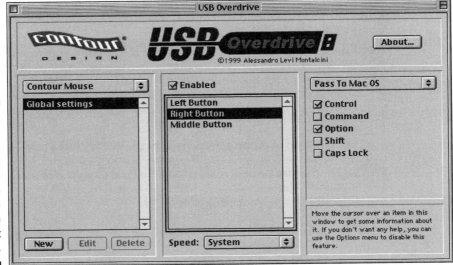

**Figure 3-3:**
Using a programmable mouse, you can assign certain key-mouse combinations to the different buttons.

✔ **My Mac doesn't sound very good.** Most Macs can be hooked up to better speakers, subwoofers, or even a home stereo receiver, if you'd like. You can also use upgrade cards or port connectors to add the capability to create MIDI (Musical Instrument Digital Interface, used to control synthesizers of all sorts) music or to record and edit digital music for audio production. Turn your Mac into a recording studio, CD production outfit, or a band to back up your hidden talents.

So, it's not all about speed. If your Mac has quality problems that you'd like to address, you can do so with various upgrades and fixes. Ultimately, the idea is to get your Mac to work as well for you as it can — and that doesn't always mean speed.

# Diagnosis: Broken

What if your problem isn't a speed problem or a quality problem — but a *problem* problem? If your Mac is crashing, devices aren't working correctly, or you just think something isn't quite right, you might need to explore whether or not your Mac is broken.

This is where my skewed definition of fixing comes into play (as discussed in Chapter 1). In many cases, if a component in your Mac goes bad, you know it immediately — the computer won't turn on, won't turn off, or won't do whatever it is that you want it to do. In those cases, you need to troubleshoot to get your Mac up and running to see what has failed. Failed components — a bad disk drive or a broken monitor — must be serviced by professionals or replaced. (Start with Chapter 23, or see the hardware troubleshoot tips throughout Parts II and III.)

If you have chronic crashing or freezing while you're working with your Mac, your Mac's hardware might not be broken, just misconfigured. It's kind of like when a toaster oven turns on and off but burns the toast because the temperature control is set wrong.

After you've eliminated configuration issues, you need to dig into the software and see whether the problem is something you encounter less often with toaster ovens: a bug, corruption, or a conflict. If your Mac is behaving weirdly, look to software as the culprit.

Many software fixes are easy to accomplish for the novice-to-intermediate user. I discuss those at length in Part IV, where you see how to tackle a Mac that's ailing from software problems, file corruption, or viruses.

Another important step in your quest to determine whether a particular component or piece of software is acting up is to ask the manufacturer. The arrival of the Internet as part of many people's daily lives has made it the easier way to get in touch with Apple and other computer vendors to see what they have to say about problems with their products. Every computer manufacturer I've ever visited on the Web has a *technical support* section in their Web site, where you can get information on their products, known problems, and downloadable solutions. If that doesn't work, call and yell at them.

I'll point out the Web sites of many major Mac manufacturers as we discuss their products through the pages of this humble text. All that is coming up, right after this page.

# Part II
# The Clinic: Upgrading and Fixing on the Outside

The 5th Wave    By Rich Tennant

"It's been two days, Larry. It's time to stop enjoying the new-computer smell and take the iMac out of the box."

## In this part . . .

You stop into your local clinic, instead of the operating room, to patch up bumps, scrapes, and much of what ails you. (Plus, there's the fabulous sugar-free candy that the receptionist always has.) Just like in the real world, plenty of Macintosh add-ons and improvements can be accomplished from the outside, with nary a screwdriver or scalpel in sight. In these chapters, you find information on all your Mac's ports, including what differentiates them and how to choose the right port for the job. Then it's on to a whirlwind tour of all the upgrading and fixing you can do using those ports, from monitors to printers to audio to video to storage. Plus, you see special upgrades for the FireWire and USB ports found on the latest iMac and Power Macintosh models.

# Chapter 4

# The Port Primer

*I*f you plan to attach devices to the outside of your Mac, you're pretty much going to have to use a port. Although just licking the device and pressing it against your Mac's case might seem easier, this strategy is flawed for two reasons. First, quite a few well-funded academic studies have shown that it's very important not to lick any type of electronic device. Second, the Mac needs some way to communicate with external devices, and that's usually accomplished by plugging a cable from the device into a port on your Mac.

## Aging Tech: The Older Ports

To talk about the first set of ports — serial and ADB — I need to set the WayBack Machine to 1997 or so because most of these ports are no longer found on Macs made in 1998 or later. Since the introduction of the iMac, all of Apple's newest computer models have stopped including serial and ADB ports. These ports, then, are becoming something of a distant oral tradition, handed down through elaborate stories told by the Mac community elders.

If you have an older Mac, though, you'll still find these ports useful for connecting new or older peripherals. So let's take a quick look at the technology behind each.

# Why all these different ports?

If you have a beige Mac (those made before the new round of colorful Macs that Apple now offers), you might be wondering, "Why so many ports?" They do this to confuse us.

Actually, the main reason is that some ports are just better at certain types of connections than others. For many years, most Macs included one or two ADB (Apple Desktop Bus) ports, one or two serial ports, and an external SCSI port for adding external devices. The ADB ports, which are the slowest type, were best designed for keyboards and mice, which don't communicate a lot of data. The ADB port can connect more devices than a typical serial port does: a mouse, a keyboard, a joystick, and so on.

Serial ports are faster than ADB ports but slower than SCSI ports, making them a good fit for modems, printers, and some low-end scanners. SCSI, on the other hand, offers high-speed connections and allows for multiple peripherals, but its cables are large and the SCSI chain has to be configured and managed. So, SCSI is better suited for external drives and high-end scanners.

The bottom line is that each port tends to be specialized, offering strengths and weaknesses. In fact, all the ports I've talked about so far are basically obsolete, as far as Apple is concerned, because of their weaknesses. USB and FireWire ports have replaced these three types of ports on newer Mac models. (SCSI is still used internally for some Mac models because it remains a strong technology for internal hard drives.)

## Serial ports

 If your Mac has serial ports at all, it likely has two serial ports — a printer port and a modem port. For all practical purposes, these ports are the same. They can both accept any sort of serial device such as a modem, a serial printer, or a serial scanner. If you have an AV Macintosh (such as the Quadra 660AV or 840AV) or any Power Macintosh that includes serial ports, both of those serial ports are also GeoPorts, which means they accept GeoPort devices. (There are very few of these, as discussed in Chapter 6.)

Both these ports are also LocalTalk ports, which means they can be used to create an AppleTalk network to another computer, a group of computers, or a LocalTalk printer using LocalTalk cabling, as discussed in Chapters 10 and 18.

So what are serial ports? For Macs that include them, they're the "jack-of-all-trade" ports. They're designed for devices that require relatively low data speeds, because serial ports, at the most, support 230 kilobits per second. This is a good speed for modems and printers, but it's not fast enough for external disks or high-color scanners. They're popular for digital cameras, specialty cameras, and personal digital assistants (PDAs, such as the Palm).

### Plugging into the port

To plug in a serial device, it's generally recommended that you turn off your Mac. It's possible (although somewhat unlikely) that plugging a device into a "live" serial port could damage the device or the port. After you've powered down, align the serial connector with the port on the back of your Mac. In most cases, the logo or label on your serial cable will be facing upward (that is, you can read the label easily) when things are properly aligned. If the cable doesn't connect easily with the port, make sure you don't have it slightly misaligned.

Don't force the connector — take a look at its pins and at the holes in the port to make sure it's aligned correctly. It plugs in only one way.

After you plug in the device, you start up the Mac and install any software that came with the device. Most serial devices require that you install *driver software* in your Mac's System Folder to tell the Mac how to talk to the device. In many cases, this driver software comes in the form of a control panel, which you can access (from the Control Panels menu in your Apple menu) to configure the device. (You look at individual devices in other chapters in Part II.)

---

# The error file: Port in use

The most common problem with serial devices is the tendency for a serial port to remain in use when you try to switch from one task to another. An example might be switching from your Internet connection to a fax program set to receive a fax using your modem — sometimes an error will appear telling you that the device is in use.

The answer to this one is pretty simple: Figure out what program or driver software isn't letting go of the port. Return to the application that was last using the port and see whether you can terminate the port connection in some way — by signing off the connection or by selecting a command to reset the port or turn off the application's auto-sensing. (In some personal digital assistant software, for instance, you can tell it to stop monitoring the port for activity.)

If shutting down the offending application doesn't help, you might need to shut down the serial device (if it has a power switch), or shut down your Mac, or both. Sometimes, you need to power the Mac all the way down so that the port (or serial device) resets.

One other caveat: If you're using AppleTalk networking, make sure you don't have the port that you're trying to use for something else selected in the AppleTalk control panel. (Open the AppleTalk control panel and make sure the correct port or technology — such as Ethernet — is selected.) If you're not using AppleTalk, open the Chooser or your control strip and turn off AppleTalk to eliminate the possibility of port conflicts. And keep this in mind: If the small logic board battery in your Mac is dying, the AppleTalk settings might reset automatically. If your Mac is suddenly experiencing serial port conflicts, that battery might be the culprit. (See Chapter 23 for more on the PRAM battery.)

### *Need more ports?*

The biggest problem you'll generally encounter with serial ports is the fact that most desktop models have only two of them. (A few have only one!) Serial ports don't support more than one device per port, unlike many other port technologies. (USB, FireWire, SCSI, and ADB all support more than one device per port, in various ways.)

If you're running out of ports, here are a few solutions for the serial port blues:

- ✔ **Choose a different port.** Sometimes you can move devices around, especially those that support more than one type of connection. If your laser printer can support both LocalTalk and Ethernet, you might consider plugging the printer into your Ethernet port and using the free serial port for another device.

- ✔ **Get a manual switch box.** You can use a *manual switch box* — a box that accepts two (or more) serial devices and then enables you to switch between them with a big knob or slider switch. However, not all devices support switch boxes, especially devices that support two-way communication between the Mac and a device, such as some digital cameras, PDA connectors, and Hewlett-Packard printers (see Figure 4-1). Oh . . . and you have to remember to switch the darned dial when you try to use the *other* device from your Mac!

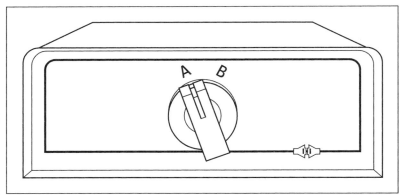

**Figure 4-1:**
Use a manual switch box to connect two serial devices to one serial port.

- ✔ **Try powered switching.** If the switch box doesn't work for you, try a *powered switching device* instead. These boxes sense which device you're trying to use (using their own control panels) and then route the data to that device. The Port Xpander from MacAlly (www.macally.com), for instance, can switch automatically between devices while supporting more devices than a typical switch box.

✔ **Add more ports.** If you're serious about your serial devices, you can add more serial ports using a PCI expansion card. (Your Mac needs to support PCI, meaning it must be based on a second-generation PowerPC processor or higher. See Chapter 14.) Keyspan (www.keyspan.com) makes such a card, which gives you four additional serial ports.

# The Apple Desktop Bus

For years (here I am in the WayBack Machine again), the Apple Desktop Bus, or ADB, was one of those technologies that set the Mac apart from the Intel PC side of the fence. Input devices were simple to plug into Macs and, using the ADB port, you could plug in two, three, or even four devices without having to worry about configuring things with drivers and settings in the Mac OS. For the most part, these devices just worked; any configuring you did was for additional benefit, not for the basic setup.

ADB is another technology whose dominance has been usurped by USB in what history will refer to as the iMac Era. Although a good technology and easy enough to use, ADB loses to USB in two ways. First, it isn't *hot pluggable*, so you need to put your Mac to sleep or power down to safely change peripheral connections. Second, ADB is very, very slow, communicating at only 154 *bytes* per second. This makes ADB suitable for only the lowest forms of peripheral life, such as keyboards, mice, and joysticks. It's also limited to three or four devices, but that's not so bad because it's difficult to use more than two input devices at once. Just try it.

## ADB connections

Modern Power Macintosh and Performa models that support ADB generally have a single ADB port. Mac II, Centris, and Quadra models, among others, often offered two ADB ports. Having two ports isn't much of an advantage, though, because you can *daisy-chain* ADB devices (plug the second device into the first and the third device into the second, and so on).

An ADB cable uses a 4-pin DIN connector on both sides for connecting devices to the Mac or to each other. No special *terminators* or other devices are required for ADB chains — just plug one device into the next in a daisy-chain configuration. Note that some devices don't include a second port; in that case, try to rearrange the daisy-chain so that the single-port device is last.

You might come across another type of ADB connector called a *passthrough* connector (see Figure 4-2). Because the ADB port can actually provide power to the devices (instead of requiring them to have their own power supplies), some devices include an ADB connector simply to power the unit. Some popular modems have used this scheme by connecting to ADB for power but to the serial port to communicate with the Mac. (Likewise, pass-through connectors are sometimes used for *copy-protection dongles*, which are used with some expensive software programs to make sure that the licensed owner of the software is the only person using it.)

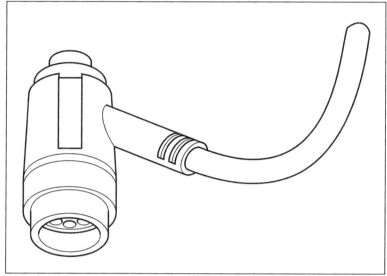

**Figure 4-2:**
Some devices use a passthrough ADB connector to draw power from the ADB connection.

Although passthrough connectors make it easy to hook up additional devices, watch out for them. The power draw makes it possible for the signals to degrade from your other devices. You might have trouble using more than a couple of input devices — such as a keyboard and a mouse — if you also have a passthrough connector plugged in.

Theoretically, the ADB is limited to fourteen daisy-chained devices. Practically, that limit is three or four devices — Apple warns that you might see degradation after plugging in three devices, but I've worked for long periods of time with four and even five ADB devices plugged in with no ill effects. (Again, you're not likely to use a mouse, a keyboard, and a joystick all at the same moment.) If you notice sluggishness while typing or mousing, you might try using one less ADB device to see whether that helps things.

As noted earlier, ADB is not hot-pluggable. Although many Mac users over the years have reported no ill effects from plugging in ADB devices while their Mac is running, Apple doesn't condone this behavior, preferring that you power down your Mac to keep from damaging ADB devices or ports. (Remember, a trickle of power courses through the port.)

## Stuff you don't need to know: ADB numbers

Internally, your Mac assigns addresses — special numbers — to each ADB device so that it can tell them apart. These numbers enable the Mac to identify the device that needs attention and listen for its input. Although it almost never comes up in day-to-day operations, I've seen one or two control panels that ask you, the intrepid user, to determine the ADB number of a device. In these cases, it can be useful to know that the Mac keyboard's secret ID code is generally device number 2, whereas a mouse is usually device number 3. (After reading this, rip this page out of the book and eat it to secure this knowledge from others.)

Want to know more ADB numbers? The limit to the length of *all* daisy-chained ADB cables should be no more than five meters, say Apple's technical specs. If you want to place your keyboard and mouse farther away from your Mac than that, you need to use special devices (discussed in Chapter 5).

# *Feelin' Kinda SCSI*

 Although SCSI (Small Computer Systems Interface, pronounced "scuzzy") is also being phased out in newer Power Macintosh configurations, it hasn't given its last hurrah yet. For centuries now (well, almost), the back of Mac models have included a convenient external SCSI that was the envy of other computer platforms the world over. Although configuration was often a bear, this SCSI port offered high enough speeds for external hard disks, high-end scanners, and removable media drives, among other wonders.

In the iMac Era (this is starting to sound like some sort of teal-and-tangerine apocalyptic vision), the SCSI port is no more, having been replaced by the higher speed FireWire port in many cases. FireWire is faster and easier to configure, and one port supports more devices than the external SCSI port of yore. But if you already have external SCSI devices or you're sticking with a tried-and-true beige Macintosh, the SCSI port is still as real and significant to you as it was in its heyday.

## *SCSI explained*

Two discussions of SCSI are relevant to Macs, and I'm going to leave one of those discussion for Chapter 17. As it turns out, SCSI is both an external and an internal connection technology. (I was just as surprised as you are.) SCSI is used to connect high-speed hard drives installed internally on many Mac models; it's still popular for such drives, especially in high-end creative environments.

As far as external upgrading goes, SCSI is a bit more limited but still popular. The back of most beige Macs and Power Macs has a single SCSI port that's designed to support external SCSI devices. This 25-pin port enables you to daisy-chain up to 7 devices. The SCSI port is capable of about 5MB per second of data transfer, making it more than fast enough for external hard disks, removable media drives, and other peripheral devices that need to transfer a lot of data.

SCSI allows up to 7 devices to coexist on a single *bus* (chain of devices wired together). In some cases, the SCSI bus is shared between internal and external SCSI devices (this is true of many, but not all, pre-Power Macintosh models; see Chapter 17). In this case, the number of external devices supported might be lower.

So, if you have an external SCSI port, you can connect somewhere between 4 and 7 external devices to your Mac, depending on your model and what sort of SCSI devices are installed under the hood. If you'd like to install external drives or scanners, SCSI is the way to go, unless you install a FireWire card.

## Installing SCSI devices

Like ADB, the SCSI bus allows you to daisy-chain devices, meaning you can connect the first device to the Mac, the second device to the first device, the third to the second, and so on. Unlike ADB, though, SCSI chains must be terminated at the end of the connection, usually by plugging a special *terminator* ("Au'll be bauck!") into the open port on the last SCSI device in the chain (see Figure 4-3).

When you install a new SCSI device, it has to have a new SCSI ID number. Amazing and exciting problems — crashes, freezes, or even hard-to-detect data problems — can result when you assign the same SCSI ID number to two different devices. Avoid doing so at all costs.

So what SCSI ID do you choose? In most cases, you can simply choose one that's available on your current SCSI bus. The best way to determine that is to open a program called Apple System Profiler, which should be installed in your Apple menu. Apple System Profiler is a tool that Apple includes with Mac OS Version 7.6 and higher to help you determine various things about your Mac, including what's on the SCSI bus.

In Apple System Profiler (see Chapter 24), you can check the Devices and Volumes section (or Device Information section, in earlier versions) to find information about your SCSI bus and available SCSI ID numbers. If your Mac has more than one SCSI bus (this is true of some Apple Macintosh and Power Macintosh models, as well as any clone or Apple machine that has a SCSI expansion card installed), the external SCSI bus will often be SCSI bus 1 (see Figure 4-4).

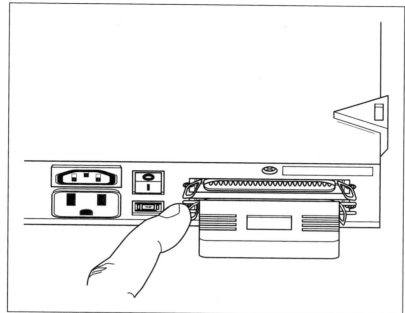

**Figure 4-3:**
A SCSI
terminator
installed on
an external
hard drive.

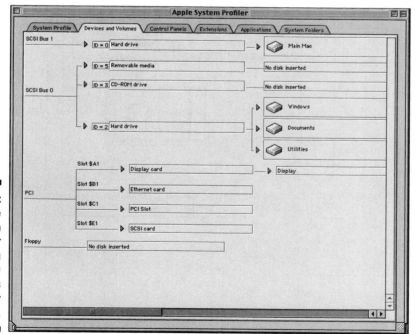

**Figure 4-4:**
The Apple
System
Profiler
shows you
the SCSI ID
numbers
currently
in use.

For your new device, choose an ID number that isn't in use and set your device to that number. How? You use the device's selector thingie. For external devices, such as hard drives and removable media drives, you generally set the SCSI number with a switch of some sort, as shown in Figure 4-5.

With the number set, shut down your Mac. Then plug the device into the SCSI port on the back of your Mac or into an available SCSI port on the *last device* in your current SCSI chain. (You'll probably have to remove a terminator to plug in the device, if your chain is already properly configured. If there's no physical terminator, you might need to turn off the termination on that last device using a switch on the back of the device.)

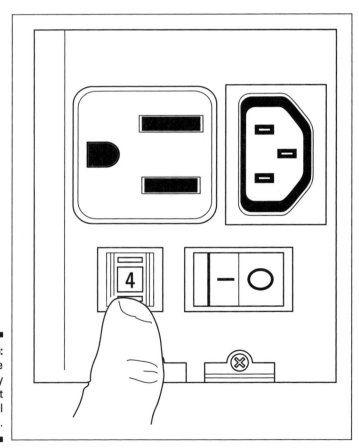

**Figure 4-5:**
SCSI IDs are usually simple to set on external devices.

After you plug in the device, plug a terminator into the other port of your new device (because it's the last device on the chain and the chain must be terminated). If the device has internal termination, switch the setting on the device so that it's terminated.

The next steps are to turn on the device, start up your Mac, and test to see whether it works. (You might need to install additional driver software.) You should be able to use the Apple System Profiler to see whether the hardware has been installed and shows up at the correct SCSI ID number.

## When good SCSI goes bad

Is your SCSI chain giving you fits? I'll let you in on a little secret. Old Mac hands call the problems associated with these connections *SCSI voodoo* because, well, SCSI can be a bit cranky.

Here's a look at some of the issues surrounding a SCSI connection and what makes them tick:

- **SCSI numbers.** Technically, the higher the SCSI ID you assign to a device, the higher the priority. In reality, it doesn't matter much, because the Macintosh itself is the only device that really has priority over the others. (And the Macintosh is automatically given SCSI ID 7 on any SCSI chain.) That said, if you have trouble with a SCSI device, you might try setting it to a higher SCSI ID — or simply a different SCSI ID.

- **SCSI cables.** SCSI cables need to be high quality, offering the proper shielding and components. Poor-quality cables are probably the fore-most cause of SCSI failure.

- **SCSI chain length.** The length of your SCSI cables (and the overall length of the SCSI chain, when you add all those cables together) is also an issue. The overall length of a SCSI daisy-chain should never exceed 20 feet, although any chain over 10 feet can exhibit problems. Likewise, cables between 1 and 2 feet long are best for connecting individual devices. If you need a device farther from your Mac, consider using a networking connection instead. (For instance, your Mac can access an external drive attached to another Mac over an Ethernet connection.)

- **Types of connectors.** The external connector on your Mac uses a 25-pin connection, but many SCSI devices use the standard (called *Centronics*) 50-pin connector (and some others might even have a Wide SCSI 68-pin connector). That means you might need to buy a 25-pin-to-50-pin (or 25-pin-to-68-pin) adapter (or cable) to connect between some devices and your Mac. Check both ends of your proposed connection and make sure you have the right connectors and cables to make the link work.

## *Terminating with care*

I hope your termination issues are painless. If you have only one or a few SCSI devices, you generally just turn on termination for the final device in the chain, and your worries end there. But that's not always the case. Sometime, you need to dig deeper into termination issues.

Here are a few issues to look out for when it comes to termination:

- **Don't terminate devices twice.** This is especially easy to do when you're dealing with devices that have internal terminators. If you double-terminate, you can cause errors or data corruption.

- **Look out for software termination.** Some devices offer termination controlled by software, not by dongles or switches. Check your device's manual carefully.

- **Watch out for TERMPWR.** Makes your skin crawl just thinking about it, doesn't it? Some earlier SCSI devices send *termination power* (TERMPWR) to the SCSI bus. Most modern Macs don't react well when forced to associate with such devices.

- **Consider devices with active termination.** These devices terminate themselves based on circumstances, often using an LED indicator to tell you what the verdict was. If you don't agree with the device's decision (or if errors ensue), you should be able to change the setting.

- **Break the rules.** You're supposed to terminate only at the beginning of the SCSI chain (usually handled for you inside the Mac) and at the end of the chain. But if your SCSI chain reaches beyond 10 feet, adding a third terminator at about the 10-foot point can be useful if you're having SCSI-related errors. Stranger than fiction, eh?

# *Universal Serial Bus*

 I keep talking about the iMac Era in this chapter, but I did you the disservice of creeping up on the main reason for such a focus. When the iMac was introduced, it was offered in one model, with one type of external upgrading port on its side. That technology was universal serial bus (USB).

At the time, this move was heralded by some as outstandingly ingenious and by others as utterly stupid, although ingenious seems to be ahead as the last votes are tallied. By putting only USB on the original iMac — and then proceeding to sell a few million of the little devils — Apple was a driving force in moving the entire computing industry to this previously undervalued standard.

What upset users of older Macs was the lack of support for SCSI devices, ADB devices, and serial devices, because USB is incompatible with each of those. And Mac owners tended to own many of those devices and weren't keen to replace them. As you see in Chapter 12, the marketplace responded, offering a number of adapters that do allow you to attach older devices to USB ports.

But there are good reasons why USB was a great technology to build into iMac and other new Mac models. USB is hot-pluggable, meaning devices can be plugged and unplugged while the Mac is running. USB is faster than serial and ADB ports, making it appropriate for a wider variety of devices. And USB can support an unlikely maximum of 127 devices per bus, which offers these Mac owners the flexibility of attaching pretty much as many USB devices as they want.

So how fast is USB? Each USB bus can transfer data at 12 megabits per second, or about 1.5 megabytes per second. This makes it capable for any number of devices, including keyboards, mice, printers, scanners, and removable media. And in a pinch, especially on iMacs that don't support FireWire, you can even plug in an external hard disk.

Want USB on your pre-iMac machine? You can install a PCI-based expansion card that gives your Mac USB ports. See Chapter 14 for details.

## *Hooking up USB devices*

USB features a 4-pin connector that can be inserted only the correct way in a USB port. (The pins aren't raised like they are on older ports and connectors, so they can't be bent.)

Two types of USB cables are available: those with two 4-pin connectors (A-A cables) and those with one 4-pin connector and one 6-pin connector (A-B cables). The A-A cable is used to connect between a USB port and a USB *hub*. The A-B connector is used to connect USB devices to USB ports. (*A* for the port and *B* for the device.)

What's this about hubs? A *hub* is a device that allows you to add more USB connections using an existing USB port. Because USB can't be daisy-chained like some other technologies, you can add only as many USB devices as you have ports. On most Macs, that's two ports — hardly enough for 127 devices.

Using a USB hub, though, you can add four, seven, or more USB ports for connecting your devices. And many hubs are powered (you plug them into the wall or your surge protector), so the hub can provide power to USB devices that don't have their own AC adapters.

How do you connect USB devices? Just plug them in! Your Mac can be on, off, sleeping, or even doing some other sort of computing when you plug in the USB device. When the Mac wakes up, turns on, or otherwise gets a free moment, it notices the USB device and attempts to load the device's driver. If the driver is present, the device should start working. If the driver is not present, you need to install it.

So I guess that's actually two steps: plug in your USB device and load its software. (You could also get clever and install the software first, and then plug in the device, so that it's recognized instantly.) Not all USB devices need a special driver (keyboards and basic one-button mice should work fine), but others will need a USB driver in the System Folder on your Mac before they are recognized.

## USB trouble

USB is reasonably trouble-free, although it's had growing pains as a new technology. For Macs that came from the factory with USB ports, one of the main things you need to do is to keep that Mac's firmware upgraded. (*Firmware* is low-level system software kept on a special chip on the Mac's logic board.) Firmware updates tend to make support for USB better, as do Mac OS updates. (Both are covered in Chapter 22.)

Aside from the system software and the appropriate software drivers for your devices, a few issues you might encounter with USB connections follow:

- **The device isn't detected.** First, confirm that the device is getting power and that it's turned on. Then make sure you've installed the device's driver software. If you have (and you've restarted, if necessary), try unplugging and re-plugging the device to see whether it's detected after re-plugging. Then try another port. If that doesn't work either, try shutting down the Mac, plugging in the device, and then restarting. If none of these works and your firmware is up-to-date, there might be a problem with the device.

- **The Mac OS complains about power.** If you see a message stating that a USB device isn't working because it doesn't have enough power, plug the device's AC adapter into the wall. You can also try plugging the device into another port on your Mac or removing some other devices from your USB hub, if that's how the device is connected.

- **The Mac OS says a driver isn't found.** You need to install the device's driver software, probably on a CD included with the device. If that doesn't work, something might be wrong with the device driver software; check with the device's manufacturer.

- **The Mac freezes.** Whoops. Sounds like a problem with the device's driver or with the USB software you have installed. Update your firmware and test again. If the Mac still freezes, make sure you're using the latest Mac OS version (see Chapter 22) and then talk to the device's manufacturer.

# FireWire

 FireWire is a technology invented by Apple and conceived, ultimately, as a replacement for SCSI. In the same way that USB offers advantages over serial and ADB ports, FireWire offers similar advantages over SCSI, especially for external upgrading.

The bottom-line differences are twofold: FireWire is faster than external SCSI and easier to use. (Nanny, nanny, boo-boo.) There isn't much in the way of FireWire voodoo — most of the time, it just works. FireWire is hot-pluggable, allows you to daisy-chain up to 63 devices, and doesn't require terminators, ID numbers, or thick cables. In fact, some FireWire devices don't require a power supply because the FireWire bus itself offers power.

How much faster is FireWire? External SCSI (in all forms included on Mac models that had it) transfers data at 5 megabytes per second. FireWire, in its first iteration, transfers data at 400 megabits per second, or 50 megabytes per second.

FireWire is a fast, easy standard for hooking up external devices, made even more popular by its inclusion on colorful Power Macintosh G3, G4, and the iMac DV models. FireWire hard drives and removable media drives are now appearing on the market in droves. Plus, FireWire is already a standard in the world of digital video (DV) camcorders. If you have a DV camcorder, it likely has a FireWire port.

 Like USB, you can add FireWire cards to an older Mac, as long as it has an available PCI slot. See Chapter 14.

## Plugging into FireWire

Let's cut to the chase on this one. FireWire supports 63 devices per bus, and FireWire devices can be daisy-chained. If you have a number of devices, some might need to run off AC power because the bus provides only 6 watts of power. Also, FireWire hubs are available, but they're really only a convenience — disconnecting one FireWire device won't break the chain if you're using a hub.

Like USB, FireWire cables come in two types. The 4-pin-to-6-pin types (4/6) are designed for connecting a digital camera (4-pin) to a FireWire port (6-pin). A 6-pin-to-6-pin cable (6/6) is designed for connecting other FireWire peripherals, including hubs, to a FireWire port.

Again like USB, FireWire devices are easy to plug in — just install any necessary driver software for the device first and then plug in the FireWire device. If the device needs its own AC power, plug that in as well. You should be up and running. If you want to check, the Apple System Profiler shows FireWire devices on its Devices tab.

## *Avoid getting burned by FireWire*

I know . . . you're thinking that this section's title is too obvious. You're right — and it doesn't even work well because there aren't too many problems you can encounter with FireWire. Again, you'll want the latest firmware and the latest version of the FireWire Mac OS extension, and you'll want to install any updates or revisions to the device driver software for your FireWire devices. (See Chapter 22 for hints on updating your Mac's software.)

Other than that, here are some FireWire thoughts:

- **Keep your lines straight.** When you're daisy-chaining your FireWire devices, make sure that none of them double-back on the chain and create a loop. Plug them in so that device one is attached to the FireWire port, device two is attached to device one, device three is attached to device two, and so on. If you create a loop, you're just askin' for trouble.

- **Keep unused ports empty.** There's no need to plug an extra cable into the last open port of a FireWire device on the daisy-chain. There are no terminators with FireWire.

- **If a device requires power from the FireWire bus, plug it directly into the FireWire port.** You can also plug directly into a FireWire hub if a FireWire-powered device is giving you trouble. The FireWire bus provides only limited amounts of power, and that power can't always trickle down an entire daisy-chain. If you have a choice, plug your device into the wall using its AC adapter.

- **Don't unplug devices while any are in use.** Remember that unplugging one device on a daisy-chain interrupts the connection to all subsequent devices; if you're currently reading or writing data to or from one of those devices, the sudden disconnect can cause trouble. Although FireWire devices can often recover from being suddenly unplugged, you might corrupt files or cause your Mac to freeze.

- **Use fewer devices.** If you're not getting the results you want, especially with FireWire-based DV cameras, plug only that device into the FireWire port while you're using it or plug the device into its own FireWire port while you use the other one for a daisy-chain. The fewer devices you have between the device and the Mac, the better the quality of the transfer will likely be.

# Chapter 5

# Keyboards, Mice, and Cool Input Devices

● ● ● ● ● ● ● ● ● ● ● ● ● ● ● ● ● ● ● ● ● ● ● ● ● ● ● ● ● ● ● ● ● ● ● ● ● ● ● ●

*In This Chapter*

▶ Shopping for input

▶ Using fancy keyboards

▶ Mousing around in unique ways

▶ Driving, shooting, or a combination thereof

● ● ● ● ● ● ● ● ● ● ● ● ● ● ● ● ● ● ● ● ● ● ● ● ● ● ● ● ● ● ● ● ● ● ● ● ● ● ● ●

"*A*h, the keyboard . . . how quaint," quoth Scotty, the intrepid engineer of the original *Star Trek* series in *Star Trek 4: The Wrath of Polyester.* (That might not have been its original title.) One day, in that idealized future of a constant barrage of aliens with odd foreheads, perhaps we, too, will talk to our computers.

Actually, that's probably about ten years away, assuming that speech ends up being a productive way to work with computers. For now, you generally chat with your Mac using the same devices we've been using for more than 15 years: a keyboard and a mouse. If you want to get fancy about it, you can add a digitizing pad or touch screen, too.

## The Wonderful World of Input

Input devices are attached to Macs using one of two technologies: ADB or USB. If you have a pre-iMac machine, you use ADB unless you've added a USB expansion card. For all non-beige Macs, you use USB for your input devices.

Do you have a blue Power Macintosh G3? In that case, you're special. That particular model includes both USB and ADB ports; which you use is completely up to you.

As mentioned, input devices vary greatly. It so happens, though, that manufacturers who make one type of input device will often make another, so I'd like to cover most of those manufacturers quickly here in this section. Plus, it's only fair because they all gave me wheelbarrows full of cash.

If you're looking to see what's out there in the world of peripherals, you might visit some of these Web sites:

- ✔ **Adesso, Inc.** (www.adessoinc.com) specializes in ergonomic keyboards and mice for Macs and PCs.

- ✔ **APS Technologies** (www.apstech.com) builds some peripherals, but they're also a catalog company and clearinghouse for special items such as advanced mice and cables.

- ✔ **Ariston** (www.ariston.com) offers USB-based input devices.

- ✔ **Kensington** (www.kensington.com) is best known for trackballs but also offers programmable mice and ADB keyboards.

- ✔ **iMaccessories** (www.imaccessories.com) specializes in USB input devices and other options for Macs that support USB.

- ✔ **MacAlly** (www.macally.com) makes a number of Mac ADB and USB peripherals, including keyboards, mice, touchpads, joysticks, and gamepads.

- ✔ **Microspeed** (www.microspeed.com) offers trackpads, mice, and Mac keyboards.

# *Love Your Keyboard?*

Over time, most Apple Macintosh computers (and all clones, as far as I'm aware) have included keyboards. (During one dark period in the early 1990s, Apple didn't provide a keyboard with their multi-thousand dollar machines, but the Mac faithful try to block that time out of their minds.) The original Macs shipped with a 58-key clacker that looked like something out of the movie *Brazil.* Later, most Macs shipped with the Apple Extended keyboard, which was a wonderful keyboard that included 104 keys. That gave the keyboard space to include a numeric keypad, a special Power key, and 12 function keys along the top of the keyboard.

The colorful Macs of the past few years (iMacs and the Power Macintosh G3 and G4 series) have a new keyboard that's nice and pretty, but some feel it is slightly cramped. (Complaints about it don't begin to rival complaints about the colorful mouse, however, which I discuss later.) That keyboard is a complete one, though, and it has the advantage of being a passive USB hub, allowing you to connect an additional USB device to its free USB port.

But new keyboards abound, offering you different configurations, built-in mousing devices, or designs to alleviate the strain and stress associated with extensive keyboarding. To use one of these devices, you simply buy it and attach it, as long as it uses a port interface that your Mac supports.

TIP

If you have USB ports on your Mac, you can even hook up USB keyboards designed for Microsoft Windows computers. In most cases, the Windows keys and other special keys will map to the corresponding Apple command key and other special keys on a Mac keyboard.

## *Shapely, contoured keyboards*

*Ergonomic keyboards* are designed to place your hands in a more comfortable, more scientifically correct posture than regular keyboards promote. Often this is accomplished by splitting the keys down the middle, forcing you to elevate your wrists slightly while keeping them more directly in front of you. It's a position you might be familiar with if you've ever taken piano lessons. (Figure 5-1 shows an ergonomic keyboard.)

**Figure 5-1:**
One of
Adesso
Inc.'s
ergonomic
keyboards,
designed to
help ease
typing
tension.

Ergonomic keyboards come in two different flavors: commercial and therapeutic. There's plenty of disagreement over exactly what sorts of keyboard designs are best for different users. You'll find that the sub-$100 market offers some ergonomic designs that may or may not be more comfortable than traditional keyboards over long periods of use. For more than $100, you can find manufacturers who make keyboards that are, presumably, based on the findings of medical professionals.

ON THE WEB

Aside from ergonomics, keyboards offer a number of different features, including wireless connections, built-in input devices, special adaptive technologies for people with disabilities, or more far-flung designs for speed and comfort. Here are a few companies that offer specialized keyboards:

✔ **Comfort Keyboard Company** (www.comfortkeyboard.com) makes the Comfort Keyboard, a fully adjustable keyboard that breaks apart and changes angles for any user.

✔ **DataDesk Technology** (www.datadesktech.com) sells, for children and adults, ergonomic and programmable keyboards that take up less desk space than typical keyboards.

✔ **Keytime** (www.keytime.com) offers keyboards in special layouts that support Dvorak and others (see the next section).

✔ **Kinesis Corporation** (www.kinesis-ergo.com) offers split keyboards, keyboards with special cupped designs, and programmable keyboards that can support special layouts such as Dvorak (see the next section).

✔ **Maltron Keyboards** (www.maltron.com) makes highly ergonomic keyboards designed for people suffering from repetitive stress disorder (RSI) as well as keyboards for people with limited use of their hands. Single-finger or mouth-stick keyboards are also available from the company.

✔ **Orcca Technology** (www.orcca.com) makes adaptive technology keyboards and mice.

✔ **Pace Development Corporation** (ids2.com/pace/) offers a fully adjustable keyboard (ADB only, it seems) that can be placed at different angles.

Want to plug standard Intel-compatible keyboards (or even mice) into your ADB-based Mac? In many cases, you can — with the right adapter. USR Systems (www.usr.com) offers their AppAdapter product, which enables Mac owners to plug in PS/2-style keyboards and mice, translating the PS/2 commands into Mac ADB data. USB mice and keyboards can be plugged right into Macs that support USB, although all the features of a Windows-oriented USB device might not be activated.

## Keyboard layouts

Built into the Mac OS is the capability to support different keyboard layouts: Change the layout, and the keys you press on the keyboard will give different results. If you want to change the language in which you're typing (so that you have access to various international characters, for instance), you can do that using the Keyboard control panel (see Figure 5-2).

In 1936, efficiency expert August Dvorak introduced a new layout meant to speed up typing while lowering the hand movement required by the standard QWERTY layout. Dvorak reportedly estimated that over an eight-hour day a typist's hands can travel 12 to 20 miles over a regular keyboard, while travelling only 1 mile using the Dvorak layout. You may or may not type faster and you may or may not be more comfortable with Dvorak; but you can try it if you want.

By selecting the Dvorak layout from the Keyboard control panel, you can immediately switch your current keyboard to support this style of typing. You might want a new keyboard so that the keys actually represent the letters you're typing, or you can also opt for some letter stickers from the computer or office supply store. Figure 5-3 shows the basic Dvorak layout.

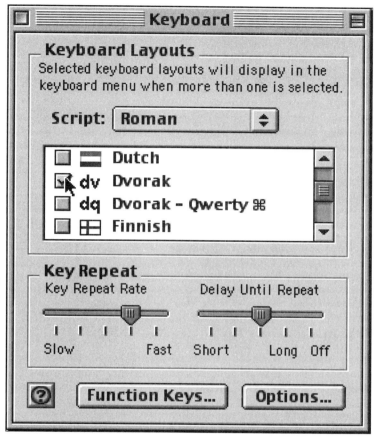

**Figure 5-2:**
Use the Keyboard control panel to change the results when you press keys.

**Figure 5-3:**
With the Dvorak layout, 70 percent of the keys you type don't require you to move your hands.

If Mac OS 9 (or higher) is installed on your Mac, the Dvorak layout is built in. All you have to do is select it in the Keyboard control panel.

If you have an earlier Mac OS version, you need to install a Dvorak layout file. All keyboard layouts are stored in the Mac's System file, which is in the System Folder. To add a layout to the Keyboard control panel, you need to drag and drop the layout file onto the System file or, in System 7.5 or later, onto the System Folder.

Need a Dvorak layout file? You can get a free one from `www.mit.edu/people/jcb/Dvorak`. You can also find shareware and commercial typing tutors that can teach you to use the Dvorak layout.

## Cleaning your keyboard

It helps to keep your keyboard clean and cola-free. But if you do spill something on your keyboard, or if you're experiencing other trouble, you probably shouldn't spend forever trying to clean it. It can be tough to get a sticky keyboard back in working order because you need to get at many moving parts as well as some electronic components. Replacement keyboards cost between $25 and $150, so trying to save a keyboard that's been spilled on is worth a little effort, but not a ton. Here's the step-by-step for cleaning a keyboard:

1. **Shut down the Mac (for an ADB keyboard) and unplug the keyboard.**

2. **Dry the outside of the keyboard with a dry towel or sponge.**

   If you spilled a sticky liquid, use a clean, damp (but not dripping) rag to clean as much of the exterior as you can.

3. **Turn your keyboard upside down and shake it to remove any excess liquid.**

   You can also use compressed air to blow liquid out from between the keys.

4. **Depending on the type of keyboard, you might be able to flip it over and remove the back plastic. If you can, mop up or shake out any other liquid, but avoid touching any circuit boards you come across — a static discharge can quickly kill a keyboard. (As if the keyboard didn't have enough trouble already.)**

5. **You can use a hair dryer (set to a cool setting, because heat could damage the keyboard) to dry the surface of the keyboard and between the keys.**

6. **Let the keyboard dry for at least a day. Then plug it in, turn on your Mac, and test it.**

If the keys on your keyboard are sticking, you can try using a small computer-component vacuum cleaner or a can of compressed air to blow out dust and dirt between the keys. (Don't get too close with the compressed air because it can cause condensation.) If that doesn't help, you can remove the keycaps on most keyboards to clean them. To remove the keycaps, you should use a keycap removal tool, which you should be able to find at a computer store.

Remove only the keycaps you need to clean under and try to remember where they go. And don't try to pry off the spacebar, which has a snake's nest of springs under it.

A keyboard can benefit from a quick spring-cleaning session, if you're the white-glove type. Shut down the Mac, unplug the keyboard, and then gently wipe the keys with a nearly dry rag containing a touch of water or rubbing alcohol. You can get between the keys using compressed air or a small vacuum cleaner (the type sold at computer stores, not the Hoover-type with a drapery attachment).

Don't spray anything directly on the keyboard. If you use any liquids for cleaning your keyboard, spray a light mist directly on the rag or cloth you're using.

## *Longer cables*

If you have an ADB keyboard, a mouse, or both, you can use a special ADB extension cable to extend its connection to the computer. There's a limit of about five meters on your entire ADB chain, though, so make sure your extension cable plus all the other cables in your ADB chain don't add up to more than that.

If you have USB devices, you can simply buy new connecting cables for your USB input devices; the limit is five meters per cable (because each cable must be connected to a USB port on the Mac or on a USB hub). Special cables can be longer if the cable includes a repeater.

For products that extend ADB and other Mac input cables by tens of meters, check out products such as the ex•tend•it series of standalone and rack-mounted devices from Gefen Systems (www.gefen.com). These products enable you to move ADB devices hundreds of feet away and switch the same keyboard and mouse for use with many different Mac OS computers.

Gefen Systems also offers a special device that allows you to switch one keyboard, mouse, and even a video connection between multiple Macs or between Macs and PCs. If you'd like to control more than one computer from one set of devices, check out their KVM Switch.

# *Mighty Mice*

The mouse you get with most Mac models (the Apple Desktop Mouse, included with models from the late 1980s until the end of the pre-iMac era) was fairly universally loved. It was a good size, rolled along nicely, and didn't offer any annoying attachments or add-ons.

With the iMac and subsequent colorful Mac models, Apple has foisted upon the world the Apple USB Mouse. The world has responded by immediately dividing into two camps: people who heatedly dislike the hockey-puck mouse and people who express cold indifference to the hockey-puck mouse. (There might be a smallish contingent of folks who, with Goldilocksian fervor, warmly regard the hockey-puck mouse as just right, but it's a statistically insignificant bunch.)

If you're interested in a new mouse for whatever reason, you'll find quite a few out there. Third-party mice are made in larger sizes and with various contours to fit in a variety of hand shapes more comfortably. You'll also find mice that are programmable, allowing you to map keystrokes or double-clicks to different mouse buttons. Some mice even use different mechanisms for the mousing itself, resulting in more accurate movements.

The precision of a mouse is measured in dots per inch (dpi). A typical mouse has a precision of 200 to 400 dpi — anything less than that is too little and anything more than that is considered very precise.

Three basic types of technology are used to create mice, some more common than others:

- **Mechanical.** A mechanical mouse has a rubber ball that comes in contact with the surface and rolls along with your movements. The sensors inside the mouse in this case are mechanical — usually small rollers that detect the direction and speed of the ball, moving the mouse pointer accordingly.

- **Optomechanical.** This works the same way as a mechanical mouse — with a ball and sensors — except that the sensors are optical, using light to detect changes in direction and speed.

- **Optical.** Optical mice are more rare, although a few new models have brought these mice to the masses. These mice use only light to judge movements, requiring very little contact with the surface.

Aside from the companies mentioned at the beginning of this chapter, Microsoft has recently introduced an optical mouse for USB-based Macintosh machines. And a few companies, such as iCatch from MacSense (www.mac sense.com), make snap-on additions for the Apple USB Mouse that make it a little larger and help fill out its shape a bit.

## *Mouse trouble*

Along with putting out some traps and cheese, you can take a few other steps to combat mouse trouble. If your mouse is trying to tell you something — by refusing to move or by making the cursor jump all over the place — it might just need a cleaning. You'll want to do this at a time when you can be without the mouse for a few hours because it will need to dry completely before use.

To clean your Mac's mouse:

1. **Shut down the Mac (if the mouse uses ADB), unplug the mouse, and turn it over.**

2. **The mouse ball is trapped inside the bottom of the mouse behind a dial that you can turn to remove. Free it! Free it now! You generally turn an Apple mouse's dial counterclockwise to loosen it, as shown in Figure 5-4.**

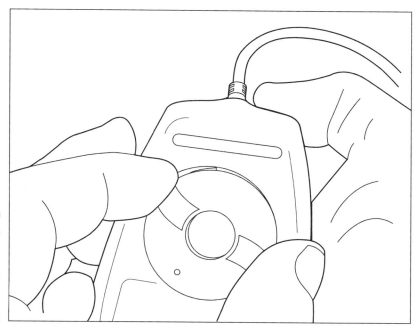

**Figure 5-4:**
Turning the dial on a Mac's mouse to open it.

3. **Turn the mouse back over and roll the mouse ball into your hand. Rinse the ball with soap and water to clean it and then set it aside until it dries completely.**

4. **Using a cotton swab and some rubbing alcohol, clean the wire rollers inside the mouse, again waiting until it dries completely.**

5. **Place the ball back in the mouse and replace the dial, turning it clockwise until it locks.**

If your mouse starts to act up again after a recent cleaning, you might want to take a look at your mousepad. If you're using a mechanical or optomechanical mouse, a clean, dry mousepad is necessary for best results. Also, feel free to change the mousepad after a few months or years — that old thing isn't offering much protection and it's starting to look a little ratty.

Still having trouble with your mouse? Maybe the problem is more than skin deep:

✔ **Are the rollers dirty?** Sometimes hair, fabric fibers, or something else can jam the little rollers inside your mouse's housing where the ball generally resides. Any sort of muck like that could affect proper rolling behavior. Tweezers or a toothpick might help you get the offending item away from the roller, but try not to bend the roller. If you do, the mouse is toast.

✔ **Is there a software glitch?** If the pointer jumps around on the screen or seems to have a mind of its own, make sure the mouse's software driver is properly installed and configured, if it has a driver. If the driver isn't the problem, you might have a system software conflict brewing. Make sure you don't have additional software installed — perhaps for a joystick or a programmable input device. (Such software would generally be in the form of a control panel.) If the mouse pointer continues erratic behavior, test for a system conflict or a virus infection, as discussed in Chapter 20.

✔ **Is it a USB problem?** If you have a USB mouse, you might be experiencing typical USB trouble — check the tips in Chapter 4 for troubleshooting USB problems. You can also try plugging the mouse directly into the Mac's USB port to make sure your keyboard or a USB hub isn't causing the trouble.

## *Other members of the mouse family*

Not everyone is a straight mouse-type person. If you feel that the mouse constrains you in some way, maybe you're simply too cool for mice. It happens to the best of us. (I, for instance, suffer from being too cool for mice.) In those cases, more drastic measures — other types of input devices — become necessary. Here's a look at some of them:

✔ **Trackballs.** These are my favorite. A trackball is sort of a mouse turned upside down: Instead of rolling the mouse around, you move the mouse pointer by pushing the ball in different directions. The advantage is that you cut down on all the movement required by a mouse, plus you save a little desk space and the $1.99 mousepad. The disadvantage is that it's tough to be quite as accurate with a trackball as it is with a mouse.

✔ **Trackpads.** Popularized by notebook computers (such as the Apple PowerBook line), trackpads are smooth surfaces that react to moisture on your finger as you glide that finger along its surface. That's how the trackpad knows to move the mouse pointer. Trackpads are generally found as part of a keyboard (MacAlly and Adesso make such keyboards). You can also find trackpads occasionally sold separately, such as the Alps Desktop Glidepoint series made by Cirque (www.glide-point.com).

✔ **Programmable mice.** Third-party vendors offer a number of different solutions to the Mac's one-button mouse. Among these are programmable mice and scrolling mice that include special buttons you can control with software. Scrolling mice are of particular interest, offering you a small shuttle between the mouse buttons that you can move up and down when pointing at a window on your Mac's screen. Moving the shuttle scrolls the page up or down, accordingly.

✔ **Graphics tablets.** Also called *digitizers,* these devices hook up through either ADB or USB, depending on the model, and allow you to use a pen as your input device. Although they're great for drawing, that's not the graphics tablet's only strength. Because they work like any other mousing device, you can use a tablet to edit documents, work with music notation, or drag clips around in your movie editing software. Plus, they look cool (see Figure 5-5). Graphics tablets run the gamut in price, usually based on the features, size, and resolution of the tablet, which is measured in lines per inch. The higher the resolution, the more detailed your drawing and mousing is.

✔ **Touch screens.** What if you could just reach out and touch your monitor to move the mouse and make selections? A number of companies have products that let you do just that. The least expensive of these connects to ADB or USB and simply overlays your monitor, letting you tap the added glass or plastic to move the mouse and make your selections. Check out companies such as Elo TouchSystems (www.elotouch.com/) and Troll Touch (www.trolltouch.com/).

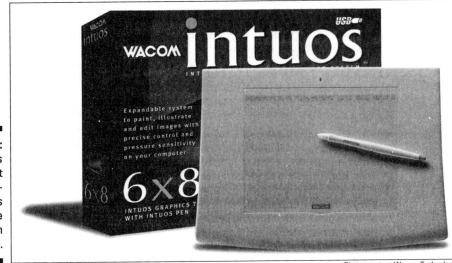

**Figure 5-5:**
Digitizers are a great way for creative users to mouse around on their Macs.

*Photo courtesy Wacom Technology*

# Serious Controllers for Gamers

If you think that a mouse and a keyboard aren't good enough for serious gaming, you're probably right. (At least, I'm not going to argue with you.) For years, joysticks and flight controllers have been used by the most avid gamers for a more realistic experience. These devices vary greatly from small gamepads (like those used for TV/console games such as Sony Playstation) to sophisticated weapon control systems that work with flight simulators and driving games.

## Types of game controllers

In general, you come across three classes of controller. Some offer different levels of specialization, but most can be categorized as joysticks, gamepads, and flight controllers:

 ✔ **Joysticks.** These days, most Mac joysticks look like the stick in an F-16. For all types of games, though, joysticks offer more precise movements, programmable buttons, and occasionally *forced feedback*. This technology actually causes the joystick to react to events in the game with shudders and shimmies.

- **Gamepads.** These controllers got popular with the Sony, Nintendo, and Sega TV console game machines. Gamepads generally offer a rocker switch that rotates in many different directions. Along with that control comes a bunch of buttons you can use for speed, firing, radar, or whatever the game does. Gamepads encourage you to use both hands completely while playing, making them less than ideal for games that require keyboard input but really useful for games that don't. Some models are easy to switch from right-handed to left-handed play, which give them a clear advantage over many joysticks (at least, for left-handed people — I've observed that most right-handed people simply don't care).

- **Flight and driving controllers.** These controllers are generally the most pricey, mostly because they're designed as knockoffs of flight controllers found in fighter aircraft. You can also find rudder pedals, thrust/weapon controls, and other add-ons that let you experience flight (or driving) as naturally as your little computer will let you.

So where do you buy? Check out Table 5-1, which shows manufacturers of gaming controllers and their Web sites. Most of these manufacturers offer both ADB and USB versions of their controllers.

| Table 5-1 | Mac Game Controller Companies | |
|---|---|---|
| *Manufacturer* | *Devices* | *Web Site* |
| MacAlly | Joysticks, gamepads | www.macally.com |
| Gravis | Joysticks, gamepads | www.gravis.com |
| Ariston Technologies | Joysticks, gamepads | www.ariston.com |
| Microsoft | Joysticks, gamepads | www.microsoft.com/ sidewinder/ |
| CH Products | Joysticks, flight controllers | www.chproducts.com |
| Suncom | Joysticks | www.suncominc.com |

Don't like the joysticks designed for Macs? Get a joystick adapter. The JoyPort adapter from Kernel Productions (www.kernel.com) enables ADB or USB Macs to use any number of joysticks and controllers from Atari, PC, Sony Playstation, and Sega Genesis machines.

## Setting up game controllers

Game controllers can be configured to work with games in three basic ways. Which one you use generally depends on the game and what it supports. Your options are to mirror mouse and keyboard commands onto the controller, use a custom driver for the controller, or use an InputSprocket driver for the controller:

- **Mouse/keyboard.** Using controls within the game, the controller's own control panel, or a third-party solution of some sort, you can convince some games that your controller is actually a combination of mouse movements and keypresses. If the fire key in the game is z, you can assign one of your buttons to be z while another is assigned to a, which the game recognizes as jump, and so on.

- **Custom driver.** Some games and controllers have drivers that are designed together. This might be the only way you'll get to use the most sophisticated combinations of controls when you're using flight and driving controllers, for instance. For the full weapon system array to work, the game might need to specifically support the controller.

- **InputSprocket.** In recent years, Apple has added a technology called Game Sprockets to the Mac OS. Game Sprockets makes it easier for game developers to focus on their cool graphics and story lines, while Apple provides standard methods for controllers to interact with games. If a game supports the InputSprocket (which is the particular Game Sprocket that works with game controllers), selecting its controller options command will bring up the standard InputSprocket dialog box, where you can assign commands to the buttons and control surfaces on your joystick, gamepad, or flight controller (see Figure 5-6).

If you have a USB controller and you're playing a game that doesn't support InputSprockets, you might still be able to configure it with a great shareware program called USB Overdrive. See www.usboverdrive.com/ for details.

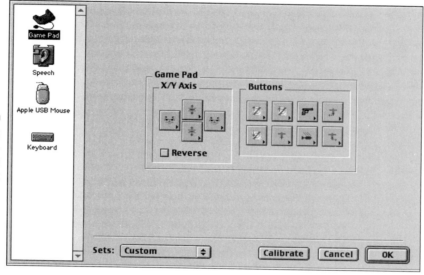

**Figure 5-6:**
The Input-
Sprocket
dialog box
gives you a
standard
way to con-
figure game
controllers.

# Chapter 6

# Modems and High-Speed Internet Access

*T*he word *modem* is really an acronym meaning *modem*odulate. It just so happens that *modulate* and *demodulate* are exactly what a modem does, so its name is a happy coincidence. (If the modem had originally been named Leopold, I would have had more explaining to do.)

The telephone system is designed to transmit sound waves. To send digital data over the phone lines, we need modems to change the data into audible tones. Those noises are received by another modem and translated back into computer data for use by the distant computer. Thus are born Internet connections and connections to online services, such as America Online.

Unfortunately, this is a rather inefficient process, which is why the modem is on its last legs for data communication. Instead, newer technologies such as DSL and cable modems create a fully digital connection, which is one reason why those connections are so much faster and why those of us who spend a lot of time online covet such connections.

In actual usage, the word *modem* gets tossed about a bit more than it should. Most people think of modems not as modulators/demodulators but as little boxes that allow them to access online services and the Internet. For instance, the terms *ISDN modem* and *DSL modem* are almost completely inaccurate, because both types of connections are all-digital — no modulating or demodulating needs to happen. I talk about such "modems" later in the chapter, but be aware that the term is used loosely.

# Modems: From the Inside Out

Modems for Macs are generally either internal expansion cards or external boxes connected to the Mac through a serial port (usually the modem port — the one with a telephone icon) or USB. If you're adding a modem to your Mac, you'll probably choose an external model because they're the easiest to find for purchasing. If your Mac came with a modem, however, there's a good chance it's an internal model, such as the modem shipped with all iMacs and many Power Macintosh G3 and G4 machines.

Modems require a connection to a standard phone line using a typical modular phone jack. (The slang down at Radio Shack for such a connection is *RJ-11*.) Many external modems also offer a second jack that acts as a passthrough connection, allowing you to connect a telephone set so that you can talk when you're not online.

External modems often use special serial cables, called *hardware handshake* cables, to connect to the Mac's modem port. In most cases, this cable is either permanently attached to the modem or connected to the modem by a special 25-pin plug on one end and an 8-pin serial connector or a USB connector for the Mac on the other end.

With many Mac modems, the power supply is an important component. Some modems will seem to work but exhibit errors when plugged into the wrong power adapters, for instance. Other modems must be plugged into the Mac's ADB port to receive power, offering a passthrough connector for mice, keyboards, and other devices.

Chapter 4 explains the difference between the ports as well as some issues that have to do with ADB and power consumption. If you don't have an ADB port on your newer Mac, avoid modems that require ADB power.

## Your modem's speed

As mentioned, modems change digital signals into analog signals. To do this successfully (and manage to talk to one another in the process), modems must be kept to certain strict standards set by a group called the International Telecommunications Union (ITU). As if that weren't bad enough, parts of the standards names are actually in *Latin*. Of all the hair-brained schemes!

Table 16-1 shows you the common modem *bits-per-second* (bps) rates and their associated standards (the Latin part). Note that the parts I've put in quotes are how the standards are usually referred to in casual shorthand. "Thirty-three dot six" and "Thirty-three six" are common ways to say "33.6" in conversation. ("Tres, tres, sixer!" would also be acceptable, but only after a really good party has gotten into full swing.)

Modem connections are always measured in bits per second. It's a common mistake by uppity just-enough-knowledge-to-be-dangerous computer users to say "baud" when referring to modems, such as "Dude, my 33.6 baud modem is lame-o." Baud and bps, however are not the same. *Baud* represents electrical changes per second over a telephone connection, which no longer has much of a relationship to the speed of a modem. (It did back during Madonna's Material Girl phase.) In other words, say "bps" or "bits per second" if you don't want to be made fun of by the type of people who know the name of the actor who played Security Guard #2 in the morgue scene in *X-Files: The Motion Picture.*

| Table 6-1 | Modem Standards, Bit Rates, and Interesting Tidbits | |
| --- | --- | --- |
| *Standard* | *Bit Rate* | *Interesting Tidbit* |
| V.21 | 300 bps | Baud and bps actually match here |
| V.22 | 1200 bps | Speed of my second modem, for a Commodore 64 |
| V.22bis | 2400 bps | Rarely found, rarely worked |
| V.32 | 9600 bps | I used to think this was really fast |
| V.32bis | 14,400 bps | Often called 14.4 |
| V.terbo | 19,200 bps | Never an official standard, but a US Robotics one |
| V.34 | 28,800 bps | Often called 28.8 for 28 Kbps |
| V.34bis | 33,600 bps | Often called 33.6 for 33.6 Kbps |
| USR X2 | 56,600 bps | US Robotics standard |
| 56KFlex | 56,600 bps | Rockwell International standard |
| V.90 | 56,600 bps | The official "56k" standard that everyone finally agreed to |

Note that *bis* is Latin that can be translated as *again* or *repeat.* In many cases, the *bis* is used to refer to an update of the original standard that allows for faster transmission rates. (The etymological origins of the scientific appendage *terbo,* incidentally, seem to point to a particularly well-received episode of *Baywatch* dubbed for Europe distribution in the early 1990s.)

In Web browsers and other software used for downloaded files (transferring them from a remote computer to your Mac), you're shown the *kilobytes per second* rate at which you're receiving the file. Ideally, you should get bytes-per-second rates that are exactly one-eighth of the bps rate of your modem (e.g., 4200 bytes per second for a 33.6-Kbps connection). But that rarely happens under real-world conditions, because the speed of your Internet Service Provider, the quality of your phone line, and the general traffic on the Internet or online service can all affect download speeds. With a typical 56-Kbps connection, you'll see transfer rates between 1500 and 5000 bytes per second.

One more darned note. Most every modem you can buy these days for upgrading is a 56-Kbps modem, but — surprise! — it's illegal for these modems to connect at rates faster than 52 Kbps. Why is it illegal? Because there's a law against it. So, you'll never see a connection over 52,000 bps. (If you do see a higher speed connection, though, and you get caught, your best bet is to shred this book and play dumb.)

# Getting and Connecting a Modem

Buying a modem is fairly simple. These days, almost every new modem is a 56-Kbps modem and all offer faxing capability and the other add-ons that have come along to make modems interesting again: voicemail, caller ID, and a close, comfortable shave.

So, if you need a modem, you should pretty much just go out and buy one. Table 6-2 shows popular Mac modem manufacturers.

| Table 6-2 | Mac-Compatible Modem Manufacturers |
| --- | --- |
| *Name* | *Web Site* |
| Global Village | www.globalvillage.com |
| Supra (Diamond) | www.supra.com |
| 3Com/USRobotics | www.3com.com |
| Best Data | www.bestdata.com |

As far as the extra features go, my theory is to buy a modem that's really well designed for *being a modem*, and let something else handle your speaker-phone, answering machine, or voicemail duties. Most of these features require you to keep your Mac powered all the time and hook your modem up to your main voice line, instead of to a secondary line that's only for data. These modem features are best targeted at very occasional home use, and I'd argue that the phone company's Caller ID box and voicemail services are probably more reliable.

That said, nearly any modem is capable of dealing with faxes and, if you expect to use that capability, it's nice to get good fax software as well as a deal on optical character-recognition software, if it's included. If you do plan to use your Mac as communications central for your home or small office, you might consider some of the other tidbits:

✔ **Speakerphone.** Some modems use their own microphone and speaker for the connection; others use the Mac's microphone (on AV, iMac, and Power Macintoshes) and the Mac's speakers. Note, however, that nearly any external modem will allow you to plug a telephone set into the passthrough port on the modem. Not only can you answer calls when they come in, but you can have your modem dial out for you (from a personal information manager program, for instance.)

✔ **Voicemail/answerer.** If your machine is on the fritz and you don't want to spend the $5 a month for the phone company's voicemail, some modems let your Mac take a message.

✔ **CallerID.** This is a handy feature you might as well turn on if your modem allows it. Usually a simple software add-on, CallerID allows your modem to translate Caller ID signals to let you know who's calling.

✔ **Flash upgradable.** Most new modems include this capability, which allows you to upgrade the basic capabilities of the modem using software. That way, just in case a new, higher speed standard comes along (or other features), you can download a program that will automatically upgrade your modem.

## Should you choose an internal modem?

Many Mac models were designed to support an internal modem. Some of these models even came from the factory with an internal modem. Performa models such as the 470 series, 570 series, 630, 5200, 5500, 6200, 6300, and 6400 and the Power Macintosh 6500 all support internal modems, as does the blue G3 and Power Macintosh G4 series.

Most of the models just described offer a special Apple *communications slot* that can accept an internal expansion card. Only communications slot, or comm slot, modems can plug into this slot. On top of that, you need to get the correct type of comm slot modem — for earlier Macs, it's the Comm slot I type; for later Macs (those that have PCI slots) you'll need a Comm slot II modem.

Unfortunately, you won't have much luck finding comm slot modems, except for a Global Village modem for the latest G3 and G4 models (which have a different type of communications slot, anyway). Companies simply don't make new modems for the Mac comm slot, and existing modems (which you might find in the classified ads on or Web auction sites) are tough to match to your existing Mac. Not to mention the fact that none of them will be the latest technology — they'll all be 33.6 Kbps or slower.

In most cases, I'd recommend an external modem for these Macs; if you already have an internal modem installed (and you want to upgrade using an external), you need to slide out your Mac's logic board and remove the comm slot modem. (It's the small circuit board with a phone jack attached to it.) Then pry the plastic guard off of the Modem port, if one is covering it. Now you should be able to use an external modem connected to the Modem port.

## *When you're faxing*

All the retail modems I've seen come with some sort of faxing capability. I'd recommend getting a second line if you plan a lot of faxes; that way you can leave your fax software on all the time to receive faxes.

In fact, the fax software you get with your modem may be its most outstanding feature. Global Village fax software, for instance, is generally well integrated with the Mac OS, going as far as to replace the Print command with the Fax command when you hold down the Option key and pull down the File menu. Some other fax software, such as FaxSTF, allows you to do this as well.

All modems typically support 9600 bps Group 3 faxing, the basic standard for most of the industry. You might also find that your modem supports 14.4 Kbps speeds for faxing. Few regular fax machines support these speeds, but some of the newer ones do.

With all fax software, faxing usually works through a virtual print driver that appears in the Chooser (see Figure 6-1). When you choose this driver and select the Print command in your software, the document is "printed" to the fax modem.

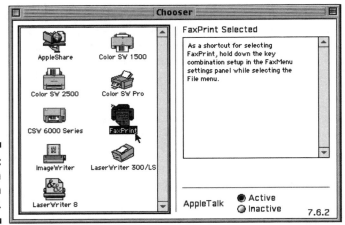

**Figure 6-1:** Selecting a fax driver in the Chooser.

If you have fax software that allows you to hold down modifier keys while you select the Print command, the software is just performing a fancy little trick that substitutes the fax printer driver for that one command. That's why the Print command is changed to Fax when you hold down keys.

Global Village (www.globalvillage.com) software is so well regarded by Mac owners that you can buy it separately for the Apple modems bundled with the iMac, iBook, and colorful Power Macintosh computers.

# Kill your GeoPort

When is a modem not a modem? Most Power Macintosh models and the Macintosh AV (660AV and 840AV) machines include a special kind of serial port, called a *GeoPort*, that makes it possible for some interesting things to happen. For one, this technology lets your Mac *emulate* a modem in software. All you need is a GeoPort adapter, shown in Figure 6-2.

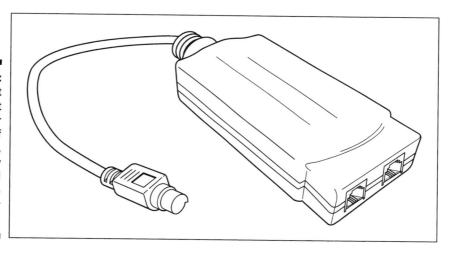

**Figure 6-2:** Here's what a GeoPort adapter looks like. If you see one, back away slowly and report it to the proper authorities.

The idea was to usher in a whole new world where your Mac is simply attached to the phone line and then wonderful things happen — speaker-phones, modem communications, faxes, voicemail — through the GeoPort adapter. Well, Apple tried it, it didn't take off, and these days they don't even update the software.

Now the problem is excising this particular demon. In some Macs, Apple shipped an internal GeoPort adapter card, and it's a drag. (Literally — it tends to slows these Macs to a crawl.) *Some* 6300, 6400, and 6500 model Macs have these adapters.

Here's how Apple tells you to figure out whether you have a GeoPort modem. Go into ClarisWorks or AppleWorks 5 and open a new *communications* session. (You can use a different terminal emulator program if you have one, but all relevant Macs shipped originally with ClarisWorks.) In the window, type **ATI1** and press the Return key. If the number returned by the modem is a 0, you have a GeoPort Telecom adapter. (A Global Village 28.8 modem returns the number 240 and their 14.4-Kbps modem returns 255.)

If you have an internal GeoPort adapter, I recommend taking it out and adding an external modem. The GeoPort is slow and requires a lot of process-ing power, which slows down the Mac itself.

If your budget keeps you saddled with your GeoPort adapter, make sure you have the latest version of the Apple Telecom software included on the CD-ROM for Mac OS 8.0 or higher. Second, make sure you have plenty of RAM in your system and add cache RAM if you can afford it (see Chapter 15). Third, try setting the Apple Express Modem control panel for 28.8 connections instead of 33.6, which, believe it or not, may speed everything up a bit.

## Installing a modem

Here's how to install an external modem:

1. **Shut down your Mac and then plug the modem's cable into the serial port on the back of your Mac.**

   You'll probably want to choose the Modem port, because doing so brings order to a chaotic world. If you're a dangerous person, you can plug the modem into the Printer port. If you do use the Printer port, make sure that AppleTalk is turned off (in the Chooser) and that the AppleTalk control panel is set so that it's not also using the Printer port (this is often the default).

2. **Connect a phone cable from the wall phone socket to the In port on a surge protector that supports a phone passthrough. Then plug a phone cable into the Out port on that same surge protector and plug the other side into your modem.**

   You can also plug the phone cable directly from the wall to the modem, but I recommend using a surge protector. Phone lines are powered, and that power can surge, killing your modem and, perhaps, your Mac. I've seen more damage from phone line surges than from any other type.

3. **Plug the modem's power supply into a wall socket or surge protector and then turn on the modem (if necessary). Restart your Mac.**

4. **When the Mac has restarted, install any software that was included with your Mac.**

   After it's installed, you might have to restart. With some modems, you have a new control panel that lets you set options for the modem. In other cases, you just have new applications to play with.

If you plan to use your modem for a dial-up Internet account, you can use the Modem control panel to set up the modem. This is most easily accomplished if your modem has a special Mac OS Modem Script. When you find that script on your modem's CD or from the manufacturer's Web site, drag it to the Modem Scripts folder (inside the Extensions folder in your System Folder).

# *Modem Doesn't Work?*

Having trouble with your modem? Time to take a quick look at some troubleshooting steps for modem-related maladies. The two major categories of modem problems are connection problems and configuration problems.

## *Step 1: Connection issues*

Is the modem getting power? Plug in the modem and turn it on. Does its power light come on? If not, check the power connections. The ADB port on earlier Macs powers some modems. If you have more than a few ADB devices, this port can get overloaded and fail to provide enough power. Try again with fewer ADB devices. If your modem still doesn't indicate that it's getting power — and it has an AC adapter — try plugging it into different wall sockets. If you still don't get power (and you're using the correct AC adapter), you might need to send the modem in for repairs.

If your modem is getting power but your communications software is not recognizing it, it's time to troubleshoot the port. One of three scenarios is possible in this case:

- **Wrong port.** You might have the modem set to use the wrong port; that is, it's not set up (in software) to use the port it's actually attached to.

- **Blocked port.** You have the modem and software correctly configured, but some other software might be trying to use the same port, resulting in a conflict.

- **Hung modem.** Sometimes modems just get confused and need to be reset before you can use them again. This happens most often when either a communications application crashes abruptly or some interference occurs on the phone line.

You set the correct port for your modem in the Modem control panel if you're using PPP or Remote Access to establish an Internet connection. Otherwise, you use the modem configuration preferences in your communications software (including the America Online application, terminal emulators, or your fax software). You need to find the setting that allows you to choose your modem's configuration profile (usually the modem's name) and ensure that it's set to the proper port. Figure 6-3, 6-4, and 6-5 show three ways to do so.

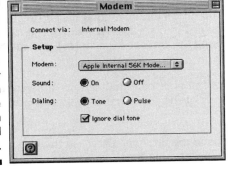

**Figure 6-3:**
Setting the configuration profile and port for your modem in AOL.

**Figure 6-4:**
Setting the configuration profile and port for your modem in the Modem control panel.

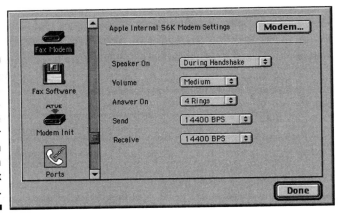

**Figure 6-5:**
Setting the configuration profile and port for your modem in FaxSTF, a popular fax program.

If you find that your modem is set to the correct port but it still doesn't work (or if you receive errors that say the "Port is in use" or something to that effect), you might need to seek out the offending application. If you use fax software, for instance, you might have to turn off the fax capabilities to keep the application from tying up the modem.

If your modem uses a serial port, consider what other of your applications might be set to use that serial port. These include PDA applications (such as the Palm Desktop software used with Palm OS devices), other modem software (you might have your AOL or terminal-communications software enabled when trying to make an Internet connection), or special software you have for other serial devices, such as scanners or digital cameras. If you have any such applications installed, check to see whether they're trying to use the same port where your modem is installed.

Finally, if the modem itself is hung, the easiest way to correct that is to flip its power switch. If the modem doesn't have a power switch (it's either ADB powered or an internal modem), you might need to shut down your Mac all the way — don't just restart — which will cut power to the modem. After waiting 30 seconds or so, restart your Mac and see whether the modem has been reset.

Zapping PRAM might also be necessary to reset a particularly hung serial port. See Chapter 23 for more info.

## Step 2: Connection trouble

If you have things configured correctly but your modem isn't connecting — or you think it's connected too slowly — I have some other issues you can attack. First, you should make sure it's getting online at all. Various indicators and issues are involved in getting online:

✔ **Check your gauges.** If you have an external modem, check its lights for indications of activity. If your modem has transmit/receive lights (labeled TX/RX, SD/RD, or with an arrow icon) and they're blinking or lit, the modem might believe it's communicating when it's not. Reset the modem, reset the Mac, check the cable connection, or try another cable. If the on-hook indicator (labeled "OH" or with a telephone or telephone poles icon) is lit, there might be a problem with the phone wiring, the serial cable, or the modem itself. Reset the modem and check the cabling. Reset the computer. If all these fail, suspect a hardware issue with the modem.

✔ **Listen for a dial tone**. If you have an internal or external modem, you should listen as it connects and dials out. (If you have an internal modem, you might need to turn up the volume on your Mac's speakers to hear it.) First, listen as the modem picks up the phone line. You should hear a dial tone, which the modem is also trying to detect. If you don't hear anything, the phone line might be connected incorrectly — plug in a phone handset and make sure the line is getting a dial tone. If you hear a stutter-tone (like the phone company uses to indicate new voicemail), the modem might choke at that point and not dial. In that case, you need to either get your messages (so that the normal dial tone returns) or set your modem to Ignore Dial Tone in the Modem control panel or elsewhere in your modem application's preferences.

✔ **Listen to the answer.** If your modem dials successfully, keep listening. First, make sure the other side of the connection is picked up by a modem or a fax (whichever you're trying to contact to). If you hear a busy tone or a muffled "Hello? Hello?! Darned fax machines!" you know you're reaching the wrong number or you need to try again later. If you hear modem or fax tones on the other side of the connection, there's a better chance that you have the right number.

✔ **Listen for success.** (This one will be tough in print.) When your modem dials out, it sends a carrier signal after it dials. That's the first tone you hear, which probably sounds like "weee, weee, weee, weee." (On a 56-Kbps modem, it sounds like "weee, dee, oo-de-doop, weee, dee, oo-de-doop.") When a modem or fax picks up on the other side, it tries to detect that carrier signal and then sends out one of its own, which is usually a more continuous, slightly lower sound, like "woooooooooooo" or "woo, woo, woo, woo." When the two agree to start communicating, a cacophony of sounds ensues "reee grog wooo aaah eeeerp," until finally the volume on your modem shuts off (in most cases).

If you hear the answering modem give out the same carrier tone as your modem, the modem might not be set to answer properly. If you hear them give out different tones but nothing else happens, there might be a configuration problem or a problem with the phone lines.

If they spend forever "grogging" within the cacophony, they're having trouble connecting, which might be an issue with the phone line or the speeds at which you're trying to connect.

If you're having trouble at the connection stage, especially when you're trying to connect to an individual friend's modem (and not a major online service), try setting the connection speed lower in your software; try 33.6 Kbps, 14.4 Kbps, or even 9600 bps for data. (In some cases, you might need to use a special modem configuration file that sets the modem to a lower speed, as in the Modem control panel.) For trouble connecting to fax machines, turn off the high-speed 14,400 bps option in your fax software.

## Step 3: Slow connection

If you get connected but you're not happy with the resulting speed, some more configuring might be in your future. Modem-related software often includes *error correction*, *data compression,* and *flow-control* commands buried somewhere in their settings boxes. The latest modems pretty much set these things up automatically, but you'll occasionally find yourself needing to choose the settings. Here's what to choose, if it comes up:

- ✔ **Error correction and compression.** Sometimes you'll have the option of turning these on or off. They should usually be turned on, unless you're having trouble establishing a connection (especially if you're trying to create a connection between your razzle-dazzle modem and your friend's old creaker). If you have a specific setting option, choose v.42bis first and then MNP-5.

  Are you waiting for an important call, but need to be online? There are no guarantees, but it's possible to make your modem connection *less* reliable by turning off error correction in the Remote Access or PPP control panel on your Mac. (You might find similar settings in other modem communications software.) If you don't use error correction, the modem is a bit more likely to lose the connection when the call waiting tone blares through, thus knocking you off and causing the phone to ring. I wouldn't exactly run the White House Situation Phone this way, but it might help in nonessential situations.

- ✔ **Flow control.** If you have a high-speed (9600 bps or greater) modem, your choices for setup are usually one of the following: CTS and RTS (DTR), CTS only, RTS (DTR) only, and None. The CTS and RTS option is the way to go if your modem will let you. If you experience problems, though, a common setting for Mac modems is CTS only.

# *Step 4: Problems during the call*

After the call is negotiated, you're likely to have a smooth connection. But be aware of a few caveats that can reset your connection or otherwise interrupt your modem sessions:

- ✔ **Call waiting.** If you dial out with a modem on a line that has call waiting active, you may be disconnected when the signal tone beeps on the line. You can often enter a code to turn off call waiting; in many areas in the United States, the code is *70. Wherever you enter the phone number you're dialing, type **\*70,555-1212** or whatever the phone number is. The comma tells your dialing software to pause for a moment before dialing the rest.

- ✔ **Noisy line.** If you hear noise when you pick up a phone handset, that line noise can affect your connection. If you have long extension cords and funny couplers to extend your lines, try to eliminate them. Otherwise, a phone technician might have to clean up your lines.

- ✔ **Excessive errors.** If your connection drops for no reason, downloads cut off in mid-transfer, or things occasionally slow to a crawl, check the line for indications of noise. If the line seems okay, make sure you've chosen the correct modem profile in your software and that you've entered error correction and flow-control settings. Finally, try connecting at a lower bps rate.

Don't forget to check your modem's manual, where you'll likely find more troubleshooting hints specific to your particular modem brand and its internal commands and characteristics.

# Fast Internet Access . . . Go Wide

The whole modulating and demodulating thing has left modems at a disadvantage. Namely, the technology has come up against a brick wall, where modems now go about as fast as they're going to go. As the Internet grows and the tasks we ask of it become more complicated, though, the speeds offered by modems are simply not enough.

So, we're forced to turn to higher bandwidth alternatives. *Bandwidth* refers to the connection's capability to download more data at one time and is generally measured in Kbps or even megabits per second (Mbps) for wider alternatives. These technologies are all digital in nature, giving you a direct network connection to your Internet service provider. So, if you're downloading large files or accessing multimedia over the Internet, the speed and quality of your connection will easily out-do the best modem connections.

For the sake of simplicity, we often say that different modems and connections are *faster* than one another, when that isn't always the case. What's more important is the width of the pipe through which data is sent. A 14.4-Kbps modem might not be *slower* than a 56-Kbps modem if both of them are downloading a 10K file, because the file would fit within the bandwidth of each modem. A 100K file would transmit more quickly using the 56-Kbps modem, though, because more of the file can fit through the 56-Kbps pipe at once. The same is (basically) true of so-called higher speed connections such as cable and DSL connections; they fit more data at once.

So, what technologies are available? Three that you might encounter are ISDN, cable modems, and DSL.

If you're lucky enough to have direct Ethernet access to the Internet through a T-1 or T-3 line, you have a Get Out of This Chapter Free card. I discuss Ethernet and TCP/IP settings and technologies in Chapter 18.

## ISDN: What's in a name?

When Integrated Services Digital Network (ISDN) technology was conceived in the 1960s, it seemed like a good idea. The thought was to overhaul the existing telephone infrastructure to make it fully digital. This would bring about untold advantages such as digital services, videophones, and even high-speed data transfer.

Unfortunately, the switchover to ISDN didn't happen as was originally antici-pated, so the phone system (in the U.S.) has never become completely digi-tal. In major cities (and many other countries), you can often have a digital phone line installed, and it offers some advantages over typical modems. If you don't have DSL or cable modem offerings in your area, ISDN is a reason-able solution.

Basic Rate ISDN (typical for home, home/office, and small business) generally offers about 128-Kbps connections and allows you to connect to the service using a special ISDN modem (actually a *terminal adapter*). These connections can be for a single Mac using a serial or USB connection or for a group of Macs connected through an Ethernet network. You generally order ISDN ser-vice from your phone company, which will likely set up your terminal adapter and configure your software. (ISDN connections, like modem connections, tend to be dial-on-demand instead of always-on connections.)

If you're considering an external ISDN adapter, USB ports offer plenty of speed, but serial port speeds depend on your Mac model. The serial ports in AV and Power Macintoshes are capable of up to 230 Kbps, so it shouldn't be limiting to an ISDN connection. Some Quadra models and older Macs, how-ever, are limited to 57.6-Kbps connections and might have trouble reaching high speeds with external ISDN adapters. In these cases, you might be better off with a technology that uses Ethernet, such as those described next.

## *Turn to the Internet Channel?*

Think how happy those cable company executives were when some engineer told them that they could send Internet data over existing cable TV wiring — and charge for it! It's true, and the latest implementations offer high-speed, always-on connections that can make it simple for a household to get fast access. Now think how happy you'll be if you find out that your local cable company actually offers this service. Woo-hoo!

Internet access over a cable modem (which actually does do some modulat-ing/demodulating, but is a much more complex beast than the regular tele-phone modems I discussed previously) can sometimes reach speeds of 2 Mbps or more, although that can be limited in interesting ways.

Because of the nature of the way cable TV is brought to neighborhoods, most cable-based Internet access offers a certain amount of bandwidth to a group of subscribers. So, the more Internet service subscribers in your neighbor-hood — and the more active they are on their connections — the less band-width you might have for your connection. (In other words, try not to gloat about your huge downloads at neighborhood BBQs. And try to keep the topics light and distant from computing — sports, politics, international rela-tions.) Even if your neighbors do catch on, you'll probably still enjoy your surfing because the average connection speed will usually hover between 500 to 1000 Kbps, or at least 10 to 20 times faster than a modem.

Cable-based Internet access also tends to be a bit one-sided, with *downstream* transmissions to your modem faster than *upstream* transmissions to the Internet Service Provider. After all, cable was originally designed to be only one-way, bringing TV signals to your TV. Today's cable modem implementations offer upstream connections, but they're often not the same bandwidth as the downstream and might not be suitable for tasks such as Web serving.

About 10 percent of the cable modems deployed are telco-return modems, meaning they accept only downstream data and you have to use a phone modem to send data upstream. These are rare and are being phased out in most cases, but don't be shocked if you come across one.

It's also worth noting that most cable modem service requires that you use the cable company as your Internet service provider. That might mean changing your e-mail addresses, Web page location, and other externals, not to mention a bunch of settings on your Mac.

Most cable modems (or routers) connect to your Mac through the Ethernet port or provide Internet access to your Ethernet hub, if you have more than one machine networked together using Ethernet. You then use the TCP/IP protocol (set to Ethernet in your TCP/IP control panel) to access the Internet. It's usually that simple, although you may still have the cable guy out to set up the modem, because they just like to do that sort of thing.

## DSL: Revenge of the POTS

To differentiate it from other phone line technologies, the copper wiring and other systems that make up what we think of as a telephone connection is called the Plain Old Telephone System, or POTS. For some time it was thought that higher speeds weren't possible over regular phone lines. Digital Subscriber Line (DSL) technologies, however, have changed that, allowing for very high speeds over existing phone lines.

In fact, if you get DSL service, your current phone line becomes an always-on, high-speed networking connection *without* interrupting your existing phone service. You can use the same line for data and voice at the same time, because the data is transferred at a frequency that's above human hearing.

The bandwidth provided varies based on the technologies used for the connection, as well as the length of your *subscriber loop* (the wiring that reaches your home or office and services your area). To get DSL service, you need to be within between 12,000 and 18,000 feet of your phone company's equipment station, which means it's rolling out in cities and larger towns first.

Like cable, DSL upstream and downstream speeds differ. But unlike cable, DSL throughput isn't a shared pool and speeds can reach higher, if you pay for them. Bandwidth ranges from 256 Kbps to 6 MBps, depending on the implementation by your phone company and the service you pay for. Most home and small business subscribers will see downstream speeds of 512 to 1024 Kbps and upstream speeds around 128 Kbps.

DSL technologies connect to your Mac through Ethernet, meaning you can use a DSL modem to connect directly to your Ethernet-enabled Mac, or a DSL router that connects to your Ethernet hub. With a router, you can offer Internet access to any Mac on the network; you simply set the TCP/IP control panel to Ethernet and enter some numbers. Service technicians install DSL service, and you're likely to get the DSL equipment from either the ISP or phone company where you order service.

If there's anything the service person might need to know, it's your Ethernet ID number. (For more on Ethernet cards and ports, see Chapter 18.) You can find this number in a few different ways. On iMacs, you find the number behind the port door (on first-generation models) or on the label on the bottom of the machine. Power Macintosh G3 and G4 machines include the number on the back of the machine. If you have an AppleTalk network set up, you might be able to find the Ethernet ID by choosing Ethernet from the AppleTalk control panel. Then choose Edit ➪ User Mode ➪ Advanced. Click the Info button that appears. In the Info window, find the Hardware address.

# Chapter 7

# On Monitors, or Murphy's Law
# of Vertical Hold

● ● ● ● ● ● ● ● ● ● ● ● ● ● ● ● ● ● ● ● ● ● ● ● ● ● ● ● ● ● ● ● ● ● ● ● ● ● ● ● ●

### In This Chapter
▶ Monitoring the video basics
▶ Adopting and caring for your monitor
▶ Dealing with blurs, splotches, and fuzzies

● ● ● ● ● ● ● ● ● ● ● ● ● ● ● ● ● ● ● ● ● ● ● ● ● ● ● ● ● ● ● ● ● ● ● ● ● ● ● ● ●

*I* know too many people who scrimp on their monitors just to keep things a little cheap. I say, No! Get as much monitor as you can afford because, aside from the keyboard, it's the one aspect of your computer that you're really going to spend the most time with. (If you have an all-in-one Mac, you don't really have the option of changing your monitor, but you can still change its settings and clean it. Plus, if you have an iMac, that monitor is *outstanding!* Love that screen.)

In this chapter, you find out how monitors work and what you should look for in a new one. Later, I cover some troubleshooting tips, including how to fiddle with the dials. Of course, look out for Murphy's Law of Vertical Hold — the more you mess with the dials on a TV (or a monitor), the worse the picture gets. At least many monitors have a Reset button!

## Monitor Basics

Every Macintosh available has video circuitry built in or included on an expansion card that's designed to paint the screen dot by dot. This circuitry determines what each dot should look like at a given moment of time, including whether it's on or off (on a black-and-white screen) or what intensity of red, green, and blue the dot will represent to form a particular color.

This process creates an image called a *bitmap*, where each *pixel*, or picture element, of an image is stored in computer memory. This map is then handed over to the monitor (which is plugged into the video port on the Mac or card), which begins the process of turning on dots at the correct intensities. In a CRT (cathode ray tube) monitor, dots are turned on by an electron beam that sweeps across the back surface of the monitor's glass to draw each line of the screen image.

It sounds complicated, but a typical Macintosh actually draws the screen between 60 and 120 times per second, depending on the capabilities of the display and computer. (The screen is redrawn so often because the intensity of the phosphors fades very quickly.) Because the human eye detects changes at a rate of only about 30 times per second, these higher rates (called the *refresh rate*) give the illusion of movement when you, say, drag an icon across the screen.

With an LCD (liquid crystal display) monitor, only the drawing process is different; each pixel is simply turned on or off, with the intensity of red, green, and blue information determining the exact on-screen color of each pixel. LCDs don't refresh because the image isn't draw on phosphors; instead, each pixel stays on until it's changed again.

Some older monitors were called *interlaced* monitors because they worked the same way a television does, by drawing every *other* line of the screen image and then filling in the alternating lines on the second pass. These monitors were cheaper to make but tended to result in visible flicker. If someone tries to sell you an interlaced monitor at a garage sale, smile politely and then fake illness.

When you're shopping for a monitor or considering the specs of your current monitor, you need to look at some basic issues. With CRTs, concern yourself with the refresh rate, the resolutions supported, and the dot pitch that the monitor offers. With LCD monitors, only resolution is relevant, but LCDs deal with resolution slightly differently. In fact, sometimes they're downright nasty about it.

## *The refresh rate*

As mentioned, the number of times a Mac's screen is redrawn per second is called the *refresh rate,* often measured in hertz (Hz). The higher the refresh rate, the more rock-solid the display seems, with no hint of flicker or strobing.

Most modern monitors are called *multiscanning* monitors because they're capable of synchronizing to different refresh rates and screen resolutions. This means they offer different experiences and picture quality depending on the settings you choose in the Monitors (or Monitors & Sound) control panel.

You'll want to set refresh rate carefully, though, because a refresh rate that's beyond a monitor's tolerance can damage the monitor. Most of the time, the Monitors control panel won't let you overdrive your monitor, but you should check your monitor's manual for its tolerances, just to be safe.

## *The resolution*

As discussed, your Mac creates a bitmap image of the screen to describe how it should look to the monitor. Each bitmap is a fixed size: so many pixels wide by so many pixels high. That's the *resolution:* width-pixels by height-pixels.

The first question that pops to mind is, "Who could possibly care?"

On earlier monitors, the resolution is fixed by the monitor. The original black-and-white Macs, for instance, offer a fixed resolution of 512 pixels by 384 pixels. Multiscanning monitors, however, offer a range of different resolutions that you can set using the Monitors control panel. By changing the resolution of the screen, you change the number of pixels that appear at one time. There are at least three decent reasons to do that:

- ✔ **Use fewer pixels.** If you lower the resolution of your screen, it'll use fewer pixels to create its bitmap. With fewer pixels, the computer is less taxed when drawing graphics, making it possible for it to change and display those pixels more quickly. That's why many 3-D games, for instance, switch to a lower resolution (such as 640x480) before starting a game.

- ✔ **Get more screen real estate.** If you set your monitor to a higher resolution, all icons and windows become smaller because each pixel is smaller. That means you'll see more of the screen at one time. A screen viewed at 1024x768 can show you more information in a window, for instance, than can a screen displayed at 640x480. (See Figures 7-1 and 7-2.)

- ✔ **Get the picture just right.** Okay, Goldilocks, you've seen screens too big and too small. If you get the screen resolution just right, though, you get it close to WYSIWYG (an impossible acronym meaning What You See Is What Your Get and pronounced "wizzy-wig"). When your monitor is set close to its WYSIWYG resolution, the size of documents on-screen will be about the same as a printed document.

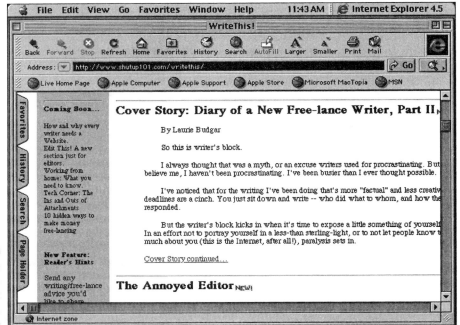

**Figure 7-1:**
A screen shown at 640x480.

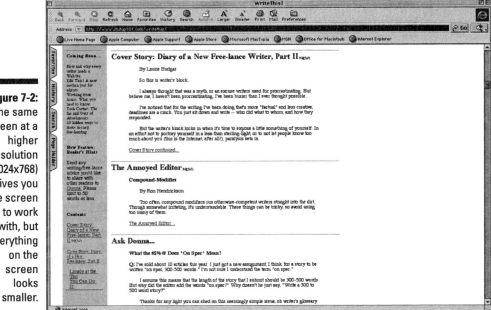

**Figure 7-2:**
The same screen at a higher resolution (1024x768) gives you more screen to work with, but everything on the screen looks smaller.

The question, then, is at what resolution should you set your monitor? My recommendation is simple: Try the WYSIWYG resolution, as shown in Table 7-1. (The table shows the typical viewable area of the monitor being discussed and the size that the monitor is probably advertised as being.) If you don't like the resolution, raise or lower it to the next level and see whether that fits your taste more.

In this crazy world of ours, most CRT manufacturers advertise their monitors not at the actual screen size (the size you would view) but instead at the overall size of the screen, even though you can't see the parts of the screen hidden behind the monitor's plastic. The size of the screen that you *can* see is called the *viewable area*. LCD displays have no issue with viewable area, though, so their true resolution is the same as their viewable area. (So, if you're buying an LCD display, ignore that third column as if it were someone you were thinking of going steady with in the fourth grade. And don't blame me — I didn't make up the rules of young love.)

**Table 7-1    Ideal (WYSIWYG) Monitor Resolutions and Viewable Areas**

| Resolution Setting in Monitors Control Panel | Best for Viewable Areas Nearest to . . . | Which Manufacturers Often Advertise as . . . |
|---|---|---|
| 512x386 | 8.9 inches | 9 inch |
| 640x400 | 10.5 inches | 12 inch |
| 640x480 | 11.1 inches | 14 inch |
| 800x600 | 13.9 inches | 15 inch |
| 832x624 | 14.4 inches | 16 or 17 inch |
| 1024x768 | 17.8 inches | 19 inch |
| 1152x870 | 20.0 inches | 21 inch |
| 1280x1024 | 22.8 inches | 24 inch |

Resolution works differently with LCD displays because they're generally designed with an optimum resolution in mind. For instance, most 13.5" LCD displays look best at 800x600 resolution; 15" LCDs often look best at 1024x768. When you change resolutions on LCD displays, the display must either use less of its available screen space or *antialias* the display image (make on-screen curves a little fuzzy) to create the illusion of a different resolution. Although this can be okay for gaming and some other occasional uses, you'll have trouble working with an LCD in any resolution but its native one. So make sure you've worked with and loved an LCD monitor's native resolution before you commit to it with hard-earned dollars.

## Dot pitch

One other consideration when comparing CRT monitors is the dot pitch on color monitors. *Dot pitch* is a measurement in *fractions of millimeters* of the distance between the red, green, and blue dots that make up a single pixel on a color monitor. (There's no dot pitch on grayscale or LCD monitors.) That's right — 0.2 mm can ruin your whole day!

You'll find a good, solid dot pitch of .28 mm on most multiscanning monitors. Image quality is affected when you get over .40 mm, but such monitors are blissfully tough to find these days. If you come across a dot pitch of .26 mm or lower, you're probably looking at a monitor based on Sony's Trinitron technology. Sony uses a different approach to the aperture grille that enables the pixels to shine through to the screen, resulting in a sharper image that almost always looks better than traditional CRT monitors (which use *shadow-mask* technology). At least, I like 'em.

# Buying and Caring for a Monitor

So now that you know all this useless stuff about monitors. How do you buy one? Here are some tips:

- ✔ You need a good monitor, so be ready to buy the best monitor that offers the best refresh rates, resolution support, and dot pitch that you can afford. Also, buy the largest monitor you can afford.

- ✔ Judge the quality and clarity of the monitor in a computer store before buying. Also, read the reviews in Mac magazines and on Mac Web sites. If you can, convince the salespeople in the store to put your favorite monitors side-by-side so you can judge them. If they won't move the monitors, maybe your hundreds of dollars can buy more respect at the next store down the street.

- ✔ Straight lines on the screen should look straight. Colors should be vibrant, not washed out. Changing the brightness control shouldn't warp the image terribly or blur text on the screen.

- ✔ Play with the Monitors control panel to see whether the monitor syncs well to other resolutions or if switching is difficult. (Some monitors will sync correctly to different resolutions; others will leave it up to you to make the final adjustments to the picture every time you switch.)

If you have a pre-G3 Macintosh, the monitor port is probably an Apple RGB connection; G3 and later Macs include a VGA port, which is standard for Intel-compatible PC monitors. It doesn't really matter, though — you can shop for any multiscanning monitor. If the monitor's cable doesn't match your Mac, you can get a VGA-to-RGB adapter (These are shown in the next section.)

## Fancy tricks with monitors and TVs

Want to go beyond the monitor? If you'd like to put your monitor's image on a TV — either for presentations or for big-screen gaming — you'll need a *scan converter*, which is a device that takes the monitor's output and makes it compatible with a TV's inputs. (It works with other devices such as VCRs, too.) Scan converters are made by Focus Enhancements, (www.focusenhancements.com), Aver-Media (www.avermedia.com), and others.

## *Installing the monitor*

After you've chosen the monitor you want to use with your Mac, installing it should be a fairly simple matter. You just need to answer a few quick questions before you connect the cables:

✔ **Is this a multiscanning monitor?** Older Apple-branded monitors and a few others capable of connecting to Mac OS computers are not multi-scanning, meaning they're designed to accept only one resolution and one refresh rate. You can use such a monitor with most modern Macs, but you shouldn't try to change resolutions, even if the Monitors control panel will let you.

✔ **What type of cable does the monitor have?** If your monitor is Apple-branded (in most cases) or is a Mac-only monitor with cabling exclusively for Mac, it uses an Apple RGB port adapter (see Figure 7-3). Otherwise, the monitor is probably a VGA-compatible monitor. (VGA is the Intel-compatible video standard. The port is shown in Figure 7-3 as well.) If you have a VGA monitor and an RGB port, you need a special adapter (a VGA-to-RGB adapter, discussed a little later in this section).

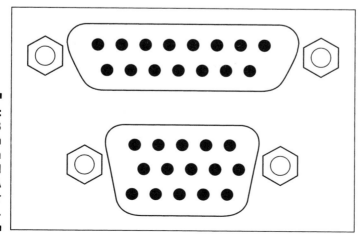

**Figure 7-3:** Apple's RGB connection (top) and a standard VGA connector (bottom).

✔ **Does your Mac have a nonstandard video port?** Quadra AV and early Power Macintosh models offered special video ports for AppleVision AV displays. (The connection enables both video and audio information to travel directly to the monitor.) Unfortunately, without an adapter, these ports aren't compatible with any displays other than AppleVision models. The adapter is included with these computer models, or you can buy such an adapter separately.

✔ **Does this non-Apple monitor offer any sync limitations?** Depending on the age and capabilities of a VGA-compatible monitor, you might need a particular adapter that limits the resolution, color depth, or refresh rate to certain levels. In particular, it's best to find out whether the monitor's manufacturer offered a special Mac adapter for the monitor. If so, you should have that adapter on-hand.

After you have all that figured out, make sure your Mac is shut down. Plug your monitor into a surge protector or a wall outlet. (If your monitor has a shielded plug that won't fit a wall outlet, plug it into an outlet on the back of your Mac. This offers the advantage that the monitor will shut down automatically when the Mac does.) Now you're ready to connect the monitor's cable to your Mac's video port.

If you're planning to connect an Apple monitor and an Apple-branded Mac, you should have no trouble; just connect the monitor's video connector to the RGB or VGA port on the back. Tighten the monitor connector by turning the thumbscrews. (They don't need to be Spanish Inquisition tight, just secure.)

Some newer Mac models offer both an RGB port and a VGA port as a convenience. You can't use both ports at once, but you can use the port that works best with your monitor. Just plug it in and go.

---

# Make it squeaky clean

Your monitor might look like a window but that doesn't mean you should use typical window cleaner to wipe it off. Most manufacturers recommend a static-free cleaner that's specifically designed for monitors; regular chemical cleaners can remove the antiglare coating found on some monitors. (Check your monitor's documentation.)

You should also shut down the monitor first, spray liquid only on the clean, lint-free cloth you're using (not on the monitor itself), and avoid any sort of abrasives. Be doubly careful around an LCD display because its front is plastic, not glass, and will mar or scratch even more easily. Finally, here's a hint from Helo-weezy: An anti-static dryer sheet that's already been through the dryer is a great rag for wiping a CRT clean!

If you're attaching a standard VGA-compatible monitor to your Mac, you might need an adapter. Although many types of adapters exist (including some that might be made by your monitor's manufacturer for your particular monitor), the easiest adapters to work with are universal adapters made by Sony, Interex (www.interex.com), Griffin Technology (www.griffintechnology.com), and a number of other manufacturers (see Figure 7-4).

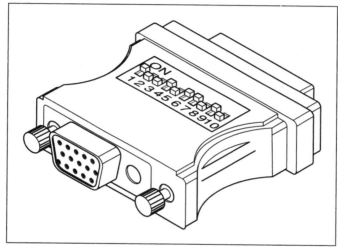

**Figure 7-4:** A universal RGB-to-VGA adapter for attaching VGA-standard monitors to Mac OS computers.

Using small switches on the adapter, you can set it to a specific resolution that the monitor supports. Then, in most cases, the Mac syncs to that resolution as it starts up. If the monitor is a multiscanning monitor, you can generally set the adapter to a multiscanning setting and then use the Monitors control panel to set the desired resolution. After it's set, connect the adapter to the monitor cable and then connect the whole adapter-cable combo to your Mac's video port. Tighten as necessary and then start up your Mac.

# *Monitor on the Blink?*

If you're having trouble seeing things correctly on the monitor, you need to first isolate the problem by making sure it's not a more general Mac issue. (For instance, you might not be getting a picture on the monitor because your Mac isn't starting up!) Then, you can troubleshoot the monitor and its settings.

*Do not open your monitor to service it.* I won't be talking about that level of fixing in this section because the inside of a monitor is reserved for seasoned professionals. The monitor's innards pack quite a punch — up to 30,000 volts — even when unplugged for days. Instead, I focus on the outside, where it's much safer.

## Nothin', nada, zip-o

A blank screen can result from quite a few circumstances or problems. Start by eliminating those that fall outside the responsibility of the video subsystem. For instance, make sure your Mac is plugged in, that it's turning on correctly, and that it hasn't crashed or frozen in sleep mode. For instance, does the Mac seem to start up (or restart) in response to keyboard commands or its power/reset buttons? Do you hear the fan or hard drive whirring? If those things aren't happening, your problem is probably with the Mac, not the monitor. If the Mac seems to be working fine, though, you can move on to the video subsystem.

After you've decided that the problem is with the video subsystem, you can troubleshoot the monitor itself to see if it's the problem. Here are the places to start:

✔ **Check the power.** Check the monitor's power cable to make sure it's plugged into both the monitor and the wall socket or your surge protector. With some Apple models, you can plug the monitor directly into the back of the Mac, so check to make sure that connection is secure. Check that the monitor is turned on. If your monitor has an LED light on the front, it will probably glow when the monitor is receiving power.

The LED on many monitors glows green when the monitor is on and receiving an image from the video card. Amber (orange-ish) often suggests that the monitor is working but not receiving a picture from the video circuitry because the Mac is off, is in sleep mode, or has something wrong with the video card or cable.

✔ **Check the cable.** Check the cable that connects your monitor and Mac. Make sure it's connected and not too stretched, pinched, or frayed. Also make sure the pins on the cable's connectors aren't bent or broken off.

✔ **Review the settings.** Most monitors have external controls for brightness and contrast; use those to see whether they've just been dialed down below visible. (It's usually best to adjust one control at a time.) If your monitor has a Reset button, push it. That returns the monitor to factory default values, which should restore the image to something you can make out on screen.

✔ **Restart the Mac.** Most Mac models attempt to recognize the monitor as they start up, and they won't always sync correctly with a monitor that's plugged in after the fact. If you've connected the cable or something else has changed, you might need to restart your Mac before it will display an image on-screen.

How do you restart the Mac cleanly if you can't see the screen? Press the Power key on your keyboard and then press the Return key. If all goes well, you'll hear the Mac shut down and power off. If that doesn't work, you might need to shut down the messy way — press Control+⌘+Power on the keyboard or press the reset button on your Mac.

✔ **Zap PRAM.** Monitor settings are stored in parameter RAM — a portion of RAM that the Mac keeps for its own private storage of settings. If you restart the Mac and hold down ⌘+Option+P+R until you hear two more restart sounds, you'll reset the Mac to its lowest monitor resolution setting. (You'll also need to reset some control panels; zapping PRAM is discussed in Chapter 23.)

If these options don't net any results, the monitor might be broken. Test it using different power cables. (The black power cables that connect most monitors to an AC socket are the same as the power cables used to connect most Mac models to an AC socket and should be interchangeable.) You should also pick the monitor up and test it using a wall socket on the other side of the room, just to make sure you didn't throw the circuit under your desk. If you don't seem to be getting any power to the monitor — no clicking or humming sounds, no glowing LCDs or screen fuzz — it's time to head to a repair shop.

If your monitor does seem to turn on, the problem is either with your monitor cable or with your video circuitry. The best way to test this is with another computer. Shut down the second computer, plug in your monitor, connect them to one another, and start up the computer. If you don't get an image, something might be wrong with your monitor's cable.

If you still don't get an image, the trouble is with your Mac's video circuitry or video expansion card. These are tough to test on your own. If you've recently installed VRAM or a video expansion card, make sure it's seated properly (see Chapters 14 and 15 for details.) Otherwise, it's time to bundle up your Mac and take it to a service center to see whether they can revive your video.

According to Apple's technical documents, Macs in the 400, 600, or 6100 series (including both Performas and Power Macintosh models) will offer no video if the PRAM battery is dead. So, if video isn't working on those models, suspect the battery. See Chapter 23 for details.

## Ginger and Fred, it ain't

If your Mac's monitor looks like your television when you're watching the premium cable channels you haven't paid for — with the screen flickering at odd angles and appearing to roll over constantly — you have a sync problem.

Somehow, your Mac has managed to set itself to a resolution, a refresh rate, or both (in the Monitors or Monitors & Sound control panel) that your monitor doesn't support.

How do these things happen to otherwise upstanding computer components? Here's the quiz:

✔ **Is everything plugged in nice and snug?** You won't always get the results you want if your monitor cable is hanging precariously out of the video port on your Mac.

✔ **Is it really a multiscanning monitor?** Sometimes the Monitors control panel will let you set the resolution to a level that isn't supported by your monitor because it isn't capable of that particular resolution or it isn't really a multiscanning monitor. If you can, change back to a lower resolution or the one you were using before.

If you've just chosen a resolution in the Monitors control panel and your monitor can't sync to it, don't panic — wait about 10 seconds without touching the mouse or keyboard. The Mac OS should return to the previous resolution automatically.

✔ **Was the monitor connected at startup?** The Mac attempts to detect the monitor and sync to it at startup. If the monitor wasn't there (because you've connected it or reconnected it without shutting down the Mac first), it might not sync. Try restarting the Mac.

✔ **Is your adapter set correctly?** Most sync problems come from setting an RGB-to-VGA adapter incorrectly. The Macintosh is sensing the adapter, not the monitor itself, so the adapter must be set to a resolution and refresh rate that your monitor can handle. Try using adapter settings for a more basic monitor (640x480 at 60 Hz, for instance) if you have trouble with other settings.

You can damage some monitors by attempting to drive them at resolutions or refresh rates they don't support. If you have your monitor's documentation handy, check it out to see what the limits are for your monitor.

If you have a sync problem, try forcing the Mac to restart. Again, if you can't see the screen, try pressing the Power key on your keyboard and then pressing Return. If that doesn't work, press Control+⌘+Power, press the Mac's reset button, or cycle the Mac's power switch. When the Mac starts up, it should sync to the monitor. If it doesn't, check the connection and try all over again.

If the monitor still doesn't sync, restart the Mac and zap parameter RAM by holding down ⌘+Option+P+R until you hear the startup chime twice more. Then release the keys and allow the Mac to start up. This should reset the video circuitry to its lowest resolution so that you can at least see what you're doing.

## Old Macs and multiscanning monitors

Some Macs in the Mac II series and the LC series, as well as the earliest Performas, weren't designed to work with multiscanning monitors. In many cases, these Macs were designed to work with only the Apple 13" RGB Display or the Apple Basic Color Display.

Many of these Macs, however, can be coaxed into working with a multiscanning monitor at 832x624 resolution, although you won't be able to change resolutions. There's a special adapter (you can find it in some Mac stores and catalogs) for the LC III, Performa 450-460 series, and early PowerBook models. This adapter works also with the Apple Display Card 4/8, 8/24, and 8/24GC.

Earlier Macs support only 640x480 resolutions and require an adapter to show an image on a multiscanning monitor. They are the LC, LC II, Performa 400 series, Performa 600/600CD, and the Macintosh IIvx and IIvi.

If syncing just doesn't seem to be in the cards, it might be because you're using the wrong RGB-to-VGA adapter (which is the most common sync problem) or that the monitor and Mac were simply not designed to work together.

## Waves, blotches, and blurs

If you have a wavy, blotchy, or blurry monitor image, you might be surprised when I tell you that you might be able to fix that. Monitors are complex devices, but some very basic issues can correct problems with their on-screen images. Of course, monitors can go bad (or they can be made poorly in the first place), so you can't fix everything. But you can try, which is all that your mother and I ask of you.

Here are some phenomena that can cause problems on your screen:

- **Magnetic interference.** Seeing waves, blotches, or splotches? (Is this starting to sound like Dr. Seuss?) If you have any sort of distortion near the edges of your screen, especially in blooms of color or waviness, it could be that some sort of magnetic interference is near your monitor. Move speakers, phones, and other electronic equipment away from the monitor. If you have more than one monitor on your desk, they can affect one other in this way — try moving them farther apart. (If you're working with multiple monitors, angle them so that their backs are far away from one another, even if their fronts are close. Also, a thick, non-ferrous cookie sheet between the two of them should clear up interference.)

Believe it or not, monitors are calibrated so that they sometimes work best when they're facing east-west or north-south. If you have distortion problems that can't be explained by external interference, see whether the image improves when you turn the monitor 90 degrees in one direction or the other.

✔ **Internal magnetic build-up.** Over time, your monitor might build up a magnetic charge *internally*, which can affect picture quality. To remove a built-up magnetic charge, you *degauss* the monitor. If you're lucky, your monitor includes a button that lets you degauss the monitor manually. Alternatively, your monitor might degauss itself whenever you turn it on or off. (That's why the monitor shimmers as it turns on until it seems to lock into place.) If your monitor doesn't have such a feature, or if degaussing yourself doesn't help much, you can take it in for service. Monitor service technicians can take the monitor apart and fully degauss it, which might improve picture quality considerably.

✔ **Strobing or pulsating.** Does your monitor have disco fever? The culprit might be fluorescent lighting, if you're in the office. If you can, try setting the monitor to a higher refresh rate (85 to 90 Hz, for instance) in the Monitors control panel. If you can't change the refresh rate, see whether you can change the lighting a bit: Put a regular incandescent lamp on your desk. If trouble persists, you might need to get a new monitor.

✔ **Blurriness.** Over time, your monitor can loose *convergence,* which means the electron beam begins to miss the small dots it needs to hit to display a crisp image on-screen. If things are blurring a bit, especially in splotches away from the edges, you might be able to adjust the *convergence focus.* Some monitors have buttons or dials on the front for adjusting focus; others have a recessed screw on the side of the monitor that you can get at using a long, thin screwdriver. (Note that Murphy's Law of Vertical Hold is bound to grab you if you try adjusting the focus. Good luck.) If you can't find an external focus control, it's likely that the focus controls, convergence controls, or both are internal, in which case you'll likely need to take it in to a service technician for adjustment.

Convergence problems at the very edges of your monitor's screen are considered normal, which is why many monitors come from the factory with a black border around the screen image. The electron beam originates from the center of the screen (toward the back of the monitor's deep enclosure), so it's more spread out when it shoots for the edges, resulting in poorer convergence.

## *Trouble with colors*

Trouble with color can come in different flavors — it could be that your monitor isn't set correctly for its surroundings, that the colors are washed out, or that you're seeing all too much of one particular color. Here's the executive summary of steps you can take:

✔ **Correct the gamma.** The *gamma* for your monitor is a number used to determine how, exactly, the monitor interprets brightness. Due to certain limitations in monitor technology, a monitor generally won't display brightness linearly (meaning that each step up in brightness requested doesn't always equal a complete step up in brightness displayed). If you have a color monitor and you're running Mac OS 8.1 or earlier, choose Macintosh RGB Color Display for the gamma setting in the Monitors & Sound (or Monitors) control panel.

✔ **Create a profile.** In later Mac OS versions, color is more of an issue. In the Monitors & Sound (or Monitors) control panel, find the Color button. Press it to see the different color profiles you can select from. If you haven't yet, you'll find that it's a good idea to create a new color profile — you can do this by clicking the Calibrate button. The Monitor Calibration Assistant then walks you through creating a profile (see Figure 7-5). Calibration does two things. First, it enables you to set your monitor for the current lighting conditions in your work area. (You can set different profiles for morning and afternoon, for instance, and switch between them for best color.) Second, a ColorSync profile helps you get more accurate matches between your monitor's display and color printouts, if you have a color printer that supports ColorSync.

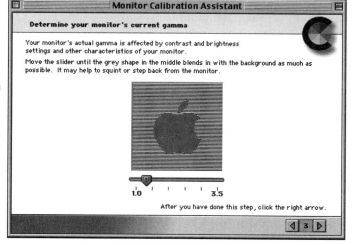

**Figure 7-5:** Follow the on-screen instructions to create a monitor profile in Mac OS 8.5 or later.

✔ **Fix the sync.** If you're seeing too much red, green, or blue, perhaps your monitor cable is poorly connected or going bad. Try tightening the connector to the port. If your video circuitry is on an expansion card, you might need to open the Mac up and make sure that the card is seated well. (See Chapter 14.) If the cable and connection seem fine, you might have a problem with the monitor; maybe that warranty is still in place.

Some Macintosh II and early LC models send out a sync-on-green signal that most VGA monitors don't find the least bit amusing. If you're seeing a lot of green, you might need to hook up an adapter between your Mac and the monitor (try Griffin Technology at www.griffintechnology.com) or upgrade the Mac OS to a newer version that's supported for your Mac model.

## *How the pros do it: Brightness and contrast*

Adjusting brightness and contrast correctly improves both the colors and readability of your Mac's display. If your Mac has an integrated monitor or you're using an Apple ColorSync or AppleVision display, brightness and contrast are handled in the Monitors or Monitors & Sound control panel.

For others, though, some manual adjustment might be necessary. Here's the best way to do that:

1. **Place an image on the screen that you can use as a reference.**

   You can use either a grayscale image (one with various levels of gray, black, and white) or a color image. If you use a color image, it should be composed of very familiar colors.

2. **Turn the brightness and contrast of your monitor all the way down.**

3. **Turn the contrast up until you see the complete image displaying strong blacks, rich colors, or both.**

4. **Turn the brightness up until any white portions of the image are pure white but comfortable and not too bright.**

   If you have a piece of bright white paper around, hold it up to the screen to check it against the monitor. You don't want the white too gray, nor do you want it too bright and shiny. Also, try to avoid pushing the brightness up to 100 percent because this can shorten the life of the monitor.

# Chapter 8

# Making Pretty Pictures: Scanners and Digital Cameras

*In This Chapter*

▶ Finding out how scanners do what they do

▶ Comparison shopping for a scanner

▶ Installing your scanner

▶ Disciplining an unruly scanner

▶ Buying into the digital camera frenzy

As far as I'm concerned, scanners and digital cameras work by *magic*. Some experts disagree, though, claiming to know how scanners and cameras turn real-world objects into computer documents that you can view and edit on your screen. Those people have even measured the vital signs of cameras and scanners so you know which ones to buy and how to troubleshoot them when they fail.

Unfortunately, I'm not one of these expert people. So I'll be psychically channeling one for the duration of this chapter; I'm sorry in advance if the voice switches from first to second person and back again. (This person might also be slightly less funny than I am, but it can't be helped.) On the upside, this leaves my regular personality free to play mental gin rummy against myself, which is great, because I've been on a roll for the past few days.

## What Scanners Do

A *scanner* is a device that creates a digital image file from an original (often a photograph or a printed document). The scanner creates the image by passing a light along the surface of a piece of paper (or similar object) while *charged-coupled device* (CCD) sensors or *contact image sensors* (CIS) follow behind it, picking up the information and turning it into ones and zeros. The resulting digital file can then be translated into different file formats, retouched to add something onerous, and placed in the desktop publishing document you've created for your weekly conspiracy-theory newsletter.

Most scanners can perform scans that incorporate different amounts of color and light information. For a *black-and-white* scan, the scanner simply determines what portions of the document are white and what portions aren't. This results in a scan that you might use to fax a printed document or for line-art that has no shading particular detail.

To create a *grayscale* scan, the sensors use a white light to determine how much lighter and darker parts of the image are in relation to each other. This results in different levels of gray in the final image file.

To perform a color scan, the scanner emits colored light: red, green, and blue. (Some scanners use a color filter over the sensor instead of a different colored light.) The software then detects how much red, green, and blue is in a given dot on the original and creates an image file that mixes those colors to get the right result.

In the past, these three-color comparisons were performed in three passes of the scan head, once each with red, green, and blue. Today's scanners, however, measure the colors quickly enough to gather the necessary data in one pass. This makes it possible for scans to come out more quickly with the same amount of color information.

# Buying a Scanner

Scanners come in different shapes and sizes, just like happy children. Scanners for Macs come in two interface basic flavors: USB and SCSI. (By the time you read this, FireWire scanners may have hit the market; they have advantages similar to USB but are even faster.) If you have a choice, SCSI scanners might be a bit faster, but USB scanners are easier to hook up. (In the past, some scanners were made to use the serial port, and you might still come across one in the used classifieds or at computer swap meets.)

Beyond the interface, the look of the scanner can be different, too:

✔ **Flatbed scanners.** You see these most often. Flatbed scanners look like the top of a photocopier, with a plastic lid that covers a glass bed. You lay documents on the glass, face down, and then close the lid to do your scanning. Figure 8-1 shows a typical flatbed scanner.

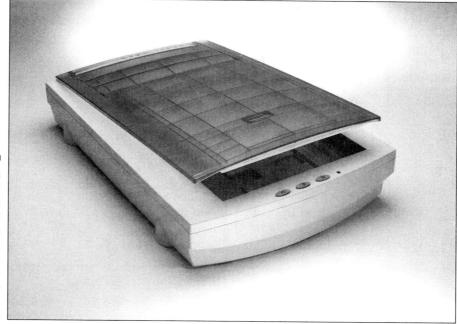

**Figure 8-1:**
A flatbed
scanner can
resemble
the top of a
photocopier,
albeit some-
times in teal,
like this
UMAX MX3.

Flatbed scanners can often accept add-on accessories such as sheet feeders (for scanning multiple documents at once) and devices that allow you to scan slides or larger transparencies. If these capabilities are important to you, shop for a flatbed scanner that supports them. Scanner accessories can be expensive, though, so you're likely to use them only in a professional or organizational setting.

✔ **Handheld scanners.** You won't find many of these anymore, but I have to include them so that people don't write me letters saying, "Hey, why didn't you include handheld scanners in your discussion of scanners?" Handheld scanners are a little like barcode readers in department stores; you pass the scanner over the document (using your hand). It's tough to keep the scanner in a straight line and you can't scan full-sized printer documents easily, which is why they have passed into obscurity.

✔ **Sheetfed scanners.** These lower-quality, lower-cost scanners were popular in the Olden Days when flatbed scanners were more expensive. Sheetfed scanners pull a document past the scanner head in much the same way a fax machine does. (Most of them offered similar quality.) You don't see too many of these anymore, though, because flatbed scanners have come way down in price.

✔ **Photo scanners.** These scanners allow you to scan a 3x5 or 5x7 photograph into a digital image. They're generally compact, easy to work with, and one-trick ponies.

✔ **Slide/film scanners.** Slide scanners allow you to scan 35-mm slides (and sometimes film negatives) into color images. This is often the best way to get professional-level images into your desktop publishing documents. Otherwise, if you're scanning slides for lesser uses, you can often use an attachment for a flatbed scanner.

Some past scanner makers that are now out of the Mac scanner business include Hewlett-Packard, Visioneer, and Apple itself. You might still find such scanners available at dealers and in the classified ads.

You'll find that most scanners, both high and low end, are flatbed models, although their prices, quality, and accessories vary. Aside from slide scanners, few manufacturers are making Mac-compatible handheld scanners and photo scanners.

Table 8-1 shows some popular scanner manufacturers that make Mac-compatible models and the types of scanners they make.

| Table 8-1 | Companies, Scanner Types, and Their Web Sites | |
|-----------|-----------------------------------------------|---|
| *Company* | *Web Site* | *Type of Scanner* |
| Agfa | www.agfa.com | Flatbed |
| Epson | www.epson.com | Flatbed |
| Kodak | www.kodak.com | Slide/film |
| Linocolor | www.linocolor.com | Flatbed |
| MicroTek | www.microtek.com | Flatbed, page |
| Nikon | www.nikon.com | Slide/film |
| Polaroid | www.polaroid.com | Slide/film |
| UMAX | www.umax.com | Flatbed |
| Visioneer | www.visioneer.com | Page |

# How well does it scan?

The quality of a scanner is often measured by its vital statistics: resolution, number of colors supported, and scanning speed. Some of these numbers can be a bit confusing (in fact, they're designed to trip up regular citizens like ourselves), so let's be careful out there.

First, you should look at the *true*, or *optical*, resolution of the scanner. This number represents the dots per inch that the scanner's scanning mechanism uses to receive information. On less expensive scanners, this number might be 300 dpi or 600 dpi; more expensive scanners offer optical resolutions of 1200 dpi or higher.

Although most scanners advertise two resolution numbers, such as 300x600 or 600x1200, the first number is the only one that represents the optical resolution. The second number simply tells you how many steps the scanner mechanism takes as its scans the image. Ideally, the more steps, the better the image, but returns diminish if the optical resolution is low.

So, if you've ever seen a 9600 dpi scanner advertised for pocket change, you have a right to be skeptical. That's why you have to watch out for a number called interpolated resolution. *Interpolated resolutions* are arrived at by sophisticated software routines that create artificially smaller dots for a smoothing effect for the overall image. This might make some scans look better, but it's no substitute for a higher optical resolution, especially for high-end photo and artistic scans.

Most inexpensive scanners work with *24-bit* color, meaning they can digitize as many as 16.7 million colors, which is the upper range of the number of colors humans can distinguish. The 24 bits are divided three ways so that 8 bits, or any of 256 unique values, can be assigned to each red, blue, and green level for a particular dot's color. More sophisticated scanners work at 30 or 36 bits per pixel, so such scanners can distinguish billions of colors. It might seem like overkill, but these scanners can sometimes offer even more detail within the colors of the scan.

Ultimately, though, the number of colors is less important than the quality of the scanner and its scan head. One measurement of quality is *dynamic range*, a number from 0.0 to 4.0 that tells you the range of tones that the scanner can display. Inexpensive scanners have a dynamic range around 2.5; the closer to 4.0 this number is, the higher the quality of your scan. (Check the scanners packaging, documentation, or other product information for its dynamic range.)

## The DPI conspiracy

You hear dots per inch and resolution numbers bandied about concerning all different types of computer peripherals — monitors, printers, scanners, and cameras. You'll be happy to know that, in most cases, the numbers aren't related. Wouldn't it be great if a 600 dpi scan would look perfect on a 600 dpi printer? Sorry, it just doesn't work that way.

Scanner resolution and printer resolution aren't the same thing at all. Instead, a closer relationship exists between a scanner's resolution and the *lines per inch* (lpi) that your printer is capable of printing. You can probably determine your printer's lpi from its printed documentation. Then create your scans at 1.5 times your printer's lpi. Home/office printers tend to have an lpi around 70.

Most of the time, you'll scan somewhere between 150 and 200 dpi for most inkjets and laser printers. If you're scanning a black-and-white line-art image, scan it at the full resolution (300 dpi or 600 dpi) of the printer. If you're scanning an image you want to enlarge, though, multiply that base dpi by the ratio at which you'd like to expand the image. (For instance, if you're going to make the image 5/4 the original, scan at 250 dpi instead of 200.)

## *What comes with the scanner?*

Another factor to consider when shopping for a scanner is what software, if any, comes with it. In many cases, scanners include a special program for operating the scanner, or creating photocopies, or managing a number of scans at once. However, such manufacturer-specific software might be of dubious value — I'd say half the programs I've installed from scanner manufacturers are buggy at best and worthless at worst.

Instead, you might opt to use professional image-editing software and a *plug-in* for the scanner, as described next.

Here's a list of the other software you should look for from a scanner:

- **Image-editing software.** A lot of scanners come with an Adobe editing program: PhotoDeluxe, PhotoShop LE (Limited Edition), or the full version of PhotoShop. If you got the full version, count your stars, because it's worth many hundreds of dollars. I prefer PhotoShop LE over PhotoDeluxe, but that's because I find PhotoDeluxe's user-friendly interface grating (and it offers fewer actual editing controls).

✔ **Scanning plug-in.** Aside from the image-editing software included, find out whether PhotoShop-compatible plug-ins are available or whether the standard plug-ins are completely supported. Scanning from within PhotoShop (or a program designed to work with PhotoShop's plug-ins) can be a great way to quickly get your scans into the Mac and edited to taste, without using an intermediary scanning program. If you have such a plug-in, you can scan by simply choosing a command in the File menu (see Figure 8-2).

TWAIN stands for *technology without an interesting name*; it was some comedian's acronym for a mechanism that integrates standard scanning commands with scanners and image-editing programs. If you scanner is TWAIN compliant, you don't need to use its software to get basic scans; instead, you can use the TWAIN commands within your image-editing program.

**Figure 8-2:** A plug-in adds scanner-specific commands to Adobe PhotoShop or a similar image-editing program.

✔ **Optical Character Recognition (OCR) software.** These applications, which come with some scanners, read scanned documents — such as a memo or a page from a printed book — and turn the scanned text into computer text that you can edit in a word processing program. The idea is to do away with retyping documents. In most cases, OCR programs are 90 to 95 percent accurate, depending on the quality of the original document, the scanner's capabilities, and blind luck. (It also helps if the original document is printed in a common font, such as Times or Courier and hasn't had coffee spilled on it.) Figure 8-3 shows an OCR application in action.

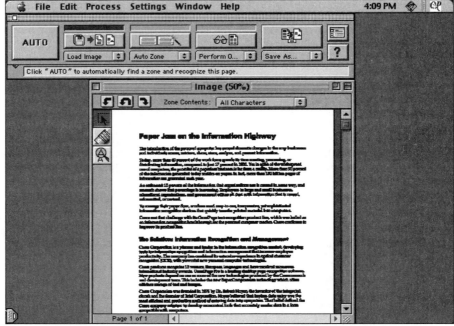

Figure 8-3:
An OCR
application
allows your
Mac to read
scanned
documents,
turning them
into editable
text.

# Installing a Scanner

Scanners are generally either SCSI or USB; which you choose depends completely on which ports you have available. If you happen to have a choice between USB and SCSI, you might find USB easier to configure. You also come across the occasional serial-port scanner, especially if you're shopping the used market.

Some scanners ship with special pins or locks that must be disabled before the scanner is turned off. This is less common on newer, inexpensive models, but it's something to look out for before you plug the scanner in. Check the documentation for a dial or pin that needs to be adjusted before you start up the scanner.

Serial and USB scanners are generally simple to install:

✔ **Serial scanner.** In most cases, you simply power down your Mac, plug the scanner into an available serial port, and restart the Mac. Then install any software that came with the scanner. If you have trouble with the scanner, troubleshoot it as you would any other serial device, as discussed in Chapters 4 and 6. (Most serial scanners, page scanners, and other specialty devices turn on when you feed a document into the scanner. Often, they don't have power switches, although they do generally need to be plugged in.)

✔ **USB scanner.** If you're installing a USB scanner, you might find it useful to install the scanner's software first. That way, a driver is present when you plug in the scanner. The software will likely require you to restart your Mac. After that's occurred and the Finder has loaded successfully, plug the scanner into an available USB port on the side of your Mac, your Mac's USB keyboard, or your USB hub. Turn on the scanner, if necessary. The scanner should be automatically detected. (If you see a message saying there's no driver for the device, you either didn't install the software that came with the scanner or the software isn't working correctly.) If you don't see any error messages, you should proceed to your scanner software and test to see whether it will scan successfully.

Again, if you happen to have a FireWire-based scanner, it will connect pretty much the same way a USB scanner does, except you might choose to daisy-chain the scanner to your other devices. Otherwise, install the software, connect the scanner to an available FireWire port, and start scanning.

To install a SCSI scanner, you must first decide what SCSI ID to use. (See Chapter 4 for more on managing SCSI.) Then you're ready to begin the process:

1. **Shut down your Mac.**

2. **On the back of the scanner, select a SCSI ID number for your scanner.**

3. **Plug one end of the scanner's SCSI cable into the scanner and plug the other end into your Mac's SCSI port.**

   If you have other SCSI devices, remove the terminator from the last SCSI device and plug your scanner into that device. (If the last SCSI device doesn't have a physical terminator, check for a switch and make sure termination is off.)

4. **Unless the scanner has internal or automatic termination, you need to terminate it manually. Plug a SCSI terminator into the scanner's other SCSI port or flip its termination switch on the back of the scanner.**

5. **Plug the scanner's AC power cord into a wall socket or a surge protector and turn the scanner on.**

   You should see lights, hear the scanner warm up, or both.

6. **Turn on your Mac.**

7. **Install any software that came with the scanner and then restart your Mac if the installed software requires it.**

Want to make sure the scanner is recognized? Open Apple System Profiler and check your SCSI devices. If you don't see the scanner, you might need to power down, change SCSI ID numbers on the back of the scanner, and start up again.

# *Scanner Trouble*

If you have trouble with your scanner, it will probably be in one of two areas: the interface or software. Both SCSI and USB can be a little cranky, so if you're having problems indicating that the scanner either is not being recognized or is being recognized intermittently, troubleshoot the connection. You can see some hints on this in Chapter 4.

For SCSI problems, make sure you consider the following additional issues:

- **Turn it on.** You might not always think of this step, because you don't often turn off other SCSI devices. Make sure that the scanner is turned on and, if necessary, that you restart the Mac so it rescans the SCSI bus. You can rescan the SCSI bus also from Apple System Profile — choose Commands ➪ Update All Information — or by using a shareware or freeware SCSI utility.

- **Check the termination.** Some scanners have odd termination schemes, including switches, internal termination with no visible indicators, or odd passthrough terminators. Again, read the scanner's documentation carefully.

- **ID clear on both buses?** If you have two SCSI buses in your Mac, some scanners get picky and want their SCSI ID to be free on both buses. So make sure no device is using the SCSI ID you've chosen for your scanner on either bus.

As far as software goes, check the age of the software you're using for your SCSI scanner; some of that software can be old and infirm. It might also require extensions to the Mac OS. If you're having trouble getting the scanner recognized, try reinstalling all its software from the installation CD or disks. Also try the manufacturer's Web site or customer service line to see whether updates are available.

For USB scanners, make sure you're using the latest Mac OS version and Mac firmware updates for your particular Mac model. If the scanner isn't working when plugged into a passive hub or the iMac's keyboard, try connecting it directly to one of the USB ports on your Mac.

## Keep the scanner squeaky clean

To clean a flatbed scanner's glass, use a slightly damp, soft cloth and wipe the surface. Don't spray liquids directly on the glass. You should also avoid abrasives and corrosive chemicals; a little glass cleaner sprayed on the cloth should work fine. Let it dry thoroughly so that it doesn't heat up when the scanner is on and so your documents come out of the scanner as crisp and clean as they went in.

Dust can accumulate inside the scanner, under the glass. If your scanner's user guide includes instructions for removing the glass and cleaning it, you can do so; otherwise, removing the glass might void your warranty. Cracking or breaking the glass will necessitate a pricey fix, so be careful when handling it.

# Become a Digital Shutterbug

Digital filmless cameras are probably the wave of the future. With ever-improving specifications and ever-decreasing prices, a *digital still camera* is becoming a more and more likely accessory for the home or small business user. Over time, digital cameras might even become less expensive than traditional cameras. After all, after you buy the camera, you can take as many pictures as you like without ever buying film or paying processing fees again.

A digital camera is a lot like an upright scanner. Using CCDs and a camera lens, the camera quickly scans the world around it. You usually see the image in an LCD viewfinder, which shows that the camera is picking up the world around it live as you point it at different things. When you see the snapshot you want to take, press the button.

The image is stored in the camera's memory. This memory can be fixed in the camera or removable. Some removable memory is in a standard format (CompactFlash or SmartMedia) that can be read by USB-based devices and accessed like a removable disk.

In other cases, you hook the camera up to a USB or traditional serial port and copy the files from the camera. After you have the images in your Mac, you can use an image-editing program to edit, crop, and save them in any image format desired. From there, you can include the image in a printed document, place it on the Web, send it to friends through e-mail, or do whatever you'd typically do with scanned pictures. What could be more fun?

## *Shopping for a digital camera*

To figure out digital cameras, you need to do a little shopping. Cameras are still on the pricey side, although camera retailers aren't quoting the insane Department of Defense budgeting numbers that they used to. Ranging from a few hundred dollars for a point-and-shoot to thousands for a professional camera, you definitely have some shopping to do.

Pro-level photographers often use digital *camera backs* for their digital photography, allowing them to continue to use their priceless lenses to take digital images. If you have a professional need or money to burn, look into a digital camera back for yourself, which will allow you to attach a traditional camera body to a filmless base for digital pictures.

No matter what the price range, you should ask some basic questions when comparing the quality and performance of digital cameras:

- ✔ **Resolution.** Digital cameras tend to be measured in their megapixel rating, meaning how many millions of pixels they're capable of storing per image. Low-end cameras often offer resolutions up to 1152x864. Higher end cameras offer 2.1 megapixel or so resolution, meaning 1600x1200. Any camera capable of megapixel resolutions in this range is acceptable for 5x7 printed images; lower resolution images (such as 640x480) can be used for Web pages and for sending through e-mail.

  Watch out for interpolation, the same software trick used in scanners to up the resolution and make it seem more impressive than it is. Check the camera's documentation carefully to make sure the advertised resolution is an *optical* resolution.

- ✔ **Optical zoom.** Cameras offer different levels of true zoom capabilities, called *optical* zoom because the camera's optics are responsible for zooming in and out. This is in contrast to *digital zoom*, which the camera emulates by using software routines.

- ✔ **Storage.** All digital cameras use some sort of memory to store images — in many cases it's *flash,* or nonvolatile RAM — which means it doesn't need external power to maintain its contents. In today's digital cameras, images are often stored on CompactFlash or SmartMedia memory cards, which are read using devices that attach to your Mac. Both are standard for memory cards that can be bought from a variety of vendors, so you can fill one up with pictures, swap it for a second card, and keep shooting without being forced to download images to your Mac first. Other cameras use their own memory cards (proprietary standards) or other storage mechanisms — even floppy diskettes!

✔ **Compression.** Hand-in-hand with storage is the compression format. Most cameras use the JPEG image format, which allows you to choose different compression formats. The more compressed the images, the more will fit in the camera — and the lower the overall quality of the images. If quality is a priority, choose a camera that offers different compression options.

✔ **Interface.** If you plan to hook up your camera to your Mac to download images directly, you may want one with a serial or USB connector. Serial, however, is slow for transferring megapixel images, which might take up hundreds of kilobytes even with compression. USB is somewhat faster.

You'll come across other features, too, such as red-eye reduction, digital stabilization, and other ways to get video out of the camera, including RCA-style or S-video jacks to connect the camera to a VCR or a TV. (I've seen some cameras you can use as a camcorder if you hook them up to a VCR and record its input.) Still others might be able to record audio or small segments of video in MPEG or QuickTime formats. And if you plan to take action shots, a burst mode that lets you grab three or five shots quickly is a must.

Ultimately, though, the keys to a good camera are the quality of the lens and the optics. If you already know cameras, you know what to look for: a good flash, exposure settings, macro settings, and similar controls. The best advice I can give is to shop customer-friendly stores that will let you work with and test the camera. Also, consult the popular computer and electronics magazines to see which cameras are ranked the highest and offer the best quality.

Who makes cameras? Most scanner manufacturers listed previously in this chapter also offer digital cameras. Plus, traditional camera makers such as Minolta, Canon, Olympus, Kodak, and Polaroid tend to have digital offerings.

## Using the camera with your Mac

Your camera might also come with bundled software that you might find interesting, including a plug-in for PhotoShop or perhaps even PhotoDeluxe or PhotoShop LE. If your cameras uses a direct USB or serial connection, you're likely to need to *acquire* the images in some way, using either the camera's special access software or a plug-in (see Figure 8-4) that works with an image-editing program, such as Adobe PhotoShop. Often, this software shows you *thumbnails*, or small postage-stamp versions of your photos. You select the thumbnails that represent the images you want to copy to your Mac and then invoke the download command. (The process is different in each program.)

When you use a PhotoShop plug-in, you generally access it through the Acquire command in the File menu.

**Figure 8-4:**
Canon's
PowerShot
software
lets you
capture
images from
Photoshop
and other
image-
editing
software.

Again, with some cameras, this won't be necessary; if you use a standard CompactFlash or SmartMedia reader, you simply copy image files (in JPEG format) between the memory card and your Mac's hard disk. The reader attaches to your Mac (usually via USB) and, when you plug in a SmartMedia or CompactFlash card, the card appears on the desktop as if it were a typical floppy diskette. Double-click its icon and you have access to all your picture files.

## Capturing video

Aside from digital still cameras, you come across a few other cameras that let you get images into your Mac. And you can find other solutions that let you get images from *analog* (non-digital) camcorders or cameras into your Mac:

✔ **Videoconference cameras.** Although you don't have to use them exclusively for videoconferencing, these small, inexpensive video cameras are tethered to your Mac, feeding a rather low-quality image into a window on your Mac. Such cameras connect through serial or USB and let you take pictures of yourself making goofy faces, mostly. You can use them for other things, too — such as impromptu talent shows — and save the results as QuickTime movies. Then send them through e-mail or removable disk to friends. Hewlett-Packard (www.hp.com), UMAX (www.umax.com), and iREZ (www.irez.com) all offer such cameras for Macs.

✔ **Video capture devices.** If you need to turn camcorder video into QuickTime movies (which you can then edited and play back on your Mac), you need video capture capabilities. In desktop Macs, this is usually accomplished with an expansion card, especially for professional-level video capture (see Chapter 14). If you have an iMac or you prefer to use USB, you can use a USB-based video capture device from XLR8 (www.xlr8.com), iREZ, or Eskape Labs (www.eskapelab.com). Such a device enables you to get video into your iMac so that you can edit it and post it on the Web, send it through e-mail, or burn it to a CD if you have a CD-RW drive (see Chapter 11). With some of these devices (although not all of them), you can even send the image back out to a VCR after it's edited.

# Chapter 9

# Sound Off with Your Mac

• • • • • • • • • • • • • • • • • • • • • • • • • • • • • • • • • • • • • • • • • • • • • • • • • • • • • •

## In This Chapter

▶ Uncovering the types of Mac sound

▶ Discovering MIDI

▶ Rolling your own recordings

▶ Speak and ye shall be heard

▶ Hooking up with some decent speakers

• • • • • • • • • • • • • • • • • • • • • • • • • • • • • • • • • • • • • • • • • • • • • • • • • • • • • •

*P*robably my favorite story from Macintosh lore is the introduction of the original Mac by Steve Jobs. In 1984, at the introductory press conference, Jobs opens up the carrying case in which the original Mac had arrived (they had carry cases back then — maybe a bit of wishful thinking) and plopped the Mac up on a table. He turned the Mac on and, after startup, it said aloud, "Welcome to Macintosh. It sure is great to get out of that bag." The speaking computer apparently pleased the observers tremendously.

The Mac has been making and editing sounds ever since then, as both a hobbyist's tool and a major component of many professional-editing suites. These days, you can do three basic things with sound and a Mac or iMac: record and play back sound, write music and control MIDI devices, and speak or listen to your Mac.

## The Glorified Cassette Deck

For a computer to record sound, it must *digitize* that sound, turning it into the ones and zeros that make up a computer file. In an analog recording (say, a cassette tape), you record sound waves. When you digitize, however, you record digital information that describes those sound waves. This digital information is stored as a computer file, which you can then copy, edit, and play back on your Mac.

To get that information down in digital form, a computer must *sample* the sound wave amplitude many times in a second — so many times that the human ear can't distinguish the difference between an analog recording and a series of digital samples played one right after the other.

If you sampled an audio source (singing, talking, breaking glass) only a few times per second, you'd notice staggered, incomplete sound. Digital sound files are sampled thousands of times per second — this is the *frequency* of the sound, measured in kilohertz (kHz, or thousands per second). Frequency, along with a number of other factors, determines the quality of a digitized sound.

## Quality is the thing

Most phone calls are digitized these days. What travels over the phone line is not your voice but a digital representation of your voice, sampled thousands of times per second. With phone calls, the frequency is often relatively low — 8 kHz for digital calls. Although you can tell what's being said and who said it, a phone call generally doesn't give you the full tonal quality of a person's voice. (Which is painfully obvious when someone calls to serenade you with "It Had to Be You." Not that I'd know from experience.)

Audio-CD quality is generally considered to be 44.1 kHz, which translates into about 44,100 samples per second. Actually, that many samples per second is beyond human perception, but they make the recording sound better because the elements you don't perceive still smooth out the parts you do hear.

But lower frequencies can be useful, too, because the lower the frequency, the smaller the data file. Digital audio recorded at 22 kHz sounds like an FM radio broadcast; audio recorded at 11 kHz sounds like an AM radio signal. If you were recording audio, you might opt for a lower frequency to cut down on the space required for the audio file.

Aside from frequency, other factors contribute to the quality of a digitized recording, including the bit depth, channel depth, and compression scheme. Ultimately, these factors play out a tug-of-war between a smaller data file and a higher quality:

- **Bit depth.** Sound is usually sampled at either 8 bits or 16 bits, with the latter offering higher quality. Each sample must be represented by a number; in the lingo, choosing that number is called *quantizing* the sample. An 8-bit sample has only 256 possible numbers to represent the sound, so errors are introduced by rounding. A 16-bit sample has more than 65,000 possible numbers, meaning the representation is more accurate.

- **Channel depth.** A sound recorded in stereo takes up twice as much space as a mono sound, making for a larger but higher quality sound file.

✔ **Compression.** Quality is also affected by the compression scheme used to make the data file smaller. *Compression* uses sophisticated mathematical formulas to discard redundant data in a digital file so that it takes up less storage space.

So, the best sounding files would be recorded at 44 kHz or higher, in 16-bit samples, in stereo, and with no compression. At that rate, though, the sound file would take up about 176KB per second, or about 10MB for one minute of sound. That's about how much space music requires on an audio CD. It makes sense: An audio CD has about 740MB of raw storage capacity, which is why you can get only about 74 minutes of music on a single CD.

That's fine for a CD, but when you want to create a computer file of music, you probably need to conserve a little more hard disk space than that. So you use compression schemes when your record and save audio files. Which compression scheme you use depends on the type of audio file you're trying to create.

## Audio file formats

Ultimately, the point of digitizing an audio source is to get it saved as a computer file. After it's saved, you can use applications on your Mac to play back the audio, edit the audio, or even move it to another medium, such as by burning your own audio CDs. All this is possible if you know the code.

Here are the major file formats you might encounter in audio recording:

✔ **MP3.** This is the standard that's getting all the interest these days. Part of the MPEG ( Moving Picture Experts Group) standard for audio and video file formats, MP3 is the special compressed file format that makes audio files much smaller (at a ratio of 12:1), without noticeably affecting the audio quality. That makes MP3 files great for transmitting over the Internet and storing on your hard drive or on data CDs. The popularity of this format has spawned a new category of hardware and software designed to help you create your own Mac-based (or portable) music stations. If you've ever worn out the Pause button on your cassette deck making mix cassettes, MP3 is right up your alley.

✔ **AIFF.** Apple's own audio format, the Audio Interchange File Format, is designed for high-end audio work, allowing for CD-like quality with a minimum of compression. If you're going to edit professional audio, you'll probably work with this format at some point. The files are compressed at 3:1 or 6:1 ratios. ( The compressible version of the file format is called *AIFC.*)

✔ **WAV.** This is the Microsoft Windows standard, which is popular for short sound samples on Web pages and elsewhere on the Internet. If you're creating a sound for your Web page, you're likely to save it as a WAV file.

You might encounter other sound file formats, such as AU, which is standard on many UNIX platforms, and System 7 sounds, which is the sound format used for Apple's HyperCard and for the Alert sounds in the Mac OS. And, if you're working with high-end sound-editing software, you might store your files in proprietary sound file formats such as Sound Designer II, which is written by DigiDesign (`www.digidesign.com`), or SoundEdit by Macromedia (`www.macromedia.com`).

## *Recording your own cuts*

To record audio, you need hardware and software to help you out. Actually, the software is more critical for sound recording because a lot of the sound hardware is already built in. If you have a CD-ROM or DVD-ROM drive, for instance, you can record audio from CDs.

All iMac, Power Macintosh (and equivalent Performas), and Macintosh AV machines offer an audio-in port that's capable of recording audio at CD quality. (Early Macs are sometimes limited to 8-bit audio recording and playback.) You just need to hook up your Mac to any amplified source (a receiver, a mixing board, or a special microphone) through its audio-in port. The audio-in port is generally labeled with a small microphone icon.

On some Mac models — notably the Power Macintosh 8500 and 8600 and original G3 minitowers (in beige) — you'll find RCA-style phono jacks for left and right channels of audio. On other Macs, you have just the one microphone port, called a stereo mini-plug. If you'd like to split that connection into two phono jacks, you need an adapter from your local electronics store. (If you're using a stereo receiver, you need to connect your Mac to the receiver's audio-out connectors, not to its speaker connectors.)

After you've hooked up the hardware to record from, you need software to manage the recording. Recording software ranges from low-end sound shareware and freeware programs to mid-range and professional editing suites. Plus, there's a new category of hobbyist tools for managing, playing back, and encoding MP3 files.

Many Macs come with a small program called SimpleSound — located in the Apple menu or in the Applications folder on your hard disk — that lets you record small System 7 sounds. Designed mostly for recording Alerts (quick sounds Macs make to get your attention), you can still use this program to record small sound effects or other files. Other Macs allow you to record alerts from within the Sound or Monitors & Sound control panel.

Here's a look at some of the different software you can use for recording and audio file translation:

- ✔ **QuickTime Player.** Depending on the version of QuickTime you have, you might be able to use the MoviePlayer or QuickTime Player program to play and convert audio files, including audio tracks from a CD. (In QuickTime 3.0 or higher, you need to upgrade to QuickTime Pro, which costs extra from Apple.) Choose File ➪ Import, find the audio track on the CD, and click Convert. After the sound file is converted, you can export it in many different formats (see Figure 9-1).

**Figure 9-1:**
The QuickTime Player lets you turn CD tracks and other audio files into sound-only QuickTime movies.

- ✔ **Freeware or shareware.** You can download popular programs such as SoundMachine, SoundApp, and Sound Sculptor from online file archives. For little or no money, these programs can translate between file formats and allow you to record and edit sound files. (See Chapter 24 for more on downloading shareware.)

- ✔ **Professional sound editing.** ProTools from DigiDesign and SoundEdit 16 from Macromedia are two popular ways to edit professional-level sound using your Mac. These multitrack editors allow you to process the sound, add effects, create a sound track, and then output the results to professional recording equipment.

- ✔ **MP3.** Software designed to work with the MP3 format runs the gamut from player programs (such as Macast Lite, www.macast.com) to full-featured commercial MP3 encoders such as SoundJam (www.soundjam.com), which enables you to turn CD and AIFF audio files into MP3 files. Figure 9-2 shows SoundJam.

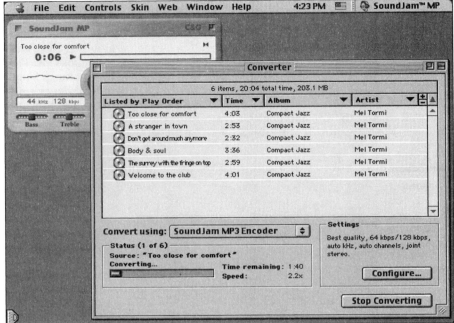

**Figure 9-2:**
SoundJam
lets you
play,
encode,
and manage
MP3 files.

## Professional sound is in the cards

A Mac's built-in sound is acceptable for many sound-related pursuits — I've used it myself for editing audio for use on both Webcasts (audio over the Web) and real-live radio shows. But for true professional audio, you might want to upgrade your Mac's capabilities with an expansion card or device.

NuBus or PCI upgrade cards can do two things for you. First, they can give you a better array of ports, such as RCA-style phono jacks, to give you better quality connections for your channels of audio input. Second, cards and components can allow you to input multiple tracks of audio at once, thus using your Mac as a digital mixing board where each individual track can be managed independently.

For example, if you were recording a rock band with a single audio-in port, you'd have to mix the instruments — guitar, keyboard, bass — using a mixing board *before* the audio gets into the Mac. That limits your ability to isolate the tracks and make the guitarist louder or add some sound effects to the bassist's riffs. With equipment that supports multiple audio inputs, you can bring in each individual track and computerize it to death.

Such hardware solutions are offered by Korg, DigiDesign, Lucid Technology, and Emagic, among others. They work in tandem with audio software from Macromedia or DigiDesign to manage all those sound tracks. See Chapter 14 for details on upgrading with expansion cards.

## Playing with MP3

It's always interesting to watch computer technologies grow. MP3 evolved from the MPEG layer 1 and MPEG layer 2 standards, both of which offered increasingly impressive compression techniques. When MP3 hit, it wasn't something that had never been done before. It had simply reached a way-station of mass-market potential.

With MP3 file format and compression, it's possible for anyone to create CD-quality sound files that are small enough to transmit over the Internet. What does that mean? According to the popular press, it means the death of the recording industry, for two reasons. First, piracy of CD audio is easier than it has ever been — you can use SoundJam to copy tracks right off CDs, save them as MP3 files, and then share them with your friends. (However, you *shouldn't* do that because it ultimately hurts the artist.)

Second, and perhaps more importantly, MP3 makes it possible for musicians to distribute their work directly on the Internet. If you like the band, go download their MP3s. They can charge you directly and make a tidy little profit for themselves. It might even be more than the record company would give them.

It will take a while for the recording industry to implode (assuming it ever does), but there is other fuel for the MP3 fire. Not only can MP3s be transferred over the Internet and then burned on a recordable CD (see Chapter 11), but a new class of hardware, the portable MP3 player, is making it possible to download MP3s to a lightweight device and go jogging (see Figure 9-3).

**Figure 9-3:**
The Diamond Multimedia Rio 500 allows you to store MP3s and play them back within the portable player.

*Photo courtesy Diamond Multimedia, Inc.*

The Diamond Multimedia Rio 500 (www.diamondmm.com/) works with SoundJam MP to transfer files to and from the player; the player offers 64MB of RAM for storing music or audio files and can be upgraded with memory cards to 96MB or more (a song tends to be 3 to 4MB long). Plus, you can swap the cards in and out of the player to effectively expand the amount of storage. The Rio 500 is the first player to support the Mac, and there seems to be no doubt that many more portable MP3 players are on the horizon.

## Sound-in issues

Not hearing anything when you record? A setting in the Sound or Monitors & Sound control panel lets you set whether or not the device you're recording from plays through to the speakers. Enable this option if you want to hear what's being recorded on monitor speakers. Or, in most cases, you can plug headphones into the Mac's headphone (or sound-out) jack.

Likewise, you might need to set the Sound-in device in the control panel to make sure you're recording from the correct device, whether it's a built-in microphone, an external microphone, or another device, such as the internal CD player.

If you have an external CD-ROM or DVD-ROM drive, you might have come across an interesting limitation: By default, you can't play and record from CDs in the drive. That's because internal drives tend to have a special audio cable that connects to the logic board; an external drive, by definition, can't connect to the logic board.

If the external drive has an audio-out port, you can use a cable (with stereo miniplug connectors) between that port and the Mac's microphone port. That should allow you to record from the external drive. Or you can connect the drive to a stereo receiver that's also connected to your Mac, and record from it that way.

# It's MIDI Time

MIDI, the Musical Instrument Digital Interface (said "middy"), is actually a computer language of sorts, such as Adobe's PostScript used in many printers. Using the MIDI language, you can write music in a MIDI program. You can then use software to send commands through a MIDI interface to your MIDI-capable synthesizers. Call it a player piano (or a guitar, drum machine, or effects processor) on steroids.

The real power lies in the capability to control multiple synthesizers at once. Using different *channels* to communicate over a daisy-chain of connected MIDI devices, you can create as large or varied an orchestral sound as you like. Plus, MIDI can work in reverse, too, annotating the notes you play on your synthesizer, writing music as you play it (see Figure 9-4).

MIDI files are simply a series of instructions to a MIDI synthesizer for the playback of a song. That means you can't record human voices or any sort of analog sound or music to a MIDI file. It also means that these instruction files are very small and easy to store or transmit over the Internet. Using MIDI playback software, you can play any Standard MIDI Format (SMF) file on your Mac. (These files usually have the .MID or .MIDI extension appended to their names.)

A library of MIDI instrument sounds is built into QuickTime Version 2.5 and higher, enabling you to use the MoviePlayer or QuickTime Player to play a standard MIDI file through your Mac or iMac's speakers. If you're an intrepid Web user, you'll find MIDI files you can download from sites around the world. You'll also find shareware and commercial MIDI players that enable you to manage your own library of MIDI song files.

**Figure 9-4:** Allegro, from Coda Music, creates music notation from a MIDI keyboard.

If you'd like to get into making MIDI files yourself, you need only a few different components to get started. Here's a quick list:

✔ **A MIDI interface.** A MIDI interface allows your Mac to connect with and control MIDI devices, such as synthesizers. MIDI interfaces are often small boxes, about the size of a deck of cards, that connect to the serial or USB port on your Mac. The interface has MIDI ports that you can use to connect to one or more synthesizers. See Figure 9-5 for an example of a basic MIDI interface. This one is from Mark of the Unicorn (www.motu.com).

**Figure 9-5:**
The FastLane USB MIDI adapter connects MIDI devices to a USB-equipped Mac.

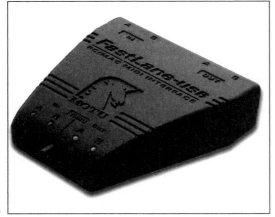

*Photo courtesy MOTU*

✔ **A MIDI-capable synthesizer.** You need at least one keyboard or other sound module that offers a MIDI interface if you want to make some music. Look for MIDI connections on the device, in the form of 5-pin IN, OUT, and (often) THRU connectors on the back of the instrument. You connect a 5-pin MIDI cable from the synthesizer to the MIDI interface. Plus, if you have additional synthesizers, you use the THRU port to connect them in daisy-chain fashion (unless your MIDI interface supports multiple inputs and outputs).

✔ **MIDI-capable software.** Your Mac will just sit there wondering what all this jumble of data on the serial port is for if you don't have some software to interpret it. MIDI software comes in two general flavors. *Sequencer* software controls one or more channels of MIDI data, allowing you to rearrange notes, change the tempo, and so on, and then play back the song on connected synthesizers. *Notation* software is designed to transcribe played notes into musical notation. These functions can be present in the same software program. Companies that make MIDI software include Opcode, Coda Music Technology (www.codamusic.com), Emagic (www.emagic.de), and Mark of the Unicorn (www.motu.com). You can also find some shareware and freeware notation software in popular download libraries.

After you've set up these components, you can begin to create MIDI music. Playing notes on the keyboard (or entering them in the software) creates a song. Depending on your equipment, you often create multiple *channels* of MIDI instructions, each of which corresponds to a different instrument in your setup. (If you have one general-use keyboard synthesizer, it can likely interpret multiple channels at once, so it can play the guitar, piano, and drum parts, for instance, all at once.) To save your work or distribute your song, you create and save to a MIDI file. That file can then be played on other MIDI instruments or in MIDI playback software.

You might run across a few terms you want to understand if you're shopping for MIDI equipment. *Polyphony* is the number of discrete notes that can be played at once — 32 or 64 notes are typical. *Timbre* refers to the number of simultaneous instruments that can be played by the synthesizer; this is often advertised as *channels*. A single MIDI controller can handle 16 channels, as can some general-purpose synthesizers. The pros, however, often prefer a device that handles only one channel but reproduces its instrument's sounds very well.

You might be wondering how one synthesizer can know how to properly play back another synthesizer's commands. The General MIDI standard codifies 128 basic General MIDI instrument sounds, or *patches*, each of which is required to have the same code number. So, for the first 128 instruments, any General MIDI device will know what instrument sound to use. Most store-bought synthesizers support General MIDI, but if you're shopping used or pro-level equipment (where eccentricity often beats out compliance), you should double-check for General MIDI support, if it's important to you.

Aside from the 128 standard voices, a General MIDI compatible device must meet other criteria. The instrument should support at least 24-voice polyphony, must support different instruments on all 16 channels, and must respond to certain basic General MIDI commands, such as fine-tuning and pitch bend. If a keyboard qualifies, it can display a "General MIDI" logo.

# Speak, Mac, Speak!

Three types of speech technology exist to make your Mac jabber and listen using a synthesis of our highly developed vocalization-based communications system.

Most Mac models can speak text aloud, simply translating words in a text document (or elsewhere, such as in alert boxes) into an audible format. Macintosh AV and Power Macintosh models also support speech recognition, called *Speakable Items* by Apple, which allows you to control some aspect of the Mac interface using spoken commands and a special microphone. The third type, dictation, requires add-on software and, sometimes, a new microphone. Dictation software is the most powerful type of speech recognition, allowing you to create written documents by speaking the words instead of typing them.

Here's a look at all three:

✔ **Text-to-speech.** Text-to-speech technology is offered through the Speech control panel (and associated extensions) in Mac OS 7.6 and higher. If installed and enabled, text-to-speech enables applications to speak text aloud, if the application supports it. (Test this in SimpleText by opening a document and choosing Sound ➪ Speak All.) This is also the technology used for Talking Alerts, which enable the Mac OS to speak Alert text out loud. Talking Alerts is also controlled from the Speech control panel, as are the voices used for text-to-speech.

The Mac OS extension **MacinTalk** determines the sophistication of your Mac's text-to-speech capability. MacinTalk 2 works with Macs from the Mac Plus on. MacinTalk 3 requires a 33-MHz 68030 processor or better. And MacinTalk Pro, which offers the best quality, requires a 68040 or PowerPC processor.

✔ **Speakable items.** Apple's speech recognition software generally needs to be installed separately, although you'll find its installer on the Mac OS installation CD (in Mac OS 7.6 and higher). After you install the software, you can turn on Speakable Items using the Speech control panel and then use the Speakable Items and Feedback options to configure speech recognition. Using a PlainTalk microphone (a special microphone included with most Power Macintosh models) or the microphone built into your iMac or other all-in-one Mac models, you can speak commands and your Mac will respond to them.

iMac models that currently run Mac OS 8.1-8.5 require English Speech Recognition 1.5.4 and an upgrade to Mac OS 8.6 or higher to use Speakable Items. You can get Version 1.5.4 with the Mac OS 8.6 update or by purchasing an upgrade to Mac OS 9 or higher.

✔ **Dictation software.** Think of it: Your very own stenographer. Until recently, there wasn't much on the market that would enable your Mac to type what you say out loud, but that's changing. IBM's ViaVoice (www.ibm.com/software/speech/) for Macintosh supports dictation of 60,000 words, plus a trainable dictionary. It also includes a special headset microphone that you can plug into your microphone port. VoicePowerPro (www.voicepowerpro.com) offers discrete speech recognition, meaning you have to pause between each word, but it can dictate and control parts of the Mac interface. Other announced software includes products from MacSpeech (www.macspeech.com).

# *Speakers: The Missing Link*

So far I've talked about all these great sound technologies that give your Mac amazing audio prowess. But by and large, Mac models offer tinny, under-powered, completely unimpressive speakers to play all these great sounds. MP3s through the five-cent paper speaker in your Power Mac? What's the point?

For that swingin' hi-fi experience, you'll want to add some external speakers to your Mac. Or if you already have an impressive stereophonic setup, you can wire your Mac directly to a stereo receiver and pipe audio through that way. Now it's beginning to make some sense to play those audio tracks through your Mac.

 If you plan to connect speakers to you Mac's sound-out port, you'll need to use powered, shielded computer speakers. The magnets in speakers can distort the picture on your monitor and, under certain circumstances, erase magnetic media such as floppy disks. So shielded speakers are recommended for placement near your computer. Because the sound-out port is a line-level port (it isn't amplified), the speakers need their own power.

If you already have a stereo system you like, use that same sound-out port to connect your Mac as easily as you connect another component on your stereo receiver. (You'll probably hook it up to the Auxiliary inputs.) A trusty Y-connector will help you wire the Mac's stereo mini-plug to RCA-style phono inputs.

You can also use USB speakers with a USB-equipped Mac. With USB speakers, your Mac sends a digital signal all the way out to the speakers. This eliminates some of the noise that's introduced when an analog signal is sent from your Mac's sound-out port to external speakers.

USB speakers aren't terribly popular for Macs yet, but a few options are beginning to appear. For instance, the slot-loading iMac (and iMac DV) offers support for a special Harmon-Kardon-designed subwoofer (called the iSub) that adds much needed bass response to the iMac's built-in speakers. Yamaha and other vendors offer USB speakers, including subwoofers, for Macs.

 Not hearing anything through your USB speakers or your stereo receiver? You might need to set your Sound or Monitors & Sound control panel to recognize them. Find the entry for Sound-out, and then make sure the appropriate device is selected.

# Chapter 10

# Houston, We Have a Printer

. . . . . . . . . . . . . . . . . . . . . . . . . . . . . . . . . . . . . . . . . . . . . . . . . . . .

*In This Chapter*

▶ Buying decisions

▶ Getting your Mac and printer to chat

▶ Upgrading your printer — and fixing it, too

. . . . . . . . . . . . . . . . . . . . . . . . . . . . . . . . . . . . . . . . . . . . . . . . . . . .

Could there be more printers? You'd think something as simple as creating a printout wouldn't require all this effort by multinational conglomerates to churn out all these different printer types with their print heads, cables, connectors, and software. What's the point? Seems to me we need just one printer and we're good to go.

I guess the question is, which *one?* Printers vary in price, performance, and capabilities, allowing you to print inexpensively for small-office or school work, or very expensively for color proofing of high-end design work or magazine pages. Whatever your printing needs, you can find a printer meant just for you.

## *Matchmaker, Matchmaker, Get Me a Printer*

Forget everything else for a moment and breathe deeply. Concentrate on the sound of my voice. You're getting sleepy. You're concerned only with the purchase of a printer, and you realize that your needs are coming into focus. All you have to ask yourself is one simple question. Will you need color?

If you need a color printer, you're likely shopping for a color *inkjet*. Nearly all inkjet printers on the market today offer color printing, so it shouldn't be tough to find one. If you have high-end publishing needs, you might opt for a *dye-sublimation* printer. Or if you have a Corporate Gold Card burning a hole in your pocket, you might opt for a color *laser* printer.

If you have no need and no desire to print in color, you'll have to think a little harder. Inkjets are still cheaper at the outset, and they offer good, speedy black-ink printing. But affordable *grayscale* laser printers offer high-speed, high-quality printing that is very cheap on a per-page basis. Plus, laser printers can often be used on a network more easily (as can some, but not all, inkjets) and accept attachments such as additional paper feeders and envelope feeders. On the high-end, workgroup laser printers offer very high-speed printing and add-ons that make them worthwhile in an office setting with many network users.

## Which printer is more your type?

Before we get too deep into the terminology, though, I'll define some of it. Traditionally, printers have been defined according to the technology that's used to get images and text on the page. Because I don't have the energy to break with tradition at this moment, I'll describe the different methods used to get ink on the page.

### Laser (or page) printers

Laser printers, first of all, don't use ink. They use toner, like a photocopier. And they don't always have lasers, either, so they're better described as *page printers*. (Some page printers use LED or LCD technology, instead of a laser, to create the page.)

## It's all about measurements

Printer speed is measured in *pages per minute,* or *ppm*. The more pages a printer finishes with per minute, the faster it is. Or, put another way . . . uh, I can't think of another way.

Another measurement of a printer's worth is resolution, codified into *dots per inch,* or *dpi,* horizontally and vertically. The higher the resolution of a printer, the more crisp and clear the printout, in most cases. A resolution of 360x360 is the low end of acceptable for inkjets. A good laser starts at 600x600, and a decent inkjet starts at 720x720 dpi. Even higher resolutions — 1200x600 and 1440x720 — are becoming popular for printouts

that shine. (They still don't reach to professional typesetting levels, which spiral upward toward 5000 dpi for magazine covers.)

Another interesting stat on your printer's trading card is *lines per inch,* or *lpi*. This is the measurement used when printing *halftone images* — images composed of black dots that are varied to give it the appearance of many shades of gray. The more lines per inch, the better the grayscale reproduction of photographic images. Lines per inch is closely related to the resolution for scanning images, as discussed in Chapter 8.

A page description is sent to the printer, which begins to build an image of that page from the description. Laser printers create an image of the entire page before printing, which is why they can be a touch slow to start printing. They also require their own RAM and on-board processors, which is part of why they tend to be more expensive than inkjet printers.

When the page is ready, paper is fed into the printer while the printer's laser begins to draw the page image by electrically charging particles on a rolling drum. That drum picks up toner particles wherever a charged particle has been drawn, and that toner is transferred to the sheet of paper as it is pulled across the drum.

For black-and-white printing, laser printers offer some interesting advantages:

- ✔ **Speed.** Laser printers are generally faster than other types of printers, although inkjets have improved their speeds lately. New, low-end lasers print around 8 ppm. Workgroup lasers (more expensive models for networked groups) tend to print between 16 and 24 ppm or faster.

- ✔ **High capacity.** Laser printers offer bigger paper trays, and toner cartridges tend to last for thousands of pages printed. Workgroup lasers are designed for networked situations where many people need to print lots of documents.

- ✔ **Cost per page.** If you're going to be killing entire forests, laser printers can be cheaper over time. (I hope you're willing to buy recycled paper.) Inkjet cartridges tend to be expensive given that they often offer only enough ink for a few hundred pages, whereas laser toner cartridges often print thousands of pages, making them cheaper on a per-page basis.

- ✔ **Flexibility.** Because lasers tend to be designed for office tasks, laser printers tend to offer higher end peripherals such as dedicated printer-server capabilities, paper feeders, and high-capacity paper trays. More expensive workgroup printers even feature copier-like features, such as collating and stapling.

Color laser printers are also becoming more common and popular, as prices begin to come down somewhat. Color laser printer prices are still measured in multiple thousands of dollars but are creeping downward. Compared to inkjet printers, however, color laser printing is reserved for professional uses and as a plaything for the idle rich.

### Inkjet printers

Most home and small-office users will opt for an inkjet printer, which gives you color printing capability without too many drawbacks. Inkjet printers use tiny nozzles to spray wet ink onto the page as the printer pulls the paper along a paper path. The nozzles use a number of different technologies to get ink out of its cartridge and onto the page — and most companies are firmly convinced that their method offers the best quality and laser-like output. You be the judge; check the output of different printers in the computer store when you're shopping.

Inkjet printers *do* use ink, believe it or not, which is stored in special cartridges that usually include the print head. When you replace the cartridge, you also replace the print head, which is convenient but adds a bit to the cost of ink. Over time, printing with an inkjet can be more expensive than printing with a laser printer, especially if you frequently print in color.

The ink is a special composition that dries quickly enough to keep from streaming (wicking) down the page. The spacing of the nozzles is an exacting science, allowing the print head to move quickly along the page while maintaining a resolution of between 300 and 1200 dpi, making many inkjets the rival of laser printers as far as print quality goes.

So, the inkjet's printing advantages stack up like this:

- ✔ **Color.** By mixing together three or four colors of ink (usually the CMYK colors — cyan, magenta, yellow, and black), inkjet printers can print in full color without requiring highly sophisticated or expensive hardware. That makes them economical for color printouts or for *proofing* — seeing how a high-end project will look in color before sending it to a professional printer (especially if the printer supports PostScript).

- ✔ **Initial cost.** Inkjet printers are often cheaper, partly because they don't have their own RAM and processors. Instead, they tend to rely on the Mac itself to build the page and feed the image to the printer. (Most inkjets have a small amount of *buffer* RAM just so they can keep up with the flow of data from the Mac.) In most cases, the printing can take place in the *background*, allowing you to continue working with your Mac. As long as you're printing, though, you'll likely experience some slowdown while the Mac works to create that page.

Inkjets tend to be a little slower than laser printers, but not by much. Low-end inkjets print text-only pages at 4 to 6 ppm, with high-priced models reaching 12 ppm. Color printing tends to be slower, sometimes much slower, depending on the printer.

Inkjets can offer some interesting flexibility to the printer manufacturer, partly because of their low cost. Recently, Canon, Hewlett-Packard, and Epson introduced all-in-one inkjet printers that also come equipped with a scanner and fax capabilities (see Figure 10-1). Used both on their own and connected to your Mac, these machines can fax, copy, print, and scan, all from the same machine. They're a good purchase for small offices, as long as you remember the adage, "Jack of all trades, master of none." Also, don't forget that if the printer is in the shop, your fax machine, copy machine, and scanner go with it!

**Figure 10-1:**
Epson's
Stylus Scan
2000 offers
multiple
capabilities
built around
an inkjet
printer.

*Photo courtesy Epson Corp.*

## Color proofing printers

Other printer types are more one-trick ponies, designed to offer color output that looks very high end, often for magazine layout artists who want to see what their work will look like after it's printed. Here are the technologies:

✔ **Dye sublimation.** In this process, the printer melts ink from a ribbon onto special paper. The color is defused into the paper; other colors can be melted directly on top of the first colors. Dye sublimation creates a continuous color image that mimics a photograph. In fact, an emerging niche for dye sublimation (called *dye-sub* by folks in the *business*, which is called *the biz*) are printers designed to print images captured using digital cameras, such as those offered in the Sony Mavica line (www.sony.com).

✔ **Solid ink.** These types of printers use dyed wax — sticks that resemble crayons — melted into a glossy ink that's then transferred to the page. The result is a very bright color image that doesn't always require special paper. These printers also tend to be expensive, at least compared to inkjets, although a reasonable cost-per-page can make them useful for color-printing professionals and offices that need high-quality color proofing. ALPS (www.alps.com) and Tektronix (www.tektronix.com) are two manufacturers of such printers.

### Dot-matrix printers

Dot-matrix printers are the classic clackity-clack printers of yore (say, about the time of the movie *War Games*). Dot matrix used to be the prevailing standard; now, you pretty much see them in gas stations.

One good reason to keep a dot-matrix printer around is if you have one. A dot-matrix printer makes text appear by striking a ribbon with small pins, usually using either 9 pins or 24 pins to create a single character. (24 pins offer higher quality.) Because the pins impact the page (through the ribbon), dot-matrix printers are useful for multipart forms. If you need to print anything in triplicate, find yourself a dot-matrix printer if you can.

## The language your printer speaks

Another important factor is determining your compatibility with a new printer is the language it uses to create the page. (Actually, you probably won't care much, because you're unlikely to speak the language yourself.) Printers use one of three languages to communicate between the Mac and the printer. Which language the printer uses can dictate how it connects to your Mac, the types of fonts it uses, and even how much the printer costs. Here's the rundown:

✔ **QuickDraw.** Early Mac-only printers spoke QuickDraw, the same language used to describe screen images in the Mac OS. This made it easy for the Mac OS to build the page image and feed it to the printer. These printers were mostly dot-matrix printers and inkjets, although some personal Laser printers made by Apple and Hewlett-Packard used QuickDraw.

✔ **PCL.** PCL (Printer Control Language), developed by Hewlett-Packard, is becoming a popular cross-platform solution. Driver software written for the Mac OS allows it to print in PCL, making it possible for a slew of USB-based printers to be marketed for Macs as well as PCs. You might come across the occasional USB laser or Ethernet-based printer that communicates with Macs through PCL, but most PCL printers are inkjets.

✔ **PostScript.** Adobe's PostScript language is used in the majority of laser printers that support Macs, and nearly all of them that are networking via Ethernet. If you have a workgroup printer that supports both Macs and Windows, it likely uses PostScript. PostScript is more exacting for graphics tasks and a favorite among design professionals. PostScript printers are more expensive, however, requiring additional RAM and processing power as well as a license fee (in most cases) from Adobe.

Most PostScript printers support both TrueType and PostScript fonts right out of the box; other printer languages might need special software, such as Adobe Type Manager, to print PostScript fonts. If you have a large collection of PostScript Type 1 fonts, you should at least consider a PostScript-language printer for best results. Otherwise, PostScript is best for graphics-oriented tasks and situations where you might need your printed output to match up exactly with a professional printer's output somewhere down the road.

For home and small-office use, a PCL printer will work just fine. And if you have a QuickDraw printer squirreled away somewhere, there's no reason to toss it as long as its quality is holding up and you don't mind the slower speeds.

## Do you connect well?

Another factor that determines what type of printer you can buy are the ports your Mac offers. With the advent of the iMac and the switchover to USB that's taken place in the Mac market, there are fewer offerings for printers connected via the serial port. If you have Ethernet, though, you might consider an Ethernet-based laser (or one of a handful of Ethernet-based inkjets), which lets you access the printer over a network connection.

Here's a look at the interfaces you encounter on printers of today and yesterday. You know . . . when all our troubles seemed so far away:

✔ **Serial.** Connecting to the Printer serial port is a time-honored tradition that no one seems to honor anymore. In the past, the serial port was used almost exclusively for QuickDraw printers. Many of Apple's popular StyleWriter and Personal LaserWriter printers used a serial connection.

✔ **LocalTalk.** Although LocalTalk uses the same port (the Printer or Modem port) as a serial printer, you're actually establishing an AppleTalk networking connection between the printer and the Mac. LocalTalk is the aging networking standard for Macs — most new networks are built with Ethernet instead of LocalTalk. Most LocalTalk printers are laser printers that use PostScript, although Apple's last line of StyleWriter inkjets (the Color StyleWriter 4000 and 6000 series) and some HP DeskWriter models used LocalTalk connections.

✔ **USB.** The port of choice for most PCL printers today is USB, which allows manufacturers to make printers that cater to both the Intel-compatible world and the Mac market. If you have USB ports and you don't intend to share your printer on a network, a USB printer (inkjet or laser) should work well. A few PostScript-based USB printers are available; most are PCL.

✔ **Ethernet.** If you need a high-speed laser or a printer to share on a network, you'll likely choose Ethernet. Ethernet printers are often the most sophisticated, and they almost always use PostScript. This makes them cross-platform, so that Windows and Mac users (and even UNIX users) can print to the same printer on a network.

If the printer you're considering doesn't offer the right connector, you can still have hope. For serial connections to newer PCL printers, you can use a special adapter and driver software. PowerPrint from Infowave (`www.infowave.com`) is a parallel-to-serial adapter that includes PCL drivers so that your Mac can connect to and print to PC-compatible printers (see Figure 10-2).

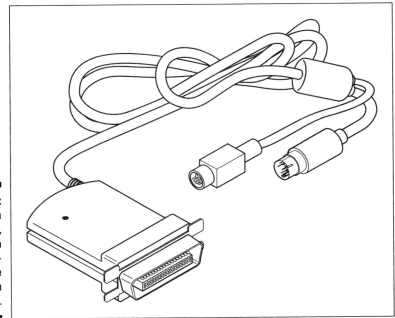

**Figure 10-2:**
With PowerPrint, you can use PC-compatible printers with your Mac.

Infowave also makes a USB-to-parallel adapter that you can use with PCL-based printers intended for the Microsoft Windows market. Although many PCL printer manufacturers are writing Mac drivers for their printers, not all models are covered. If you have a PCL printer that isn't covered, the PowerPrint USB adapter and software connects you to that printer and gets your Mac printing to it.

## Pairing up with a printer

So you've seen the technologies, languages, and connections. Have your heart set on a printer yet? When you make a long-term commitment to a new printer, you might want to know a few other things about it. What type of *consumables*, such as ink and paper, does the printer use? Find out the cost of a laser printer's toner cartridges or an inkjet's ink cartridges. Some of them vary wildly. Also find out whether the best results will require special, expensive paper, or if you need to upgrade the RAM on your laser printer to get decent results.

Also consider what add-ons are available for the printer, such as extra paper cartridges, printer servers (which help take some of the load off your dedicated servers in a networking situation), and RAM upgrades.

Table 10-1 shows some manufacturers who make Mac-compatible printers for individual Macs and workgroups.

| Table 10-1 | New Mac-Compatible Printers | | |
|---|---|---|---|
| *Manufacturer* | *Printer Types* | *Technology* | *Web Site* |
| Epson | Laser, inkjet | PCL, PostScript | www.epson.com |
| GCC Tech | Laser | PostScript | www.gcctech.com |
| Canon | Inkjet | PostScript | www.canon.com |
| NEC | Laser | PostScript | www.nec.com |
| QMS | Laser, dye-sub | PostScript | www.qms.com |
| ALPS Electric | Dye-sub | PostScript | www.alpsusa.com |
| Tektronix | Inkjet, solid ink | PostScript | www.tektronix.com |
| Hewlett-Packard | Inkjet, laser | PCL, PostScript | www.hp.com |

# Installing Your New Friend

As noted previously, you have quite a few ways to connect printers. Fortunately (for me, especially, because I had to outline this chapter), I can break down installations into two different approaches: direct connections and network connections. If your printer supports serial or USB, you perform a direct connection. For LocalTalk or Ethernet printers, you're creating a network connection to the printer, even if your Mac and the printer are the only two devices on that network.

## *Direct connection*

Serial printers — which includes USB because it's the universal *serial* bus — require direct, one-on-one communications with your Mac. These printers are more like children, unable to face the real world on their own. (Plus, they're always asking for a little more money.) Without their own processors or RAM, these printers rely on a direct connection to a Mac that can create the page image and feed the printer information as it needs it. (Actually, that makes them more like college roommates than most of the children I've met.)

Each model of serial printer requires a unique printer driver, so you want to make sure that the printer's software is available. In fact, it's a good idea to check the printer manufacturer's Web site for any last-minute updates to their printer driver software.

Many serial and USB printers don't come with the actual cable needed to connect it to your Mac. For serial printers, you'll want a serial cable, often called a StyleWriter or ImageWriter serial cable, not a LocalTalk cable. For USB printers, you most likely need a parallel-to-USB cable, unless your printer offers a USB port, in which case you'll need a standard A-to-B USB cable. Check your printer's documentation for details.

Installing the printer should be easy. You simply connect it to an available port and activate its driver software. If you have a serial printer:

1. **Shut down your Mac.**

2. **Plug the serial cable into the printer and then plug the cable into the printer port on your Mac.**

3. **Restart your Mac.**

4. **Install the software drivers that came with the printer.**

   If the printer is a StyleWriter or Personal LaserWriter made by Apple, the drivers are already installed along with the Mac OS and should appear in the Chooser.

With a USB printer, you should install the driver software first. Then simply plug one end of the USB cable into the printer and the other end into an available USB port on your Mac or on a USB hub. (USB is hot-pluggable, remember?)

Now you need to select the printer's driver:

1. **From the Apple menu, open the Chooser.**

2. **On the left side of the Chooser window, select your printer driver's icon.**

3. **On the right side of the Chooser, select the port that your printer is connected to: Printer, Modem, or USB, depending on your circumstances.**

   See Figure 10-3.

4. **Close the Chooser.**

   You're ready to print using the Print command in your application software.

**Figure 10-3:**
For serial printers, you select the individual icon for the printer's driver software and select the port that connects that printer.

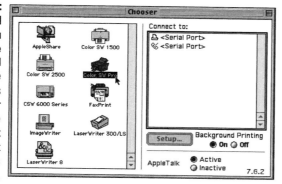

## *Network connection*

Most networked printers are PostScript printers, complete with their own processors and RAM. In a sense, these printers are actually computers, so creating a network connection to them makes a lot of sense. Instead of relying on your Mac to do the imaging, the Mac sends PostScript commands to the printer, which then takes over responsibility for imaging the page and getting it printed. The connection is less reliant on a particular Mac, making PostScript printers ideal for workgroup situations.

Installing a network printer isn't particularly difficult. For a LocalTalk connection:

1. **Shut down your Mac.**

2. **Plug the LocalTalk cable into your Mac's printer port and into the printer's LocalTalk port.**

   If you'll be using the printer on a workgroup network, connect it to a PhoneNet adapter (or a similar transceiver). Then connect the transceiver to the network. (See Figure 10-4).

3. **Restart the Mac.**

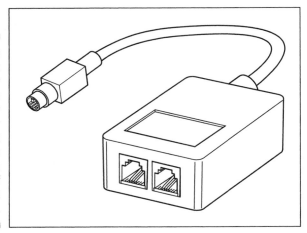

If it's just your Mac and the LocalTalk printer, you have two options: directly connect the LocalTalk cable to each, or use a transceiver on each device with PhoneNet cable between the two and terminators on each transceiver. The PhoneNet connection is likely to be more reliable, but I've had plenty of luck just directly connecting the cable.

If you're connecting more than one Mac to the printer, you must configure each with a transceiver and connect them together in a daisy-chain configuration with terminators on the two ends of the chain. (See Chapter 18 for more on networking.)

Need to network a LocalTalk printer to an Ethernet network? You need a *bridge*, which is hardware or software to help you move data between a LocalTalk and Ethernet connection. Software is more demanding, but it's free in the form of Apple's LaserWriter Bridge, available for download from Apple's Software Update library (asu.info.apple.com). For hardware, Farallon (www.farallon.com) makes the iPrint adapter, which lets you hook up either a serial or a LocalTalk printer to an Ethernet connection, depending on the model of adapter you buy.

For an Ethernet printer, you need to consider some options. If you're connecting one printer and one Mac, and both support *10BaseT* cabling (see Figure 10-5), you can connect them to one another with an Ethernet *crossover cable*, which enables you to connect without an Ethernet hub. Just connect the cable to the Ethernet port on the Mac and the Ethernet port on the printer.

In other situations, you'll connect the printer to your Ethernet hub using *patch* cable. This allows all Macs connected to that hub to see and use the printer. (Crossover cables are often bright yellow; patch cables are often gray or black.)

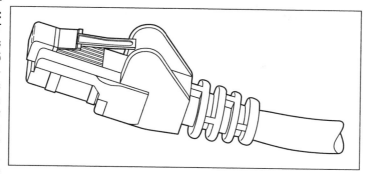

**Figure 10-5:** 10BaseT cabling uses an RJ-45 plug to connect; it looks like a phone cord, only thick with a bigger connector.

If you're using a *10Base2* (also called BNC or coax) cabling system, you often connect two segments of the coax cabling to either side of the printer's 10Base2 connection, thus adding it to the daisy-chain of networked Macs. You might need a special transceiver for this type of connection if your printer doesn't have built-in 10Base2 support. See Chapter 18 for more on this type of network.

With nearly any networked PostScript printer, you don't need to install special driver software. Instead, you install a *PostScript Printer Description (PPD)* file, which can be used with the standard LaserWriter 8 driver. If your printer came with a PPD, install it in the Printer Descriptions folder inside the Extensions folder in your Mac's System Folder.

After that, you're ready to set up your printer. Here's how:

1. **From the Apple menu, open the Chooser.**

2. **On the left side of the window, select the LaserWriter 8 driver.**

   If your network is divided into AppleTalk zones, select the zone in which the printer resides. (More on zones in Chapter 18.)

3. **The networked printer should appear on the right side of the window. Select it and then click the Create button.**

   The Create window appears.

4. **Click Auto Setup to configure your printer.**

   If Auto Setup fails, you can manually select a PostScript Printer Description by clicking the Select PPD button. Use the Get Info, Configure, and other buttons to alter the printer description is necessary. When you've finished setting up, click OK.

5. **Click the Chooser's close box to close it.**

   The setup takes place. An alert appears telling you to choose Page Setup in your applications — this is a good sign because it suggests that the changeover went well. Then a desktop printer icon appears on the desktop (in System 7.5 and above).

So how do you test the printer? Try printing! If it works, you'll have a printed document and you'll quickly begin to lose interest in this chapter. (I know where you're loyalties lie, traitor.) If you have trouble, keep reading.

# Upgrading and Fixing the Printer

Printing doesn't always come off without a hitch — in fact, any time you get networking protocols, PostScript, and fonts all in the same room, there's bound to be some chaffing. Plus, many printers don't come from the factory fully decked to the gills with capability. If your printer doesn't do everything you need it to, it's time to consider upgrading it. Here now, in seemingly random order, is a discussion of both issues.

## Poor person's network printer: Sharing

Although they're designed for direct connections, many of Apple's serial-based printers can be shared over a network. Unfortunately, few USB-based printers can be shared, but that might change. (One shareware solution, called EpsonShare, can be used for Epson's USB printers. See Chapter 24 for more on shareware.)

You can share a StyleWriter or a Personal LaserWriter by selecting the printer in the Chooser, selecting its port, and clicking Setup. You'll see the Sharing window. Select the Share this Printer option and give the printer a name. (If paper is like gold to you, you can assign a password so that only members of your secret society can print to the shared printer.) Click OK and close the Chooser.

Other users on your network (LocalTalk or Ethernet) can now select that same printer driver and, lo and behold, a new entry appears under the Printer port and Modem port — a network printer icon with the name you've assigned. When they select that icon and close the Chooser, your printer becomes their printer.

One caveat: When they print, your Mac is used for printer management. Your Mac needs to be on (even if it's in Sleep mode). That could slow operations on your Mac if the whole office is printing to your Mac all the time. It will also introduce the possibility of instability — I've found that Printer Share likes to crash — sometimes both machines. Convenient, eh?

## Upgrading your printer

Workgroup laser printers tend to offer the most configuration options, but inkjets are increasingly taking on more demanding tasks and accessories are coming along for the ride. Likewise, many printers benefit from RAM upgrades and other software and hardware add-ons that increase capabilities. Such items address issues like the following:

- **Paper handling.** Options include high-capacity paper trays, special feeders for envelopes, and add-ons for printing to transparencies.

- **Duplex printing.** Some printers can support add-ons that allow you to more easily print to two sides of the page. (Printing to more than two sides of the page becomes a multidimensional physics issue.)

- **Networking options.** If your printer didn't ship with networking capabilities, you might be able to add an internal upgrade card or printer adapter of some sort. Such upgrades might include a hardware print server that can offload the page-queuing responsibilities from your server computer.

- **RAM upgrades.** Add more RAM to support graphics-heavy pages, to support pages that require many fonts, or if your printer complains with *Not enough RAM* errors.

Most of these upgrades are proprietary, which means you need to get them from your printer's manufacturer and count on that manufacturer to help you set up and support the upgrade.

RAM is usually available from different sources, though, because many printers support standard RAM types. Adding RAM can speed up your printer a bit, especially if you print graphics or if the printer is shared in a networked environment. It might also allow you to access dormant features, such as increased print smoothing or higher-end graphics printing capabilities.

Some printers use special compression techniques to get the most out of their installed RAM. Upgrading the RAM in these printers might allow them to stop compressing so much and to cache incoming pages, thus speeding things up.

## Fixing your printer

If your printer won't print or won't communicate or you're experiencing other problems, you've likely turned to this page in anger. Calm down. It's not my fault. It's the fault of the printer manufacturer and all its subsidiary companies. My suggestion: Divest yourself of all stock in such companies. If you like, I'm happy to take those shares off you hands — you don't even have to pay me. Just sign the back of the certificate.

Let's take a look at the issues surrounding printer trauma and see whether we can nail things down. Usually, the biggest problem with a printer, assuming you remembered to turn it on, is making sure you have the right cable connected and the software configured to talk to it via that cable.

### Printer can't be found message

If you get a *Printer can't be found* message, first, make sure your printer was turned on and that it was finished warming up before you tried to print. Then try the following checklist for other possible solutions:

- ✔ **Is everything plugged in?** Make sure you have the LocalTalk, serial, USB, or Ethernet cable properly plugged in. Ensure that you've set the correct port in the Chooser. If you have a serial-port switch box, make sure it's correctly dialed so that the printer's connection is active.

  Also make sure you're using a LocalTalk cable for LocalTalk connections or a StyleWriter-type printer cable for a serial printer, and that you haven't mixed up the two types of cabling in some way. (They're similar — both fit your printer and modem ports.) If it's a USB printer, try unplugging and replugging; take other USB troubleshooting steps as discussed in Chapter 4.

- ✔ **Is everything turned on and happy?** Make sure the printer is turned on and that it isn't showing an error (paper jam, memory problem, and so on). Try turning the printer on and off or pressing its reset button.

- ✔ **Is the printer configured correctly?** Many workgroup printers allow you to choose between PCL and PostScript languages; make sure the printer is set up to receive PostScript if that's what your Mac is trying to send to it. Likewise, if the printer offers more than one connection type (serial, Ethernet), make sure the type of connection you're using is chosen. (You'll often change these settings using the buttons or the LCD screen on the printer itself.)

- ✔ **How is the Chooser taking this?** First, make sure the Chooser is showing your printer driver. If it's not, you might need to install the printer software. Next, make sure you've selected the appropriate port for a serial printer. If you're using a networked PostScript printer and you've selected the LaserWriter 8 driver, the printer should appear on the right side and you should select it. If you don't see the printer, make sure you've selected the appropriate AppleTalk zone, if necessary. If you still don't see the printer, make sure it's properly configured.

- ✔ **Is the desktop printer working correctly?** If the desktop printer isn't highlighted with a thick, black border, it's not the currently selected printer. Select that printer in the Chooser or select the printer icon; then choose Printing ➪ Make Active Printer from the Finder's menu.

✔ **Are the necessary extensions present?** In the Extensions Manager, make sure you've selected to load your printer driver as well as the Desktop Printing Extension and the Print Monitor (both are necessary if you're using Mac OS 7.6 and above and an Apple printer). If your printer has its own Print Monitor (such as the HP Print Monitor), make sure it is selected to load in the Extensions Manager.

The *Printer can't be found* message is almost always a configuration issue — the printer isn't plugged in or turned on, the cable was pulled accidentally, or the wrong port is selected in the Chooser. It's also possible that something is wrong with the printer driver software or a PRAM setting. Try reinstalling the printer driver and check the manufacturer's Web site for an updated version. If that doesn't work, zap PRAM, as discussed in Chapter 23. You can also try the troubleshooting steps in the next section.

### Printer port is in use message

The *Printer port is in use* message often indicates a configuration problem, but there can be some hidden problems that cause it. (It happens most often to serial printers.) The printer is likely not connected to the right port in the Chooser or that port is being monopolized by another program. You can take some steps to test this one and get at the solution:

1. **If you have a switch box, make sure it's set to the printer's connection and try to print again.**

   You might need to restart your Mac first.

2. **Check the Chooser.**

   Make sure your printer driver is selected and set to the correct port.

   You might also have AppleTalk active and LocalTalk or Printer Port chosen in your AppleTalk or Network control panel (depending on your Mac OS version). If AppleTalk is set to the same port as your serial printer, you can't print to it. Use the AppleTalk or Network control panel to disable it for that port. If you don't otherwise have a network, turn off AppleTalk in the Chooser.

3. **If you have a modem, a personal digital assistant, a scanner, or another device that uses a serial port, make sure that device's software is not set to use the same port as your printer.**

   A lot of this software configures itself automatically and sits in the background — check your PDA software, fax software, modem control panels, and so on.

   Try starting up your Mac with extensions off (hold down the Shift key after the startup tone) and attempt to select the correct driver and port in the Chooser. If the printer now works, it's possible that an extension or control panel that you're not aware of is using the printer's port.

4. **If the problem occurred right after a printer failure, it's possible that the driver crashed or hung the port. You might need to power all the way down to reset the port — sometimes you even have to zap PRAM, as discussed in Chapter 23, to clear an errant port.**

5. **If all this fails, test the printer on the Modem port and see if it works.**

   If you get all the way through these steps (and the previous section's steps), chances are the problem is due to a bad serial port.

### Problems with PostScript

If you're lucky enough to have an advanced PostScript printer, you're also unfortunate enough to be living in the world of obscure PostScript errors. Thankfully, you have me. I don't know any more about it than you do, but I'm a friendly face and I have a crack team of unpaid research assistants. Here, then, are a few common reasons for PostScript errors:

- ✔ If you send multiple documents to a printer that can't handle them, you get a timeout error. In this case, try sending fewer pages at one time or turn off background printing in the Chooser. (You'll have to wait for printing to complete before you can get control of your Mac again.)

- ✔ You might get PostScript errors if you choose too many nonstandard options in the Page Setup dialog box, or if you're trying to print with hairline margins and odd paper sizes.

- ✔ Allowing unlimited downloadable fonts either in an application's Page Setup or in the printer's PPD file can cause PostScript errors, as can using too many fonts in one document.

- ✔ A corrupt font can causes PostScript errors that might seem random. If you don't know what to make of your errors, but you notice that they happen only with certain documents, look to see whether they're using the same font.

One of the leading causes of errors in laser printers is a lack of RAM, especially if you're getting font errors or timeouts or if your printer prints incomplete pages. Consider upgrading the RAM if you experience errors that keep your pages from printing properly.

### Freezes and crashes

If your Mac is exhibiting consistent freezes or crashes when trying to print, the problem is likely corruption. Here's where the corruption can occur and how to root it out:

✔ **Corrupt document.** If you get an error, freeze, or crash while a particular document is printing, that document might be corrupt. This might also be the case if you see an error message that says there was a problem but let's you "Try Again" and then shows you the error again almost immediately. To remove the document, double-click the desktop printer icon and drag the document to the Trash. You can also delete the document from the PrintMonitor Documents folder inside your System Folder.

✔ **Background printing.** If your Mac crashes while attempting to print documents in the background, you might have a corrupt document or you might have problems with the PrintMonitor or Desktop PrintMonitor. Test by turning off background printing in the Chooser. If the printing works, the problem is background printing. Make sure you have free space on your hard disk — PrintMonitor requires scratch space. Also, you can try assigning more RAM to PrintMonitor or Desktop PrintMonitor. Select either in the Extensions folder and then choose File ⇨ Get Info. In the Show menu, choose Memory. Set the Minimum and Preferred Sizes to slightly higher numbers.

✔ **Preferences file.** If you have repeated problems printing different documents that don't seem to be corrupt or have corrupt fonts, you might have corruption in your printing preferences files. The fix is to delete the Printer Prefs file or folder from the Preferences folder in the System Folder. If your printer is a non-Apple printer or an inkjet, the preferences file might be named after that printer or company.

You should be using the latest printer drivers with your printer, especially if you've updated the Mac OS recently. If you continue to have trouble, test for more general problems and conflicts, as outlined in Chapter 20.

## *Maintaining your printer*

It's not just software that can affect your printouts — the hardware can offer the occasional glitch, too. You can keep glitches at a minimum, though, with some TLC:

✔ Print only on items approved for your printer type, especially labels and transparencies. In laser printers, nonapproved printing mediums can melt and stick to the innards.

✔ Avoid cheap, lightweight paper because it can be dusty and tear easily as it moves through your printer. Buy at least 20-lb paper of medium or better quality.

✔ If your printer isn't pulling paper through well — it slips and jams often, for instance — take it in for service. You can often get the rollers worked on affordably. (My editor gloats that she "lightly sanded the rollers with very fine sandpaper" and it fixed the problem on her printer. Are you that brave?)

✔ Open up your printer and see whether you see ink or toner inside. Temperature, humidity, and other factors can affect how cleanly the printer prints and how often it should be serviced.

✔ Printing to the second side of a used sheet of paper is environmentally conscious of you, but not always best for your printer. Toner can reheat and flake off pages in a laser printer; inks that aren't completely dry can roll off inside inkjets. Plus, paper that's been through the wringer can be more difficult to pull through the printer the second time. Instead, use clean paper (or paper with less printing on the scratch side) and recycle that white paper vigilantly!

✔ With inkjet printers, don't just pull the plug (or more likely, don't just throw the switch on your surge protector). Inkjets need to go through a power-down cycle, purging the cartridge and storing it away, for best performance. Let it power down by shutting down the Mac and then pressing the printer's power button, if it has one.

# Chapter 11

# Removable Media: Zips, Floppies, and CDs

- - - - - - - - - - - - - - - - - - - - - - - - - - - - - - - - - - - - - - - - - -

- - - - - - - - - - - - - - - - - - - - - - - - - - - - - - - - - - - - - - - - - -

*L*ike drinking fine red wine, adding a removable drive to your Mac is a good idea on three levels. A removable drive adds storage capacity to your Mac, it allows you to formulate an all-important backup strategy, and it gives you another option for transferring files between computers. (Drinking fine red wine is good because it complements many meals, the tannin helps fight heart disease, and a couple of glasses will help your friends gloss over the embarrassing 40 minutes of karaoke you subjected them to last night.)

Most Macs — and all Power Macintosh machines and equivalent Performa models — have CD-ROM drives. Many Macs also have floppy drives; others ship with Iomega Zip drives. But what if you want something between those extremes — a way to store hundreds of megabytes on a single disk of some sort? Or, perhaps you're interested in creating your own CDs.

All that is possible and a good idea. I encourage you to look into *some* sort of high-capacity storage, if only to keep your data a bit more secure with back-ups. In this chapter, you look at the different types of drives, their capacities, and how to get a removable installed. Then you focus on building a backup strategy for safeguarding your data.

## *A Little Disc'll Do Ya*

I'll begin with CD technologies. The ubiquitous little CD is all grown up in media, forming the basis for any number of data and content distributions. The CD is the standard in audio (although MP3s aren't far behind, as discussed in Chapter 9). A CD-ROM drive of some sort is found on nearly any computer made these days. And new technologies, such as recordable CDs and high-capacity DVDs, are becoming common both in computing and in home audio/video.

Here's an overview of the various technologies:

- ✔ **CD-ROM (compact disc read-only memory).** CD-ROM is the prevalent technology today. CD-ROM discs must be *burned* in a manufacturing process that imprints the disc with small *pits* (tiny indentations). Using a laser, the drive translates each pit as slightly less light reflective than the *lands* (the sections that remain flat) on the disc. These light levels represent the ones and zeros that make up digital files. A typical CD uses this technology to store around 650MB of computer data in the form of audio, video, or computer applications and files. CD-ROMs can't be written to using a regular Mac; they must be "burned" using special manufacturing equipment.

  Did you notice that I said a CD-ROM has 650MB of storage space in this chapter, but I said it has 740MB of storage space in Chapter 9? Makes you wonder if I'm lying about my voting record from my early days in Congress, too, doesn't it? Actually, the statements can be reconciled; it depends on your definition of storage space. A CD-ROM uses a different file format for computer data than for raw audio data (used with audio CDs). All the overhead required to store computer files and make them show up in the Finder eats up that extra 90MB.

- ✔ **CD-R (compact disc-recordable).** With this technology, you can write your own data to CD-R media using a CD-R drive. Instead of physical pits and lands, the CD-R includes a layer of organic dye that is burned by a laser. This resembles the pits and lands of a CD-ROM closely enough that most CD-ROM drives can read CD-R discs. This only allows you to burn the disc once, though, so CD-R is a *WORM* (Write Once, Read Many) technology. You can, however, save multiple *sessions* on a single CD-R until it's filled up; you just can't save over data that's already been recorded. This might seem like a huge limitation, but CD-R discs are so inexpensive that CD-R is probably the best way to archive your data or send data to friends and colleagues without too heavy a financial burden.

- ✔ **CD-RW (compact disc-rewritable).** CD-RW discs are similar to CD-R discs, except they you can write to them more than one; that is, you can overwrite the data on the disc. This is possible because the rewritable layer replaces the organic dye with a chemical compound that crystallizes when heated to a particular temperature but returns to a non-crystal state after being heated to an even *higher* temperature and then cooled. The only drawbacks are that CD-RW discs are more expensive and not as compatible with run-of-the-mill CD-ROM drives; many newer drives can read them, but older CD-ROM drives might not. Still, this is a great solution for rotating backup and personal storage.

✔ **DVD-ROM (digital versatile disc read-only memory).** In some ways, DVD-ROM is just a bigger, meaner version of CD-ROM technology. Capable of storing between 4.7GB and 17GB of data, DVD is becoming a standard in two places: as the replacement for CD-ROMs in computing and as the replacement for VHS tapes and LaserDisks in the home video arena. DVD-ROM drives are backward-compatible with CD technologies, so they can generally read CDs, CD-Rs, and CD-RWs. Working in tandem with a MPEG-2 decoder (either hardware or software), a DVD drive can be used to play back digital video movies. The iMac DV and Power Macintosh G4 ship with DVD-ROM drives in most configurations; Apple will likely ship all Mac models with DVD-ROM drives from now on.

✔ **DVD-RAM (digital versatile disc random-access memory).** Want to make your own DVDs for data storage? A DVD-RAM drive allows you to create DVD discs in 2.6GB and 5.2GB capacities (depending on whether both sides of the disc are used). DVD-RAM media can't always be read in early DVD-ROM drives and can't be read at all in CD drives. DVD-RAM is great for high-capacity backup, with the potential to back up some hard disks with a single DVD-RAM disc.

Most external DVD-ROM (or DVD-RAM) drives can't be used for playing DVD movies. The simple reason is that any DVD movie player needs an MPEG-2 decoder, which is generally a PCI expansion card that needs to be installed internally. If you have an available PCI expansion slot, you can install a decoder and an internal DVD-ROM drive or, in rarer cases, an external drive that can connect to the card. If you don't have a PCI slot available, you're able to use the DVD-ROM drive only for reading data discs. (See Chapter 14 for more on PCI cards.)

## *Measuring CDs: Speed and go seek*

Most CD drives of any technology are advertised and compared according to their *transfer rate*, or the average rate at which they transfer data. Of course, the marketers don't use the actual speed at which the drive transfers data — marketers like happy, simple numbers. Instead, a system was arrived at to compare data transfer rates using a *multiplier*. Thus, CD drives are advertised as *2x* or *24x* drives, which means very little, as it turns out.

Okay, the numbers mean something. Early CD-ROM drives (I remember them like it was 1990) spun at the same speeds as audio CD players, which netted a transfer rate of about 150K/sec. Since then, drives are measured by how much faster their data rate is than that original, so a *2x* drive transfers data at 300K/sec and a *24x* drive transfers data at 3.6MB/sec.

Of course, these numbers are completely theoretical. The transfer rate of a CD drive is dictated by the interface used (for instance, a USB connection can transfer data at a maximum of only 1.5MB/sec), how much cache RAM you have, the humidity, whether or not it's Tuesday — tons of things. Plus, drives faster than 12x use a constant velocity, so the maximum data rate is applicable only at the very outer edge of the CD; data closer to the middle of the disc might transfer at half that rate.

So, although a 24x drive is a good upgrade over a 2x drive, you won't see much benefit if you already have an 8x or 12x drive. If you have money burning a hole in your pocket, I'd recommend a CD-RW or DVD drive of some sort instead of upgrading your mid-range CD-ROM drive.

If you're a real stickler for numbers, you can also compare CD drives based on the *seek time* of the drive, which measures the average number of milliseconds a drive takes to move to a new section on the disk. The lower the number, the better. This is especially important if you use discs for tasks that jump around a lot — any type of reference title such as a legal database, phone book, or encyclopedia — as opposed to linear tasks such as installing software or playing back video.

## *Select your spinner*

Most external CD drives use one of three technologies, which you might be familiar with: SCSI, USB, or FireWire. If you have an older Mac that offers only SCSI, choose SCSI for your external CD drive. SCSI offers plenty of speed for any CD technology, and you get great performance — assuming you avoid any SCSI voodoo issues (see Chapter 4).

If you have FireWire or USB, you probably already have an internal CD or DVD drive that's plenty fast enough. In that case, either FireWire or USB is fine for setting up an external CD-R or CD-RW drive. (USB is a bit on the slow side for removable media, so I'd choose FireWire.)

One thing to consider before opting for an external drive is whether you're willing to install an internal drive. If you don't have a CD-ROM drive, you probably have an available drive bay, at least in Centris, Quadra, and later models. An internal CD-ROM drive is quicker, can play audio CDs through your Mac's speakers (which an external CD drive can't do), and takes up less desk space.

An external drive, though, offers the convenience of being able to pick it up and take it with you. This can be an advantage, especially if you're looking into a rewritable CD drive of some sort. Just pick it up and take it to another Mac if you need to do some backup — no need to buy multiple drives.

# Installing CD Drives and Burning CDs

Actually, I'm not going to tell you how to install an external CD drive yet, because it's the same as installing any other external removable drive, which I cover later in the creatively named section "Installing an external removable drive." I just didn't want you getting cranky because I didn't tell you how to install the external CD drive in the CD drive section. Patience, I implore you!

I'll discuss one thing about installing CD-ROM drives: the CD-ROM driver software. To mount CDs on the desktop (so that you can double-click them to get at the files), the Mac OS needs to have CD-ROM driver software present. For built-in drives, that's generally the Apple CD Driver or, in newer Mac OS versions, the Apple CD/DVD Driver. But not all non-Apple drives support this driver.

Read your drive's instructions (and technical support issues on the manufacturer's Web site) carefully if you're having trouble getting CDs to mount. In particular, you might need to manually update, or *patch,* the driver using software from the manufacturer, especially if you've recently upgraded the Mac OS. (See Figure 11-1.)

**Figure 11-1:**
This patch operation was necessary to update my external CD-RW drive to be compatible with the latest Mac OS version.

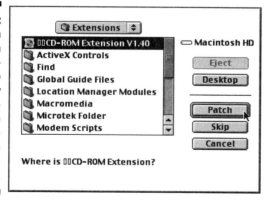

Popular CD driver companies include FWB Software (www.fwb.com) and CharisMac (www.charismac.com). If you have a third-party CD drive, the driver software was likely written by one of these companies.

## *Burn, baby, burn*

After you have a CD-R/CD-RW drive installed, burning your own CD isn't exactly like copying files to a hard disk or removable media disk. In most other cases, removable media appear on the desktop, where you double-click them to open a window, and then you drag files to that disk to copy them. CDs don't always work that way (although they can, as discussed shortly).

If you're using *premastering* software to burn a CD, you often have to copy data to the drive in steps. Data is copied to a CD-R or CD-RW in a *session*, which you need to set up beforehand by determining which files you'd like on the CD. Using your burning software, you create a list of the files you want to copy. When you're ready to burn the data to the disc, the program builds an image of the disc, copies as much data into its cache (RAM allotment) as possible, and then begins to write the data to the disc.

You also determine the format in which the data will be stored on the disc. If you're creating a Mac CD, use HFS; for a CD that can be read by Microsoft Windows, use ISO 9660. You can also experiment with a UDF volume, which can often be read by newer drives in both Mac and Windows environments. (Macs can generally read ISO 9660 volumes, too, although the files will lose some Mac-specific characteristics such as icons and information about the program that created the file.)

Now the burning process sets in. Depending on the speed of your drive, the connection, and other factors, this can take quite a while — with a USB drive and a full disc, you'll wait 20 minutes or more. It's important to note that you can't do anything else with the Mac during this time — even automatic background tasks can interrupt the burn and ruin the disc you're creating. Figure 11-2 shows Charismac's Discribe, a CD-mastering program, in action. Aside from CharisMac, Adaptec makes popular premastering software, including Adaptec Toast and Adaptec EasyCD Creator.

You'll find that premastering software is also often adept at copying an entire existing CD to a recordable disc, if you'd like to back up your discs (or copy audio CDs). Likewise, many mastering programs are capable of extracting audio tracks from audio CDs and burning them onto a recordable CD — that way, you can create your own mix CDs, if you like. (Of course, you should observe copyright laws in doing so.) Just make sure you're formatting in an audio CD format, not in HFS or ISO 9660. If you want to burn an audio CD from audio files already stored on your Mac, you generally save them as 16-bit 44-kHz AIFF files. A sound-editing program or MP3 utility should be able to help translate audio file formats and prepare them for burning to a CD; see Chapter 9.

**Figure 11-2:**
Discribe
enables you
to burn a
premas-
tered CD-R
or CD-RW.

Premastering isn't the only way to create CDs. Software from Adaptec called DirectCD allows you to use *packet-writing* technology to write data to a CD-R or CD-RW on the fly, without gathering all your files for the burn. DirectCD makes it possible to mount a CD-R or CD-RW disc on the desktop, just like other removable media. You then simply drag and drop files onto the disc.

Why not create CDs this way all the time? The major issue with packet writing is compatibility — not all CD-ROM drives support the UDF (Universal Disc Format) that's used to make this drag-and-drop burning work. The CD-R or CD-RW drive you use must support UDF if you plan to use the disc with it. Many modern drives do, and UDF support is built into Mac OS 8.1 and higher, so this should become less of a drawback as time wears on. For now, though, premastered CD-Rs are better for sending out to friends and colleagues than are UDF CD-Rs.

If you have all the requisites for DirectCD, you simply install it and configure its control panel. You're then able to drag files you want to store on a CD-R directly onto that disc in the Finder. Note that DirectCD must specifically support your drive; Adaptec's maintains a list of compatible drives on its Web site (www.adaptec.com).

The latest versions of popular Mac backup applications, such as Retrospect Backup, support writing directly to some CD-R and CD-RW drives. This can be a major convenience, making it much easier to automate backup to record-able CDs. See Chapter 21 for details on automating your backups.

## *Ouch, that's hot!*

Although they shouldn't be too hot to the touch (even though they're *burned* . . . get it?!) writeable CDs can be problematic at times. Creating a CD is a demanding process that monopolizes your Mac for the duration of the burn, even on very powerful models. It's not uncommon to waste a few CD-R discs (or have to erase and rewrite a few CD-RW discs) before you get the hang of using your drive with your Mac. Here are some tips if you encounter trouble:

- ✔ **Don't run anything else.** Your software might even warn you of this. If you quit all other applications — and even restart with extensions disabled, by holding down the Shift key after the Mac's startup tone — you might have better luck burning CDs. Any actions by another application during the burn process has the potential to interrupt the burn, which often makes the disc useless.

- ✔ **Assign the program a lot of RAM.** Your disc-mastering software uses a cache (in RAM) to store as much data as possible before the burn. This helps ensure that there's enough data to write in a continuous stream to the disc, which is mandatory for success. If you assign the program more RAM (see the section on configuring application memory in Chapter 15), you give the program more RAM to work with, so it can cache even more data.

- ✔ **Make sure you have hard disk space.** In some cases, the disc-mastering software might need to create a disc image on your Mac's hard disk; this is particularly true if you're trying to duplicate an entire disc. In that case, at least 700MB of free space (and ideally more) should be available for storage on your hard disk. You might need to delete some files or archive them to CD-R first (which might become a catch-22 if you're running way low on drive space). Also, your drive should be free from errors and recently defragmented (see Chapter 21) for best performance.

- ✔ **Use the built-in tests.** It might seem like a pain, but you should run the mastering software's read and write tests, at least for the first few burns. This will give you a good idea as to whether or not your Mac and drive connections are going to succeed when this little CD-burning square dance gets underway. If your Mac repeatedly fails the tests, it might be an indication that you need to disable extensions and virtual memory, change preferences in the program, upgrade other components (such as RAM or your processor), or consider a different CD-R or CD-RW drive.

✔ **Update your software.** CD-R and CD-RW technologies are reasonably new to the industry, as are the USB and FireWire standards. The bottom line: You're likely to run into some sort of snag, even though you'd think this would all work when you pull the drive out of its box and hook it up. Vigorously scour the support section, Frequently Asked Questions (FAQs), and other portions of your manufacturer's Web site, including downloading and installing any update software. This is even truer if you've recently updated the Mac OS or if you're using a new Mac model that might not have been fully tested when your drive was manufactured.

✔ **Read your manual.** One of the most important things to know about your disc-mastering software is how it handles sessions and volume formats. Be confident that you know how to set up a new session (often by recording a new *track* of data) to avoid either overwriting your existing data (on a CD-RW) or inexplicably creating more than one volume on the disc. The more you understand your software and the CD burning process, the better luck you'll have.

# Working with Removables

One of the most hotly debated features of the iMac was something it didn't include — a floppy drive. Until that point, all Macs had featured at least one, but the iMac design team, led by CEO Steve Jobs, felt it was a waste. With a capacity of only 1.4MB of data, the floppy drive had outlived its usefulness, said Apple, because it couldn't possibly be used to back up the multigigabyte drives of modern Macs. What's more, it was an unreliable technology that could hold only a few word processing documents or even fewer image files. Because all programs are installed using CDs these days, the floppy was an anachronism.

How you feel about that is between you and your therapist (or your Mac user group). The fact is, many new Macs don't have floppy drives, which is either a curse or an opportunity, depending on your point of view.

Now, when it comes to removable media, you have a choice. I would encourage you to get some type of removable media. A high-capacity disk of some sort allows you to back up the data on your Mac — and the data is often more important than the Mac itself, especially in a business situation.

Removables offer a range of speeds, prices, popularity, and attractiveness — some are downright *purty* — so you have some decisions to make. And if you're a hopeless romantic, a conservative, or both, you can even add a floppy drive to that new-fangled Mac — or get your old one in fighting shape.

Aside from the CD burners mentioned previously in this chapter, you have three types of drives to consider for backup and file transfer purposes. These are removable cartridge drives (like we've been talking about), magneto-optical drives, and tape drives. In this section, you examine each in turn.

## Removable cartridge drives

Removable cartridge drives are probably the only type that fulfill all three promises of external storage media — they expand your Mac's storage capacity, they enable you to back up your files, and they're useful for transferring files to others. Magneto-optical and tape drives are both a bit more specialized than that. If utter fulfillment is important to you, read on.

Removable cartridges sometimes look like floppy diskettes (see Figure 11-3) and other times look like hockey pucks. But it's not quite fair to classify these as the same as floppy diskettes, for two reasons. First, removable cartridges tend to use different technologies than floppies to store data. Second, there's pretty much nothing whatsoever that's floppy about them, so let's just *let go* of that term, if you please.

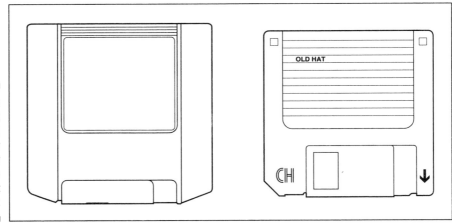

**Figure 11-3:** A Zip disk (on left) looks similar to a floppy diskette (right) but thicker.

Here's a look at the major brands and technologies in the removable cartridge world:

✔ **Iomega Zip.** Probably the most popular, Zip cartridges come in two capacities, 100MB and 250MB. Drives that support 250MB can also read and write 100MB cartridges, but earlier drives can deal with only 100MB cartridge. Although the Zip format remains an Iomega technology, a number of different companies make Zip compatible drives with all sorts of interfaces, including USB, FireWire, and SCSI. Zip drives tend to transfer data more slowly than hard disks, but the speed is usually acceptable for backup and transfer tasks.

✔ **Iomega Jaz.** Not as popular as Zip, the Jaz drive supports media in 500MB, 1GB, and 2GB sizes. Although Jaz is great for adding storage and backup capacity to your Mac, the expense of each cartridge makes them unlikely candidates for swapping with colleagues. Jaz disks often rival external hard disks in speed, and the media offers large capacities, making Jaz good for routine backup.

✔ **LS120.** Also called *SuperDisk*, drives that adhere to this standard can read and write to both standard floppy diskettes and special 120MB diskettes. Although speeds are improving, LS120 tends to lag behind Zip in this arena. Multiple vendors make LS120 drives, but they tend to use USB as the interface of choice.

✔ **Orb.** After a rocky start (where Orb drives were announced months before any made their grand appearance in the world), the Orb standard is beginning to fulfill its promise. It offers the one-two punch of reasonably inexpensive media and 2.2GB storage space. Available in SCSI, FireWire, and USB versions (as well as internal models), the Orb is made by Castlewood and other manufacturers. It isn't terribly time-tested, though, so its reliability remains to be seen.

Aside from these removables, some companies also make external USB-based floppy drives for iMac and Power Macintosh users who really miss or need the floppy drive. Table 11-1 shows popular removable cartridge drive manufacturers and the drive standards they offer.

| Table 11-1 | Drive Manufacturers and Their Products | |
|---|---|---|
| *Manufacturer* | *Types of Drives* | *Web Site* |
| Iomega | Zip, Zip 250, Jaz | www.iomega.com |
| Imation | LS120 | www.imation.com |
| VST | LS120, Zip, floppy | www.vsttech.com |
| Newer Technology | Floppy | www.newertech.com |
| ClubMac | Orb, Zip, Jaz, floppy | www.clubmac.com |
| Ariston | Floppy | www.ariston.com |
| Microtech International | Zip, floppy | www.microtech-pc.com |

## *Magneto-optical drives*

Magneto-optical (M-O) drives aren't as popular as Zip and LS120, but they offer a few advantages. The media is considered reasonably impervious to dust, moisture, and magnetic fields. The M-O format isn't controlled by a single company (unlike Zip and Orb), so you can get the discs themselves from more vendors. These two factors combine to make M-O drives good for backup and archiving, especially for long-term storage. They're less useful for transferring files because you can't always rely on your colleagues to have access to an M-O drive. And even if they do have an M-O drive, it might have trouble reading your disks.

The late 1990s saw a break in M-O technology, allowing it to increase both transfer rates and storage capacities. M-O drives now approach hard drive speeds. Capacities for new drives range from 640MB to 4.6GB, although many drives remain backward compatible with 230MB and 128MB cartridges. Companies that offer external M-O drives include Pinnacle Micro (www. pinnaclemicro.com), Fujitsu (www.fujitsu.com), and APS Technologies (www.apstech.com).

M-O drives come in SCSI, USB, and FireWire versions. You can also install an M-O drive internally, if you have the inclination and wherewithal. See Chapter 17 for more on installing internal drives.

## *Tape drives*

Tape is another cartridge that isn't particularly suited to sharing files with your buddies because, well, it's slow. Tape drives are for backup and archiving — data is written sequentially, as if recorded to an audiocassette. This sequential process makes it tough to get at a particular file on a moment's notice — you have to rewind or fast forward to get to it.

Also, tape drives are *near-line* solutions, meaning nothing gets mounted on the desktop for you to click in the Finder. Instead, you need to use a utility program, usually a backup application such as Retrospect, to access the files on the tape.

Have I scared you off yet? No need — tape fills the backup role very nicely. For one, tape comes in capacities up to 80GB or more — yowza — meaning you can easily back up your whole hard disk. With a tape in the tape drive, you might not even have to think about your backup often, meaning you'll actually do it. People rarely do things they have to think about, unless it's counting money.

Tape cartridges are generally cheap and perfect for off-site backups — media locked in a fireproof safe or down at the bank in your safety deposit box — in case of emergencies.

In a quest to understand tape, you need to know about three standards (or, if you get bored, just read until your eyes glaze over):

- **Travan/QIC.** Travan is the popular standard for low-cost storage that's backward compatible with the old dog of tape backup, QIC. Travan drives let you use tapes between 1.6 and 4GB in capacity, while remaining backward compatible with QIC tapes. (You often see capacities of up to 8GB advertised, based on 2:1 compression of your backed-up data.) Even higher capacity drives that rely on the Travan NS (network series) standard are available, pushing capacities to 20GB (compressed) or more.

- **DAT.** DAT (digital audiotape) was designed for expensive CD-quality recordable cassettes that never really took off (at least, they don't have many DAT decks for cars). The 4-mm tapes were re-purposed for expensive data storage. Tapes come in capacities marked DDS-1 through DDS-4, with DDS-4 reaching up to 40GB per tape (compressed). Speeds on these drives tend to be much slower than other tape drives, reaching 1.2MB/sec with a stiff wind at their backs. Most of these drives use SCSI or Fast SCSI external interfaces.

The various SCSI levels aren't discussed until Chapter 17 because they rarely have any bearing on external devices — all Macs that Apple ever shipped with a SCSI port had a plain, old 5MB/sec SCSI port. In order to have a Fast SCSI (10MB/sec) port, you'd need to add a SCSI expansion card that offered the port. If you had such a card, you'd be able to hook up Fast SCSI devices and experience their full grandeur. With the regular SCSI port, you can still attach such drives, just at lower top-end speeds.

- **DLT.** If DAT is expensive, then DLT is really *impressively* expensive. It offers higher capacities and higher speeds than DAT and is considered ultra reliable, thanks to an internal process that constantly cleans the tape and a head that never touches the tape. For high-end network solutions, DLT makes sense. For regular folks, it's a bit much, with capacities reaching up to 80GB and transfer rates up to 20MB/sec on high-end drives.

For most home and small-office situations you'll opt for a Travan tape drive, which can get you 8GB of backup on a single tape. Drives are a few hundred dollars, some feature USB interfaces, and the tapes are reasonably inexpensive, especially in smaller capacities. All different types of tape drives are offered by Lacie (www.lacie.com), ClubMac (www.clubmac.com), Aiwa (www.aiwa.com), and Arriva (www.arriva.com) among others.

# Connecting External Drives

If you've installed any other external devices on your Mac (or if you've read any of the other chapters in Part II), you already know how to install an external removable drive. It's a piece of cake! All you need to do is wire it up, install the driver software, and then head over to the manufacturer's Web site and look for answers when the golly-blamed thing doesn't work. (I'm kidding — I hope.)

## SCSI drives

For a SCSI drive, here's the drill:

1. **Open up the Apple System Profiler (see Chapter 24) or another SCSI utility. Find an available SCSI ID number for your drive.**

   To access the SCSI device information in the Apple System Profiler, choose Select ➪ Device Information.

   Some Macs have an internal and external SCSI bus; you need an available SCSI ID on the external bus.

2. **On the back of the drive, change the SCSI ID to its new value.**

   Some devices, such as external Zip drives, don't offer the full range of ID numbers — they might offer only 5 or 6, for instance (see Figure 11-4). If that's the case, you might need to rearrange your other peripheral's ID numbers to suit.

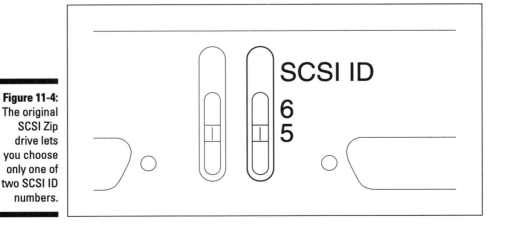

**Figure 11-4:**
The original SCSI Zip drive lets you choose only one of two SCSI ID numbers.

3. **Shut down your computer.**

4. **Plug the SCSI cable into the SCSI IN port on the back of your removable media drive.**

   If the drive doesn't have a port specifically labeled SCSI IN, you can likely use either of the two SCSI ports on the drive.

5. **Plug the other end of the SCSI cable into your Mac's external SCSI port.**

   If you have other devices on your SCSI chain, plug your removable drive into the last device on the chain. Make sure you remove the terminator from that device (or otherwise turn off termination) because your removable drive is now the last device in the chain.

   You don't have to make your removable drive the last device in your SCSI chain. If you want to put it in the middle, do so, just make sure your drive isn't terminated and that the end of the SCSI chain is. See Chapter 4 for more on SCSI termination.

6. **If the removable is the only device or the last device in the SCSI chain, terminate it.**

   Either add a terminator to its SCSI OUT port, flip the termination switch, or if the drive offers auto-sensing termination, do nothing.

7. **Plug the drive's AC adapter into an available socket on your surge protector.**

8. **Turn on the drive and wait for it to spin up.**

   If it doesn't have a power switch, don't try to turn it on. It might take days before you give up.

9. **Start up your Mac.**

10. **With the Mac activated and the drive on, install any software that came with the drive.**

    Many removable drives need driver software installed so that the disk can appear on the desktop when inserted. You might need to restart your Mac after you've installed the software.

If the installation went well, try inserting a disk in the drive. If it's recognized, you might be asked to format the disk; otherwise you can just double-click it in the Finder to begin using it.

If you do have the option of formatting it, go ahead and format it as a Mac OS Standard volume, unless it's a large (over 250MB) disk. In that case, you might choose to format it as a Mac OS Extended volume, provided that you don't expect to ever have to use the disk with a Mac running Mac OS 8.0 or earlier. (Mac OS 8.1 is required for compatibility with Mac OS Extended format.)

If the media isn't recognized, begin by opening Apple System Profiler or your SCSI utility and making sure the drive itself is recognized. If it isn't, you should troubleshoot as you would for any SCSI device — see Chapter 4.

If the drive is recognized but the media isn't, something is wrong with the driver software or the media you're using. Check to make sure you didn't forget to install the driver software and consult the manufacturer's Web site to make sure you don't need to install a newer driver. (While writing this chapter, I installed a USB CD-RW drive that ended up needing a new driver for media to appear on the desktop in the Finder. After I installed the updated driver, it began working like a charm.)

## USB and FireWire

For USB and FireWire drives, the same advice applies as for other USB and FireWire devices. Install the driver software first and then power up the drive by connecting its AC adapter to a socket on your surge protector. (Some removable drives might not even have a power adapter.) Next, plug the drive into an available USB port on your Mac or on a USB hub. For FireWire devices, you can plug the drive into an available FireWire port on the Mac or into the last device on the FireWire chain.

If the drive is recognized, you can see it in the Apple System Profiler. You can then insert media and see whether the media is recognized. If asked, you might need to format the media. If the media isn't recognized, you might need to restart your Mac so that the device driver you installed is activated.

If you have trouble, you can troubleshoot the same way you would troubleshoot any USB device, as discussed in Chapter 4.

On slot-loading iMacs, Power Macintosh G4 models, and newer Macs going forward, each USB port is a separate bus. That means each has 12 megabits per second of bandwidth to play with. Because external drives are demanding, you might consider connecting the USB removable drive to one of the USB ports on the side of the Mac without attaching other devices (if you have few enough devices). That way, the drive can always get as much throughput as possible.

## The infamous click of death

Although all removable drives have their share of problems (for instance, when SCSI Orb drives use early driver software, they sometimes seem to appear twice on the SCSI chain), Zip disks were hit with a nasty one. Called the "Click of Death" because of the symptoms, the problem is still somewhat mysterious. If you use a Zip drive, you need to be aware of this issue.

What happens is simple: In some Zip drives (Iomega always points out that it's "less than 1%"), the drive heads can become misaligned. When this happens, the drive is no longer useful. But if a disk is in a drive that's become misaligned, the drive can mess up the disk. If you insert that disk in *another* Zip drive, the new

drive can be misaligned *by that disk*. Now you're upset.

If you hear constant click-click-clicking when you insert a disk, remove it immediately. Iomega then recommends that you try a second disk — preferably a fresh disk with no saved data. (The second disk can be ruined by this test, so make sure it doesn't have important stuff on it.) If the second disk doesn't click, the problem is probably isolated to the first disk; unfortunately, that first disk is pretty much unusable. If the second disk clicks, the drive is the problem. Contact Iomega for information on returning the drive, because it's probably misaligned. And don't use those disks in other drives from now on.

# Trouble with Removables

Trouble with a removable drive can be frustrating, especially because your data is probably important to you and you'd like to feel that it's stored away safely. Most problems with removables are easy to troubleshoot, though. Here are some standard issues:

- ✔ **Buggy drivers.** Removable drives often exhibit trouble when something is going on with their driver software — either the software is conflicting with another driver or it needs to be updated for a new Mac OS version. And sometimes the software is just buggy and needs to be updated by the company. In those cases, you need to visit the manufacturer's Web site and download a new driver.

- ✔ **Dueling drivers.** Sometimes two different versions of a driver can conflict. If you use an Iomega Zip or Jaz drive, for instance, you might encounter this problem. If you start up the Mac while a cartridge is in the drive, the Mac OS uses the cartridge's driver instead of the driver in the System Folder. If the cartridge's driver is older, you'll start to get errors when you eject that cartridge and attempt to insert cartridges that use a newer version of the drive. The best plan is to upgrade all your cartridges to newer drivers, if you can, usually by using the drive's utility program (see Figure 11-5). Another approach is to make sure you don't start up your Mac with removable cartridges in their drives. (Unless, of course, you're *trying* to start up from the Zip or Jaz disk. In that case, that disk should have the latest driver installed.)

**Figure 11-5:**
A removable drive's utility application can often update drivers, reformat the disk, and even set preferences such as when to automatically eject the disk.

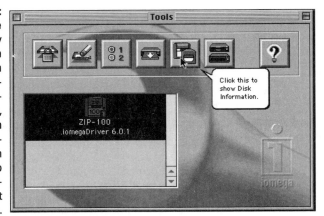

- ✔ **Special erase.** Although removable media drives can often be formatted using the Mac's Special ➪ Erase Disk command, you might have better luck with utilities included with the drive. In general, these utilities will augment a typical Mac format's capabilities, such as verifying the integrity of the media.

- ✔ **Mounting DOS media.** If you plan to use your removable drive with DOS-formatted disks, I recommend that you upgrade to Mac OS 8.1 or higher. In that version, PC Exchange was updated to more readily recognize and mount DOS-formatted media in many removable media drives. If you can't upgrade, one way to get PC-formatted media to work with your drive is to head over to the PC Exchange control panel *before* you insert the DOS-formatted media. Choose the Options button and click once on the removable drive. Click OK and PC Exchange will keep the DOS-formatted drive from loading its own driver so that it doesn't cause trouble with the Mac OS.

# Chapter 12

# The New Guard: More on USB and FireWire

*T*he way that Apple introduced USB and FireWire to the Macintosh market was about as significant as the technologies themselves. Breaking with the received wisdom of the PC market, Apple opted not to offer the new ports alongside the more familiar ADB, SCSI, and serial connections found on older Macs. Instead, the company forced users down a new path with the original iMac, which offered only USB ports. Soon after, the Power Macintosh G3 was released with only USB, ADB, and FireWire — no serial or SCSI ports. Subsequent Power Macintosh models have dropped ADB, offering only the two latest technologies.

Was this plan wrong? In the short term, it caused some complaints. Users with *legacy* peripherals — those that used the older technologies — found that their devices weren't compatible with Apple's latest offerings. If your printer's serial port is no longer offered on the newest Macs, it makes the price of a new system that much more prohibitive. Some Mac owners opted to make their statement by not upgrading to Apple's Macs, but others gave in and dug deeply for the cash to buy both a new Mac and the new peripherals that worked with it.

In the longer term, this plan has moved the Mac market very quickly to modern technologies. Both USB and FireWire are good speedy methods for connecting devices to computers — much better than their predecessors. Modern Macs — although not problem-free by any stretch of the imagination — don't suffer annoying glitches caused by aging port technologies. Plus, both technologies offer new advantages, such as USB's support for many different devices and FireWire's hidden talent with digital video, which I explore later in this chapter.

Eventually, the third-party market filled in the gaps for legacy devices. It turns out that you can build an adapter for most anything, including serial, SCSI, and ADB devices that need to be connected to a USB-based iMac or Power Macintosh. A number of companies have pitched in with solutions that help you connect older printers, removable drives, scanners, and even external hard drives to these new-fangled ports. If you're not yet ready to buy new peripherals, perhaps it's time to *adapt*.

# *The Talented Mr. USB*

With the popularity of the original, USB-only iMac, the universal serial bus (USB) got saddled with quite a bit of responsibility. Almost immediately, users pining for a cute little iMac also wanted to use with it their printers, external drives, scanners, cameras, and personal digital assistants. Fortunately, entrepreneurial manufacturers responded, some of which made their name (or made a new name for themselves) offering adapters for USB.

## *Adaptable technologies*

As it turns out, USB is fairly adaptable. Companies were able to come out with devices that enable you to connect serial, SCSI, ADB, LocalTalk, and even Intel PC-based parallel port devices to the USB ports on your Mac. These connections provide a convenient way to deal with the occasional device that doesn't natively support USB.

Any adapter has a few weaknesses, however. For the most part, these adapters require special driver software that needs to be well written and maintained by the manufacturer — a hit-and-miss proposition at best. Before buying any adapter, I recommend digging into the manufacturer's support Web pages to see whether they list compatible devices and problematic devices. And make sure you're buying Mac adapters — USB adapters are gaining popularity for PC users, too, and don't always include Mac driver software in the box. (Look for the Mac OS icon or cover copy that says the product is Mac or iMac compatible.)

Also, some technologies are more suited to adaptation than others — although you might get a SCSI device to work through your USB port, for instance, you might run up against some limitations. Here's a look at some of the traditional Mac technologies and how well they adapt to USB:

   ✔ **Serial.** USB-to-serial adapters are probably the most prevalent, because they're the easiest to implement and tend to be the least demanding. Serial's top-end limit of 230 Kbps (with most serial devices requiring only half of this bandwidth), keeps serial fully within USB's 12 Mbps limit. USB and serial ports are both *serial* technologies, so there isn't too much adaptation that has to happen. For the most part, USB-to-serial adapters simply work, although some work better than others. Very few of these adapters provide MIDI, GeoPort, or LocalTalk support, for instance, and some devices that *poll* the port (that is, the device contacts the port repeatedly waiting for software to respond, instead of waiting until software contacts the device) won't work or require special workarounds. Figure 12-1 shows a two-port USB-to-serial adapter.

**Figure 12-1:** The Keyspan serial adapter lets you connect a printer, a PDA, or another Mac serial device to a USB-based Mac.

*Photo courtesy Keyspan, Inc.*

Don't buy a PC serial adapter by mistake; Mac serial ports are DIN-8 ports. Make sure the adapter says DIN-8 or Mac-compatible somewhere on the box.

✔ **Parallel.** USB-to-parallel adapters enable you to connect devices that offer only a parallel port to your USB-equipped Mac. In most cases, this works only with select parallel printers. Because most parallel devices are designed for Intel-compatible PCs, you need driver software to use a parallel device; only a few printer manufacturers have written such drivers. If your parallel printer offers a Mac driver, though, using a USB-to-parallel adapter should work fairly well. (In fact, this was the method used for the first iMac-compatible printers — PC printer manufacturers just quickly wrote some Mac drivers for their parallel printers).

The PowerPrint drivers written by Infowave allow you to connect a number of parallel printers to your Mac through a parallel-to-USB adapter, as discussed in Chapter 10.

✔ **ADB.** If you have a mouse, a keyboard, a joystick or another ADB device that you'd like to hook up to your iMac or newer Power Macintosh machine, you might consider a USB-to-ADB adapter. These devices require their own drivers but tend to be less problematic that some other adapters. Although most ADB devices adapt well to USB, you might have trouble with some high-end input devices (such as pen tablets) and some password-protection dongles. Also, not all ADB-powered devices will work correctly.

✔ **SCSI.** USB-to-SCSI adapters are fairly popular among iMac owners who also have an external hard drive, external removable drive, or scanner that they're bringing with them from an earlier Mac relationship. Some of these devices offer support for only one SCSI device; others can support an entire chain. In fact, some offer to make your SCSI chain hot-pluggable (in the USB tradition), which is a nice touch. Unfortunately, USB isn't as fast as SCSI, so your performance, especially with hard drives, is worse using the adapter. Also note that adapters can come in 25-pin and 50-pin (Centronics) varieties, depending on your needs, as discussed in Chapter 4.

Aside from those basic offerings, a few companies have even more clever gizmos. The Compucable iDock series is a swivel stand that you place under your iMac and hook up to using a USB cable. The iDock offers a USB hub, serial ports, a parallel port, and even a floppy drive in some configurations. New Motion offers a similar device (also creatively named the iDock) as well as the gDock, which sits on top of a Power Macintosh G3 or G4 and offers additional ports, a USB hub, and a removable drive bay that supports ATAPI drives.

ATAPI is, put simply, removable IDE, a technology for internal CD-ROMs and other drives. It's discussed in Chapter 17 and will, blissfully, make only one more annoying appearance in this chapter.

Microtech offers SmartUSB, a USB-to-ATAPI converter cable that allows you to connect its external ATAPI devices (mini versions of Zip, CD-ROM, and hard drives) to a Mac's USB ports. Belkin's USB Videobus allows you to connect an analog camcorder (using RCA audio/video plugs) and digitize video through USB.

## *Taking the adapter plunge*

Your mission, should you choose to accept, is to shop carefully for adapters by checking the manufacturer's Web site (or customer support line) for specific compatibility with your device. As a rule, adapters are not as trouble-free as most devices designed for USB from the outset — you'll find that many require workarounds to work effectively, including updates to the Mac OS, updates to your Mac's firmware, and vigilant downloading of the latest drivers for the adapter.

Table 12-1 shows adapter manufacturers and their products. See Chapter 22 for more on updating the Mac OS and your Mac's firmware.

| Table 12-1 | Manufacturers of USB Adapters and Their Products | | |
|---|---|---|---|
| **Company** | **URL** | **Adapters** | **Notes** |
| Ariston Technologies | www.ariston.com | USB-to-serial USB-to-parallel USB-to-SCSI | Offers 2- and 4-port serial adapters; offers 25- and 50-pin SCSI adapters |
| Belkin Components | www.belkin.com | USB-to-serial USB-to-parallel USB-to-SCSI | The adapters snap and stack together to support multiple devices at once |
| Compucable | www.compucable.com | USB-to-serial iDock series | Serial adapter supports GeoPorts; iDock offers serial, parallel, and floppy drive (in some configurations) |
| Entrega Technologies | www.entrega.com | USB-to-serial USB-to-SCSI | Also offer PC serial adapters that can be used with downloadable Mac drivers in some cases |
| Griffin Technology | www.griffintechnology.com | USB-to-ADB | |

*(continued)*

**Table 12-1 (continued)**

| Company | URL | Adapters | Notes |
|---|---|---|---|
| iMaccessories | www.imaccessories.com | USB-to-parallel | |
| Keyspan | www.keyspan.com | USB-to-serial USB-to-PDA cradle | PDA-specific adapter plugs directly into the cradle using PC-style DB9 serial port instead of the Mac DIN-8 port |
| Microtech | www.microtechint.com | USB-to-SCSI USB-to-ATAPI | Offers 25- and 50-pin versions |
| New Motion | www.newmotion.com.tw | iDock gDock | Offers serial and parallel ports in unit; some units support ATAPI drive |
| SecondWave | www.2ndwave.com | USB-to-SCSI | |

# FireWire Gets Friendly

Like USB, FireWire is adaptable to other technologies, although fewer tend to be offered. Although FireWire is higher speed than USB, adapting some technologies to FireWire — such as ADB, serial, and parallel — would be overkill. That means you see two basic types of FireWire adapters: SCSI and A/V.

And, while I'm on the topic, I'd like to briefly touch on a FireWire capability that doesn't require an adapter but might seem a little out of character at first — connecting your FireWire-enabled Mac to a digital camera.

Like most any Mac technology, FireWire is kept even friendlier if you stay on top of its software updates. If you're using Mac OS 9 or higher, the Software Update will help you find updates. Otherwise, a quick check of www.apple.com/firewire/ will give you the latest scoop.

# *FireWire adapters*

FireWire-to-SCSI adapters make a lot of sense — FireWire offers speeds that can support a SCSI device's 5MB/sec throughput. And, if you have a Mac with FireWire built in, it doesn't have SCSI built in. That's just a general rule.

FireWire-to-SCSI adapters are available from Orange Micro (www.orangemicro .com), which also offers PCI expansion cards that add FireWire to older Macs. (See Chapter 14.) FireWire adapters for digitizing video — connecting RCA-style or S-video connectors from analog video sources such as camcorders and VCRs — have been promised by a few different vendors but haven't appeared yet as final products. Their viability might be in question.

Another adapter with interesting potential is the FireWire-to-ATAPI adapter. I've seen only prototypes, but Iomega, for instance, will be using such an adapter to hook up external ATAPI drives (Zip, ZipCD, and others) to Macs with FireWire ports. Other manufacturers will surely follow.

# *The digital video connection*

Digital video (DV) camcorders have hit the consumer market with a sudden thud of inevitability. Reaching below $1000 (right on down to $500 in some cases), these camcorders have another important factor in common — support, out of the box, for FireWire. Almost coincident to this phenomenon, many folks with a little cash to burn are desperately seeking their "inner Hitchcock."

Together, DV camcorders and FireWire are ushering in a revolution of sorts, called *desktop video*. Digital video cameras offer a high-quality picture that you can easily transfer to a home computer. Using the computer, you can edit the movie using transitions, music, special effects — everything the studios have been doing for years. If you're any good, you've created a broadcast-quality video clip for a few thousand dollars in the initial investment. This is very different from creating video just a few years ago, which would either require low-quality VHS or prohibitively expensive Betacam equipment and equally costly editing studios.

Nearly any DV camcorder offers a FireWire port. It might be called something different — FireWire is Apple's trademark for the technology. (It was initially developed by Apple but has since become an industry standard, called IEEE 1394.) You'll see the port called DV, or 1394, or i.Link, or Lynx, or something else. In most cases, the camera accepts a standard 4-pin FireWire connector, allowing it to chat with your Mac through a FireWire port.

With the correct software, that connection means you can copy the video from the camera, over the FireWire connection, and to your Mac's hard drive. This is a fabulous new upgrade from earlier video technologies. With analog camcorders (even pro-level equipment), the image has to be *digitized* — the analog pictures are interpreted by computer hardware that translate the image into a computer file. In a DV camera, the image is *created* as a computer file and stored in the DV format. No analog film or tape is involved — the images are registered through the lens and laid down to magnetic tape (or some other storage device) as a computer file.

Because a DV movie clip is already a computer file, FireWire is just a fast way to copy that file to your Mac. Then you can use software — Apple's iMovie including with the iMac DV (see Figure 12-2), Apple's Final Cut Pro, or offerings from Macromedia (www.macromedia.com) or Adobe (www.adobe.com) — to edit the DV clips, add sound effects, add transitions, and so on. When you're finished, you can store the edited DV file as a QuickTime movie or translate it to various video formats (for posting on the Web or sending through e-mail, for instance). Or you can send it back out the FireWire connection to your DV camcorder, which can then play it on TV or feed it to an analog VCR for taping.

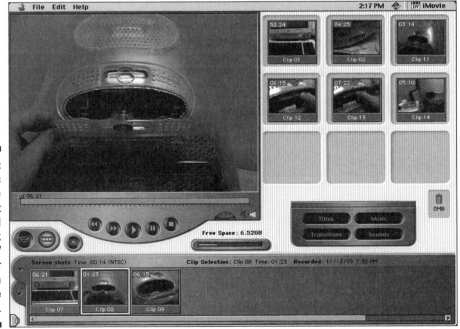

**Figure 12-2:**
Apple's
iMovie
makes it
easy and
fun to work
with a DV
camcorder
and a
FireWire
connection.

If you have FireWire ports built into your Mac or iMac DV, connecting a DV camcorder is simple — just plug it in using the appropriate FireWire cable. (A cable appropriate for a camcorder comes with the iMac DV.) You might also want to explore your camcorder's compatibility with the video software you decide to use — the software controls the camera, allowing you to play back clips from the camera on-screen, fast forward, reverse, and import clips from the camera to your Mac.

If the camera offers a FireWire port (or any IEEE 1394-compliant port, regardless of the name used) and it's compatible with your editing software, you shouldn't have any trouble connecting it. Cameras don't have to offer any specific Mac-compatibility or software drivers. DV is a universal standard recognized by any Mac or PC that offers FireWire connectivity. The usual suspects in consumer video products make DV camcorders: Canon, Sony, Kodak, Nikon, Panasonic, JVC, and others.

# Part III

# Advanced Surgery: Getting inside Your Mac

The 5th Wave     By Rich Tennant

"THERE YOU ARE SIR. ONE MACPAINT, A MACWRITE, A MAC-
ACCOUNTANT, TWO MACSLOTS, A MACPHONE AND A MACDRAW.
WOULD YOU LIKE FRIES WITH THAT?"

## In this part . . .

Fortunately, Mac surgery doesn't require the same steady hand required for surgery on people. (I'd be upset if my surgeon ended up with an extra part after he closed me up as often as I've ended up with an extra screw after sewing up my Macs.) You don't even need to be comfortable with common household tools such as a forklift and a jackhammer. All you need is a little know-how and a healthy respect for static electricity. In these chapters, you see how to get inside your Mac, install upgrade cards, augment your Mac's memory, boost the processor, and add internal storage drives. You even see the basics of Macintosh networking and break open an iMac or two and check out the exciting things you can add to your little high-tech beachball.

# Chapter 13

# Getting inside Your Mac or iMac: The Surgeon's Handbook

*In This Chapter*

▶ Discovering the type of doctor you are

▶ Implementing standard tools for the Mac troubleshooter

▶ Tips for not killing yourself or your Mac

▶ Ins and outs of opening standard Mac cases

*F*or a few years now, I've co-hosted a TV call-in show dedicated to answering people's questions about both Intel-compatible PC and Macintosh upgrading and fixing. And just as often as we get a caller who is incredibly excited about getting inside his or her system, I come across another who simply does not want to be told that he or she needs to open the case and mess around in there.

I've talked to folks who'd rather scrap the whole system and burn some credit card plastic on a new Mac before they'd open up their existing one to fix or improve it. But it doesn't have to be that way. You can do it.

## How Steady Is Your Hand?

Just in case you need some reassurance, here it is: You can easily perform most internal upgrades or component-level troubleshooting on your own. Most procedures barely even involve a screwdriver, and the upgrades that do require some assembly are still designed for regular folks to accomplish (at least, in most Mac models). Remember that most troubleshooting actually happens at the keyboard anyway, unless you're trying to replace a failed component.

I look on upgrading (or replacing broken components) as having three basic levels. Anyone can accomplish any of these, but if getting inside your Mac makes you uncomfortable, you can decide to leave the more complex operations to the professionals. Here are the three types of upgrading and troubleshooting:

✔ **External upgrades and configuration.** Using your Macs ports, this rarely requires any special tools. Most of the time, you plug in the peripheral, connect it to your Mac, and install some software. These are discussed in Part II.

✔ **Slot upgrades and changes.** You have to open up your case for these, but beyond that it's straightforward. You plug a circuit board into an available slot or socket, secure it, and close the Mac back up.

✔ **Component upgrades and changes.** In these cases, you might have to replace a component on the logic board or elsewhere inside the case. That component might be a CPU chip, a daughtercard, a battery, or a drive mechanism. These replacements might require special instructions, multiple screws, and care in plugging in delicate wires. But they're still fairly easy to accomplish and, what's more, the victory is made sweeter by the difficulty of the task.

External upgrades are a cakewalk, as you may have already seen in Part II. Going inside your Mac is a little tougher but still not impossible. All you need are the right tools, a good workspace, and a little forethought. With those, everything should go smoothly.

## Nurse . . . screwdriver!

You do have to admit that, in many ways, computers are weird. What other major electronic devices are we actually *encouraged* to take apart and mess with ourselves? Any individual caught taking a screwdriver to the back of a television set is immediately branded an engineer or a daredevil, if not worse. The idea of popping a few more chips into your VCR is equally ludicrous. But it's par for the course with most computers, even though you paid many times over for your Mac what you pay for a TV.

But a fact is a fact. If you plan on getting inside your Mac, you need some tools. I recommend you have on hand a Phillips-head screwdriver, a set of Torx screwdrivers (only for some early Mac models), a small flashlight, a paper clip, antistatic containers or bags, and a grounding strap.

Although many Macs have quick-release cases designed to be opened with your fingers, it seems that a Phillips-head screw pops up sometimes when you least expect it. You'll need such a screwdriver for some cases, for many internal drives, and to release and secure internal upgrade cards. Certain Mac models also require a Torx screwdriver, especially the older all-in-one classic Macs.

I recommend a flashlight just because it can be tough to see into many cases, especially when you're looking for the glint of a screw you've dropped in the machine.

The single most useful tool around a Mac is the paperclip. You can use this bendable little marvel to set small switches (especially on internal SCSI drives), reset certain Mac models, and manually eject CDs and removable disks from problematic drives. Have at least a few handy.

A trend in newer Macs is the need for a coin to turn a large screw to open some part of the case. You probably have the coin around somewhere, though, so I'll leave it out of the checklist. It will be amusing, though, if one day you're out on the street corner trying to make change so you can add some RAM to your iMac. ("Change for a dollar? Anybody?")

Static electricity discharge — the type you used to create as a kid by shuffling your feet across the carpet and touching a doorknob or a sibling — can be very damaging to computer components. (For instance, one little zap can kill an entire, expensive RAM module.) That's why I recommend using the anti-static plastic bags that come with your upgrade components. If you're swapping a device, place the old device immediately in the bag that the new device came in. If you don't have an antistatic bag handy, you should be able to get one at a computer store.

You'll also want a grounding strap if you're digging into your computer's innards. A grounding strap (available from computer and electronics stores) generally wraps around your wrist and attaches to a metal ground, such as a screw on your Mac's case, to keep you from discharging static electricity into your computer components.

## Pull the plug on your patient?

When a computer is plugged in properly, it's electrically grounded. (That's what that third prong is for on the computer's wall plug.) So, if it's grounded and shut off while you're working inside it — the theory goes — touching any metal part of the computer's power supply or chassis will discharge static.

All of this is true, and I've successfully upgraded computers while they were still plugged in. I've also dropped a screwdriver on a computer's main circuit board (not a Mac, thankfully) and seen the ensuing light show that blew out important parts of that computer's innards. I didn't get much of a jolt myself, but it certainly seemed like the potential was there. And anything dropped or spilled in the open compartment — although it might cause damage anyway — will certainly cause even more if the computer is plugged in.

My glib advice on the matter is this: Keep your Mac plugged in if you're more worried about your components getting shocked than you are about your body getting shocked. If you feel very strongly that your person should not be exposed to any extraneous voltages — or if you think it's even remotely conceivable that something might be dropped in the open computer — work with the machine unplugged and wear a grounding strap instead.

## *Tips for successful surgery*

I know it's a running gag in American pop culture, but could you imagine a book called *Brain Surgery For Dummies?* It would be cute and happy, with little animated doctor icons and stuff. And it'd have friendly little section headings almost exactly like this chapter's. In fact, if they ever do come up with such a book, maybe I'll have some legal grounds here.

Here's some advice culled from years of experience (by actual experts) along with some stuff I've made up. I think you'll still find it useful:

- ✔ **Take your time.** Studies show that most tasks, aside from computer book writing, take 2.5 times as long as you expect them to. (Computer book writing follows a different metric, whereby the writer gets 2.5 times less sleep than the average human does.) Be prepared for a quick upgrade to take longer than you expect and set up a block of uninterrupted time accordingly. Most importantly, don't *ever* make big changes before an important deadline!

- ✔ **Back up your important data.** A lot of people look at me funny when I recommend this — after all, they're only adding a video card! How could that affect their data? My usual answer is: *How did you get in my office?* The fact is, any upgrade can lead to downtime for your computer through a misconfiguration or an unforeseen circumstance. Even if you're not messing with the hard disk, if the Mac has to go into the shop for a few days, you'll be happy to have a recent Zip or CD-R with you data so you can work on another computer in the interim.

- ✔ **Make space for upgrading.** Crawling under your desk to get at your Mac's case? Along with enough time to do the job, you need to have enough space to do it well. Clear an area 5 feet by 5 feet (or so) on a largish table so you can see all the components and keep track of what you're doing. (It's also nice to have enough room to sit or stand comfortably.) You'll also want a little room for this book, too.

- ✔ **Don't spill.** Keep the Cheetos and RC Cola as far away from the Mac as you can stand to have them.

- ✔ **Try not to sparkle.** Electrically ground yourself when upgrading any computer components. A wrist or ankle grounding strap is best. Otherwise, you should touch a metal part of your Mac's case while it's still plugged in and then don't move around much (especially on carpet) to keep from generating more static.

- ✔ **Don't get too touchy-feely.** Handle circuit boards by the edges to avoid touching leads, contacts, connectors, and components on those boards. Also, store your circuit boards in antistatic bags, where they won't be stacked, have metal dragged across them, and so on.

✔ **Keep a bowl or coffee cup handy.** Ashtrays that people inexplicably bring home from casinos can also be useful for this task: managing loose screws. You'll be tempted to store these screws in your mouth or between the shags of your shag carpet, but that certainly isn't recommended. You will *not* remember what each screws was for and where you put it. Instead, a few coffee cups or similar storage devices help you keep track of screws and other tidbits.

✔ **Save and label everything.** You can use masking tape or office-supply labels to remind you what a wire is for and the orientation of its connector.

✔ **Think things through.** I've actually been sitting there, with my only computer in two pieces on my desk, thinking to myself "I'll just hop on the Internet for more instructions." What's the problem with this scenario? Consider whether you'll be a similar bind, and download and print instructions or troubleshooting advice ahead of time (or have another computer ready for those tasks). And if you read through the instructions first, you might see something in Line #20 that you need to prepare for now, before you start disassembling things.

✔ **Make one change at a time.** You're doing the big changeover — RAM, a processor card, a video card — and you want to see all that souped-up performance at once. Fight the urge. If you change one component at a time, you'll have better luck tracking down trouble if it occurs. Perform the upgrade or fix, button everything up, and test your Mac. Then break it all down again and perform the next upgrade. Saving time by changing more than one item will waste time if you need to troubleshoot.

✔ **Don't leave the case off.** All Mac cases were designed by engineers to help airflow over the components to keep them cool. Running your Mac with the case off for any length of time might cause the components to run hotter than necessary. (Yes, even though there's lots of air flowing, it might not be flowing correctly.) You can leave the case off some Macs while you're testing to see whether the upgrade or fix was successful; after that, though, button things up quickly.

# Open Up and Say Ah!

I don't have enough room to cover how to open every Mac's case (that's better left to *Macworld Mac Upgrade and Repair Bible*, which has nearly a thousand pages to burn!), but I hit some of the highlights in this section. If you have your Mac's original *User's Guide,* you might find hints in there, as well.

If you have a Mac OS clone (such as those from Power Computing, Motorola, or Umax, among others), you'll find, for the most part, that you remove a few screws on the back of the case and lift the top off the case's chassis. I'll show you an example a little later in this section.

Planning to open up your iMac? Check out Chapter 19, where I detail the instructions for getting inside and upgrading the little bugger.

Apple cases have gone through many different iterations, sometimes bouncing back and forth between the theory of ultimate user accessibility and closed-case designs to keep the intrepid user out. In this section, I stick to machines designed to be opened by mere mortals.

In fact, it's easy to pin down Apple's upgrade-friendly machines in three basic categories, which I call the slip-and-slide, pop-top, and open-sesame designs. If your Mac doesn't fit one of these categories, refer to your documentation or *Macworld Mac Upgrade and Repair Bible* for details on your system.

## The slip-and-slide design

When Apple wanted to make a consumer-friendly, upgradable Mac in the past, it often resorted to the slip-and-slide design, where the logic board of the Mac simply slides out for easy upgrading. Usually, you either pull down tabs or remove screws on the back of the Mac, and then you grab a handle or handles and pull the logic board. It slides out, revealing all the available slots (RAM, cache RAM, and upgrade card slots, usually).

Macs that fit this category follow:

- **Mac Classic and Color Classic** have small tabs that are pressed down to pull away the rear panel (see Figure 13-1). Remove the retaining screws and then pull the small handle to pull out the logic board.

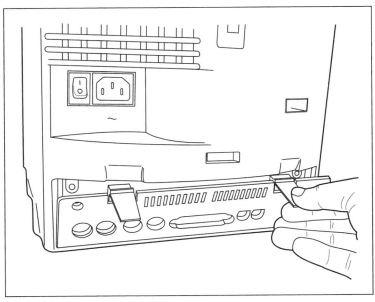

**Figure 13-1:**
The Mac Classic and Color Classic were the first to include a rear panel that pulls away to reveal a pull-out logic board.

✓ **Quadra, Centris, and Performa 630, 6200, and 6300** have two small tabs on their rear panel that you push down while rotating the panel downward to open it (see Figure 13-2). Then, after removing the retaining screws, extend the metal handle and use it to slide out the logic board (see Figure 13-3).

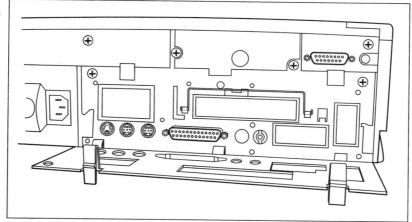

**Figure 13-2:** The 630, 6200, and 6300 enclosure has a pull-down panel, revealing a small metal handle for sliding out the logic board.

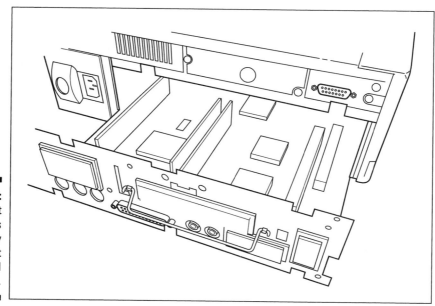

**Figure 13-3:** Slide-out logic boards make it easy to get at internal components.

✔ **LC, Performa models 520, 550, 575, and 580, and MacTV** have two retaining screws that you must remove first. Then you use the tabs to open the back panel. Grab the exposed metal handle and pull straight back to slide out the logic board.

✔ **Performa and Power Macintosh 5200, 5300, and 5400 series** have two retaining screws that you must remove. Then reach under the back plate, locate the tabs, and press down to release them. Lift the plate up and off the back panel and then grab the metal handle and pull straight back to slide out the logic board.

✔ **Performa 6400 and Power Macintosh 6500** have two retaining screws that you must remove. Then grab the plastic handles and slide the logic board out of the back of the Mac.

After you have a logic board out of one of these Macs, make sure you keep the area as static free as possible and don't bend, warp, or put pressure on the logic board. When you've finished upgrading, you slide the logic board back in — check to make sure it's aligned properly and don't force it if it simply doesn't want to slide. It should slide fairly easily in its slot until it meets with the connector deep in the machine; then you might need to give it a little extra push to secure the logic board completely. (Once secure, the logic board should be flush with the back of the Mac, ready to accept its retaining screws or plastic panel.)

You might have noticed that these slide-out logic boards don't give you access to internal areas of the Mac where you might install a hard drive or a removable drive. Very perceptive. The fact is, some of these cases aren't designed to allow you entry for upgrading the drives because most of these Macs don't offer available drive bays (areas where you can install internal drives).

Some do, however. Among those noted, the 630, 6200, and 6300 will allow entry from the front (see Figure 13-4) as will the 6400/6500 machines (see Figure 13-5). On the 6400/6500 series, you push up on the buttons underneath the bottom of the case's front, and then you pull the front away from the machine. It's tough to do and it makes a lot of noise.

The 6400/6500 also features a front bay for an internal SCSI removable drive (such as a Zip or an Orb) on models that didn't ship with a preinstalled Zip drive. (If you like, you can remove the Zip drive.)

If you're worried about doing harm by prying open these cases, you can simply opt for external drives, using the Mac's external SCSI ports. There's much less mess that way. If you do damage the plastic on your Mac, though, it's usually easy and inexpensive to replace through an Apple dealer or service center.

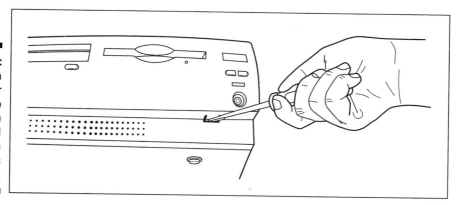

**Figure 13-4:**
Use a screwdriver to press up slightly on the tabs and release the front of this case.

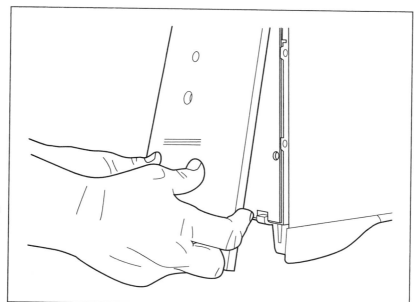

**Figure 13-5:**
Prying open the 6400/6500 series.

## *The pop-top design*

Apple has made some machines that were designed to be workhorses, with the assumption that the user or a system administrator would need to get inside them every once in a while. These machines were designed to be opened up and rooted around in, so you'll find, for the most part, that they're easy to work with when you're upgrading internally.

The only caveat? Because most of the Macs that fit this design scheme are older, they tend to have a screw or two to contend with. Others have tops designed to pop off, but they might take some digital maneuverability (good hands).

Macs that fit this general description follow:

✔ **Mac II, IIx, and IIfx** open by pushing the plastic buttons in the top corners of the back of the Mac and lifting the top off the Mac's chassis. These machines might have a center-mounted retaining screw to remove before popping open.

✔ **Mac IIcx, IIci, IIsi, and Quadra 700** open by lifting up on the tabs and pulling the top (or side) away from the Mac's chassis. Watch for a single retaining screw on many of these models.

✔ **LC, LC II, LC III, Quadra 605, and Performa 400 series,** or the pizza box Macs, also have a single retaining screw and a tab. They're best opened, however, by reaching across from the front and popping the tabs up (see Figure 13-6).

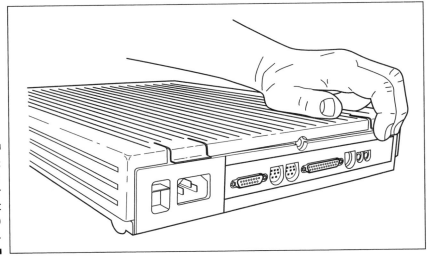

**Figure 13-6:**
Many Mac models offer tabs that you pop up to release.

✔ **Mac IIvx, IIvi, Centris 650, Quadra 650, Performa 600, and Power Macintosh 7100 series** all have a single retaining screw and a top that doesn't quite pop as much as it just slides off the chassis, as shown in Figure 13-7.

✔ **Centris 610/660AV, Quadra 610/660AV, Power Macintosh 6100, and Performa 6110 series** all have pretty typical pop-open cases with two tabs in the back. The tabs take a little muscle to pop open, but there's no retaining screw. Just pop the tabs and pull the top up and slightly forward to remove it from the chassis (you need to get that front plastic to clear the CD-ROM and floppy drives).

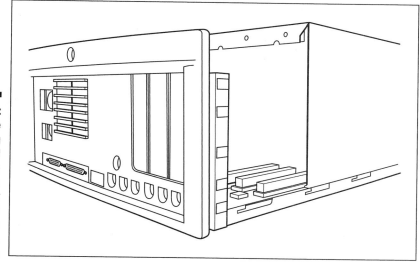

**Figure 13-7:**
Remove the retaining screw and then slide the case slightly forward and lift it off the chassis.

✔ **Quadra 800, Quadra 840AV, Quadra 900 series, Power Macintosh 8100 series, 8500, and most Mac OS clones** are the most boring designs, offering a tower case with top and side panels that come off as a unit. Remove the four retaining screws (thumbscrews or Phillips screws) on the back of the Mac. Then lift the top up and forward to pull it of the Mac's chassis (see Figure 13-8).

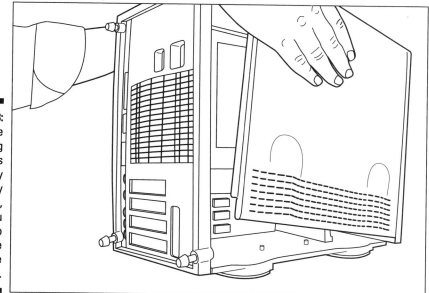

**Figure 13-8:**
These boring tower cases are usually pretty easy to get into, but you have to remove some screws first.

Most pop-top cases go back on even easier than the way they came off — you line up the top carefully and press down on the case until the tabs snap into place. On non-tab cases, you need to place the top of the Mac back on the chassis from the front (make sure everything lines up correctly on each side, too), slide it toward the back of the Mac until it's flush, and then replace the retaining screw(s).

On cases that don't have tabs, you might want to tilt the case onto the chassis in the exact reverse of the way you got the case on. Remember that the case needs to line up correctly with your drives up front as well as with the hole(s) for the retaining screw(s).

## The open-sesame design

As time has worn on, Apple's professional-level Macs have become easier and easier to get into. For the pros, Apple assumes that getting inside the Mac is a given — you have to upgrade RAM, cards, and other internals every once in a while — so the engineers have made it progressively easier.

Here are the easy-open designs:

- ✔ **Power Macintosh 7200, 7300, 7500, 7600, and G3 desktop** all have a desktop enclosure (as opposed to a minitower) that opens *all* the way up to reveal the logic board. You begin by reaching under the front panel of the case to locate the tabs, and then you push the tabs up and slide the case toward you, as shown in Figure 13-9. The case comes completely off. Next (with the Mac unplugged), swing a small metal foot around so that it's sticking out from the outside edge of the drive cage (the metal cage where the internal drives are installed). Finally, release the green tabs (push them down) and swing the drive cage all the way out of the chassis to reveal the logic board.

- ✔ **Power Macintosh 8600, 9600, and G3 tower** all have a small button on the top of the case that, when pushed, enables you to pull the side away from the Mac. Now turn the case so that it's resting with this open side up, and then release the two tabs that hold the drive cage in place. Swing the cage out of the Mac's chassis to reveal the logic board.

- ✔ **Power Macintosh blue G3 and Power Macintosh G4** are the most innovative so far, with a side door that simply falls open. Place your finger in the hole on the side of the Mac and pull up on the door's latch. Open the door to reveal the Mac's logic board and available drive bays (see Figure 13-10).

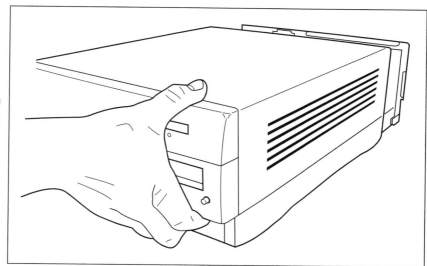

**Figure 13-9:**
You slide the top off the case first, and then you can swing it open to access the logic board.

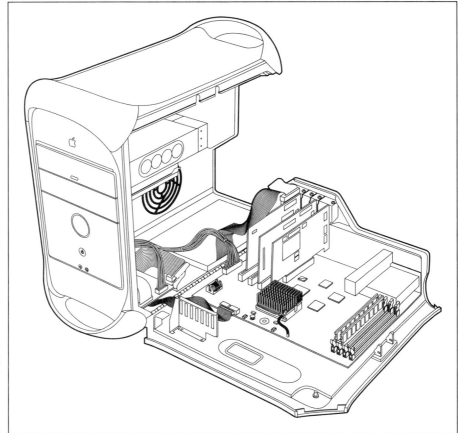

**Figure 13-10:**
The blue G3
and the
Power
Macintosh
G4 are both
amazingly
easy to get
into for
upgrading
and trouble-
shooting.

# Chapter 14

# Playing Cards: Upgrading with PDS, PCI, and NuBus

*W*hen the original Mac 128k design was finalized, a conscious decision was made, most say by Steve Jobs personally, to avoid including an expansion slot. The thinking seemed to be that Macs were supposed to be the easiest computers in the world to use, so they shouldn't have confusing internal expansion capabilities.

Fifteen years later, Jobs was once again CEO and, once again, they built an iMac without an expansion slot? Co-ink-ee-dink? I don't think so.

But the promise of upgrade slots is a siren song: Buy a card, plug it in, and you have a whole new capability for your Mac. Wouldn't it be cool if your brain worked this way?

Upgrade cards aren't as easy as adding external devices, but they're pretty simple nonetheless. What sort of stuff can you add? With an expansion card, you can give your Mac USB or FireWire ports, faster video, multimedia, networking capabilities, or quite a few other capabilities.

In this chapter, you check out the different technologies used for upgrade cards. Then you look at a slew of possible upgrades and the companies that make them. I end with a double-lux and death-spiral finale in which I fling you across the ice as if you were a discarded matador's cape.

# Expansion Cards: PDS, NuBus, PCI, and More

By the time Apple got around to the Mac SE, just a little while after the original slotless Macs, the company opted to give it a special PDS slot. The Mac II rolled out with six NuBus slots, which was almost an apology for the original Mac's lack of slots.

Since that time, all Mac models except the Mac Classic, Mac TV, and iMac have offered slots, although the technologies have varied: PDS, PCI, NuBus, AGP, communications slot — even a special slot on some Performas for a TV tuner.

Some of these upgrading technologies are getting a little long in the tooth. Apple hasn't made a machine with NuBus or PDS slots in over five years, so it's getting tougher to find expansion cards that will fit in those slots. These days, most upgrade cards are designed for a PCI slot, which is both faster and a cross-platform standard, with PCI cards available on both Macs and Intel-compatible PCs. But you can't add PCI slots to an older Mac.

What are all these technologies and what do they mean? Stay tuned.

## Processor Direct Slots

The Processor Direct Slot, or PDS, was introduced in the Mac SE, where it allowed the user to add a video card for presenting video on an external, larger monitor. Eventually, it was also useful for processor upgrades and cards that boosted the speed and RAM capacity of the Mac. Like PDS slots in other Mac models, the PDS slot in the Mac SE was specific to the Mac SE and cards had to be designed to support it.

By definition, a processor direct card must be tailored to a specific machine or series of similar machines. (For instance, an LC PDS card has to be different than the Mac SE PDS card, which has to be different than a Power Macintosh 6100 PDS card.) This differentiates PDS from NuBus or PCI, which are both expansion bus technologies. Because the processor communicates with expansion cards through the expansion bus, the cards can be more easily interchanged than PDS cards.

PDS connectors are usually black and look like actual slots, accepting a card with a flat circuit-board connector that slips into the slot. All Macs with PDS slots have only one PDS slot.

PDS survived for quite a while; even the first generation of Power Macintosh machines, for instance, offer PDS slots that are used these days for G3 and G4 upgrades. Later PowerPC-based Performa models also sport a PDS slot, although it can't be used for processor upgrades and was never used for much else, as it turns out.

## NuBus cards

NuBus doesn't have a direct connection to the processor; instead, it's an *expansion bus technology* that allows compatible cards to work with a wide variety of processors. It's sort of like having to go through an assistant to talk to the big boss.

NuBus is a 32-bit-wide expansion technology; even early Macs had fairly sophisticated expansion capabilities compared to their Intel-compatible brethren. (If your assistant is 32 bits wide, it means he or she hasn't seen enough manual labor since you decided to have all the coffee catered by MoonCash Coffee. In fact, that's a huge problem around my office — the only exercise my assistant ever gets is carrying in the ice sculpture every day.)

NuBus slots are usually gray in appearance and are actually *sockets* that accept pins from the card. The bottom of the card has a plastic housing that fits over the connector when plugged in.

The theoretical limit in one Mac is sixteen NuBus slots, although no Mac has ever had more than six — and that only happened in the Mac II and Mac IIfx. Having even five NuBus slots (Quadra 900 and 950) was rare. More often, Macs were configured with three NuBus slots or one slot, especially in tighter cases.

NuBus cards are self-configuring, so you simply install them in their slots and start up your Mac to use them. The Mac OS gives each NuBus card a number and then manages interaction between the CPU and the cards through *bus interface units,* which are chips on the logic board.

The last Macs to include NuBus slots were the first-generation Power Macintosh models (6100, 7100, and 8100), including Mac OS clones based on those technologies (the Radius 80 and the Power 100 and 120 machines). After that, Apple switched to the PCI standard, which is still in use today.

## Peripheral Component Interconnect

Any Mac based on a second-generation PowerPC processor (a 603- or 604-level processor) or newer, as well as a few PowerPC 601 stragglers, such as the Power Mac 7200, offer the *PCI expansion bus* instead of NuBus slots. The PCI, or

Peripheral Component Interconnect, standard enables faster connections than NuBus cards, making it better for demanding tasks such as digitizing video and network or Internet communications cards.

Although 64-bit PCI is possible, it's usually implemented as 32-bit technology, like NuBus, but it runs at 33 MHz, which means it can transfer up to 133MB per second.

Intel originated the PCI standard, so PCI has the advantage of being cross-platform. In many cases, the same PCI card can be used in a Mac and in a PC, as long as each platform has drivers written specifically for it. That's made the Mac upgrade card a bit more competitive, because we can get hand-me-downs from PC manufacturers looking to squeeze a few extra bucks out of a card they've designed for PC users. Of course, plenty of Mac-only cards are available, including some that, ironically, allow your Mac to run Windows applications, such as those manufactured by Orange Micro (www.orangemicro.com).

PCI cards come in two basic sizes 7 inches (short) and 12 inches (long), depending on how much circuitry needs to be crammed on the board to get its features working (see Figure 14-1). Some Mac models don't support a 12-inch PCI board, so you'll want to check your Mac's documentation before buying one.

**Figure 14-1:**
PCI cards can range in size.

PCI slots are similar to PDS slots (that is, they look like *slots,* not sockets) although they're generally white instead of black. Most PCI-based Macs have either three or six slots, although some Mac models (often Performa models) have one PCI slot that accepts only short cards.

More recent Macs have offered some interesting PCI updates. In Power Macintosh G3 and G4 machines, the main PCI slots now support 64-bit cards running at 33 MHz (just in case you come across one). The Power Macintosh G3 also offers a special 32-bit, 66-Mhz slot that's used for the included video card.

## Accelerated Graphics Port

The Accelerated Graphics Port, or AGP, has become popular in more recent Mac models, including the slot-loading iMac or the Power Macintosh G4, as 3-D graphics requirements have become more intense. AGP is based on the PCI standard but is designed specifically for demanding graphics.

It's a 32-bit-wide port that runs at 66 MHz, translating into double the bandwidth (266MB per second) of regular PCI. And that's just for 1x AGP. The standard has been extended to 2x (or 133 MHz, meaning 532MB per second) and even 4x (1.07GB per second). The Power Macintosh G4 offers a 2x AGP slot (except for the slowest model, the 350 MHz Power Macintosh G4, which offers the same 66 MHz PCI slot as a Power Macintosh G3).

The AGP slot is similar in appearance to a PCI slot but shorter (see Figure 14-2). On Mac models, the AGP slot tends to be filled with an ATI graphics card, which ships standard with all current Power Macintosh G4 models. That doesn't preclude you from putting a different card in that slot, although you'd have to remove the current video card first.

## Special utility slots

PCI, NuBus, and PDS are standard types of upgrade cards in Macs, but they're not the only types. Apple isn't above tossing us a curve ball, especially in the form of extra one-hit-wonder slots designed for a particular upgrade.

Almost all these slots have appeared in the Performa line of computers (although some have sneaked into all-in-one Power Macintosh models, such as the 5400 and 5500 series, that shared their innards with similar Performas). These home- and education-oriented Macs offer special slots designed for networking and modem cards (communications slot), adding a TV tuner, and capturing digital video. The upgrade cards that Apple offered for these slots were a little cheaper than the typical PCI or NuBus version.

These days, you can still find Ethernet upgrades for the comm slot, but it's tough to find upgrades for the video or tuner slots, unless you look on the used market. And be aware that there are two different versions of the comm slot — Comm Slot I and Comm Slot II (based on PCI). If you buy a used modem, for instance, make sure it fits the comm slot in your Mac.

It so happens that the Power Macintosh G3 and G4 include a special internal modem slot, although the slot is different from the Performa's communications slot. If your Power Mac didn't ship with a modem, you can get an internal model from Global Village (www.globalvillage.com) that will fit the slot easily. You can also find cards that use that port to add an old-style serial port to your newer Mac, such as the gPort from Griffin Technology (www.griffintechnology.com).

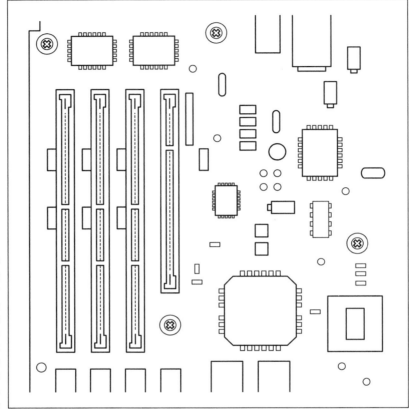

**Figure 14-2:**
In a Power
Macintosh
G4, the three
slots on the
left are PCI;
the fourth
slot (on the
right) is AGP.

# Installing Expansion Cards

Regardless of the type of card you're installing, the process will probably be similar. At the most, you have one less screw to worry about with some cards. In any case, give yourself around 15 minutes for the upgrade, including a little time to test it out. Also keep track of your screws and, if you're the studious type, make sure you have a good backup of your important data.

Here's how to add an expansion card:

1. **Shut down your Mac and electrically ground yourself, preferably with a grounding strap, as discussed in Chapter 13.**

2. **Open the Mac's case and locate an empty expansion slot.**

   Take a good look at the slot and make sure that it's the right type for the card you bought.

3. **Remove the slot's screw and metal dust plate, which covers the hole in the back of the case.**

   For some upgrades, such as many PDS cards, this won't be necessary because the slot doesn't butt up against the back of the machine. In a few cases, you might need to install a special adapter in the slot. (For instance, the Power Macintosh 6100 requires a special adapter to change its PDS slot into a NuBus slot; if you're installing a PDS card, though, the adapter isn't necessary.)

4. **Position the card so that its interface is directly over the slot.**

   If you have a NuBus card, the card's plastic lip should fit over the slot on the logic board. With a PDS or a PCI card, make sure the card is lined up correctly over the slot.

5. **Press down lightly and uniformly on the top corners of the card until it's firmly in place.**

   If one end is higher than the other, parts of the connector might not be making proper contact, and the card will fail to work.

6. **If you like, you can plug in your keyboard and monitor and quickly turn on the Mac (with the case off) to test for the new card.**

   You might need to install software before the card can be used, although you're most likely to be able to see it in the Apple System Profiler with or without its software loaded. If it does show up in the System Profiler, shut down again and close up your Mac.

That's it. If the card has been installed correctly and you've installed the software that came with it, you should now be able to configure the card and use it to accomplish wonders, according to the card's nature.

Which brings us to an interesting point. What-all *can* these expansion cards do? Can they sing the blues?

# The Wonderful World of Expansion Cards

Expansion cards can take on a wide variety of duties, most of which extend your Mac's capabilities. Adding expansion cards can give you more external ports, speed up your video, add networking capabilities, or even turn your Mac into a multimedia workstation.

In this section, I briefly move through the different technologies you can add with an expansion card. (I save a few for other chapters, such as SCSI and IDE cards in Chapter 17 and networking cards in Chapter 18.) This might not be an exhaustive list, but I promise it was exhausting to compile. Come with me. Take my hand.

---

## Troubleshooting expansion cards

You won't encounter much troubleshooting with expansion cards; most of the time they just work. If you're having trouble with a card, you have three primary issues to worry about.

First, if you can't find the card at all (it doesn't show up in the Apple System Profiler, for instance), you might not have the card properly seated in its slot. Shut down, open things back up, and make sure the card is properly installed. Don't screw it down too tight in the back, though. Just secure it to the case.

Second, you might occasionally encounter a card that's picky about its slot. If your Mac has PCI slots, the slot closest to the center of the logic board is often the *bus-mastering slot,* or the slot that has more control over traffic on the PCI bus. If your card wants to be in that slot, you might need to move things around to accommodate it.

Third, think software. A lot of expansion cards require a control panel, a Mac OS extension, or both to work properly. If that software is conflicting with other software, you might have trouble. If adding the card seems to have contributed to more crashing and other bad behavior on your Mac, troubleshoot for a conflict, as discussed in Chapter 20.

---

# *Adding video capabilities*

Nearly all Macs ship with built-in video, either in the form of chips on the logic board or an included expansion card. Depending on your Mac model and your needs, this video circuitry might be more than adequate.

But if you find that you can't get enough colors on your screen, you can't go to high enough resolutions ,or you'd like to use more than one monitor, you need a video expansion card. Such a card gives you another video port out the back of your Mac, allowing you to explore higher speed, higher capability video. Nearly all third-party video cards are *accelerator* cards, which can speed up 2-D and 3-D graphics — even games — on your existing Mac.

### *Choosing the right video card*

After you've decided you want a new video card, you need to consider some factors:

- ✔ **Upgrade card technology.** You have to get a card that will fit an available slot in your Mac. Cards are generally available in PDS (for some early Macs), NuBus, and PCI varieties. All but PCI video cards might require you to do some hunting because there aren't too many NuBus and PDS cards sold anymore.

Don't forget about the AGP slot if you have a Power Macintosh G4 (or higher). You need to replace the card that your Mac shipped with, but you might get better performance if you plug a new, high-end accelerator into that 66 MHz slot.

✔ **VRAM.** Buy a card with the most VRAM that you can afford, up to a point. Although 8MB of VRAM will give you millions of colors for most resolutions, 3-D accelerator cards can use even more RAM — 16MB, 32MB, or more — to speed up screen draws and 3-D elements.

✔ **Acceleration.** Look for acceleration but don't overspend if you're not a computer artist or a serious gamer. For regular tasks, look for a card that accelerates 2-D draw. High-end professional cards generally accelerate QuickDraw 3D (also called Rave) tasks; gaming cards often offer VooDoo (also called Glide) or OpenGL acceleration to speed up the gaming experience. Which type of 3-D acceleration you choose depends on the type of acceleration that your games support. (Some adapters support more than one type of acceleration with driver software.)

You install a video adapter card in the same way you install any upgrade card. The only issue is the port coming out of the back of the card — it must fit your monitor. If it doesn't, you might need an adapter. Macadapter (www .macadapter.com/) and Griffin Technologies (www.griffintechnology .com/) are both good sources for adapters.

Table 14-1 shows some popular video adapter manufacturers and their products.

| Table 14-1 | Video Adapter Manufacturers for Macintosh | | |
|---|---|---|---|
| *Company* | *3-D Acceleration* | *Slots Supported* | *Web Site* |
| ixMicro | Glide, RAVE | PCI | www.ixmicro.com |
| ATI | OpenGL, RAVE | PCI | www.ati.com |
| VillageTronic | Glide, RAVE | PCI, NuBus | www.villagetronic.com |
| Formac | OpenGL, RAVE | PCI, AGP | www.formac.com |

## Getting double vision

If you've installed a new video card, you likely have two sets of video circuitry (the new card and the old video you already had) at your disposal. If you also have two monitors, you can connect them both and use both monitors at once — the capability is built right into the Mac OS. With two monitors, you can literally mouse from one to the other, effectively doubling (or more) the amount of screen real estate you have for windows and applications.

## Step into some serious VooDoo

Among the competing acceleration standards is VooDoo technology offered by 3DFx, Inc. Many VooDoo accelerators aren't video adapters — that is, they can't be used on their own to connect a monitor. Instead, they work with your existing video card. (Usually, you plug the video card into the accelerator card using a two-sided monitor cable, and then you plug your monitor into the accelerator card.)

Because they aren't full-featured video cards, they don't have to be as Mac specific. PCI-based VooDoo accelerators are available from many different PC manufacturers; all you need is Macintosh driver software (and a Flash ROM updater), which can be downloaded for free from www.3dfx.com. So, get yourself any VooDoo3 2000 or VooDoo3 3000 accelerator and download the drivers. (Note: In the future, 3Dfx might also support newer VooDoo4 and VooDoo5 standards with downloadable Mac drivers.)

Start up your Mac with the two monitors connected. Then open the Monitors or Monitors & Sound control panel. If the Mac OS has recognized both monitors, they appear in the control panel, with each screen numbered 1, 2, and so on.

How you manage the two monitors depends on your Mac OS version. In some, you see a simple window that allows you to arrange each monitor (Figure 14-3). In later OS versions, you see control panels for each monitor (Figure 14-4).

**Figure 14-3:**
In earlier Mac OS versions, you arrange the monitors using a single control panel.

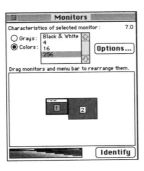

In either case, you'll be able to *arrange* the monitors using the control panel so that you can determine which monitor is on the left and which is on the right (or top and bottom, if you desire). If you're not sure which monitor is which, click the Identify button and each monitor's number will appear on-screen. Arrange the monitors so that the mousing is logical — when you mouse off the right side of the leftmost monitor, for example, you want to show up on the left side of the rightmost monitor.

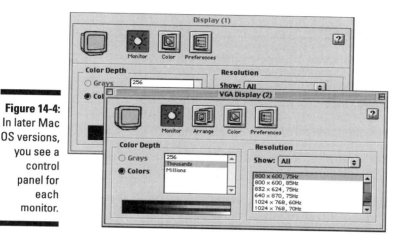

**Figure 14-4:**
In later Mac OS versions, you see a control panel for each monitor.

You can use the control panel to set the resolution of each monitor separately; they can have different resolutions and color depths with no adverse effects. Also in the control panel (usually in the Arrange section), you can drag the menu bar from one screen to the other. The menu bar determines which is the main screen, where applications launch and commands are accessed.

## *Video capture and TV cards*

Beyond computer video, expansion cards can infuse your Mac with the capability to digitize video, play back video, and tune in TV channels right on your screen. In fact, your Mac may have these capabilities built in, or you might be able to add them with a special card. In other cases, a regular NuBus or PCI card will let you get TV signals into your Mac.

Before we get too deep into this, check out Table 14-2 for some manufacturers of such cards.

| Table 14-2 | Manufacturers of Video Editing and Tuner Cards | |
|---|---|---|
| *Manufacturer* | *Type of Cards* | *Web Site* |
| Digital Origin | Video editing | www.digitalorigin.com |
| Avid | Video editing | www.avid.com |
| Aurora Video Systems | Video editing | www.auroravideosys.com |
| Pinnacle Systems | Video editing | www.pinnaclesys.com |

*(continued)*

### Table 14-2 *(continued)*

| Manufacturer | Type of Cards | Web Site |
|---|---|---|
| Media 100 | Video editing | www.media100.com |
| ATI Technologies | TV tuner | www.ati.com |
| ixMicro | TV tuner | www.ixmicro.com |
| Formac | Video editing, TV tuner | www.formac.com |

### *Joining the video-in club*

Want to edit movies? You can get a video clip off a camcorder and into your Mac in two basic ways. The easiest way is using FireWire, as discussed in Chapter 12. Unfortunately, this solution requires not only FireWire ports but also a DV camcorder, which not all of us have.

If you have a regular analog camcorder (of the VHS, Super8, or Betamax variety) or even a pro-level analog camera, you need to *digitize* that video to get it into your Mac for editing. The digitizing process turns an analog video signal into a digital computer file, so that the video can be edited using software. Digitizing requires special hardware, which may or may not be built into your Mac. Macs that include built-in digitizing capabilities are Quadra/Centris 660AV, Quadra 840AV, Power Macintosh 6100AV, 7100AV, 8100AV, Power Macintosh 8500, 8600, and the original beige G3 minitower. All these models have RCA video-in and -out connectors; some also have S-video connectors.

In the Performa line, many models offer a special upgrade slot for video expansion, ideally filled with a card Apple used to sell called the Apple Video Card. Models include the Performa 630, 5200, 5300, 5400, 5500, 6200, 6300, 6400, and 6500. (Quadra and Power Macintosh models with those same model numbers also include the video slot.) In fact, some of those models may have shipped with the card installed; if you have RCA-style video ports on your Performa, you have the card installed.

In other cases, you need to add a video card. Then you can connect a VCR, a TV, or a camcorder to the video-in ports on the card using either RCA-style connectors or S-video cable (which offers better quality). Next, using software, you import the video, turning it into a QuickTime movie (in most cases) or another type of movie file. Finally, you can edit the video and add effects to it using video editing software such as Final Cut Pro (Apple), After Effects (Adobe) or VideoShop (Strata, www.strata.com).

When you finish editing, you hook up a recording device (again, a camcorder or a VCR) to the video-out ports on your Mac or on your video expansion card, and then you send the video out to the device. It's laid down to tape so that it can be played back using typical video equipment.

### Or just watch TV

Couch potato? Now you can be a desk chair potato, too, with a TV tuner card. Install such a card and you can plug in a cable TV, an antenna, or even a game console (such as a Sony Playstation or Nintendo set) and tune in the TV picture right on your desktop.

In some cases, you get a remote control (especially for Macs with built-in infrared ports). In other cases, your TV tuner software is also able to capture video to a file. In still other cases, the software isn't able to do any of these things: You just sit there with CNN (or more likely, the Sci-Fi channel) on your Mac desktop.

On AV Macs (those with built-in video capabilities) and Macs with an Apple TV tuner card, you can use the Apple Video Player software to watch TV. In conjunction with the TV tuner card, the player can be used to change channels and assign on-screen descriptions for each station. On AV Macs, you need an external tuner (such as a VCR), which you hook up to your Mac's video input. Then you can use Apple Video Player to watch television (or even a videotape) on-screen. In either case, you can use the player for screen captures or to digitize video clips.

## Add-a-port

If you have an available PCI slot in your Mac, you can add all those ports you've been wishing your Mac had: multiple serial ports, USB ports, or even FireWire. Or if you're lucky, you can find cards that offer a combination of these. All you do is plug in the card and start up your Mac: Suddenly you have additional ports for your devices. (Some require that driver software be installed.) Table 14-3 shows some such cards.

| Table 14-3 | Manufacturers Offering Port Expansion Cards | |
|---|---|---|
| *Manufacturer* | *Type of Ports Added* | *Web Site* |
| Adaptec | FireWire | www.adaptec.com |
| Promax | FireWire | www.promax.com |
| Swann | FireWire | www.swann.com |
| Entrega | USB | www.entrega.com |
| Macally | USB, FireWire | www.macally.com |

*(continued)*

**Table 14-3 *(continued)***

| Manufacturer | Type of Ports Added | Web Site |
|---|---|---|
| XLR8 | USB | www.xlr8.com |
| Ariston | USB, FireWire | www.ariston.com |
| Keyspan | Serial ports, USB | www.keyspan.com |
| Apple | FireWire | www.apple.com |
| OrangeMicro | FireWire, USB and FireWire combo | www.orangemicro.com |

Remember that the more physical ports on the card, the more devices you can easily connect. That said, having more than one USB port, for instance, doesn't necessarily mean you have more than one USB bus. Dual-bus USB cards enable you to boot off USB devices (using Mac OS 9 or higher), so you might consider that possibility in your shopping.

# Chapter 15

# Improving Your Memory

*R*AM is the first upgrade you should consider if you plan to get inside your Mac, which is why I've brilliantly decided to bury this chapter deep in the middle of the book. (It seemed to make sense during all our planning meetings.) After you've figured out how to get inside your Mac, you might find that a RAM upgrade is your first, and most important, upgrading step.

In this chapter, I talk about how to get more RAM, what RAM you need, and how to install it. Then, even when you do have more RAM, you need to set up your applications so they take advantage of it. Finally, with all the time left over thanks to the speed-up from our RAM upgrades, maybe you can grab a ball and head out to the park for a little game of catch. Just you and me.

# Get More RAM!

Sure, RAM won't fix a tragically slow Mac. But it will help almost any Mac. The more RAM you have, the less *virtual memory* (hard disk swapping) your Mac uses. Accessing data on the hard disk is slower than accessing it in RAM, so the more hard disk swapping there is, the slower your Mac computes.

Plus, you can never have too much RAM. It's like cola in my household; if it's there, I'll drink it. Even if you have plenty of RAM to keep your Mac from swapping to disk, you can still use additional RAM for a variety of reasons. A RAM disk, for instance, lets you store documents and applications in a *virtual* disk — actually, it's a portion of RAM. Files stored in this part of RAM act as if they're on a removable disk but can be accessed much more quickly. You can use a RAM disk to speed up games (by storing their data files on the RAM disk), speed up Web browsers (by storing their cache files on the RAM disk), or for any files that you'd like to be able to read and write to very quickly. (See Figure 15-1.)

**Figure 15-1:**
A RAM acts
like a
removable
disk.

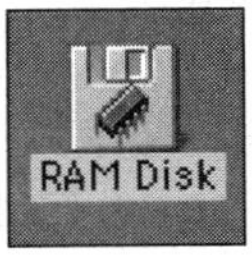

So how much RAM is enough? The rules become outmoded quickly. Today, Apple ships most of its systems with 64MB of RAM, standard. If you plan to run Mac OS 9 or higher, 64MB is a workable minimum. For any sort of graphical, multimedia, or gaming tasks, 96 or 128MB is recommended as a good starting point. For professional-level computing, especially in multimedia (such as image manipulation or digital video production), 128MB should be a minimum, with 256MB a common number.

Apple is now routinely releasing Macs that can support over 1.5GB of RAM, so the days of half-to-full gigabyte systems are upon us. If you're a pro-level Mac user, don't be surprised if you begin to find that 256MB of RAM is a good amount for a mid-range machine.

## How much RAM do you have?

Not sure how much RAM you have? The quick way to find out is to switch to the Finder and choose About this Macintosh or About this Computer from the Apple menu. (Different Mac OS versions have different commands.) The result is a dialog box, such as the one shown in Figure 15-2.

In this dialog box you see *Built-in Memory,* which represents the amount of actual, physical RAM that's installed in your Mac using memory chips. You also see the *Virtual Memory* number. This represents the total amount of main memory your Mac has at its disposal, including both real RAM and hard-disk swapping space.

If you have a lot of physical RAM, you can leave virtual memory set to a small number — usually 1 megabyte over the Built-in Memory number. This allows you to take some advantage of virtual memory without allowing too much swapping to disk. If you have *gobs* of memory, you can do away with virtual memory altogether. This is often ideal for multimedia production: working with CD-R, MP3, digital video and other such tasks. You turn virtual memory on and off (along with setting the amount to use) in the Memory control panel, shown in Figure 15-3.

Physical RAM

**Figure 15-2:**
The About
this
Computer
dialog box.

Total memory

If you have tons of RAM (128MB, 256MB, or more), you can try turning virtual memory off; you get a nice speed boost. (Turn it back on if you get out-of-memory errors.) If you have a decent amount of RAM (64MB to 128MB), you can set virtual memory at 1MB over the physical RAM amount (for instance, 65MB in a 64MB system). If you're hurting for RAM, set virtual memory up to 10MB over installed RAM, as in 40MB or so for a Mac with 32MB installed.

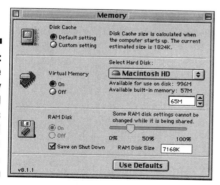

**Figure 15-3:**
The
Memory
control
panel lets
you parcel
available
memory.

Aside from setting virtual memory, you can also determine how much RAM is used for a cache and how much is used for a RAM disk. The *cache* allows for slightly speedier processing, enabling the Mac to store often-used data in a special portion of RAM. (This is different from *cache RAM,* which is discussed later in the chapter.) The RAM disk, as mentioned, can speed things up as well.

So, you see immediately that having a ton of memory can be a good thing. After you have it installed, you can turn down virtual memory, turn up cache, and turn on a RAM disk, making things that much more sprightly.

Back in Figure 15-2 you might have noticed something else — the About this Computer dialog box also shows your open applications and how much RAM each is using. This can be useful in your quest to determine how much RAM you need. Each Mac application requires a RAM setting — not enough RAM and the application will run slower or even crash. Too much RAM, and you're taking away from other applications. Changing an application's RAM allocation is a common troubleshooting technique. Fortunately, we've got it covered, later in this chapter.

# Types of RAM

Before you can head out and buy yourself some new RAM, you need to know what sizes and shapes it comes in. Over the years, new RAM technologies have changed the way RAM is installed in many Mac models — the age and technology behind your Mac determines what type of RAM needs to be installed in it.

## Module sizes

When you go to look into RAM types, you see them advertised three or four different ways. Although they might be superficially similar, it's important to get the right type of module for your Mac. Here's a look:

- **SIMM (single inline memory module).** SIMMs come in 30-, 64-, and 72-pin varieties, and were used in nearly any model built before the early 1990s — everything from the Mac Plus, through the Mac II series, and on up to the first Quadra 700, 900, and 950 models. All of these used 30-pin SIMMs, with the lone exception, before 1991, of the Mac IIfx, which required a very weird 64-pin SIMM. Later models used 72-pins SIMMs, which were wider and could run a little faster — in fact some of these models were designed to run with 60 nanosecond (ns) SIMMs, although others required 70 or 80 ns SIMMs.

- **DIMM (dual inline memory module).** Similar to a SIMM, a DIMM just packs more RAM on a slightly larger module. With the second generation of Power Macintosh machines came 168-pin DIMMs. These original DIMMs were generally rated at 60 or 70 ns and ran in 5400, 6400, and 6500 series machines as well as Power Macintosh 7200, 7300, 7500, 7600, 8500, 8600, 9600, beige Power Macintosh G3, and the 20th Anniversary Macintosh.

✔ **SO-DIMM (small outline — dual inline memory module).** The original iMac and some PowerBook modules have used these smaller, 72-pin or 144-pin versions of DIMMs. They can run very quickly — 10 ns — and fit into tighter spaces on the logic board. They're also a little pricier, thanks to their compact size.

✔ **PC100.** This is actually a 168-pin DIMM, but one designed specifically to work on a 100 MHz logic board, such as those in the blue Power Macintosh G3, slot-loading iMacs, iMac DV models, and the Power Macintosh G4 series.

RAM modules are generally standard across the computing industry, so you can, for instance, buy PC100 DIMMs designed to work in both Macs and PCs. Your model might have somewhat specific ratings, though, so it's best to buy your RAM from an authorized dealer who has a good idea what your Mac model needs. (You can also consult the table later in this chapter for general guidance.)

### DIMM technologies

On top of the different circuit board sizes and nanosecond ratings, working with DIMMs introduces some additional RAM technologies you'll encounter when trying to upgrade. Here's a quick list:

✔ **Fast page mode (FPM)** is probably the most typical type of DIMM in Power Macs. Most Macs support FPM as a least-common denominator, with only a few models requiring other types. (G3 Macs require still another type, SDRAM). FPM speeds up operations over traditional DRAM by organizing RAM into rows and columns.

✔ **Extended data out (EDO)** RAM works on the same principle as FPM except that it leaves its output buffer on while accessing memory, allowing the memory controller to access one memory address and look ahead to the next memory address at the same time. This results in about a 10 percent speed boost for read operations, which is a slight gain in speed but probably not noticeable in day-to-day work. EDO is a subset of FPM, so EDO usually works in any system that supports FPM. If your Mac already has FPM and you add EDO, EDO RAM acts as FPM in the mixed system. The Power Macintosh 4400, 5500, and 6500 require EDO RAM, as does the Performa 6400/200 with a built-in Zip drive.

The only (pre-G3) Power Macintosh model that specifically forbids EDO RAM is the 7200, which can be damaged by EDO DIMMs. Also, note that the 4400 series requires 3.3-volt EDO memory whereas the Power Macintosh 5500, 6500, and 6400/200 computers require 5-volt EDO. The two types of EDO memory are NOT interchangeable, according to Apple's tech support.

✔ **Synchronous dynamic random access memory (SDRAM)** has a clock speed that's synchronized with the Mac's CPU, eliminating the difference between memory speed and processor speeds. Data is delivered continuously to the processor and no wait states are introduced, resulting in memory access speeds that are 20 percent faster than EDO. SDRAM (5 volt) is supported in the Power Macintosh 4400 for video RAM only. It's also used in the beige Power Macintosh G3 desktop and minitower machines. SO-DIMMs and PC100 DIMMs are also SDRAM-based, so all modern Macs use this technology, too.

### iMacs and new Power Macs

The original iMac series (the tray-loading models) require SDRAM-based SO-DIMM modules; fast page mode (FPM) or extended data out (EDO) RAM won't work with iMacs. You might also have to watch the SO-DIMMs on an iMac 233 (the original Bondi Blue model), which is only certified by Apple to handle 64MB SO-DIMMs. Apple Support admits that the iMac 233 might work with larger SO-DIMMs, but it's a good idea to check with your retailer, too, and make sure they warranty the DIMM as compatible.

SO-DIMMs are not all alike, with both 72-pin and 144-pin versions available, as well as different speed ratings and other certifications. Your best bet is to find a vendor that offers SO-DIMMs that are specifically marketed as iMac-compatible.

The blue-and-white Power Macintosh G3, slot-loading iMac, and Power Macintosh G4 machines use PC100 modules. Ready for a mouthful? If you're buying RAM for one of these machines, here's what you're looking for: 64-bit bus, non-parity, 168-pin, 3.3-volt, unbuffered, PC-100 compliant, 8 ns refresh rate.

PC100 DIMMs have speed ratings that vary from 3-2-3 (the slowest) to 3-2-2 to 2-2-2. Although all are supported on Apple's models, 2-2-2 DIMMs are the fastest and are recommended by Apple. The Mac sets its speed to that of the slowest DIMM in the machine, so if you do want the best performance, make sure all your PC100 modules are 2-2-2 DIMMs. (In fact, for the highest speeds possible, you might have to remove the 3-2-2 DIMM that might have shipped with your Power Macintosh G3 or G4.)

According to Apple Tech support, a long line of statistics are not supported on the PC100 DIMM for the Power Macintosh G3 and G4 series. PC100 DIMMs with registers, buffers, PLLs, or EDO RAM are not supported. The maximum supported height of the DIMM cards is 2 inches. You should also avoid DIMMs with fewer than 4 or more than 16 chips, according to Apple support, even if the DIMM is supposed to be PC-100 compatible.

# *Your Mac's RAM requirements*

If you're ready to dig in and change the amount of RAM in your Mac, you need to figure out how much RAM your Mac can handle. Wouldn't a table help right about now? Check out Table 15-1 for guidance and wisdom.

| Table 15-1 | | | Apple Mac Model RAM Upgrades | | | |
|---|---|---|---|---|---|---|
| **Model** | **Base RAM** | **Max RAM** | **Slots** | **Type** | **Speed** | **Groups of...** |
| Classic | 1MB | 4MB | 2 | 30-pin SIMM | 120 ns | 2 |
| Classic II | 2MB | 10MB | 2 | 30-pin SIMM | 100 ns | 2 |
| Color Classic | 4MB | 10MB | 2 | 30-pin SIMM | 100 ns | 2 |
| Col.Classic II | 4MB | 36MB | 1 | 72-pin SIMM | 80 ns | 1 |
| Plus/SE | 1MB | 4MB | 4 | 30-pin SIMM | 150 ns | 2 |
| SE/30 | 1MB | 32MB | 8 | 30-pin SIMM | 120 ns | 4 |
| Mac II | 1MB | 20MB | 8 | 30-pin SIMM | 120 ns | 4 |
| Mac IIx | 1MB | 32MB | 8 | 30-pin SIMM | 120 ns | 4 |
| IIcx | 1MB | 128MB | 8 | 30-pin SIMM | 120 ns | 4 |
| IIci | 1MB | 128MB | 8 | 30-pin SIMM | 80 ns | 4 |
| IIsi | 1MB | 17MB | 4 | 30-pin SIMM | 100 ns | 4 |
| IIvi, Iivx | 4MB | 68MB | 4 | 30-pin SIMM | 80 ns | 4 |
| IIfx[*] | 4MB | 128MB | 8 | 64-pin SIMM | 80 ns | 4 |
| Mac TV | 4MB | 8MB | 1 | 72-pin SIMM | 80 ns | 1 |
| LCPerforma 200 | 2MB | 10MB | 2 | 30-pin SIMM | 100 ns | 2 |
| LC II, Performa 250, 400, 405, 410, 430 | 4MB | 10MB | 2 | 30-pin SIMM | 100 ns | 2 |
| LC III/III+, 475, 520, 550, 575; Performa 275, 450, 460, 466, 467, 475, 476, 520, 550, 560, 575, 577, 578 | 4MB | 36MB | 1 | 72-pin SIMM | 80 ns | 1 |

*(continued)*

**Table 15-1** *(continued)*

| Model | Base RAM | Max RAM | Slots | Type | Speed | Groups of... |
|---|---|---|---|---|---|---|
| Performa 600 | 4MB | 68MB | 4 | 30-pin SIMM | 80 ns | 1 |
| Performa 580, 588, LC580 | 8MB | 52MB | 2 | 72-pin SIMM | 80 ns | 1 |
| Performa 630, 630CD, 635CD, 636CD, 637CD, 638CDLC630, Quadra 630 | 4MB | 36MB | 1 | 72-pin SIMM | 80 ns | 1 |
| Performa 630DOS, 631CD, 640DOS | 8MB | 52MB | 2 | 72-pin SIMM | 80 ns | 1 |
| Quadra 605 | 4MB | 36MB | 1 | 72-pin SIMM | 80 ns | 1 |
| Centris 610, Quadra 610, 610DOS | 4MB | 68MB | 2 | 72-pin SIMM | 80 ns | 1 |
| Centris 650, Quadra 650 | 4MB° | 132MB° | 4 | 72-pin SIMM | 80 ns | 1 |
| Centris, Quadra 660AV | 4MB | 68MB | 2 | 72-pin SIMM | 70 ns | 1 |
| Quadra 700 | 4MB | 20MB | 4 | 30-pin SIMM | 80 ns | 4 |
| Quadra 800 | 8MB | 136MB | 4 | 72-pin SIMM | 60 ns | 1 |
| Quadra 840AV | 4MB | 128MB | 4 | 72-pin SIMM | 60 ns | 1 |
| Quadra 900, 950 | 4MB | 256MB | 16 | 30-pin SIMM | 80 ns | 4 |
| PM 6100, 6100AV, 6100/DOS; Performa 6110, 6112, 6115, 6116, 6117, 6118 | 8MB | 72MB | 2 | 72-pin SIMM | 80 ns | 2 |
| PM 7100, 7100AV | 8MB | 136MB | 4 | 72-pin SIMM | 80 ns | 2 |
| PM 8100, 8100AV, 8110, 8115 | 8MB | 264MB | 8 | 72-pin SIMM | 80 ns | 2 |
| PM 8100/110 | 16MB | 264MB | 8 | 72-pin SIMM | 80 ns | 2 |

| Model | Base RAM | Max RAM | Slots | Type | Speed | Groups of... |
|---|---|---|---|---|---|---|
| Performa 5200, 5210, 5215, 5220, 5260, 5270, PM 5200/75 | 8MB | 64MB | 2 | 72-pin SIMM | 80 ns | 1 |
| Performa 5260, 5270, 5300, 5320, Power Mac 5260/100, 5260/120, 5300/100 | 16MB | 64MB | 2 | 72-pin SIMM | 80 ns | 1 |
| Performa 5400, 5400/160, 5400/180, 5410, 5420, 5430, 5440, PM 5400/120, 5400/180 | 16MB | 136MB | 2 | 168-pin DIMM | 70 ns | 1 |
| PM 5400/200 | 24MB | 136MB | 2 | 168-pin DIMM | 70 ns | 1 |
| PM 5500/225, 5500/250 | 32MB | 128MB | 2 | 168-pin DIMM | 60 ns | 1 |
| Performa 6200, 6205, 6214, 6216, 6260, 6290 | 8MB | 64MB | 2 | 72-pin SIMM | 80 ns | 1 |
| Performa 6210, 6218, 6220, 6230, 6300, 6310, 6320 | 16MB | 64MB | 2 | 72-pin SIMM | 80 ns | 1 |
| Performa 6360, 6400/180, 6400/200, 6410 | 16MB | 136MB | 2 | 168-pin DIMM | 70 ns | 1 |
| PM 4400/160 | 16MB | 96MB | 3 | 168-pin DIMM | 60 ns | 1 |
| PM 4400/200 | 16MB | 160MB | 3 | 168-pin DIMM | 60 ns | 1 |
| PM 4400PC | 32MB | 160MB | 3 | 168-pin DIMM | 60 ns | 1 |
| PM 6500 series | 32MB† | 128MB | 2 | 168-pin DIMM | 60 ns | 1 |
| PM 7200 series | 8MB | 256MB | 4 | 168-pin DIMM | 60 ns | 1 |
| PM 7215/90 | 16MB | 256MB | 4 | 168-pin DIMM | 70 ns | 1 |
| PM 7220/200 | 16MB | 160MB | 3 | 168-pin DIMM | 60 ns | 1 |
| PM 7300/166, 7300/180 | 16MB | 512MB | 8 | 168-pin DIMM | 70 ns | 1 |

*(continued)*

### Table 15-1 *(continued)*

| Model | Base RAM | Max RAM | Slots | Type | Speed | Groups of... |
|---|---|---|---|---|---|---|
| PM 7300/180PC, 7300/200 | 32MB | 512MB | 8 | 168-pin DIMM | 70 ns | 1 |
| PM 7500, 7600 | 8MB | 512MB | 8 | 168-pin DIMM | 70 ns | 1 |
| PM 7600/200 | 32MB | 512MB | 8 | 168-pin DIMM | 70 ns | 1 |
| PM 8200/100 | 8MB | 256MB | 4 | 168-pin DIMM | 70 ns | 1 |
| PM 8200/120 | 16MB | 256MB | 4 | 168-pin DIMM | 70 ns | 1 |
| PM 8500 | 16MB | 512MB | 8 | 168-pin DIMM | 70 ns | 1 |
| PM 8600 | 32MB | 512MB | 8 | 168-pin DIMM | 70 ns | 1 |
| PM 9500 series | 8 or 16MB | 768MB | 12 | 168-pin DIMM | 70 ns | 1 |
| PM 9500/180MP, 9600/200, 9600/ 200MP, 9600/233 | 32MB | 768MB | 12 | 168-pin DIMM | 70 ns | 1 |
| PM 9600/300, 9600/350 | 64MB | 768MB | 12 | 168-pin DIMM | 70 ns | 1 |
| PM G3 beige Desktop | 32MB | 192MB | 3 | 168-pin DIMM (SDRAM) | 10 ns | 1 |
| PM G3 beige Minitower | 32MB | 384MB | 3 | 168-pin DIMM (SDRAM) | 10 ns | 1 |
| PM G3 (blue) | 32MB | 1GB | 4 | PC100 | 100 MHz | 1 |
| PM G4 | 64MB | 1.5GB | 4 | PC100 | 100 MHz | 1 |
| 20th Anniversary Mac | 32MB | 128MB | 2 | 168-pin DIMM | 60 ns | 1 |
| iMac 233, 266, 333 | 32MB | 256MB | 2 | 144-pin SO-DIMM | 10 ns | 1 |
| iMac 350, iMac DV | 64MB § | 512MB | 2 | PC100 | 100 MHz | 1 |

*The IIfx requires its own special 64-pin SIMM.*

° *The Quadra 650 later came with 8MB of base RAM, which raised its limit to 136MB.*

†*The Power Macintosh 6500 Small Business Edition bundle came with 48MB of RAM; the 6500/300 offered 64MB.*

§ *The iMac DV SE model shipped with 128MB of base RAM standard.*

All Mac models ship with a base amount of memory — sometimes this memory is soldered onto the logic board and sometimes it's installed as a module. Generally, all models also offer at least one other slot for upgrading RAM. In some cases, you need to install more than one SIMM at once for the upgrade to work correctly. That's noted in the "Groups of" column in Table 15-1.

Also, before you decide to buy new RAM, you should pop open you Mac and visually make sure that you have available RAM slots. Even if you only have 4 or 8MB of RAM, it's possible that the RAM is distributed in such a way that it's filling all your available slots. If you don't have slots available, you might need to replace existing RAM in your system with a larger module.

GURU, a freeware program from NewerRAM (www.newerram.com), offers information and advice on upgrading the RAM in nearly any Mac model. Some models even include diagrams to make it clear exactly how to maximize your Mac's use of RAM.

# Installing RAM

Although installing RAM means opening up your Mac and dealing with its innards, you probably won't have much trouble. RAM is considered user-serviceable in Macs — upgrading it doesn't affect your warranty and is pretty easy to do. On many models, Apple even makes it easier by exposing the RAM slots and making them easier to get at.

That's not to say you shouldn't be careful with RAM modules, which are particularly susceptible to static electricity discharge. Here are some tips:

✔ Electrically ground yourself and keep your RAM modules away from static, liquid, or other trauma.

✔ Store RAM in the antistatic pouch it came in (or, if you're replacing older RAM, store the older module in the antistatic pouch that the new RAM arrived in).

✔ Don't touch the contacts (the gold or tin pins) on a RAM module. Instead, handle it by the top corners.

✔ Don't force RAM into its socket — if it doesn't go in fairly simply, you might have it turned the wrong way. As a general rule, SIMM modules go in at a 45-degree angle and then tilt up to 90 degrees. DIMMs are installed straight into the socket (at a 90-degree angle to the logic board). Nearly all modules have notches that help you line them up with the socket, which means they install in only one direction.

As mentioned in Chapter 13, it is dangerous to go inside the early Macs — Plus, SE, and SE/30 — because of their exposed monitor housing. Consider taking these Macs to a qualified service center.

## Installing a SIMM

If you're installing a SIMM in an older Mac, here's what you should expect:

1. **Shut down the Mac, ground yourself electrically, and unplug the Mac.**

   If you've read Chapter 13 and decided that you're a leave-it-plugged-in person, more power to you. (Excuse the pun.)

2. **Open the Mac's case.**

3. **Find an empty RAM module slot.**

4. **Make sure you have the module turned in the right direction.**

   The module should fit into the memory slot at a 45-degree angle to the logic board. (See Figure 15-4.) The module might also have notches that determine the direction that you should install it; if it doesn't fit, turn it around.

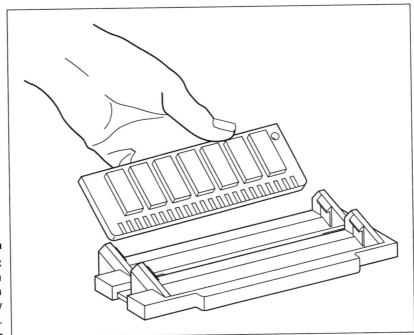

**Figure 15-4:**
Inserting a
SIMM in a
memory
slot.

5. **With the module pushed into the memory slot at a 45-degree angle, tilt the module up until it locks into the slot at 90 degrees.**

   In some cases, little metal or plastic hooks grab the module and hold it in place.

6. **Insert any other modules if your Mac requires more than one at a time.**

Now close up the Mac and restart. If you get past the startup tone (and don't hear other, odd tones), wait until the desktop appears, and then choose the About this Computer or About this Macintosh command from the Apple menu. Check the Built-in Memory entry to see whether the new amount of RAM is reflected. If it is, you've succeeded!

If the RAM isn't recognized, shut down and make sure you've seated the RAM correctly in its slot. If you have empty slots, try another slot. If the RAM still isn't recognized, make sure your Mac model doesn't require that two (or more) SIMMs be installed at once or doesn't require memory banks to be filled in a specific order. (Your Mac's manual or the GURU software can help with this.) If that's not the problem, the memory module might be bad — take it to a service center for testing.

RAM doesn't really *go* bad — it's a solid-state technology. It can *be* bad — either defective from the manufacturer, damaged after a static electricity discharge, or damaged by power surges. If you're having trouble with RAM, you'll usually experience that trouble at startup time. See Chapters 23 for help.

If you have an older Mac — Mac SE/30, Mac II, Mac IIx, or Mac IIcx — you might need to turn on 32-bit addressing to get full use of your RAM upgrade. If you don't see the full amount of your added RAM in the About this Macintosh window, open the Memory control panel and turn on 32-bit addressing. (If you don't have that option, you might need to custom install the 32-bit System Enabler or update to System 7.5.5.)

## Installing a DIMM

Installing a DIMM is a little different than installing a SIMM. It's all about how you line things up:

1. **Shut down the Mac, ground yourself electrically, and unplug the Mac.**

2. **Open the Mac's case.**

3. **Find an empty RAM DIMM slot.**

4. **Visually line up the notches on the bottom of the DIMM with the ridges in the DIMM slot on the logic board.**

   If the two don't match up (so that the DIMM would fit in the socket), turn the DIMM around.

5. **Push the DIMM straight down into the slot.**

   Don't insert it at an angle. If all goes well, the release levers on each side of the DIMM lock into place. (See Figure 15-5.)

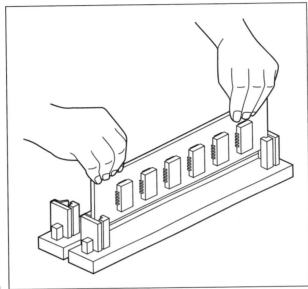

**Figure 15-5:**
Installing a
DIMM —
look Ma,
no angles!

To release the DIMM, you simply push down on the locking levers on each side of the DIMM slot. This should pop the DIMM right out.

Sometimes you get a RAM module that just doesn't fit — don't force it. You should buy your RAM modules from dealers who understand Macs and offer a return policy — sometimes you get the wrong module, or sometimes a module that's supposed to be right simply doesn't fit. Check your Mac's stats again, and then return the module if necessary.

# Augmenting Other Memory

Aside from main memory, your Mac uses RAM in some other ways as well. Cache RAM is used to speed up main memory a bit — if your Mac doesn't have optimum cache memory, you might see a nice boost after you install some. Video RAM improves your Mac's capability to display colors and resolutions, enabling you to install bigger monitors and get more accomplished in your graphics programs.

# Cache RAM

In Chapter 2, I briefly discussed cache RAM, the type that's used for high-speed access to small bits of relevant data. Earlier Power Macintosh, PowerPC-based Performas (such as the 6200, 6300, and 6400) and many Quadra-level machines benefit from a cache RAM upgrade. These Mac systems can accept cache RAM upgrades that are placed in a special cache RAM slot on the logic board. The upgrade is simple — it's pretty much the same as installing a RAM DIMM, except you use the special cache RAM socket.

Check your manual to see whether your Mac has a socket for cache RAM — if it does, you can install it just as you would a regular RAM module. The cache RAM module *isn't* a regular SIMM or DIMM, though; it's special high-speed memory that needs to be designed for your particular Mac model. Cache RAM is often rather expensive ($50 to $100 per megabyte), but you'll use less of it. You'll also usually find it only at Mac-specific dealers.

Older Mac modules can accept a cache PDS card, which usually helps to speed the machine up by 10 to 20 percent or so. If you won't be using your Mac II's PDS slot for a processor card, consider a cache RAM card, which gives you a smaller speed boost but is also cheaper. ( Try www.micromac.com, www.milagromac.com, or www.nexcomp.com.)

On some Macs, the cache RAM socket has been used by enterprising upgrade manufacturers to offer a G3 or G4 upgrade for aging Macs. Models such as the 4400, 6360, 6400, 6500, and Twentieth Anniversary Macs as well as many Mac clone models benefit from these processor upgrades, which are discussed in Chapter 16.

# VRAM

Video RAM ( VRAM ) is an animal similar to cache RAM — you need to get special modules for your particular Mac model. VRAM gives your video circuitry more memory to work with, allowing it to display more colors or higher resolutions than it can without the upgrade. Chapter 7 discusses these technologies in more depth.

Not all Mac models can accept a VRAM upgrade. However, many Quadra models, mid-range Power Macs, the original Power Macintosh G3, and the original iMac can be upgraded, as can many Mac OS clone models. VRAM upgrades vary somewhat in their implementation: Some Macs require special cards, others require SIMMs, and still others have more specialized modules. Again, your Mac manual, a Mac dealer, or the GURU software should be able to help you decide whether your Mac can accept a VRAM upgrade.

# Configuring Application Memory

What if people could actually dedicate some brain-power to specific tasks? Suppose you could take a chunk of your memory and set it aside for counting cards in Vegas or memorizing trivia for one of those big-money game shows? Or what if you could just clear out high-school gym class memory, for instance, and use it to store French lessons?

If you have a decent chunk of RAM in your Mac, parceling it up is the next step to running things efficiently. Aside from turning off virtual memory or using a RAM disk (as discussed earlier in the "Get More RAM" section), you also need to configure your applications to take advantage of the new RAM. Here's how to increase the allotted RAM for a particular application, for increased efficiency or to combat out-of-memory errors:

1. **Shut down the application (choose File ⇨ Quit in the application's menu.)**

2. **In the Finder, locate and highlight the application's icon.**

3. **Choose File ⇨ Get Info.**

   The Get Info window appears.

4. **In the View list, select Memory.**

5. **In the Preferred Size box, enter a larger number.**

   Start by adding 10 to 15% more RAM. The application is allotted the additional RAM only if that much RAM is available.

6. **Click the close box.**

Launch the application again; the Mac OS should give it the new memory amount. Test the application and see whether the error has been solved.

If you're having other memory problems, try and remember that there's more coverage in Chapter 20. (You might want to jot that down quickly.)

# Chapter 16

# The Need for Speed: Processor Upgrades

*I*f you're interested in changing the way you work with your Mac, you might have turned directly to this chapter. After all, the processor is the brains of your Mac — so upgrading the processor will make it smarter, right? Well . . . it will make it faster in most cases, especially if you already have plenty of RAM. (If you *don't* have plenty of RAM, you have to read Chapter 15 before you read this one. I don't want to give away the surprise ending.)

The processor isn't the bottleneck for all Mac slowdowns, but it can be a big contributor to many of them. Do you notice the programs themselves "thinking" slowly — graphics programs that take a long time to render images, games that run too slowly to be fun, Web pages that take forever to redraw, or spreadsheets and charts that take too long to tally? In that case, you might be in need of a processor overhaul. If you happen to have the right Mac model, upgrading the processor is simple. For other models, unfortunately, processor upgrades are impossible.

## Making Processor Upgrade Decisions

Not all Macs are easily upgraded. Most offer a solution of some sort, but a few exceptions exist. Others Macs offer more than one way to upgrade them; which you choose depends mostly on your budget and the features you'd like. First, though, you might want to think through whether or not you want to upgrade at all.

The two basic reasons to upgrade the processor are better speed and compatibility with newer applications. Most processor upgrades fit the better speed category; they raise your Mac's speed from, say, a PowerPC 604e to a PowerPC G4. That's a nice boost to keep your Mac humming for another year or two.

The second reason to upgrade the processor is for better compatibility. PowerPC upgrades for Quadra-level (and other pre-PowerPC) Macs don't speed up too many operations. (The speed boost exists but isn't terribly significant compared to the modern G3 or G4 processor.) Instead, they offer you the opportunity to use *PowerPC-native* applications — those written specifically to run on Macs with PowerPC processors.

Note, though, that upgrading to a PowerPC G3 or G4 processor might not get you over one particular compatibility hump: the capability to run Mac OS X. Apple says Mac OS X won't be compatible with Macs that have been upgraded to G3 or G4. (And since it hasn't been released at the time of this writing, I have to take Apple's word for it.) So, before buying such an upgrade, check around and see whether anyone has figured out how to get it to work with Mac OS X. Your first stop might be my www.mac-upgrade.com/ Web site, where I post new info.

## Types of upgrades

The next step is figuring out which type of processor upgrade will work with your Mac. (Sometimes you might even have a choice between one type of upgrade or another.) If you're upgrading your processor, you can take one of these approaches:

- ✔ **Expansion card.** Many earlier Mac models have a special *processor direct slot* (PDS) that can be used for a processor upgrade. Although not all models with a processor direct slot can use it for an upgrade, many can, from the Color Classic to the first-generation (6100, 7100, 8100) Power Macs. Figure 16-1 shows a PDS processor expansion card. This type of upgrade always requires a Mac OS extension to work properly. Also, PDS cards must be specifically designed for your model of Mac — they aren't interchangeable.

- ✔ **Processor (CPU).** A Mac's processor is usually either *soldered* on the motherboard — which means it's affixed by heating metal that then cools to form a seal — or socketed. With a *socketed* processor, you can lift the processor out and replace it with another one. This is exactly the approach taken to upgrade many Mac II-models. It's also the approach used to upgrade many Power Macintosh G3 machines to higher speeds.

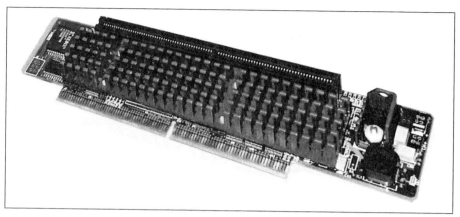

✔ **Daughtercard.** If your Mac supports a daughtercard upgrade, you're lucky. These are like expansion cards, but they hold the processor and often the secondary cache on the card. This makes it possible to simply slip the current processor daughtercard out of your Mac and slip the new one in. These upgrades usually don't require additional software, which makes them more compatible and stable that many other upgrades.

A popular twist on the idea of the daughtercard is the *carrier card.* These daughtercards place their processors in a ZIF socket, allowing you in the future to upgrade just the processor. Ideally, such a card lets you continue to upgrade your processor again and again without replacing the daughtercard.

✔ **Cache slot upgrade.** Whereas daughtercards are an obvious and easy way to upgrade the processor, cache slot upgrades are a feat of cleverism (to coin an *ism*). For quite some time, many Mac models — led by the popular Performa 6400 and the Motorola series of Mac clones — seemed utterly un-upgradable. (The Mac market tends to call these *upgrade-challenged.*) Enterprising engineers figured out that they could add an upgrade through the cache RAM slot on those Macs, effectively boosting them to G3 (and sometimes G4) speeds. These upgrades always require a Mac OS extension, so they're a little less reliable than some others. But it's a great way to get G3 in upgrade-challenged Mac models.

✔ **Logic board.** The best and the worst upgrade is a logic board replacement. In some cases, the only way to give a Mac a speed boost is to swap its logic board. And doing so gives you a whole new Mac — only the case stays the same. Unfortunately, swapping a logic board is difficult, and logic boards are tough to find. (Often people will ask me, "Why not just buy a newer computer and then swap the logic board into the older computer," to which I invariably reply, "Why not just buy the newer computer and use it?")

Logic board upgrades are difficult — most often best left to professionals. The exception is the slide-in/slide-out logic board that many Mac models use, discussed in Chapter 13. Some of those can be upgraded with newer logic boards just by performing a little sliding magic. Micromac (www.micromac.com) offers a number of these for older Performa models.

If your Mac model offers an upgrade path, the upgrade is likely very easy to perform. Most Macs that can be upgraded are *easily* upgraded; those that can't be upgraded are only upgraded with *decidedly more difficulty.* In fact, the only way to upgrade some Macs is to learn to count very quickly on your fingers, effectively making your Mac a dual-processor model.

## *Where to get upgrades*

When the PowerPC G3 processor first came on the scene, a slew of upgrade companies appeared to sell G3 upgrades to the owners of daughtercard-based, second-generation Power Macs and Mac OS clones. As the boom wore on, some of these companies went out of business, while others starting getting creative, finding ways to upgrade even older Macs through PDS or cache RAM slots.

---

### Your bus speed

How quickly you get to school depends on the speed of your bus; the same can be said for how quickly your Mac's upgrade processor runs. Allow me to explain before I segue across four lanes of traffic like that again.

Your Mac's logic board has a system bus that transfers data between the processor and RAM. The speed of that bus determines the potential speed of your processor because the processor must be a multiple of the bus speed. For instance, if your bus runs at 50 MHz (standard for many second-generation Power Macs), you need a processor that runs at 350, 400, or 500 MHz. If you have a 40-MHz bus, you need a processor that runs at 240, 320, or 400 MHz. (In some cases, a 1.5 multiplier will work, too.)

What this means is that a slower bus can affect the top-end speed of your processor upgrade. A Power Macintosh 6100/60, for instance, has a bus speed of 30 MHz. Because most G3 upgrades are limited to an 8x multiplier, the top speed in most cases is 240 MHz for a G3 upgrade in a 6100. (Some manufacturers have pushed G3 and G4 upgrades to 9x and 10x multipliers.)

Bottom line? Shop carefully when you're upgrading an older, slower Power Mac. In the case of a 6100, for instance, a 300-MHz G3 might be no better than an upgrade advertised at 240 MHz, because neither will run faster than 240 MHz in that machine. Read the fine print and ask the customer support rep for the highest speed your Mac model will support.

Those companies that remain tend to offer specialized high-speed processors or a full array of various upgrades. Sonnet Technologies, for instance, offers not only the latest G4 upgrades but also upgrades for Quadras, Mac IIs, and various Performa models. Micromac almost exclusively serves the low end with upgrades for older 68020 and 68030 processors. In fact, Micromac offers a lot of solutions for Macs that can't otherwise be upgraded.

Take a look at Table 16-1, which shows some of the manufacturers of Mac processor upgrades and the types of products they offer. (Note that Bottom Line and Other World Computing are retailers that offer their own branded upgrades.) Also, the product levels shown in the table are the currently offered models (at the time of writing), not every model ever offered by the company. Many of these manufacturers once offered 604e upgrades, for instance, that they no longer make or sell.

| Table 16-1 | Processor Upgrade Manufacturers | |
|---|---|---|
| *Company* | *Level of Products* | *URL* |
| Sonnet Technologies | 030, 040, PPC, G3, G4 | www.sonnettech.com/ |
| Bottom Line (Railgun) | G3, G4 | www.blol.com/ |
| Other World Computing (Z-Force) | G3, G4 | www.macsales.com/ |
| Newer Technologies | G3, G4 | www.newertech.com/ |
| PowerLogix | G3, G4 | www.powerlogix.com/ |
| XLR8 | PPC, G3, G4 | www.xlr8.com/ |
| Micromac | 030, 040, PPC | www.micromac.com/ |

Micromac offers a special MacSpec database you can use to determine whether your Macintosh model (especially older Mac models) offers an upgrade path. See www.micromac.com/macspec/ to look up your Mac.

# The Big For Dummies Guide to Processors and Upgrades

Now for the big table, Table 16-2. In this one, you see pretty much every Mac model ever made and its current upgradability. When a particular Mac is upgradable, all currently available (at the time of writing) methods for upgrading that model's processor are listed in the Upgradable? column. So skim the list and see how your Mac fares. (Note that new upgrades are always possible, so if yours appears in the list as non-upgradable, you might want to stop by my Web site, `www.mac-upgrade.com/`, to make sure no new upgrade technologies have been discovered.)

In the table, *030* stands for 68030 and *040* stands for 68040. Likewise, *PM* stands for Power Macintosh and *L2* stands for cache slot. Finally, note that if a computer is already a 68030 and it's upgradable to a 68030, this is usually because the upgrade doubles the speed of the processor (or better). The same is true for some 68040 upgrades.

| Table 16-2 | Macintosh Processor Upgrades | | |
|---|---|---|---|
| *Mac OS Model* | *Original Processor* | *Upgradable?* | *Upgrade Technology* |
| Mac 128/512/Plus | 68000 | No° | n/a |
| Classic/Classic II | 68000/68030 | No° | n/a |
| Color Classic, Color Classic II | 68030 | 040 | PDS, logic board |
| SE, SE/30 | 68000, 68030 | 030 | PDS |
| Mac II | 68020 | 030 | CPU |
| Mac IIx, IIcx, IIci, IIsi | 68030 | 040 | PDS |
| IIvi, IIvx | 68030 | 040* | PDS, logic board |
| IIfx | 68030 | No | n/a |
| LC, LC II | 68020, 68030 | 030, 040 | CPU, PDS, logic board |
| LC III/III+ | 68030 | 040 | PDS, logic board |
| LC 520, Performa 520 | 68030 | 040 | PDS, logic board |
| LC 550, Performa 550, Performa 560 | 68030 | 040 | PDS, logic board |
| Performa 200 | 68030 | No | n/a |
| Performa 250, 275 | 68030 | 040 | PDS |
| Performa 400, 405, 410, 430 | 68030 | 040 | CPU, PDS, logic board |
| Performa 450, 460, 466, 467, 600, 600CD | 68030 | 040 | PDS, logic board |
| Performa 475, 476, 575, 577, 578, LC575 | 68LC040 | No* | n/a |

| Mac OS Model | Original Processor | Upgradable? | Upgrade Technology |
|---|---|---|---|
| Performa 580, 588, LC580 | 68LC040 | PPC 603* | Logic board |
| Mac TV | 68030 | No | n/a |
| Performa 630, 630CD, 631CD, 635CD, 636CD, 637CD, 638CD, LC630, Quadra 630 | 68LC040 | PPC 603* | Logic board |
| Quadra 605 | 68LC040 | No* | n/a |
| Centris 610 | 68LC040 | 040, PPC 601 | CPU, PDS |
| Quadra 610, 610DOS, 650 | 68040 | 040, PPC 601 | CPU, PDS |
| Centris, Quadra 660AV | 68040 | 040 | CPU |
| Quadra 700, 900 | 68040 | 040, PPC 601 | CPU, PDS |
| Quadra 800, 950 | 68040 | PPC 601 | PDS |
| Quadra 840AV | 68040 | No° | n/a |
| PM 6100, 6100AV, 6100/DOS, Performa 6110 series | PPC 601 | PPC G3, G4 | PDS |
| PM 7100, 7100AV | PPC 601 | PPC G3, G4 | PDS |
| PM 8100, 8100AV, 8110, 8115 | PPC 601 | PPC G3, G4° | PDS |
| Performa 5200, 5210, 5215, 5220, Power Mac, 5200/75 | PPC 603 | No | n/a |
| Performa 5260, 5270, 5300, Power Mac 5260/100, 5300/100 | PPC 603e | No | n/a |
| Performa 5260/120, 5280, 5320, PM 5260/120 | PPC 603e | No | n/a |
| Performa/Power Mac 5400 series, 5500 series | PPC 603e | PPC G3 | L2 |
| Performa 6200 series, 6300 series | PPC 603,603e | No | n/a |

*(continued)*

**Table 16-2** *(continued)*

| Mac OS Model | Original Processor | Upgradable? | Upgrade Technology |
|---|---|---|---|
| Performa 6360, 6400, PM 6500 | PPC 603e | G3 | L2 |
| PM 4400, 7220 | PPC 603e | G3 | L2 |
| PM 7200, 7215 | PPC 601 | PPC 604e† | Logic board |
| PM 7300, 7600 | PPC 604e | G3, G4 | Daughtercard |
| PM 7500/100 | PPC 601 | PPC G3, 64 | Daughtercard |
| PM 8500, 8600, 9500, 9600 | PPC 604/604e | G3, G4 | Daughtercard |
| PM 9500/9600MP | 2 PPC 604e | No§ | n/a |
| PM G3 | G3 (PPC 750) | G3, G4 | CPU |
| PM G4 | G4 (PPC 7400) | G4 | Daughtercard |
| iMac (tray-loading) | G3 | G3 | Daughtercard |
| *Power Computing Systems* | | | |
| Power 100/120 | PPC 601 | G3, G4 | PDS |
| PowerBase | PPC 603e | G3 | L2 |
| PowerWave, Power Curve, PowerCenter, PowerCenter Pro, PowerTower Pro | PPC 604 | G3, G4 | Daughtercard |
| *Umax Systems* | | | |
| c500, c600 | PPC 603e | G3 | L2 |
| j700, s900 | PPC 604e | G3, G4 | Daughtercard |
| *Motorola Systems* | | | |
| StarMax 3000, 4000, 5000, 5500 | PPC 603e, 604e | G3 | L2 |

*Noted models at one time could be upgraded using a PowerPC 601 upgrade card from Apple that is no longer available at the retail level but might still be found on the used market.

°Apple offered a logic board upgrade in the past but it's no longer available at retail.

† The 7200 series can be upgraded to a 7500 using a logic board upgrade (Micromac); it can then be upgraded as if it were a 7500 to a G3 or G4 processor via a daughtercard.

§ In the past, a daughtercard upgrade to higher speed 604e processors has been offered but is no longer available at retail.

## Upgrading unofficially: Logic boards and faster clocks

Stuck with an officially un-upgradable Mac? There might be an unofficial path, as long as you're willing to take your warranty into your own hands. (Assuming your Mac is even under warranty anymore.) First, you can try a logic board swap. Many Mac models with sliding logic boards (especially older Performas and all-in-one LC models) can be quickly upgraded to a faster Mac. These upgrades don't always work, but I have seen pre-PowerPC Performa models running with PowerPC 603e processors.

In other cases, the logic board upgrade might be more difficult but doable, especially if you buy an upgrade kit and get a professional to install it. So where do you find the boards? Try

Shreve Systems (www.shrevesystems. com/), NEXCOMP (www.nexcomp.com/), or MilagroMac (www.milagromac.com/ upgrades.html) for starters. Used Mac Web sites or auction sites are also good bets.

If you're really nuts, you can try something else called *clock chipping*, a trick Macheads perform to replace the existing quartz oscillating clock on the logic board with a faster clock. (You can find the upgrades from www.micromac.com and others.) You might get a decent speed boost but be aware that clock-chipping a processor too high can introduce errors, affecting stability. I'd look to RAM and cache RAM upgrades instead of clock chipping.

As Table 16-2 shows, most Macs have a current processor upgrade path. If you're serious about upgrading the processor, you're likely to succeed.

So what about the iMac? At the time of writing, an upgrade for the iMac had just been announced by Newer Technology (www.newertech.com) for tray-loading iMac models; an upgrade for the slot-loading iMac is yet to come but might be possible. See Chapter 19 for details on opening the iMac to access its logic board.

# Performing the Processor Upgrade

Ready to roll? If you've decided on the type and speed of your processor upgrade, you're ready to dig into your Mac and do a little heart transplanting. I hope your processor upgrade came with some decent diagrams and instructions — many of them do. (You can also use Chapter 13 to help you get inside your Mac.) Although logic board upgrades are outside the scope of this text, I do talk about cards and CPU upgrades in this section.

Because I'm the wordy type, though, I have some advice up front:

✔ **Back up your data.** I know you don't want to back up your Mac, but you have to. If your processor upgrade blows up and your shirt collar catches fire, you might try to put it out with your hard drive. In that case, you could lose data. (Other data-loss scenarios are possible.) If you experience any trauma and have a good backup, you'll think of yourself as smarter and better looking.

✔ **Electrically ground yourself.** A processor or processor card is expensive. A grounding strap — from a good electronics store — is cheap. Get one and ground yourself before digging into your Mac.

✔ **Handle with care.** A lot of these upgrades come with antistatic bags; leave the upgrade in its bag until it's time to install. Then put the older processor in that same bag for storage. Plus, when you try to sell that old processor in the classifieds, that antistatic bag makes you look like a pro.

✔ **Consider a clean install.** If you're installing a new processor and you have a good backup, a clean installation of the Mac OS (after it has recognized the processor upgrade) might be a great way to get a little more performance out of the card. Just don't forget to reinstall any extensions you need for the upgrade card.

My final advice: Know your limitations. If you'd just rather not *go there,* girlfriend, no one will make fun of you if you opt for a professional. It's okay to take your Mac to a service center to get a processor upgrade. A good service center is likely to fully test and perhaps even warranty their work.

## *Performing a card trick*

The easiest upgrades are those that come on a card of some sort. In these instances, you're likely to encounter little trouble or resistance. All you need to do is find the right slot, plug in the card, and if necessary, install some software.

### *Daughtercard upgrade*

Because a daughtercard upgrade doesn't require a software extension, installing it is just a matter of getting inside your Mac and swapping the new and old daughtercards. Here's a list, complete with little numbers:

1. **Shut down your Mac, unplug it, ground yourself, and then open the Mac.**

2. **Locate the current daughtercard, which should include the current processor and a huge heat sink.**

   Look for big metal protrusions.

3. **Grab the daughtercard at its top corners and pull it straight up and out of the Mac.**

4. **Get the new card out of its antistatic bag and line it up with the daughtercard slot.**

5. **Press the new card down into the slot; it should slide in fairly easily.**

   Upgrade cards require a little wrist, but not much elbow. Check the alignment if pressing the card in seems tougher than it should be. If appropriate for your card, this is also the stage where you'll set any switches or jumpers on the card to set the bus speed and processor multiple. (Check your manual; most cards don't require this.)

6. **Close up the Mac, plug it in, and start it up.**

   Do things seem speedier?

7. **Check the Apple System Profiler (in the Apple menu) for indications of a new processor.**

   Look in the Hardware Overview section of the System Profile page.

8. **You can also run any software utilities that come with the card to test its newfound speed improvement.**

Note that you might also need Mac OS or application software updates to take advantage of some of the speed boost. For instance, you'll need PowerPC native applications to take full advantage of an upgrade to PowerPC from a 68040. Likewise, programs need to be updated to take advantage of the Altivec features of the G4 processor. Or if you happen to have a dual-processor upgrade card, you need to update your software, Mac OS, or both to take advantage of both processors. (In most cases, these will be plug-ins for high-end applications such as Adobe PhotoShop.)

If your upgrade came with software that allows you to tweak the bus speed of your Mac, doing so might offer better speed for the processor. (In some other cases, you might need to tweak these settings using little jumpers or switches on the card itself.) You can use the software to tweak the card, but my advice is to leave the card within recommended settings; if you run the upgrade at too high a speed, you risk overheating it and corrupting data. Check the upgrade card's manual for details and advice.

## PDS upgrade

The next easiest upgrade is a PDS upgrade; it's pretty much like installing a NuBus card, although the upgrade card is occasionally a bit larger. All you need to do is locate the PDS slot inside your Mac — and, if something is in the slot, remove it. For instance, some older Mac II models have a cache RAM upgrade in the slot; it has to go before you can use the upgrade card.

The following issues might crop up:

- ✔ On the Power Macintosh 6100, 7100, and 8100, you might have to remove the DOS compatibility card or the AV card if one is installed. Some PDS upgrades for these machines offer adapters that allow you to continue to use a video card. In other cases, you might need to switch your monitor to the built-in video circuitry or add a NuBus video card.

- ✔ Some Macs also require an adapter (the Mac IIsi comes to mind, as well as the Power Macintosh 6100 and some other Macs in pizza-box cases), so make sure you get the adapter when you purchase the accelerator.

- ✔ Earlier Macs often have a cache upgrade or, occasionally, a video card upgrade in the PDS slot. You have to remove it. If it's a video card, you need to connect your Mac to the built-in video port on the back of the Mac or upgrade with a NuBus video card.

Here are the steps for a PDS upgrade:

1. **Shut down the Mac, ground yourself, and pull out the power cord. Remove the Mac's cover.**

2. **Locate the PDS slot — it should be labeled.**

   Make sure you've chosen the PDS slot and not a NuBus slot.

3. **If a card is already in the slot, remove it.**

   Make sure it isn't connected to any wires through the back of the case and then grab the card at each top corner and pull straight up.

4. **Make sure you've discharged static electricity and then open the static-free bag that contains the upgrade card. Remove the card.**

5. **Line the card up carefully over the PDS socket.**

   Note how the notches in the PDS connector on the card match up correctly in only one direction relative to the PDS slot.

6. **Press the card into the socket (see Figure 16-2).**

   It should go fairly easily — if you find yourself forcing it, you might have the card facing the wrong direction. Look at the connector on the card and on the logic board to orient the card correctly and then install the card again.

7. **Close up the case (or you can test for a short time with the case open), plug the Mac in, and start it up.**

8. **Install that software and then restart the Mac.**

   You probably won't experience a speed boost until you install the software that came with the accelerator. After you've restarted, you'll have a faster Mac.

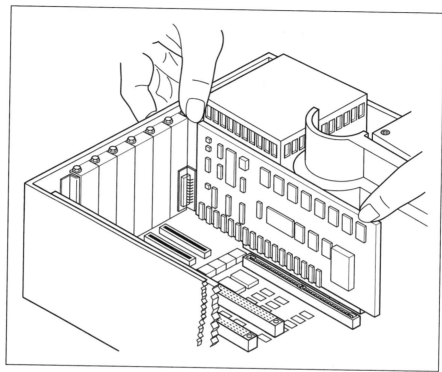

**Figure 16-2:**
Put pressure on each top corner of the card evenly to press it into place.

## Cache slot (L2) upgrades

For the most part, an L2 upgrade is about the same as a PDS upgrade. If there's any difference, it's that the cache slot is almost *always* filled with a cache memory module that you need to remove. You need a Mac OS extension for an L2 upgrade to work correctly.

1. **Install the software before installing the card.**

   Otherwise, the Mac might have trouble starting up with the card installed.

2. **Shut down your Mac, unplug it, ground yourself, and then open the Mac.**

3. **Locate the current cache module, which looks like a RAM module but is located in a slot off to its own.**

4. **Grab the cache module at its top corners and pull straight up to release it.**

   This isn't always easy — they can be firmly planted. (Some folks recommend using a flathead screwdriver to pry it up at the bottom corners, but you must be *very* careful not to mar or crack the logic board or connector.)

5. **With the cache module uninstalled, line up the processor upgrade and slide it into the cache slot.**

If it doesn't go in fairly easily, check to make sure it's properly aligned and try again.

6. **Now, close up the Mac, plug it in, and start up.**

7. **After startup, you can launch any utilities that came with the card to see how extensive the speed-up is.**

## CPU upgrades

CPU upgrades aren't difficult, but they are delicate. For that reason, I recommend that most people let a professional do the upgrade. You could bend or break one spindly pin and mess up a $500 processor chip.

If you do forge ahead, you'll find that newer Macs (such as the Power Macintosh G3, both blue and beige) offer a ZIF socket for upgrading. After you've removed the heat sink (often by removing a small tension clamp), you can get at the ZIF socket. These sockets include a small lever; when lifted, the lever releases its hold on the CPU chip. You can then lift the CPU out fairly easily (see Figure 16-3).

Performing this upgrade affects your warranty, so check your Apple documentation and make sure you want to do that. On the Power Macintosh G3, Apple puts a small label over the processor (on the blue G3, it's over the bus settings), indicating that breaking the seal voids your warranty.

When you replace the CPU, you line up the new CPU with the ZIF socket — if lined up correctly and if the lever is still in the up position, the CPU should drop right into the socket with no pressure at all. (Hence the name ZIF, or Zero Insertion Force.) If the CPU seems to require pressure, it's not lined up correctly. Check the pins against the socket again — you might have the CPU rotated 90 or 180 degrees in the wrong direction.

After the CPU slips into the socket, push the lever back down and the CPU is locked into place.

With older Macs, a CPU upgrade requires a chip puller and some patience. Slowly work the chip out of the socket: Move to one side, lift a slight amount, move to the next side, and lift a slight amount. Follow the instructions that came with the upgrade kit closely, move slowly, and avoid bending a pin on the processor.

If you do bend a pin while performing a processor upgrade, stop immediately and take the whole thing to a service center. If the pin is bent but not broken, they might be able to salvage or repair the chip.

**Figure 16-3:**
Lift the ZIF socket level and remove the processor card to upgrade it in a Power Macintosh blue G3.

# Tweaking and Troubleshooting the Upgrade

If you have trouble with your processor upgrade, check the documentation carefully and make sure you installed the software correctly. Depending on the type of upgrade you have, you might need to take other steps, such as running software that disables additional cache, removing your cache RAM module (on some PDS and L2 upgrades), or tweaking the bus speed or cache settings of the upgrade.

Here are a few other thoughts on processor upgrade performance:

✔ Remember that you've replaced the processor, which might confuse the Mac OS, especially in older Macs with issues such as 32-bit addressing (Memory control panel) and the 040 cache settings (040 Cache control panel). You might find that the best plan is to reinstall the Mac OS.

✔ If you really feel like you're not seeing much acceleration, troubleshoot the card by isolating the card's extension and restarting (assuming your upgrade requires an extension). Then, test a particularly tough processing challenge (such as recalculating a spreadsheet, creating a complicated chart, or performing a PhotoShop special effect). After that, test with the extension enabled and see whether the card does things faster. If not, check to make sure the extension is loading as the Mac starts up.

✔ If it's not a software problem and the speed-up doesn't seem to manifest itself in any software testing, shut down the Mac, ground yourself, and open the Mac up to make sure that you seated the card correctly.

✔ Allow me to reiterate: If you don't have enough RAM, you might not see the speed boost you're expecting. You need plenty of RAM to take advantage of a processor upgrade.

✔ Don't forget to check the upgrade card manufacturer's site for software updates and technical documents. The software for upgrade cards is low-level, meaning it needs to be updated often to keep up with Apple's changes in the Mac OS. Also, the manufacturer might note certain common incompatibilities — some upgrade cards have trouble with certain video cards, SCSI adapters, or Mac OS extensions, among other known problems.

# Chapter 17

# Adding Closet Space: Hard Disks and Internal Drives

· · · · · · · · · · · · · · · · · · · · · · · · · · · · · · · · · · · · · · · · · · · · · · · ·

## In This Chapter

▶ Finding out about more darned letters: IDE, SCSI, and ATAPI

▶ Choosing the right drive for your Mac

▶ Installing and using the new drive

· · · · · · · · · · · · · · · · · · · · · · · · · · · · · · · · · · · · · · · · · · · · · · · ·

*1*n Chapter 11, I talk at length about wine, patience, and romance. I also mention adding removable drives through external ports on your Mac. If you want additional storage space for your files, Chapter 11 is certainly high on the recommended reads in this book.

But wouldn't it be nice if you could add storage *inside* your Mac? Consider the possibilities: double or triple your hard disk space, for starters. You could get a faster hard disk, perhaps. You could swap out the CD-ROM drive for a CD-burning variety. Or if your Mac has room, you might even pop in an internal Zip, Jaz, or Orb drive and slide removable disks right into your Mac. Wouldn't that be cool?

Yup, and it ain't tough, neither, cowboy. In fact, it shouldn't require much more than a screwdriver, a little smart shopping, . . . and a dream.

## Alphabet Soup: IDE, SCSI, or ATAPI

Just in case I got you excited with that rousing intro, I'm afraid I'll have to bring things to a screeching halt and start defining technologies again. Sorry. Before you can get too deep into the innards of your Mac, you need to know the type of internal drive you can buy and how you install it.

Three different technologies are used for internal drives: IDE, SCSI, and ATAPI. Which you use depends somewhat on the device you chose but mostly on the type of connectors you have inside your Mac.

IDE is used on many new Macs (and, for years, in Performa and similar models) and, depending on the Mac, you might be able to swap your internal disk with a new IDE drive or perhaps add a second IDE drive. ATAPI is the removable drive version of the IDE standard; if your Mac supports an internal IDE hard disk, there's a fighting chance that it also supports internal ATAPI devices, enabling you to add a Zip, CD-ROM, or similar removable.

Most other Mac models are SCSI through-and-through, allowing you to add both SCSI-based hard disks and SCSI-based removable drives. If that's the case for your Mac, at least you'll have a little easier time shopping. To begin, look at the different technologies.

# IDE or ATAPI

Integrated Drive Electronics/AT Attachment (IDE/ATA) is the most popular internal drive interface for Intel-compatible PCs, and its popularity has boomed in the Mac market since Apple began using IDE for nearly all its internal drives. IDE used to be considerably slower than SCSI, but newer IDE drives offer speeds comparable to all but the fastest SCSI drives. Another difference: IDE offers only two devices per bus (in most implementations), whereas SCSI allows seven devices per bus.

ATAPI is the removable standard based on IDE. You can think of it as IDE for internal drives that use removable media, from CD-ROM and CD-R drives to Zips, Jaz, and others. ATAPI drives are quick, reasonably easy to install (assuming your Mac supports them), and becoming more common in Macs.

If you want to use an IDE drive, you first need to know whether your Mac supports internal IDE devices. (And if it doesn't, you need to decide whether you want to install an IDE upgrade card.) Then you need to figure out what level of IDE technology you should look for when buying an internal drive. They vary and getting the right drive can result in much better performance, depending on your Mac model.

## Choosing IDE hard drives

The IDE/ATA folks have had a lot of fun coming up with faster, meaner interface technologies over the years. Common terms include ATA-2, ATA-3, EIDE, Ultra ATA, and ATA/66. The problem is that these terms are a tug-of-war between standards and marketing terms, both of which are important if you want to look hip to others during discussions at cocktail parties.

IDE is a reasonably flexible standard in which the drives and the controllers are both backward-compatible. That means a new ATA-33 drive should work fine (but not optimally) in an older Mac that supports only Fast ATA. Likewise, an older EIDE drive should work fine (although, again, not at peak performance) in a new Power Macintosh G4, even though that Mac supports drives up to ATA/66 speeds.

Let's wade through all this terminology together:

- ✔ **IDE/ATA.** This is a generic term that suggests IDE technology in general, but it also describes the original standard in PCs. This specification calls for a single bus that can support two drives in a master and slave configuration. These drives max out around 8MB/sec.

  Sorry for the unfortunate *master* and *slave* terms, but they're not my fault. The terms suggest how two IDE devices are configured when they're on the same IDE bus; one is the master and one is the slave. It doesn't really matter which is which — in fact, the slave drive doesn't in any way depend on the master drive. They could just as easily have been called Number 1 and Number 2, but some engineer didn't think that through.

- ✔ **ATA-2.** This is an actual standard but unfortunately it's not always used by drive manufacturers, who prefer the marketing terms *Enhanced IDE, Fast ATA,* or *Fast ATA-2* because they think they're cool. All these drives offer speeds up to 16MB/sec.

- ✔ **Fast ATA.** This often refers to a subset of the ATA-2 specification, but it's basically a marketing term. These drives are supported by the Quadra/LC/Performa 630 family, the LC/Performa 580, and the Performa/Power Macintosh 5200, 5300, 6200, and 6300 series.

- ✔ **Fast ATA-2.** These drives are generally considered identical to the ATA-2 standard. Support for ATA-2 and Fast ATA-2 drives is suggested in Apple tech notes for the Macintosh Performa and Power Macintosh 5400 and 6400 series.

- ✔ **EIDE.** Enhanced IDE is the Western Digital marketing standard that's often considered an official standard but isn't. EIDE drives are specifically supported on the original (beige) Power Macintosh G3 series, although EIDE drives are generally backward compatible and can be used in most earlier Mac models.

- ✔ **Ultra ATA.** Also called Ultra DMA or DMA-33, these drives can transmit data up to 33.3MB/sec. Apple has generally shunned Ultra ATA in their tech notes until the Power Macintosh blue G3, which supports a single Ultra ATA hard drive. (Some G3 models can support two such drives in a master/slave configuration, as discussed in the section "Can I add a second IDE drive?")

- ✔ **ATA/66.** ATA/66 is the latest IDE standard and allows drives to transfer data at speeds up to 66MB/sec. Power Macintosh G4 models support these drives.

- ✔ **ATAPI.** This is the IDE standard for removable drives. Macs that ship with ATAPI CD-ROM (or DVD-ROM) drives include the Power Macintosh 4400, G3, and G4 models. All but the 4400 offer support for a second ATAPI device.

When you're looking at buying a drive, focus on the individual statistics, not the standards or marketing names. In a nutshell, all Macs require IDE/ATA drives that feature *logical bus addressing (LBA)* support and an enhanced *identify drive* command. That means, essentially, that they should meet at least the ATA-2 standard. If your model supports a faster drive, by all means feel free to get it.

### Can I add a second IDE drive?

One of the burning questions for upgraders is not just whether they can swap their existing IDE drive with a new, larger one but whether they can add a second IDE or ATAPI drive. Some models support a second drive as long as there's room inside the case. But the switch between SCSI and IDE has created some oddities over time.

If you happen to have a blue Power Macintosh G3 that doesn't include a standard Ultra ATA drive (some configurations ship with an Ultra2 SCSI card and SCSI hard drive as the main drive), you can add an internal Ultra ATA drive. (Or, you could add SCSI drives, thanks to that SCSI card.) Otherwise, you can't add a second Ultra ATA (or any type of IDE) drive to a revision A Power Mac G3.

The revision B Power Macintosh G3 (manufactured after May 1998) is a different story. It's cabled for two Ultra ATA drives and even includes a special drive bracket above the installed drive to accommodate a second drive, as shown in Figure 17-1. (The drive must be 1-inch high.) In those machines, you can set up a slave IDE drive. The Power Macintosh G4 also supports a second Ultra ATA or ATA/66 drive internally.

**Figure 17-1:**
The revision B includes a bracket and connector to support a second drive in slave mode.

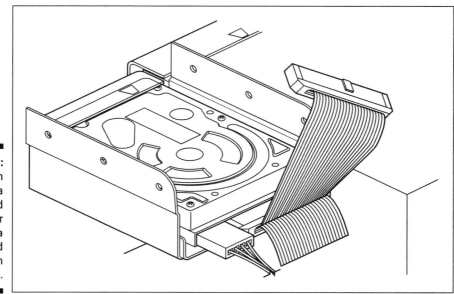

These same Macs (colorful Power Macintosh G3 and G4 machines) can accept a second ATAPI device (again, in slave mode) unless Apple has preinstalled an Iomega Zip drive.

When you add a second IDE or ATAPI drive, you need to place it in slave mode, usually using a small jumper on the drive itself, as shown in Figure 17-2. You then plug it into the existing IDE cable (if your Mac supports two devices, it should have an available IDE connector on the cable), as discussed later in this chapter in the "Installing a New Drive" section.

If your Mac doesn't support a second IDE drive, you can still add one using an IDE upgrade card. They're not as popular for the Mac as SCSI upgrade cards, but a few manufacturers, including ProMax (www.promax.com), make them.

You can use just about any brand of IDE hard drive with a Macintosh, especially with Mac OS 8.0 or later. Apple's Drive Setup application can format and install a disk driver for pretty much any IDE model. ATAPI drives are a little different, though. Before installing an ATAPI removable in your Mac, make sure it has drivers available. Third-party companies such as FWB (www.fwb.com) and CharisMac (www.charismac.com) offer drivers that support ATAPI CD-ROM and CD-R/CD-RW drives.

**Figure 17-2:**
If you're installing a second IDE or ATAPI drive, you must physically set its jumper to slave mode.

## SCSI revealed

In other chapters, I cover external SCSI (Small Computer Systems Interface) devices. You might be either pleased or horrified to know that SCSI devices also exist *inside* many Mac models. In fact, the overwhelming majority of Macintosh models ship with internal SCSI hard disks, although recent models generally offer IDE drives.

If you have a Mac SE, Mac Classic series, Mac TV, Mac II series, LC series, Centris, Quadra (except the 630), almost any Power Macintosh (before G3 and G4), or an early Performa model, you have internal SCSI drives. Even some models that offer IDE hard disks feature a SCSI expansion bay, such as the Power Macintosh 6400 and 6500. (Sometimes that bay is filled by an Apple-installed Zip drive.) The beige Power Macintosh G3 ships with an IDE drive but includes cabling for internal SCSI devices so that you can add SCSI hard drives or removables.

On top of all that, if you want to add an internal SCSI drive using the existing technology, you pretty much just need to figure out whether your Mac shipped with regular SCSI or Fast SCSI support. Then you can get an appropriate SCSI drive.

For optimum performance, though, you have to sift through some techno-babble to figure out which hard drive is best for you. If you really need fast performance, you might want to look into a faster SCSI hard drive and an expansion card that can support it. Let's look at some fascinating SCSI specs.

### SCSI specifications

The SCSI world has had three standards: SCSI (or SCSI-1), SCSI-2, and SCSI-3. These names aren't particularly important but they do make computer scientists feel superior to you and me.

More important are the SCSI *transfer protocols*, which sort of coincide with the SCSI standards. As with IDE, optimum performance is achieved when the SCSI chips on your logic board (or the SCSI card you've installed in a PCI slot) support the same technology that your SCSI drive does. When you go to buy a SCSI disk, then, you can worry about those protocols, arranged here in a handy bullet list:

- ✓ **SCSI.** This is the generic term, but it's also used to refer to Basic SCSI, or the protocol defined by the SCSI-1 standard. At this level, data is transferred along 8-bit-wide data paths at about 5MB per second. In this case, the SCSI bus speed is 5 MHz.

- ✓ **Fast SCSI or Fast SCSI-2.** Part of the SCSI-2 specification, Fast SCSI is a transfer protocol that doubles the speed of Basic SCSI to 10 MHz, still using an 8-bit path. That results in a maximum throughput of 10MB per second.

✔ **Wide SCSI or Wide SCSI-2.** Wide SCSI interfaces are called wide because they use a 16-bit bus to transfer data. The original Wide SCSI still runs at 5 MHz, so the result is a maximum throughput of 10MB per second. But the 16-bit part means that Wide SCSI buses can support up to 16 devices per bus (instead of the regular 8 devices). Wide SCSI requires a special 68-pin cable to communicate with Wide SCSI devices. (Many Wide SCSI upgrade cards also feature a 50-pin or 25-pin external connector for adding slower SCSI devices to the bus.)

✔ **Fast/Wide SCSI or Fast/Wide SCSI-2.** Put these two SCSI-2 protocols together and you get a 16-bit bus running at 10 MHz. That results in maximum transfers of 20MB/sec, along with support for 16 devices. You still have to use a 68-pin connector for optimum internal performance, though.

✔ **Ultra SCSI or Ultra SCSI-3.** Part of the SCSI-3 standard, Ultra SCSI uses an 8-bit bus at 20 MHz for a maximum transfer rate of 20MB/sec. Again, it uses a 68-pin connector.

✔ **Ultra/Wide SCSI or Ultra/Wide SCSI-3.** As you might guess, this is a 20-MHz, 16-bit SCSI bus capable of data transfers up to 40MB/sec and support for 16 devices. This also requires a 68-pin cable for the highest speed connections.

✔ **Ultra2 SCSI.** Boosted up to 40 MHz on a 16-bit bus, this technology can transfer data at up to 80MB/sec, again requiring a 68-pin cable.

✔ **Ultra160 SCSI or Ultra160m SCSI.** The latest standard in SCSI space works some doubling magic to get the data rate up to a whopping 160MB/sec, but only when everything — the interface and the drive — are Ultra160 rated.

Technically, SCSI interfaces and drives should be backward compatible, so that a fast drive can plug into a slow interface and run at the slower speed, and a slow drive can be plugged into a fast SCSI interface and continue to work. In practice, this works with all but the oldest SCSI drives; it's best not to retrofit your screaming Power Mac with a SCSI-1 drive circa 1987.

### SCSI cards

With all this technology discussion under your belt, your task is to choose the right drive (or SCSI card or both) for the job. Most Macs offer only the barest of SCSI support, with some reaching all the way up to Fast SCSI speeds. To go beyond that, you need an upgrade card. Table 17-1 shows some popular SCSI card manufacturers.

| Table 17-1 | SCSI Card Manufacturers and Their Offerings | | |
|---|---|---|---|
| **Manufacturer** | **Card Interface** | **Speeds** | **Web Site** |
| Adaptec | PCI | Fast SCSI to Ultra160 | www.adaptec.com |
| ATTO | PCI | Ultra/Wide, Ultra2, Ultra160 | www.attotech.com |
| Orange Micro | PCI | Fast SCSI, Ultra, Ultra/Wide | www.orangemicro.com |
| SIIG | PCI | Fast SCSI, Ultra, Ultra/Wide | www.siig.com |
| La Cie | PCI | Ultra/Wide, Ultra2 | www.lacie.com |

# The Right Drive for Your Mac

Here's another table, just for kicks. Table 17-2 offers a look at the major Mac and clone models so you can see your options for upgrading the hard drive or adding a second drive in an available bay.

| Table 17-2 | Hard Drive Up | | |
|---|---|---|---|
| **Model** | **Main Drive** | **Available Bays?** | **Internal SCSI Speed** |
| Mac 128, 512, Plus | None | No | n/a |
| Mac Classic series (incl. SE and SE/30) | SCSI | No | 5MB/sec |
| Mac II series, Quadra 700 | SCSI | No | 5MB/sec |
| LC series.C/Q605, Performa 400 series | SCSI | No | 5MB/sec |
| Mac IIvi, IIvx, Quadra/Centris 650, Performa 600, Work Group Server 70; Power Macintosh 7100, WGS 7150 | SCSI | 5.25"* | 5MB/sec |

| Model | Main Drive | Available Bays? | Internal SCSI Speed |
|---|---|---|---|
| Centris/Quadra 610, 660AV, Power Mac 6100, Performa 6100 series | SCSI | 5.25"* | 5MB/sec |
| Quadra 630, Performa 630, LC 630, 6200, 6300 series | IDE | No | n/a |
| Quadra 800, 840AV, Power Mac 8100, WGS 8150 | SCSI | 5.25"*, 3.5" | 5MB/sec |
| Quadra 900/950, | | | |
| WGS 90, Power Mac 9500; WGS 9150 | SCSI | 5.25"*, two 3.5" | 10MB/sec |
| Performa 6400, Power Mac 6500 | IDE° | 5.25" | 5MB/sec |
| LC/Performa 500 series; MacTV | SCSI† | No | 5MB/sec |
| Performa/PM 5200/ 5300/5400 | IDE | No | n/a |
| Power Mac 7200, 7300, 7500, 7600, WGS 7250/7350, 8500 | SCSI | 3.5"§ | 10MB/sec |
| G3 Desktop, G3 D esktop Server | IDE° | 3.5"§ | 5MB/sec |
| PM 8600, 9600 | SCSI | three 5.25"§ | 10MB/sec |
| G3 Minitower; G3 Minitower Server | IDE° | three 5.25"§ | 5MB/sec |
| Power Mac G3 (blue) | Ultra ATA | two 3.5"; one 5.25"§ | n/a |
| Power Mac G3 (blue, rev. B) | Ultra ATA | three 3.5"; one 5.25"§ | n/a |
| Power Mac G4 | ATA/66 | two 3.5"; one 5.25"§ | n/a |

*(continued)*

**Table 17-2 (continued)**

| Model | Main Drive | Available Bays? | Internal SCSI Speed |
|---|---|---|---|
| iMac (pop-out tray) | IDE | none | n/a |
| iMac (slot-loading) | Ultra ATA | none | n/a |

*One 5.25" bay filled by factory CD-ROM on certain models

°Internal expansion bays are prewired for SCSI devices

† IDE on 580 series models

§ One available 5.25" bay is filled by a factory Zip drive on certain models

One issue to note is the size of the bays mentioned in the chart. Generally, you'll find two different sizes for expansion bays: 3.5 inch and 5.25 inch. Nearly all *internal* expansion bays (those that offer no access to the outside of the machine) are 3.5 inches in width because that's the size of all modern hard disks. Because some removable drives with external access (such as CD-ROM drives) are 5.25 inches in width, those bays are generally larger to accommodate the drives. For removable drives that aren't that wide, you often use a special adapter kit to make the 3.5-inch drive fit in the 5.25-inch bay, as noted later in the section "Installing the Drive."

In spite of this scary table, you can draw some general conclusions to make choosing a drive easier. First, if your Mac doesn't have an available drive bay, your only choice is to swap a new, larger drive for your old one. In that case, the new drive should use the same technology as the existing drive: usually either Fast SCSI or IDE/EIDE. Both types of drives are easy to find at major computer retailers.

If you have a Mac that supports SCSI, a Fast SCSI drive is probably the easiest purchase to make. They're relatively cheap, reasonably fast, and should be supported by any Mac with built-in SCSI. If you have a SCSI upgrade card (that shipped with your Mac or that you added), you should buy a drive that's supported by that card — likely an Ultra/Wide or faster.

If your Mac will support a second IDE drive, get one that meets the specs of your IDE interface. For the Power Mac G3 and G4, that's Ultra ATA or ATA/66. (Note that you can use a cheaper, slower drive, such as EIDE, if you like. You probably won't even notice much of a difference unless you're a multimedia professional.) The same advice holds if you've upgraded with an IDE interface card; add a drive that matches the card's capabilities.

Finally, a word on buying the drive itself. For IDE, you can walk into any computer store and buy an IDE drive off the shelf, as long as it will fit in your Mac's available drive bay. You can use Apple's Drive Setup to format almost any IDE drive for use with a Mac. (Drive Setup 1.7.2 or higher is recommended; if you don't have a newer version, you can download it from http://asu.info.apple.com/.)

---

## Buying an internal removable drive

Some manufacturers, such as Iomega (www.iomega.com) and Castlewood (www.castlewood.com), make internal SCSI (and sometimes ATAPI) versions of their removable drives.

If you're looking for an internal CD-R or CD-RW drive, a number of companies offer them — shop the catalogs and Mac magazines. Some intrepid Mac upgraders have managed to add ATAPI-based CD-R, CD-RW, or even DVD-RAM drives to their Macs, but doing so requires good support from the CD-burning software. Check with Charismac (www.charismac.com) and Adaptec (www.adaptec.com) to see whether they explicitly support the type of ATAPI CD drive you plan to install.

---

For SCSI drives, you should concern yourself with two things. First, you are likely to need third-party driver software for the SCSI drive, so buy it in a kit from a Mac-savvy dealer. Second, don't forget to get a drive with the right number of pins on its connector; if you're using built-in SCSI in a Mac, stick with a drive that sports a 50-pin connector. If you have an upgrade card that specifically supports Wide connections, only then should you opt for a SCSI drive with a 68-pin connector.

Wondering about the drive in your iMac? Upgrading the internal hard drive is tough but not impossible. See Chapter 19 for details on opening an iMac and getting at the hard drive.

# Installing a New Drive

Have you made all your choices: IDE versus SCSI and replacement versus add-on drive? Then you're ready to dig inside your Mac and install your new drive. First, a little preparation and then you head inside your Mac and fit that drive. Plus, I show you how to add a removable drive in an external-access bay so that you can get at it when you need to.

## An installation checklist

You should know about a few important issues before you remove or install a hard drive. The first one focuses on SCSI, but the rest are applicable to both IDE and SCSI. Here's your list:

✔ Using the Apple System Profiler, check to see what SCSI ID numbers are available in your Macintosh. (If you'll be replacing the internal drive, its number should be SCSI ID 0.) You need to choose one (and perhaps a backup) so that you can set the SCSI drive to that ID.

✔ Shut down your Mac, ground yourself, open the case, and take a look around. You need to make sure a drive bay, an IDE or SCSI connection, and a power connector are available. (Some Mac OS clone machines have more drive bays than power connectors. You can, however, get power-connection splitters from computer stores, as long as you're not overloading the rating on your power supply.)

✔ Confirm that the available drive bay is the right size for your drive. A standard 3.5-inch drive can fit in any available bay using an adapter kit, but a 5.25-inch drive needs a 5.25-inch bay.

✔ Figure out how the drive will be secured to the Mac. Some drives have special plastic or metal guides that slide into the Mac's drive bay (see Figure 17-3); others simply screw into the drive cage. If you're having trouble find the right connector or faceplate (for removable drives), try Proline Distribution (www.proline.com/) or a Mac-oriented store. If you're replacing an existing drive, you should be able to detach rails from the old drive and reattach them to the new one.

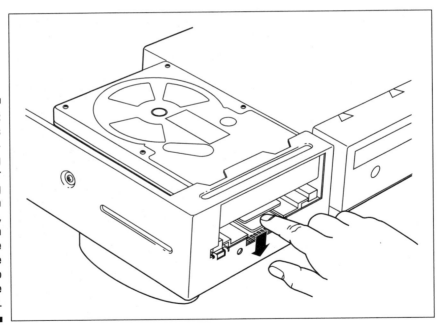

**Figure 17-3:** Many Macs use a high-end sliding system for installing drives; in this case, you push down on the lever in the front to slide the drive out.

# Removing the old drive

If your plan is to replace your old drive with a new one, you have to get the original drive out of your Mac before you can move on. It's simply a question of physics. Here are the steps for removing that original drive:

1. **Make sure you've backed up all the data you need from that drive so you can move it to the new one.**

   After the drive is in a shoebox somewhere, it becomes considerably more difficult to get data off it.

2. **Shut down your Mac, unplug it, ground yourself, and open the case.**

3. **Find the original hard drive and take a look at the type of guide it uses for attaching itself in the drive bay.**

4. **Remove the SCSI or IDE cable and the power connector from the back of the drive (see Figure 17-4).**

   Always grab the connector and pull. Avoid yanking on the cables or wires; it may detach the connector from the cable, requiring you to get a new cable.

5. **If necessary, unscrew any retaining screws that are holding the drive to its drive bay.**

   If your drive uses quick-release plastic drive rails, there are no screws to worry about.

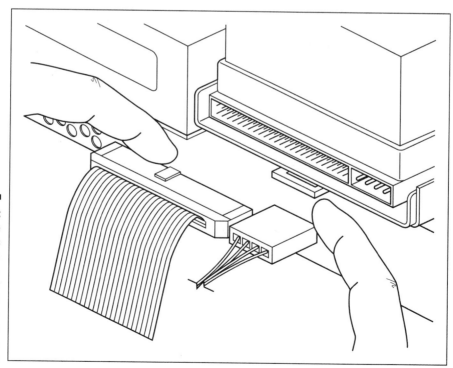

**Figure 17-4:**
Remove the connectors gently from the drive. Note their orientation for reinstallation of the new drive.

6. **Release the drive from its bay and then slide it out of the bay.**

Depending on your Mac model and the type of drive you're working with, you might find that sliding the drive out the front of its bay is easier, even if the cables are hooked up at the back of the bay.

That's it. If you plan to use the same rails for your new drive, unscrew them from the old drive and keep the screws and rails handy. Otherwise, you might want to stick the drive in an antistatic bag (perhaps the bag that came with your new drive) for safekeeping.

## Prepping a SCSI drive

Before you install a SCSI drive, you need to make sure the SCSI number is set correctly and the drive's termination is properly configured for your SCSI bus. Here are some guiding principles:

- ✔ If you're replacing your existing SCSI drive with a new model, you probably need to make sure that termination is turned on and that the SCSI ID is set to 0. (Most likely both are, but you should double-check.)

- ✔ If you aren't replacing your existing hard drive (for instance, you're installing a second hard drive or a removable drive), make sure you've chosen a connector that's on the *middle* of the SCSI ribbon cable. In this case, the drive shouldn't be terminated: Make sure termination is set to off. You also need to set the drive to a unique SCSI ID, probably using jumpers on the drive itself.

- ✔ If you're adding a second drive or a removable, make sure you have the correct rail kit for your Mac model. Likewise, a 3.5-inch drive might need an adapter kit if it's supposed to fit in a 5.25-inch drive bay. If the drive is a removable drive, you might need to install a faceplate on its mounting kit, depending on the model.

## Prepping an IDE or an ATAPI drive

Before you install an IDE drive (or an ATAPI removable drive), you should prepare it for its new life inside your Mac. If you're replacing an existing drive, make sure the new drive is set to master mode; if you're adding the drive to your Mac, it should be in slave mode. (You usually set the mode with jumpers on the drive itself.)

You might also need to check and make sure your existing IDE cable is long enough to reach the drive bay (where you'll be installing the new drive) and that it has an additional connector for the drive. If it doesn't, you might need to purchase a new IDE cable. (Note that cables for Ultra ATA and ATA/66 drives need to be of a high quality; ask around at the computer store.)

Finally, install the rails for your drive and have the correct faceplate or bezel on hand (or installed on the rail kit) if you're installing a removable. You'll use the faceplate to make sure that the removable drive lines up nicely with the front of the case.

## Installing the drive

Finally, you're ready to install the SCSI, IDE, or ATAPI drive. Sorry if this is anticlimactic, by the way.

Good preparation should make this fairly easy:

1. **Make sure that your Mac is shut down and unplugged and that you're electrically grounded. Open the Mac's case.**

   If you're installing a removable drive, you'll need to remove the plastic faceplate from the front of the available drive bay.

2. **Slide the new drive into an available drive bay.**

   Make sure you orient the drive correctly so that it will line up with its interface and power connectors. (Some Mac models have these connectors in the front of the bay instead of the back.) Also make sure that you don't slide the drive in upside down; if the drive is upside down, its securing screws or rails won't line up correctly.

3. **Connect the SCSI or IDE cable to the drive.**

   Orient the cable correctly, with the red strip on the SCSI or IDE cable lining up with the leftmost pin (pin 1) on the connector.

4. **Plug the power connector into the drive.**

   It should install in only one direction, so if you have trouble plugging the connector into the drive, try flipping it over.

5. **Make sure the drive is firmly seated in its drive and reinstall any protective plates that cover the drive bay.**

   If the drive is a removable drive, you might need to install a faceplate or bezel on the front of the Mac. Most of the time, it will snap right into the bay's opening, as shown in Figure 17-5. (Other times, the faceplate is already secured to the front of the drive.)

## Formatting and using the new drive

After a hard drive is installed and you feel confident that everything is wired together correctly, you can plug in the Mac and start it up. If all goes well, your

Mac will begin the boot-up process. (If you've replaced the internal drive, you might need to boot from a Mac OS CD this first time.) If the drive is preformatted for Macintosh, it should appear on the desktop, ready to double-click and work with.

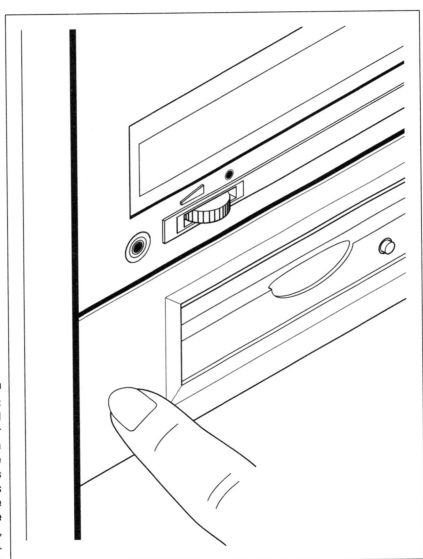

**Figure 17-5:**
The final step for installing a removable drive is snapping its faceplate into place for a good, snug fit.

If you've added a removable drive, you might need to install driver software for the drive first. Then, after restarting, pop in a disk and see whether it appears on the desktop.

If the drive (or removable disk) isn't Mac formatted, you might see a dialog box asking whether you want to erase the disk so that it can be used. Make sure the dialog box is talking about the right drive (it should have an estimate of the size of the drive), choose a format type, and click Erase.

Your formatting choices are Mac OS Extended or Mac OS Standard. Mac OS Extended (available in Mac OS 8.1 or higher) is more efficient and best for large hard drives. If you think you might ever have to uninstall the drive and place it in a pre-Mac OS 8.1 Mac, choose Mac OS Standard format for compatibility.

You might also decide to partition the hard drive, creating two or more *volumes,* each of which will appear on the desktop. A partitioned drive can be used to help organize your files or to dual-boot between the Mac OS and another operating system such as Mac OS X or Linux. To partition the drive, you need to use Drive Setup (see Chapter 24 for details) or the disk formatting software that came with your drive, such as LaCie's Silverlining Pro or FWB's Hard Disk Toolkit.

For smaller removable disks, Mac OS Standard format is fine. Larger (1GB or more) disks can benefit from the Mac OS Extended format, but remember that you won't be able to use them with versions of the Mac OS before Mac OS 8.1. See Chapter 11 for more discussion of removable disks.

# Chapter 18

# Get Out and Mingle: Basic Networking

Creating a network is a hoot. Of course, if your network is for an office environment, you need to take it more seriously: It's a fundamental variable in the utilization of leveraged corporate informational synergy. (Feel free to crib that sentence for your memo to the boss.)

But if you're talking about your home, small office, or organization, creating a network is a *hoot*.

First, you need to understand the technologies behind Mac networking — both the hardware that connects your Macs and the software that helps them chat. Then I'll show you the configuration hoops you need to jump through to connect a wired — or even wireless — network.

## The Tech behind Your Net

When you network a few machines together in your home or office, you're creating what's called a *local area network (LAN)*. A LAN is a network designed to pass documents and share printers within a fairly confined space. It's in contrast to a *wide area network (WAN)*, which generally serves to move data between local area networks. For instance, a large university might have a WAN to interconnect multiple LANs that serve individual colleges or computer labs. In this same way, the Internet can be seen as a WAN because it can be used to connect LANs (and individual computers) all over the world.

## LANs for the lost

We can divide LANs into two basic types: *client/server* and *peer-to-peer*. A client/server network is set up so that a single or a few primary computers, called *servers*, store data and make peripherals (such as printers) available. At a *client* computer (the Mac where you do your work), you sign into the server to access files, printers, and so on. When you're finished using the network, you sign off the server.

In a peer-to-peer network, every computer becomes a server. (They all get more respect, too.) If you'd like to exchange files with Billy, you sign into Billy's computer and, if you have the proper networking privileges, you can copy files from his hard disk. If Mary wants a file from your computer, she can sign into it, and if she has the proper networking privileges, she can copy the file from your computer to hers. This can go on for as many computers and users you have. Which type of LAN you implement depends on the number of people and the amount of time they spend on the network; the more demand for networked resources, the more it makes sense to have a server computer.

To create a LAN, you need some basic ingredients. First, you need hardware that connects your Mac to other Macs (or other computers). Second, you need software that knows how to communicate between computers for sharing information. Third, you need to configure everything correctly so that your Macs are actually doing something.

Macs have three basic hardware approaches and two basic software approaches to network connections. For hardware, there's

- ✔ LocalTalk
- ✔ Ethernet
- ✔ AirPort, the wireless networking hardware from Apple

For software, you can use

- ✔ AppleTalk, which has been the standard Apple networking protocol since the first Mac was sold
- ✔ TCP/IP, the networking protocol used on the Internet, as well as in many other places, that's now very popular on the Mac

But what does a networking protocol do? AppleTalk or TCP/IP is the language used to make *file sharing* or *print sharing* possible. In other words, the protocol makes it possible for your Mac to access disks and printers that aren't connected to the Mac directly, but rather via a wired or wireless network.

Let's look at the different types of hardware and software protocols. You have to decide what approach to take before you can wire things together.

# *The chatter about LocalTalk*

Originally built into every Mac, LocalTalk was the de facto standard for Mac network wiring for at least ten years, maybe a little longer. By simply hooking up a small box, called a *transceiver*, to the printer or modem port on the back of your Mac, you could wire together two or more Macs and start sharing files (see Figure 18-1). You connect the transceiver to each Mac and then daisy-chain the transceivers using wire — usually it's PhoneNet wiring, which is the same wiring used for telephone extensions.

Don't confuse AppleTalk and LocalTalk. LocalTalk is the name given to the standard of cables and connectors that creates this special Apple-style network. AppleTalk is a software protocol that tells Macs how to transfer data across a network. If you have a LocalTalk network, you use AppleTalk protocols, but they're not the same thing.

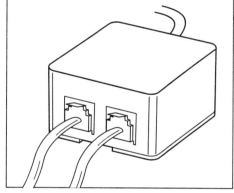

**Figure 18-1:**
A LocalTalk
transceiver
and
PhoneNet
wiring.

These days, LocalTalk is on the outs. It wasn't anything it said or did. It's just too darned slow. LocalTalk is limited to about 230 Kilobits per second, meaning a 1MB file takes about 30 seconds to transfer over such a connection (assuming it's the *only* file being transferred). Those speeds are only about 4 to 5 times faster than today's modems, and files today tend to be on the large side.

The Power Macintosh G3, the iMac, and subsequent Macs don't even support LocalTalk — at least, not directly. In those cases, you're likely to opt for an Ethernet network or, with some of the latest Mac models, an AirPort wireless network.

In other cases, though, you might find LocalTalk convenient for hooking up a limited number of older Macs and sharing the occasional file. If you have an older PostScript printer, you probably have to deal with LocalTalk in some form or fashion — most older laser printers for Macs were designed to connect through LocalTalk.

Here are a few other fast facts about LocalTalk:

- ✔ LocalTalk has limitations. Without a repeater or a hub (devices that boost the LocalTalk signal), you're limited to 32 devices (24 using PhoneNet) and 1800 feet of cabling.

- ✔ Unlike Ethernet networks, it's rare to have a *hub* at the center of your LocalTalk network. Instead, each Mac's transceiver is connected directly to two others to create a daisy-chain (like a SCSI chain). At the last Mac on either end of the LocalTalk chain, a *terminator* is installed in the open port on those transceivers to signify the end of the network.

- ✔ LocalTalk transceivers are most often connected using PhoneNet cabling, but you can also use LocalTalk cabling, which resembles long serial cables, but with only 3-pin connectors.

The phone wiring in your house might be set up for two lines (two "pairs"), especially if the wiring is reasonably new. If that's the case, you might be able to plug a phone-line splitter into the wall. Using that second line (if you don't have service on it from the phone company), you can plug in PhoneNet cabling connected to your Mac's transceiver. Instantly, you have a home or organization-wide network (assuming you're not exceeding the overall distance limits).

## Ethernet

The standard for most networking, including Mac networking, is Ethernet. Ethernet is inexpensive to add to a computer (and most Mac models include it, as shown in Table 18-1), and it's fast, offering 10 Mbps, 100 Mbps, and 1 Gbps standards. It's also the most popular way to network other types of computers, so it's fully supported by popular networking protocols, including AppleTalk and TCP/IP. In general, if you plan to get serious about your network — and you don't mind having some wires attached to your Mac — Ethernet is the way to go.

**Table 18-1  Standard Ethernet and Ethernet Upgrade Options**

| Model | Ethernet Connector | Ethernet Upgrade Options |
|---|---|---|
| Classic Macs (Mac SE and newer) | n/a | PDS card |
| Mac II series | n/a | NuBus card |
| LC series | n/a | PDS card |
| Performa series and Quadra 630 | n/a | PDS or Comm Slot card |

| Model | Ethernet Connector | Ethernet Upgrade Options |
|---|---|---|
| Performa 5400, Power Mac 5400, 5500, 4400 | 10BaseT | Comm Slot |
| Centris/Quadra | AAUI | NuBus |
| Power Mac (NuBus), Performa 6110 series | AAUI | NuBus |
| Power Mac 6500, 7200, 7300, 7600, 8600, 9600 | 10BaseT/AAUI | PCI |
| Power Mac G3, G4 | 100BaseT | PCI |
| iMac | 100BaseT | n/a |
| Power Computing | 10BaseT | PCI |
| Motorola StarMax 3000, 4000 | n/a (optional) | PCI |
| StarMax 5000 | 10BaseT | PCI |
| Umax (J & S models) | 10BaseT | PCI |

Macs that offer a connector have Ethernet capability built in. Those that don't require an upgrade card before they can connect to a network; the upgrade cards come in PDS, NuBus, Comm Slot, and PCI varieties. (See Chapter 14 for details on these technologies.)

If the Mac offers a 10BaseT (or the faster but otherwise identical 100BaseT) connector, it can accept a 10BaseT cable plugged directly into the Macintosh. Models that offer an AAUI (Apple Attachment Unit Interface) adapter require a transceiver, which can then accept either 10BaseT or 10Base2 cabling (see the next section).

Companies that offer PCI, NuBus, and comm-slot Ethernet adapters include (www.farallon.com), Asante (www.asante.com), AESP (www.aesp.com), and Macsense (www.macsense.com). If your Mac doesn't offer an internal Ethernet solution, your best bet is a LocalTalk-to-Ethernet adapter from Farallon.

You can use your home phone wiring for Ethernet networks too, but you need special equipment. Companies such as Farallon offer Ethernet-to-HomeLine adapter kits that allow you to use your Mac's Ethernet port to connect to a HomeLine-standard network. HomeLine technology allows you to use existing phone jacks for a 2 Mbps networking connection, which is not as fast as regular Ethernet but useful for small LANs between Macs in different rooms in your house.

### Rumble in the jumble: 10BaseT versus 10Base2

If you're working with Macs that require an expansion card or an AAUI transceiver to connect, you might be asking yourself which type of cabling to get: 10Base2 or 10BaseT.

10Base2 cabling is also called *thinnet, coax,* or *BNC* (which is also the name of the connector.) The cable generally looks like the cable used to connect a television to cable TV service and comes in creative colors such as gray and black. 10Base2 cabling is the less popular of the two standards these days but offers one advantage over 10BaseT — you can use it to daisy-chain networks, just like LocalTalk. You wire the cable to your Mac's transceiver, and then you wire it to the next transceiver, and so on. At both ends of the network chain, you put a terminator on the last transceiver. Such a network can stretch 600 feet before you're forced to add a hub or a network switch.

10BaseT is also called *twisted pair* and is sometimes referred to by its connector type: *RJ45.* 10BaseT is like typical phone wire except the connector and wiring are a bit thicker. 10BaseT networks require a hub — they can't be daisy-chained. The hub offers advantages, though. Problems with one 10BaseT connection don't bring down the whole network, as they can in a daisy-chained 10Base2 network. And it's easier to add new computers to a 10BaseT network because you just plug each Mac into an available port on the hub. For a 10Base2 network, you have to fit the Mac into your daisy-chain, which might be much tougher.

A third type of technology, called 100BaseT, uses the same RJ45 connector as 10BaseT but supports 100 Mbps connections. iMacs, Power Macintosh G3 and G4 machines, and many PCI-based networking expansion cards support 100BaseT. If you want to use those speeds, you need a hub that supports 100BaseT and high-quality *(Category 5)* Ethernet cable.

### Hubs and switches

So, what are these hubs of which I speak? *Hubs* are boxes that offer ports for Ethernet cabling and indicator lights that give basic information about the data traveling over your network. Hubs can be small, 5-port models designed for little LANs or larger, powered *switches* that can be connected to form larger networks. (If you're connecting two hubs, you generally use the *uplink* port to connect them, often with BNC cabling or 100BaseT cable.)

Hubs come in different shapes and sizes. For a typical home or small office network, you'll probably be fine with a *passive* hub, which simply connects between five and ten computers for sharing data. For more intense networks, you might consider a *managed* hub, which allows you, as the network administrator, to control the hub through software. With a *switched* hub, packets are actively redirected to the correct port on the hub, offering better performance than passive hubs.

## More silly terms: Router and bridge

A bridge is something I want to sell you if you think I know what a router is. (I'm kidding.) Actually, a *bridge* is hardware that moves data from one network to another. For instance, data can't pass from a LocalTalk network to an Ethernet network without a bridge.

A *router* is similar to a bridge but smarter. It can read information in a data packet and send that data along in the right direction. Routers move data more efficiently and can deal with more complex scenarios, such as working with multiple networking protocols.

To connect LocalTalk devices (or a LocalTalk network) to an Ethernet network, you need a bridge of some sort. If your have a large organizational network, you might use a router. Or you might use a router — even a software router — if you need to provide Internet access to your entire network through a modem, DSL, or cable connection. (More on that in the "Get Internet Access on your LAN" section.)

Hubs also support different connection speeds. If you have a room full or iMacs or Power Macintosh G3 and G4 machines, consider a 100BaseT hub, which lets you transfer files at speeds approaching 100 Mbps. (Due to limitations in networking protocols, the actual speeds are slower than that, but they're faster than if you use a 10BaseT network.)

Passive and switched hubs don't necessarily have to be Mac-specific. Mac-friendly companies that offer hubs include Farallon, Asante, and SMC (www.smc.com).

# *Through thin air: AirPort*

If you have a slot-loading iMac, a Power Macintosh G4, or a portable such as the iBook or PowerBook made in 2000 or later, you might get a huge kick out of AirPort. This technology allows compatible Macs to network without wires. After you're wireless, you can move around your organization or home with a portable Mac without worrying about cables — sit on the floor, at the kitchen table, in a meeting room, or wherever and you're still on the network.

AirPort requires two components. First, you need an AirPort card installed in your AirPort-compatible Mac. These cards are generally installed in special slots that Apple has hidden in the Mac for exactly that purpose. (Sometimes Macs come with the card preinstalled.)

After you install the AirPort card, you need either another Mac with AirPort capabilities (so the two can link together in a peer-to-peer network) or an AirPort Base Station, which is a special device sold by Apple that allows AirPort devices to connect to a standard network (or, if desired, to the Internet in a variety of ways).

AirPort allows data to be transferred at speeds up to 11 Mbps at distances up to 150 feet away from the Base Station. Each Base Station can support up to ten AirPort-enabled Macs at once.

The Base Station offers a 100BaseT port for connecting to an Ethernet hub (so your AirPort Macs can access other Macs on a LAN) or to a high-speed Internet device. The Base Station also includes a modem for connecting your whole AirPort network to the Internet.

After you've configured the AirPort Base Station with its Assistant software, you're ready to connect. Each AirPort-enabled Mac must be set up to use either AppleTalk or TCP/IP (as described later). You then open the special AirPort application on each Mac and select the wireless network you want to connect to. As you roam around, you can use the AirPort application to switch between wireless networks, if you have access to more than one.

Apple's AirPort technology is compatible with the IEEE 802.11 wireless standard, so you can add third-party cards (especially to PowerBooks) to get wireless access to your AirPort Base Station or a similar network configuration.

# Configuring Your Network

So, you've chosen the type of networking cable you're going to use and you've wired the whole thing together, either daisy-chaining your Macs or connecting each Mac to a hub. In either case, you're ready to make another decision — will you use AppleTalk or TCP/IP as the software protocol for your network? Each approach has advantages and disadvantages, which I'll explain after this short message from a subhead.

## Battle of the network stars: TCP/IP versus AppleTalk

AppleTalk is the venerable grandpappy protocol of Mac networking; TCP/IP is the fast-moving cousin that's taking over the scene. AppleTalk remains a bit easier to configure, especially for a smaller LAN, and it's the only protocol that works with LocalTalk hardware. TCP/IP is recommended for networks made up of newer Macs.

The other part of your decision depends on how you set up the servers on your LAN. If you have a single server using special server software such as AppleShare IP or Mac OS X, you can use TCP/IP to easily and quickly access that server. If you're using peer-to-peer serving, only Mac OS 9 or higher offers file sharing over TCP/IP. With earlier versions of the Mac OS, you have to use AppleTalk for peer-to-peer file sharing. (Older Mac OS versions can sign into file servers over TCP/IP but can't create them.)

So, you might choose AppleTalk if you have older Macs running an older version of the Mac OS or if you have a LocalTalk network. If you have newer Macs or Macs running Mac OS 9 or higher (which offers peer-to-peer file sharing over TCP/IP for the first time) or if you just want the best performance, you might choose TCP/IP as your protocol.

There's another instance where you might need to choose AppleTalk for your networking. If you have a small network where some or all Macs connect to the Internet through a modem, you'll probably want to choose AppleTalk for file sharing. The problem is that TCP/IP is used for Internet access, and you generally can't use TCP/IP for file sharing and modem-based Internet access at the same time (unless you provide access to the network through an Internet router, as discussed later in this chapter).

## *Setting up AppleTalk*

Configuring AppleTalk is fairly simple — you just need to turn on the protocol for each Mac connected to your network. Here's how to set up AppleTalk:

1. **Open the AppleTalk control panel to configure your Mac to access the network (see Figure 18-2).**

   Choose Apple menu ➪ Control Panels ➪ AppleTalk. (In earlier Mac OS versions, you may set up AppleTalk networking in the Network control panel.)

**Figure 18-2:**
The
AppleTalk
control
panel.

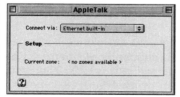

2. **In the Connect via list, choose Ethernet, Modem port, Printer port, or AirPort, depending on which type of network you have configured.**

   This is where you let your Mac know which connector or device you want to use for AppleTalk networking. (For LocalTalk networks, you choose the port you're using for the LocalTalk transceiver — either the Modem port or the Printer port.)

   The control panel takes a moment to determine whether a network exists using that type of hardware. If it finds a network, you might see a list appear where you choose the *zone* you're in. (If it doesn't find a network, it may not allow you to select that type of hardware.)

   AppleTalk Zones are used as internal dividers for large AppleTalk WANs, usually in bigger organizations. (For instance, you might have an Accounting zone and a Creative zone to encourage the advertising folks to avoid printing to the accounting folks' printer.) If you don't know which zone to choose, consult your system administrator.

3. **Close the control panel by clicking its close box.**

4. **When asked whether you want to save the change in configuration, make your selection.**

   If you choose Save, the setting is changed. You can use the File ⇨ Configurations feature to create different configurations if you routinely switch between more than one type of AppleTalk network.

That's it — AppleTalk is configured. You're ready to move on to setting up file servers and connecting to them.

If you get a message that there was an error when attempting to connect, check that you haven't chosen the wrong port in the Connect via list. If that selection is okay, check that the port is properly connected to the network. Make sure the networking cable is plugged in and all transceivers and hubs are powered and connected. If you have a daisy-chain network, make sure the entire network is connected properly and both ends are terminated.

## Setting up TCP/IP

As mentioned, setting up TCP/IP can be a bit more complicated. First, you need to open the TCP/IP control panel (choose Apple menu ⇨ Control Panels) on each Mac that will be connected to this LAN. Then you choose the type of hardware you're using for the network. Figure 18-3 shows the TCP/IP control panel.

You start by selecting, in the Connect Via list, the type of hardware you're using for your TCP/IP: Ethernet or AirPort. Then, you have some decisions to make and some numbers to fill in.

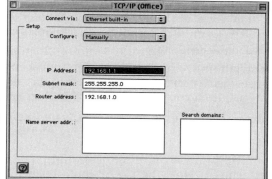

**Figure 18-3:**
The TCP/IP
control
panel.

I'll show you some default values you can use if you're configuring a small LAN. If your network is part of a larger organization or you need to provide Internet access to these networked Macs, discuss your TCP/IP numbering scheme with your network administrator. Here's what each entry does:

✔ **Configure.** In the Configure list, you choose how the TCP/IP control panel will determine the numbers it needs to operate. In most cases, you choose Manually, which allows you to enter all the numbers yourself. If you have a special DHCP server, you can choose Using DHCP Server from this list. Otherwise, you can choose the other options only on advice from your administrator. (DHCP is the Dynamic Host Configuration Protocol, a protocol for automatically assigning IP address on your network.)

If you have Mac OS 9 or higher on all your Macs and you don't need Internet access over your LAN, you can simply choose Using DHCP Server from the Configure list and then close the TCP/IP control panel. Do this on all your networked Macs and then move on to the next section, "Sharing files with the other kids." The Macs will automatically configure themselves with IP addresses and so on.

✔ **IP address.** This is the unique identifying number given to each Mac. (The number is always a series of four numbers, each between 0 and 255, separated by periods.) In most cases you need to obtain this number from your system administrator. If you're setting up a small LAN without Internet access, you can assign each Mac on your network an internal TCP/IP address that you make up for the purpose. Most such addresses start 196.168.0.1 or 196.168.1.1 and increment the last digit from there (such as 196.168.0.2, 196.168.0.3 and so on).

✔ **Subnet mask.** This number is used with the IP address on larger networks. For smaller networks, it's always 255.255.255.0 unless your system administrator tells you otherwise.

✔ **Router address.** This number is used for the router or gateway in an Internet configuration. For a local network, an exact router address isn't necessary; 196.168.0.0 or 196.168.1.0 (that is, the 0 address of whatever internal IP scheme you choose) should work fine.

If you plan to use an Internet router to provide Internet access to your TCP/IP network, you need a correct router address in this slot. See "Accessing the Internet from your LAN," later in this chapter.

✔ **Name server address.** Again, this is necessary only for Internet access; otherwise, you can leave it blank or insert a dummy address such as 127.0.0.0.

With those numbers set, you can close the TCP/IP control panel. You're asked to save the current configuration; do so. (As with the AppleTalk control panel, you can create different configurations of the TCP/IP control panel and quickly switch between them, using the File ➪ Configurations command from with the control panel.) Now you're ready to move on to file sharing.

## *Sharing files with the other kids*

You have cabling and a protocol. Now all you need is to set up your computers so that one can log into the other and access its files. You do this in one of two ways: using a professional-level file serving application to create a single server computer (in a client-server environment) or using the *file sharing* feature built into the Mac OS to share files from individual computers (peer-to-peer). I cover file sharing in this section; pro-level server software is outside the scope of this book. (Apple sells both AppleShare IP and Mac OS X Server for high-end serving. You can also using Linux, UNIX, or Windows NT to offer AppleTalk or TCP/IP file services to Macs.)

To set up built-in file sharing, you need to take a few steps. First, you turn on file sharing so that others can access your Mac over the network. Second, you create user accounts for the people to whom you want to give permission to access your computer. Finally, you determine what privileges those users have (which folders and files they can access) after they're signed on.

The first part is easy:

1. **Choose Apple menu ➪ Control Panel ➪ File Sharing.**

   With the control panel open, make sure you have an Owner's name and password for your Mac. This ensures that you'll be able to access your Mac from other computers on the network. (It also sets up a security barrier so that unauthorized users can't access all your files.)

2. **Click the On button to turn on file sharing.**

   If the button says Off, file sharing is already active.

3. **If you have Mac OS 9 or higher and you've set up a TCP/IP network, click the Enable file sharing over TCP/IP option so that your users will be able to access your Mac.**

# Choosing your friends (users and groups)

The next step in setting up file sharing is to determine which users will have access to your Mac. Although you could let anyone sign on as a *guest* user, it's generally recommended that you set up individual accounts for each person who will access your Mac over the network. This allows you to keep track of them and assign different users different levels of access to your files.

Each individual account you create is considered a *user.* You can then assign that user to one or more *groups.* When you tell your Mac that a certain group can access a particular folder on your Mac, all the users in that group get those privileges.

To manage your users and groups:

1. **Select Apple menu ⇨ Control Panels ⇨ Users & Groups.**

   (In Mac OS 9, choose the Users & Groups tab in the File Sharing control panel.) A listing of the current users and groups that have been created (if any) appears. A listing of the current users and groups that have been created (if any) appears.

2. **To create a new user:**

   a. **Click the New User button.**

   b. **In the dialog box that appears, enter a user name and password for this user.**

   c. **Click the close box.**

3. **To create a new group:**

   a. **Click the New Group button.**

   b. **Select the names of the users you want to add to that group and drag them to the open group window.**

   You can select them individually or hold down the Command key while clicking to select more than one user.

   c. **After you've added as many users as you like, click the group window's close box.**

4. **When you finish creating users and groups, you can close the control panel.**

## *Setting file privileges*

The whole point of creating users and groups is to assign those groups certain privileges to access your files. It's a little like being head cheerleader: Here's your chance, finally, to dictate who's *in* and who's *out*.

To set privileges:

1. **Make sure file sharing is turned on.**

   Choose Apple menu ⇨ Control Panel ⇨ File Sharing. Click the On button to turn on file sharing. (If the button says Off, file sharing is already on.)

2. **In the Finder, select the folder (or disk) you want to share and then choose File ⇨ Get Info.**

   That folder's Info dialog box appears. (Note that the name of the dialog box includes the name of the folder or disk you've selected.)

3. **In the Show list, choose Sharing, as shown in Figure 18-4.**

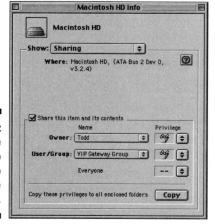

**Figure 18-4:**
Use the
folder's Info
window to
set file
privileges.

4. **To share the selected item, turn on the Share this item and its contents option.**

   This causes the item to be shared over the network.

5. **In the bottom half of the screen, select which user or group can access that item and what privileges that user or group will have.**

   In general, the Owner should be set to your user name. The User/Group can be any user or group you've previously defined in the Users & Groups control panel. The last entry, Everyone, let's you set the privilege level for *all* users who have access to your Mac.

So what are the privileges? In the small lists to the right, you can choose if that person or group will have

- **Read/write access.** The user (or group) can open any file, create files, and save files to that folder.

- **Read only access.** The user can open files in this folder but can't save changes to those files or save new files in the folder.

- **Write only access.** The user can save new files to this folder but can't open or edit any of the files already in the folder.

- **None.** The user has no access to this folder.

6. **After you set these privileges, you can choose to copy these privilege levels to all subfolders within this folder, so that they all offer the same privileges as this one. To do so, click the Copy button.**

   (You can still change the privilege levels of an individual subfolder later.)

7. **Click the close box.**

   Privileges for this folder are set.

8. **Head back out to the Finder and set privileges for any other folders you want to share (or any other folders for which you want to offer different privileges).**

## Signing on

With everything set up, you or anyone else on the network can sign onto the shared folder or disk. You have three basic ways to do this. If you're using AppleTalk for your networking protocol, available servers on your network will appear in either the Chooser or the Network Browser. For TCP/IP, you might also see the items in the Chooser or Network Browser; otherwise, you enter the IP address for the server. Here's how:

✔ In the Chooser, highlight the AppleShare icon on the left side. Any connected AppleTalk servers appear on the right side of the window. Double-click the server you want to access and then enter your user name and password.

✔ In the Network Browser, you should automatically see any AppleTalk servers. In Mac OS 9, you might have to double-click the AppleTalk *neighborhood* to see AppleTalk servers. (You might also see TCP/IP-based server neighborhoods if you have Mac OS 9; they're often listed under your local .com address, such as mac-upgrade.com.) After you find the server, double-click it to log in.

✔ To sign into a TCP/IP server, click the Server IP Address button in the Chooser or choose Connect to Server from the Shortcuts menu in the Network browser. (The Shortcuts menu is access through the small pointing-finger icon.) In the dialog box, enter the IP address for the server you want to access and then click Connect.

After you've accessed the server that you want to log in to, you see the Connect window (see Figure 18-5). You enter your user name and password and then click Connect. If you're a registered user on the server computer (or if the server allows Guest access), you see a list of the folders or disks you can access. Double-click an item and it appears in the Finder on your desktop, ready to access.

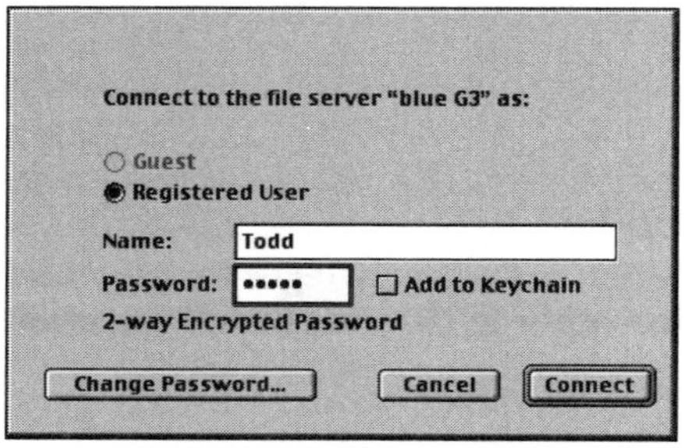

**Figure 18-5:**
The Connect dialog box enables you to log in with your user name and password.

Connect to the file server "blue G3" as:

○ Guest
● Registered User

Name:  Todd

Password:  •••••   ☐ Add to Keychain

2-way Encrypted Password

[ Change Password... ]   [ Cancel ]   [ Connect ]

# Accessing the Internet from Your LAN

If you have your LAN set up and functioning correctly, you might be interested in taking the next step — offering Internet access to all your Macs over that LAN connection. You have a few different options, depending on how your LAN is configured and what type of Internet connection technologies is at your disposal.

If your LAN has direct access to the Internet (usually through a T-1 or similar hard-wired connection), you're in luck. Generally, all you have to do is properly configure your TCP/IP control panel so that your Mac has its preassigned IP address and the proper router (or gateway) address plugged in. You also want a good DNS server address so that your Mac can resolve domain name addresses such as www.apple.com when entered into a browser. (If you don't know the correct addresses, ask your system administrator or ISP.)

If you need to provide access to your LAN using a modem, a cable modem, a DSL modem, or a similar device, you need an Internet router. This can be either software or hardware that moves data from an Internet connection to your LAN. Software options include IPNetRouter from Sustainable Softworks (www.sustworks.com) and SurfDoubler and SoftRouter products from Vicomsoft (www.vicomsoft.com), as shown in Figure 18-6.

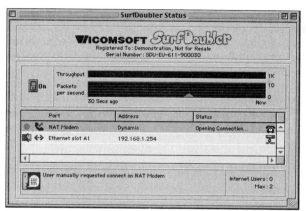

**Figure 18-6:**
SurfDoubler
lets two or
more Macs
on your LAN
access a
modem, a
cable
modem,
or a DSL
connection
to the
Internet.

These products enable one Mac on your network to connect to the Internet through a modem (even a cable, ISDN, or DSL modem). That Mac then becomes a router, passing TCP/IP data between your LAN and the Internet. All you have to do on the other client Macs is enter the correct Router address in the TCP/IP control panel, and they have access to the Net.

You can offload these responsibilities to a hardware device that acts as an Internet router. Various devices can do the trick, including routers from Ramp Networks (www.webramp.com), Macsense (www.macsense.com), Cisco Systems (www.cisco.com), and NetGear (www.netgear.com) that offer Internet access through a DSL connection or through one or more modem connections. (The routers can use two or more modems, in some cases, to offer higher bandwidth connections for your LAN.) Even the AirPort Base Station (www.apple.com) can use its built-in modem to act as a router for both wireless and Ethernet-based Macs connected to the base station.

The main advantage of a hardware router over a software router is the fact that you don't have to leave a router Mac up and running. The hardware router takes care of the connection for you, regardless of which Macs are turned on and running.

# Chapter 19

# Intimate with iMac: Special Upgrades for Your Little Buddy

*A*lthough Apple recommends that you do your iMac upgrading through the USB (or FireWire) ports, the little-Mac-that-could does sport a few internal goodies. No matter what iMac you have, you might need to add RAM, and it would be nice to get inside the Mac to do that. And after you've had the iMac for a while, wouldn't it be nice to swap its hard disk with a larger model? Or what about upgrading the processor? It's possible: You can put a nice, speedy new G3 in the tray-loading iMac.

Plus, the original Bondi blue iMacs (revision A and B) sport something else that Apple isn't keen to have you worry about — a secret slot. Using off-the-shelf upgrades, you can add a serial port, video out, or even a graphics accelerator for gaming. You just have to know where to find the slot.

## Stands for Your iMac

Among all the colorful peripheral items — mouse pads, CD organizers, tangerine-colored cheese crackers — designed to match your colorful iMac, it might seem boring to start with something like iMac stands. But I do so for two reasons. First, the iMac's screen is a little low for great ergonomics, unless you put it on top of something. (I know some folks who use a phone book, with good results. The problem is watching their faces fall when they need a local phone number.) Second, the stands are pretty cool.

Companies such as Compucable (www.compucable.com) and Contour Design (www.contourdesign.com) offer great-looking stands that bring your iMac up to eye-level and, in some cases, offer extras like a small stand for documents. If you feel you're bending your neck a bit too much, look into one of these stands.

Chapter 12 also discusses some iMac stands that include additional USB, serial, and parallel ports and, in some cases, floppy drives.

# Opening the Slot-Loading iMac

One reason Apple actually encourages you to get inside your iMac is to add RAM. With the slot-loading models, Apple actually did some engineering to make adding RAM pretty easy. You can also easily add an AirPort card to these models because both upgrades are accomplished through a convenient access door.

The slot-loading iMac sports an Ultra ATA drive (1 inch high and 3.5 inches wide). Users have reported success installing 40GB (and larger) drives. You just need the patience to remove a few panels, 22 screws, and some connectors. I recommend that you have the pros upgrade your slot-loading iMac. If you're interested in doing it yourself, however, you can find the process documented on a few iMac advocacy sites, including iMac Today (www.imactoday.com).

## Upgrading RAM

To upgrade RAM, you first need to get the right type of PC100 DIMM for your iMac — the specifics are discussed in Chapter 15. After you have your hands on the correct DIMM, you're ready to get inside and add the RAM.

To upgrade the RAM in a slot-loading iMac or iMac DV model, do the following:

1. **Shut down the iMac and place it, screen down, on a smooth surface.**

   A clean, lint-free towel between the surface and the iMac's screen is a good idea. Apple recommends you keep it plugged in for now so that you can discharge static.

2. **Locate the access door on the bottom of the iMac. Using a coin, turn the latch and open the access door (see Figure 19-1).**

3. **Touch the metal shield inside the latch area (to discharge static electricity) and then unplug the iMac.**

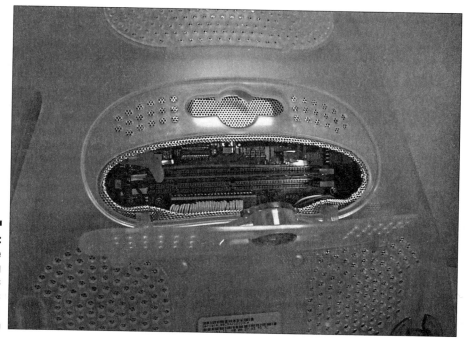

**Figure 19-1:**
Opening the
slot-loading
iMac's
access
door.

4. **Locate the available DIMM slot and insert the module into that slot.**

   It should plug straight into the slot; the small notches on the slot and the module help you orient the module.

5. **Close the access door and turn the latch to lock it shut.**

6. **Turn the Mac right side up, plug it in, and connect its keyboard and mouse. Start it up.**

   If you hear tones or your Mac fails to start, the RAM might not be seated properly. Open the Mac up and reinstall it.

7. **After the Finder appears, choose Apple menu ⇨ About this Computer and see whether your Built-in Memory reflects the new amount.**

   If your iMac doesn't seem to recognize the new RAM, you should shut down, open the iMac back up, and make sure the RAM is seated correctly. (You might try taking it out, installing it again, and restarting your iMac to see whether it works this second time.) If the RAM is installed correctly and still not working, the RAM might be bad. Take it to an Apple service center to have it tested.

## Adding an AirPort card

The slot-loading iMac is designed to accept an AirPort card, which you can use for wireless networking with other AirPort-enabled Macs (see Chapter 18). Here's how to install the card:

1. **Follow Steps 1 through 3 in the preceding section, "Upgrading RAM."**

   The AirPort card is installed through the same access door you use to install RAM.

2. **With the door open, detach the flexible antenna from the upper slot and remove its plastic coating.**

3. **Connect the antenna to your AirPort card and insert the card sideways (using the circuit board connector) in the AirPort slot, which is above the RAM slots.**

4. **Close the access door, plug in your iMac, and fire it up.**

5. **Install the AirPort software to activate and configure the card.**

An AirPort card pulled directly from an iBook or a PowerBook won't work in the iMac (or in a Power Macintosh G4). Instead, the card must include a small circuit board attachment (which comes with the card in its original packaging) for it to be installed correctly.

## Accessing video out

If you have an iMac DV model, you have another hidden port: a VGA-out port. This allows you to hook up a second monitor for *mirroring* the iMac's image to an external monitor. You can also use the port with a presentation system or a *scan converter* to place the iMac's screen image on a TV. For instance, Focus Enhancements (www.focusinfo.com) offers the iTViewDV, which allows you to put the iMac's image on TV or record to a VCR. Many other companies offer more generic scan converters, too.

To use the port, all you need to do is swap the small plastic panel that shipped on your iMac with the panel included in your iMac's packing materials:

1. **To remove the original panel, place the iMac screen-down on a soft, flat surface.**

2. **Insert a flathead screwdriver in the small slot at the top of the panel and gently pry it off.**

   You'll see the VGA-out port.

3. **Snap the second panel (with a cutaway for the port) into place.**

# Opening the Tray-Loading iMac

The original iMac design wasn't quite as friendly for upgrading because it didn't offer a convenient access door. Overall, though, it's actually a touch easier for upgrading other internals, such as the hard drive, the processor, or for the very intrepid, the CD-ROM mechanism. I cover those upgrades in this section.

These methods have worked for me in the past, but I recommend them only if you're a seasoned upgrader who isn't afraid to take your warranty into your own hands. Apple hasn't designed the iMac for easy internal upgrading. If you're at all nervous, have an authorized dealer perform the upgrades for you. It's generally pretty affordable, especially when you factor in the price tag you'd put on peace of mind.

## Adding RAM

The original series of tray-loading iMacs require a little more elbow work to get into them and upgrade the RAM. They do have an available DIMM slot, however, that you can fill with the appropriate SO-DIMM module, as specified in Chapter 15.

After you have your DIMM, you need to open up the iMac to get at the available DIMM slot. Here's how:

1. **Shut down the iMac, unplug all cables and cords, and ground yourself.**

   To guard against static when upgrading an iMac, the best plan is to wear a grounding strap.

2. **Place the iMac screen down on a soft cloth or towel on a flat surface.**

3. **Using a Phillips screwdriver, remove the screw that's inside the small handle on the underside of the iMac (see Figure 19-2).**

4. **Grab the handle and remove the plastic cover from the iMac (also shown in Figure 19-2).**

5. **Unplug the cables that connect to the main logic board.**

   If the cables are secured by clamps or screws, remove those first. Unplug all four cables (some iMacs have only three) and move them out of the way of the logic board. (The large power connector is the toughest one; push its small plastic lever *into* the connector and pull the connector away from the port. It should come out fairly easily after you have it unhooked from the port.)

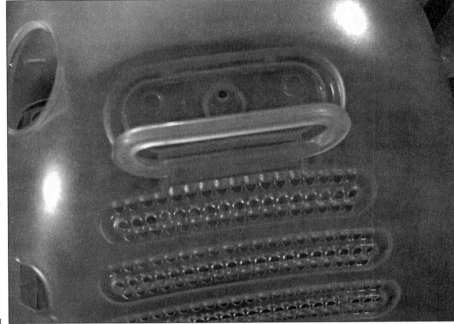

**Figure 19-2:**
Use the
handle to
pull the
plastic
cover from
the iMac.

6. **Use a Phillips screwdriver to remove the two screws that attach to the small plastic handle. Then use the handle to slide the logic board straight up and out of the computer.**

   Do the sliding slowly to avoid harming anything. When you're finished, place the logic board on a flat surface.

7. **Unsnap the metal shield by lifting it on both sides.**

   Now you should see the available SO-DIMM slot for RAM.

8. **Insert your RAM module into the slot at a 45-degree angle and then press the module down toward the logic board until it snaps into place.**

   The SO-DIMM will fit into the slot in only one way. Check the notch on the DIMM and the slot to align it correctly (see Figure 19-3).

   The original iMac 233 model could also accept a VRAM upgrade, which installs in the same way as a regular RAM SO-DIMM. The VRAM is located on the logic board, separate from the regular RAM slot. You'll have to remove the existing module to upgrade the VRAM.

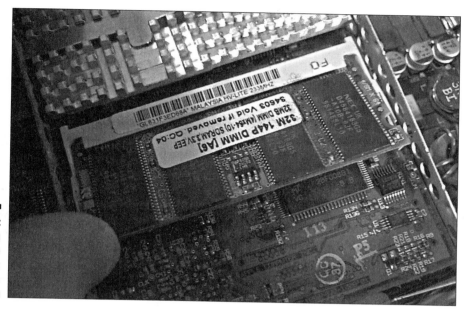

**Figure 19-3:**
Installing
the
SO-DIMM in
its slot.

9. **Reverse the procedure to close the iMac back up.**

    Note that you need to be careful when sliding the logic board assembly back into the iMac so that the CD-ROM drive door lines up correctly. Then don't forget the screws in the small handle, the screw or clamps (or both) on the four cables, and the screw on the plastic cover.

## Upgrading the processor

Late in the writing phase of this book, Newer Technology (www.newertech. com) surprised the Mac market by announcing a processor upgrade for the tray-loading iMac.

The iMAXpowr G3 466 is a daughtercard upgrade with a 466-MHz Power PC G3 and 1MB of backside cache. To perform the upgrade, you open your iMac as described in the "Adding RAM" section's Steps 1 through 6. Then you remove the existing daughtercard and replace it with the upgrade. The upgrade offers the same advantages of other processor daughtercard upgrades — namely, no special driver software is necessary.

It's not the easiest upgrade to accomplish, but Newer Technology includes written instructions and an instruction video to help you through the steps. And, now that such an upgrade has been announced, don't be surprised to see other major upgrade manufacturers follow suit with their own iMac upgrade cards.

# Upgrading the hard drive or CD-ROM drive

With the logic board/drive assembly exposed, as discussed in the preceding section (Steps 1 through 6), getting at the hard drive or CD-ROM drive is actually pretty easy. And you can upgrade both drives if you like. For the hard drive, you need a 1-inch tall (3.5 inches wide) IDE or EIDE drive, preferably in a capacity larger than 6GB. (Otherwise, what's the point?) It's best to stick with a drive rated at 5400 RPM just to keep the iMac from getting hotter than it's designed to run.

You can upgrade the CD-ROM drive to a CD-R drive with the PowerCDR upgrade from TechWorks (www.techworks.com). This special upgrade is designed specifically to replace the CD-ROM drive in tray-loading iMacs, and it even includes interchangeable colorful buttons you can add to make the drive match your iMac.

Step-by-step instructions for installation come with PowerCDR, but you might need a little help to get at the hard drive. Here's how:

1. **Follow Steps 1 through 6 in the preceding section, "Adding RAM."**

   You're ready to go once you've removed the logic board/drive assembly and placed it on a flat surface.

2. **Using your thumbs, push in on the bracket on the bottom front of the CD-ROM drive and then pull up to remove the drive.**

   Observe the guides that hold the CD-ROM drive in place; you need to line the drive up with those guides to replace it. (Note that, at this point, you have the CD-ROM drive out for swapping with the PowerCDR upgrade.)

3. **Disconnect the IDE cable from the back of the CD-ROM drive.**

4. **Remove the small metal bracket that covers the hard drive.**

   Note its orientation carefully for when you're putting the iMac back together.

5. **Remove the two retaining screws on the hard drive's rails.**

   They're close to the front.

6. **Slide the hard drive (and its rails) out of the drive cage.**

   This is a toughie. The easiest way to get the drive out is to turn the entire assembly over and note the small metal tabs (see Figure 19-4). Maneuver the drive so that those tabs are clear of their metal guards and then slowly work the drive up and out of the cage. It's a tight fit all around; work slowly to avoid hurting any of the other cables or logic board elements around the drive.

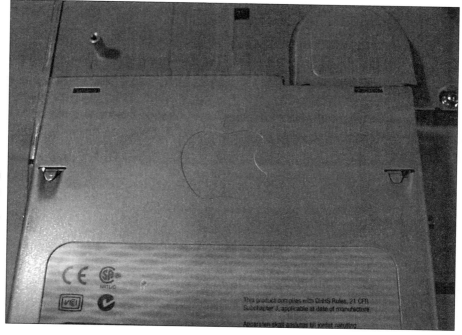

**Figure 19-4:**
On the underside of the drive cage, note the small tabs that secure the drive.

7. **Remove the IDE cable and power connectors from the back of the hard drive.**

8. **Remove the four screws that secure the hard drive to the rail assembly. Then remove the rail assembly from the drive.**

9. **Install the rail assembly on your new hard drive, plug in the IDE cable and power cable, and then reinstall the drive and rails in the drive cage.**

   Don't forget to screw the drive's rails back into the drive cage.

10. **Replace the small metal bracket and reinstall the CD-ROM drive.**

    Note that the CD-ROM drive needs to slide in a bit from the front; there's a small lip on the back of the CD-ROM drive that catches the metal bracket. Also, on the front of the drive under the tray, you'll note two small hooks that latch to the drive cage. If they're secure, it's a indication that the drive is installed correctly.

11. **Close up the iMac and test.**

    If you need help closing up the iMac, just reverse Steps 1 through 6 outlined in the "Adding RAM" section You then need to boot your iMac from a Mac OS CD-ROM; you might also have to format the drive (choose Mac OS Extended format). From there, you can install the Mac OS and replace your files from backup disks.

# The Secret Upgrades

The original revision A and revision B iMac models (but, unfortunately, no later models) shipped with a poorly kept secret: the *mezzanine* slot. This nonstandard upgrade slot, based on PCI technology, might have been intended for a future upgrade that Apple never pursued, such as video-out or an upgrade to FireWire.

What did happen, though, were some enterprising solutions from third-party vendors. Using the slot's technology, vendors offered upgrades from serial ports and VGA ports (see Figure 19-5) to SCSI and even an accelerated game card. Along with the slot, the original iMac also has a small port area that was unused, by default.

Upgrading through the slot is arduous. In general, you open the iMac as if you were upgrading RAM, and then you unmount the logic board and flip it over — the upgrade slot is on the bottom of the logic board. Then you plug the upgrade into the mezzanine slot, thread the ports through the unused port opening, and close everything back up again.

Table 19-1 details those offerings, plus some other internal upgrades. For instance, the Stealth Serial Port adds a port by replacing the internal modem in all tray-loading iMacs.

**Figure 19-5:**
On the bottom, a VGA port and a serial port, added through the secret slot.

| Table 19-1 | Internal Upgrades for Earlier iMacs | | | |
|---|---|---|---|---|
| Upgrade | Capabilities Added | Which iMac? | Manufacturer | Web Site |
| iPort | serial and VGA port | Bondi only | Griffin Technology | www.griffintech-nology.com |
| Stealth Serial Port | Serial port (replaces modem) | Any tray-loading model | GeeThree | www.geethree.com |
| iProRAIDTV | SCSI and TV-in | Bondi only | Formac | www.formac.com |
| iPresenter | Video-out port | Any tray-loading model | PowerR | www.powerr.com |
| Gamewizard | VooDoo 3-D accelerator | Bondi only | Micro-Conversions | n/a* |

*Unfortunately, MicroConversions is out of business. At the time of this writing, however, this upgrade can still be purchased through Mac retail outlets.

# iMac Troubleshooting Issues and Resetting

For the most part, troubleshooting the iMac is similar to troubleshooting most other Macs. In fact, it can be easier because the only external technologies you need to worry about are USB and Ethernet. Otherwise, iMacs are *hard-reset* (a restart of the iMac that's not accomplished through software commands) in a funny way, and you'll want to keep up on your firmware updates:

- If you're having trouble with peripherals or input devices, suspect a USB problem first. Often, unplugging and replugging USB devices (or just restarting the iMac) will solve trouble with external peripherals. (See Chapter 4 for more USB troubleshooting advice.)

- With tray-loading iMacs, resetting a hard freeze (after all other keystroke attempts have failed and you've made sure the keyboard is plugged in correctly) require an unbent paperclip placed in the reset slot on the side of the Mac (near the other ports.) The reset button is indicated by a triangle icon.

If you're sick of trying to find a paperclip to unbend when you need to hard-reset your tray-loading iMac, you can add a button. Inexpensive add-on button options are the iMacButton (`www.imacbutton.com`) or Contour Design's (`www.contourdesigns.com`) Uniswitch.

✔ With the slot-loading iMacs, you can also hold down the Power button (on the front of the iMac) to force it to shut down after a freeze (hold it down for five seconds). This has the added benefit of putting the iMac to sleep if it's not actually frozen, saving you from losing data.

✔ Finally, the iMac offers more firmware updates than most other Mac models, including updates for the modem (in early Bondi iMacs) and the CD-ROM or DVD-ROM mechanism in various models. Fortunately, Apple provides a single Tech Info article on the Web detailing the updates at `til.info.apple.com/techinfo.nsf/artnum/n58174`. (Note that the article number, 58174, shouldn't change, even if its location on the Web does at some point.)

# Part IV
# Internal Medicine and Maintenance

The 5th Wave

By Rich Tennant

"Brad! That's not your modem we're hearing! It's Buddy!! He's out of his cage and in the iMac!!"

## In this part . . .

A big part of getting a Mac working again isn't messing with hardware — it's troubleshooting the software. Like the cells, proteins, and DNA of our bodies, system software and applications give a Mac its unique personality and enable it to do things. Keeping it up and running means regular maintenance, the occasional in-depth examination, and treating illnesses — bugs, corruption, conflicts, and viruses — as soon as they set in. These chapters give you a greater understanding of the software sicknesses that can set in with your Mac, how to cure those ailments, and what to do to keep them from coming back.

# Chapter 20

# First Aid for the Mac OS and Applications

* * *

* * *

Troubleshooting your home entertainment center is rarely about pulling open the back of your TV and replacing the picture tube (or whatever the heck is back there). More often, it's about figuring out why the VCR clock blinks 12:00 or why the TV turns itself on in the middle of the night and switches itself to the cookware-shopping channel.

In the same way, Mac troubleshooting is more often about a problem with your applications or the Mac OS than it is about a blown printer or a faulty RAM module. Sure, the hardware can fail, but day to day, you're going to have more trouble with software.

The easiest way to think of software problems it to relate them to a trip to the doctor when you have some type of unidentified crud. (Now I'm writing *Internal Medicine For Dummies*, it seems.) The doctor (who knows quite a bit about illnesses) diagnoses the illness based on your symptoms and then treats that illness.

In this chapter, you do the same thing. First, you get a medical school primer on the types of illnesses to expect. Then you diagnose your Mac's illness from its symptoms. Finally, play doctor and treat the illness.

## Software Illnesses

What happens on your Mac's screen is a result of the interaction between two types of software: applications and the Mac OS system software. So if you have a software-related problem, you need to figure out whether the culprit is one or both types of software.

In some cases, you might be able to isolate the problem to a specific application. For instance, suppose Microsoft Word crashes whenever you load a particular document. That might be a corruption issue in that document or a bug in Microsoft Word. In many cases, though, a conflict exists that goes a bit deeper — a problem with the interaction between your applications and the Mac OS. Those problems, in turn, require deeper analysis. In general, software misbehaves for three different reasons:

✔ **Bugs.** At it's most basic, a bug is a mistake by the programmer. If an application or Mac OS software component does something it's not supposed to do, that's a bug. Bugs often cause crashes or hangs, although they sometimes just result in error messages or odd behavior.

✔ **Conflicts.** Conflicts occur when two (or more) software commands try to perform the same task or access the same data at once or when one component changes something that the other software is trying to use. Often, the conflict occurs between a Mac OS extension (which changes or patches the Mac OS) and an application that doesn't expect to find that extension.

✔ **Corruption.** Corruption occurs when an important file gets overwritten with either bad or nonsensical information. This can also cause crashes, hangs, or other problems. Corruption often happens as a result of a bug but might happen when an application or the Mac crashes for some other reason.

These are the basic illnesses — a bug, a conflict, or corruption. Each has its own treatment, as discussed later in this chapter. First, however, you need to diagnose which illness your Mac has, based on its symptoms.

# Diagnosing from the Symptoms

As with real doctoring, symptoms can't always point you directly to a particular disease — a fever, for instance, doesn't always mean you have the bubonic plague — but symptoms can help you figure out what sort of disease you're dealing with, as you work toward a solution.

Here's a look at the types of symptoms you're likely to encounter when your Mac's software is giving you a hard time:

✔ **Errors.** These are actual error messages, which appear in an alert dialog box and don't crash the program. After you click OK, you can still work with the program, at least in some way.

- ✔ **Crashes.** In the case of a crash, the program automatically shuts down. This might be accompanied by an error message explaining the crash. (For instance, you might get a message in the Finder telling you that the application unexpectedly quit.)

- ✔ **Freezes.** With a freeze, the screen locks up completely, usually with no error message (or, in some cases, a partial error message). With a freeze, you can't move the mouse pointer around and even keystrokes (such as Control+⌘+Power) can't reset the Mac.

- ✔ **Hangs.** A hang is similar to a freeze, at least in appearances, but with some minor differences. For instance, with a hang you might be able to move the mouse pointer around on the screen or you might see the clock in the menu bar continue to keep time. (With a freeze, you won't see anything move on the screen.) A hang usually happens with the program gets locked into a logic loop that causes it to stop responding to other input. This is not as drastic as a freeze — you might still be able to recover from it and save data.

Now, when you encounter trouble, you can probably pin it down to one of these symptoms. The key to a successful diagnosis is documenting the error and seeing whether you can reproduce it. If you're having trouble with your Mac, I recommend that you put a pad of paper next to the keyboard. When you experience a problem, write down what you last did, what applications were running, and so forth. (You can also use it for doodling while you're on the phone.)

With that information in hand, you can delve deeper into each symptom and figure out what illness your Mac has and, later in the chapter, how to treat it.

## Symptom #1: The Mac displays an error message

Error messages are easily the best type of symptom to encounter. For one thing, error messages usually don't crash your application. Therefore, although you've encountered an error, you might still be able to save your work — or even continue working without doing much. Some error messages point you specifically to the problem, such as a misconfigured printer or the fact that you're running low on RAM.

In most cases, you read the error message and see whether you can figure out what configuration or other problem might have caused it to appear. Those are happy errors, if such a concept exists. A little tougher are the slightly more vague messages you sometimes encounter, discussed next.

### *Not enough memory error message*

You'll definitely come across a *Not enough memory* error message at some point. The error is saying one of two things — either you've filled up your Mac's RAM by opening and attempting to work with too many applications or you've opened too many windows or documents in your current application and it's over its allotted memory.

When you get this message, switch to the Finder and choose the About This Computer command from the Apple menu. In that window, check the Largest Unused Block. If it's a very small number, you might need to quit one or more applications so that the others can continue to work.

If you have a decent chunk of unused memory, look at the problematic application's RAM level. If the application's entry has a full bar (indicating it's using all the RAM allotted to it, as shown in Figure 20-1), you can probably solve the problem by assigning more RAM to that application.

Instructions for assigning RAM to applications can be found in Chapter 15.

**Figure 20-1:** In this example, Communicator is using nearly its entire RAM allotment and unused RAM is very low.

If you're getting out-of-memory errors over and over, you might be encountering *memory fragmentation*. This happens when you repeatedly open and close many applications or files; after a while, it's difficult for your Mac to find contiguous bits of memory that it can use for new applications. (Some applications do a great job of cleaning up after themselves when they quit; others aren't so good, leaving little bits of locked-up memory behind.) The best plan? Restart your Mac using the Special ⇨ Restart command.

If you continue to encounter out-of-memory problems with a particular application (or you only encounter them when that application is running), a bug might be causing a *memory leak* in the application. This is when an application begins to take up more memory than it's supposed to, thus interfering with another application's memory space. For an application with a chronic memory leak, you usually need to update the application (because it has a bug), avoid using it while other applications are running, or both.

### Disk is full error message

Ideally, you get a *Disk is full* error only when your disk is actually full — you've saved so many documents or installed so many applications that no storage space is left on your hard disk. If that's the case, the solution is to delete files until you have a little more space. (You might want to archive the files and place them on a removable disk so you can get at them, if necessary.)

You might be surprised at the type of files that fill a disk quickly — aside from multimedia files such as digital video, photos, and audio clips, some of the worst culprits are email messages and download attachments you might get though email. (Check the Downloads or Attachments folder inside your email application's folder; where you may find megabytes of old files. Depending on the application, such folders might also be hidden in the Preferences folder within the System Folder.)

You can get this error also if a very old application is running and it incorrectly calculates the available disk space. Another time you might get this message is if a disk doctor utility is open while you're trying to save a document in another application. (The solution is to close the disk doctor application.) This error might also suggest virus-like activity; if you know for a fact that you have got plenty of disk space, run your virus checking program (discussed in Chapter 21).

### File not found, File system, or Type –192 error message

*File not found, File system,* and Type –192 errors usually occur when you've suddenly lost a networking connection or you eject a removable disk and then attempt to access a file on that disk (through an alias or an application's Open command). The solution is to get that connection or disk back on the desktop.

If that doesn't seem to be the case, you might be encountering some desktop database corruption. Run Disk First Aid and see whether it detects any trouble; then rebuild the desktop (discussed in Chapter 21). If those two fail, run your virus protection software and then run a disk doctor program.

### Could not open file, Type –39, or Type –199 error message

If you can't get a document to open in your application, the likely cause is corruption. The file is no longer being recognized in the file format in which is was originally saved, possibly because part of it has been overwritten.

It's also possible that the application needs a higher RAM allocation (see Chapter 15) or you're trying to use the wrong application to load the document. (For instance, you're trying load a spreadsheet document into

Microsoft Word.) In any case, you might try opening the document in a different application if you really need its contents; see the "Rooting out corruption" section later in this chapter.

# Symptom #2: The Mac crashes

When a program crashes, you might see an error message as the program disappears. Sometimes the Finder tells you that the application quit because of a Type 11 error or something similar. Surprisingly, these error messages basically mean diddly-squat, at least for troubleshooting. They're there to help programmers find bugs or conflicts in their applications. I talk about some of the messages in general, but realize that such error messages don't tell you the root of the problem like non-crashing messages sometimes will.

First, I want to talk a bit more generally about crashes. You can encounter three types of crashes. Which one you experience might help determine the root problem (at least, it might point you in the right direction). Here are the types:

- **Error message or code displayed.** This is the most controlled sort of crash; the Mac OS decide that the program did something incorrectly, so it displays an alert box (usually with a little bomb icon in it) and forces the program to quit. This can be a bug, a conflict, or corruption, although I'd lean toward bugs on this one.

- **Application unexpectedly quits.** In this case, the application disappears into oblivion, followed by a message in the Finder telling you that the application quit unexpectedly. This suggests that the application encountered corruption in a document or a preference file. If this is the case, test the document again to see whether you can replicate the crash. If the crash happened when you tried to invoke a particular command, the problem might be a bug.

- **No message displayed.** In this case, the application just disappears and your Mac might become more unstable. (Save files in other applications and restart as soon as you can.) For this type of crash, suspect corruption if it happened when working (opening, closing, printing) on a particular file; otherwise, it's likely a conflict.

## Troubleshooting the crash

When you encounter a crash, your first goal should be to save your work in other applications and restart your Mac. After any crash, your Mac might not be too stable for more than a few minutes of work.

To figure out why the crash happened, though, you must document the error and attempt to recreate it. If you figure out that it happens when a particular document is used (possible corruption) or a particular command is invoked (possible bug) or that the crash doesn't occur when you start up without extensions (possible conflict), you're on your way to solving the problem. Of course, a crash might also be a once-in-a-while occurrence that has no greater significance. Here are some questions to ask about the crash:

- ✔ **Have you restarted your Mac recently?** If not, you might have encountered some memory fragmentation or corruption in system memory. The solution is to restart and see whether things clear up on their own.

- ✔ **Have you added anything recently?** If you've added a new device, you might have also added a new device driver. Driver software is often a conflict culprit — the driver you installed might conflict with one of your applications or with the Mac OS. Check out the Read Me file and see whether the manufacturer's Web site has an update to the driver.

- ✔ **Have you upgraded the Mac OS recently?** Upgrading the Mac OS can cause conflicts and incompatibilities with your applications. If you've upgraded the Mac OS and you're suddenly having trouble with an application you used before without problems, suspect a conflict. Check the application publisher's Web site for updates or information.

- ✔ **Is the crashing consistent?** Don't forget to keep notes so you can check and see whether you're crashing when you do a particular something. If a particular document, menu command, or automated task (such as checking your email or running a backup program) was active around the same time the crash happened, maybe you're found your culprit.

Answer these questions and you might be on your way to solving your crashing problem. If it's bug-like behavior, look for an update; for corruption, toss out the document or preferences file; for conflicts, you have to do some conflict resolution.

### Type 11 or FPU not found error message

I mentioned that the error message accompanying a crash is often meaningless; Type 11 is a great example. In Mac OS 7.5.3 and higher, Apple's engineers assigned many different sorts of errors the name Type 11 during the transition from the older Motorola processors to the PowerPC processor in newer Macs. Because the same Mac OS could run on both types of processors, new errors that were introduced were assigned this number.

In Mac OS 7.6.1 and higher, the software engineers began breaking these errors out with more meaningful messages and less dramatic crashing. So, if you encountering a slew of Type 11 errors and crashes, updating the Mac OS might be a big part of the solution.

### Type 41, Finder, or bus error message

Crashes that occur before the Finder has loaded generally mean one of two things: an extension conflict or a corrupt Finder (or the corruption of another major Mac OS system file). Here's a quick list:

✔ Did you install something recently? You might have to zap PRAM or press a special reset button on the logic board (especially in colorful Power Macintosh models).

✔ If starting the Mac OS with extensions disabled (hold down the Shift key after you hear the startup chord) makes the problem to go away, suspect a conflict. To attempt to solve it, see the "Resolving the conflict" section.

✔ If starting up without extensions doesn't solve the problem, Finder preferences might be corrupt. Start up from a Mac OS CD and move the Finder preferences file to the desktop; restart from the hard disk to see whether that fixed it.

✔ If the problem isn't with Finder preferences, the problem might be the Finder, the System file, or both. Start up from a Mac OS CD and then move the Finder, the System file, and the System Resources file (if you have one) to the desktop. Reinstall the Mac OS to replace those files. Restart from the hard disk to see whether that solved the problem.

Did the error occur when you attempted to start up from a Mac OS CD? Some versions of Mac OS 8 could create this problem. Try starting up from your startup disk and then insert the CD and work with it. If you must start up from the CD, try holding down the Shift key as the Mac starts.

### Internet-related crashing

If you're crashing in multiple Internet applications, this is a special case where corruption is very often the culprit. That's because the Internet preferences file (in the Preferences folder in the System Folder) is opened and closed a lot by different Internet applications, making it highly susceptible to corruption.

So, if you're having trouble in more than one Internet application, drag the Internet preferences file to the desktop, launch your Internet applications, and see whether the problem recurs. (You might have to reset preferences in the Internet control panel or in the Internet Config application. It's a great idea to back this file up every so often so you can quickly restore it.)

If only your browser is crashing, you should suspect installed plug-ins, along with Java. You might be attempting to load a page with Windows-only code or poorly written Java code that doesn't work well in your browser. One solution might be to upgrade to a newer or different browser version.

Another file that a lot of users have trouble with is the Global History file, which is usually found in the Netscape folder, which is in the Preferences folder (inside your System Folder). Deleting that file might help with chronic Navigator or Communicator crashing. Internet Explorer stores a similar History.html file in its Explorer folder within the Preferences folder, which can also become corrupt and cause crashing.

# *Symptom #3: The Mac freezes or hangs*

Unlike an error or a crash, a *freeze* is very unlikely to be invited back to cocktail parties. The reason is simple — it's rude. Without so much as a wink or a nod, a freeze locks up the screen so that nothing moves. It's as if you pressed the Pause button on your VCR. A true freeze will even cause the mouse pointer to stop moving around, and the clock won't count forward.

A similar symptom — but a completely different problem — is an *endless loop,* or a *hang.* In this case, an application gets caught up trying to solve some computational problem without giving back control to the Mac. A hang is just a crash but looks like a freeze, except you can move the mouse pointer and the clock keeps ticking.

A freeze can be a symptom of any of our software illnesses: a bug, a conflict, or corruption. However, a conflict is the most likely cause, unless the freeze occurs while you're opening or closing a file. (In that case, suspect corruption.) Many freezes are triggered by *background processes* — software that governs printer sharing, file sharing, or background printing, for instance. Freezes can also be related to out-of-memory situations; if you boost the memory allocation, you might help avoid freezes with a particular application.

## *Diagnosis: Freeze or hang?*

The first step in your diagnosis, though, is to make absolutely sure that your Mac is frozen. It's best to avoid misdiagnosing a symptom that is actually a hang or a hardware issue. Here are some things to do when you suspect a freeze:

- ✔ **Look.** Check your mouse and keyboard and make sure you haven't kicked them loose somehow. If they aren't properly connected, you might see the mouse pointer appear to freeze. Check this carefully, so that you don't reset your Mac or do something equally drastic just because your mouse isn't plugged in. If you have USB devices, unplug and replug them to see whether you can get them working again.

- ✔ **Watch.** Keep your eyes glued to the screen for a little while. If you see any movement, blinking, or progress — such as the clock moving or icons in the menu bar blinking — you might have a hang instead of a freeze.

- ✔ **Wait.** The best plan might be to get up and grab another cup of herbal tea. Sometimes an application will get busy without giving you any indicators of activity; other times a hang will right itself after a few minutes. If you can, give it ten minutes or so, all the while watching for any activity.

✔ **Force the issue.** After you've decided that the application isn't coming back from the dead, it's time to press some keys. ⌘+period might convince the program to stop what it's doing and move on. Try pressing ⌘+S to save your work. And try ⌘+Q to get the program to quit.

✔ **Force Quit.** If the application seems completely hung, try a Force Quit. Press ⌘+Shift+Esc. If the Force Quit alert box appears, click the Force Quit button. If this works, you're returned to the Finder.

✔ **Bug out.** Finally, you can try pressing ⌘+Power. If a dialog box appears with a small prompt, type **G F** (including the space) and press Return. This might recover you to the Finder, or it might very convincingly freeze your Mac.

If any of these measures (other than plugging in the keyboard or the mouse) is successful, you should save the data in your applications and restart your Mac. It's probably very unstable and could crash, hang, or freeze again.

If none of those bullet-point solutions pans out for you, you might really be dealing with a freeze. That means there's nothing to do but restart. Using the keyboard, press Control+⌘+Power to force the Mac to restart immediately. If this doesn't work, double-check that your keyboard is connected. (If it's not, that might actually be your problem!)

If all seems correctly configured, use the Mac's hardware-reset key or button. (For details on the iMac's special reset buttons, see Chapter 19.) If that doesn't work, you might need to flip the Mac's power switch on and off (if it has one) or unplug the Mac, wait ten seconds, and plug it back in.

### Troubleshooting a hang

So what do you do about applications that hang? Actually, a hang is pretty much the same as a crash, except there's no message and the program doesn't quit itself. If you encounter a hang, troubleshoot it as if it were a crash: Note what application or new circumstances are involved and try to reproduce the problem. Suspect either corruption (a bad data file might cause an endless loop as the program tries to make sense of it) or a conflict, particularly with a background process.

In fact, sometimes you'll notice that a Force Quit will actually quit a background process or a different application from the one that seems to have hung. That strongly suggests a conflict.

### Troubleshooting a freeze

You can troubleshoot a freeze much as you would a hang or a crash, but focus on RAM issues, conflicts with background applications, and data-file corruption. Here are a few questions to ask yourself:

✔ **Was a background process running?** Was the Mac trying to print, make an Internet connection, or perform an automated task when the freeze occurred? That might be sign of a conflict.

✔ **Was a background application running?** Again, a conflict can occur with a background application, too, especially one that is trying to notify you of something. Your browser or email program might be set to alert you to new mail or an updated Web page; if that results in a freeze in your current application, there could be a conflict.

✔ **Were you opening, saving, or closing a document?** Suspect corruption in the document file.

✔ **Did the freeze occur when you launched or quit the application?** It could be the application's preferences file. Move that file to the desktop and launch the application again to test for a freeze.

✔ **How's the weather?** One reason for freezes that some people don't consider is a dramatic change in the temperature of the computer. If you're running your Mac with the cover off, if you've overclocked the processor (or installed a new processor upgrade), or if you've recently packed your computer's case full of extras drives and cards, you might be getting freezes due to too much heat inside the machine.

Freezes can occur because of hardware or driver software conflicts, too. If you were using a particular peripheral when the freeze occurred (or if you can reproduce freezes when accessing certain hardware), you might want to test that driver software for a conflict. If you've recently installed hardware, try disabling it (and turning off its extensions or control panels in the Extensions Manager) to see whether it might be contributing to the freezes.

# Curing What Ails Your Mac

After you've noted the symptoms and diagnosed the illness, it's time to treat the problem. Each type of illness — bug, conflict, and corruption — has its own regimen of treatment. And if, for some reason, your diagnosis is faulty, at least the patient probably won't die. You can go ahead and try a different course.

## Swatting bugs

The best way to fix a bug is to update the buggy program or Mac OS component. You usually do that by contacting the software author's customer service folks or by stopping off at their Web site. If a programming fix isn't available, you should let their tech support people know you're having the problem — they can help you work around it or they can alert their programmers that a problem has been found and another all-nighter and a case of Jolt cola is merited.

Aside from an update for the software, the only way to deal with a bug is to work around it. It's like the old doctor joke, "Doc, it hurts when I move my arm like this." "Well, then," the doctor says, "Don't do that." If your graphics editing program can't open a file larger than one megabyte or your compression software crashes if your folder name is too long, the necessary workarounds are obvious.

Workarounds are only temporary solutions — if the bug persists, you need to get an update to the program or just quit using it and choose another, better programmed application. Before you give up hope, though, you should also make *absolutely* sure it's a bug. A lot of buggy behavior comes from conflicts, not bugs.

Don't overlook the Read Me file, which is a text file that most software developers include on the CD, on the disk, or in the folder where their application is installed. The Read Me file often discusses bugs and known conflicts in the application, often including a history of what's been fixed. This can be helpful in helping you figure out what, exactly, is the problem with a given piece of software.

## *Rooting out corruption*

Corruption comes in many different flavors when you're talking about computing. Here's a quick look at some of the common places you'll find corruption (aside from the obvious places such as City Hall and various HBO original series):

- ✔ **Documents.** Documents can become corrupt (which is often the case if your application crashes or your Mac freezes while trying to open a saved document.) If the document becomes corrupt, the best solution is to stop using it.

- ✔ **Preferences files.** Preferences files can become corrupt, which might explain why a particular application has trouble starting up or crashes soon after startup. The solution? Trash the preferences file for your application and test again.

- ✔ **Fonts.** You might not think about it, but fonts can become corrupt, too. You see this corruption pop up in two different instances — when you launch an application (when the fonts are generally recognized and registered by the application) and when you're working with that particular font. If you encounter trouble at either of these two points, suspect a font corruption issue.

In fact, any file can become corrupt over time and start exhibiting odd behavior. Most of the time, corruption is a mistake — a file is being written to just when another application crashes, causing the write operation to fail or mess

up in some way. In fact, that's why preferences files are often the culprit —
they tend to be opened and closed often by applications, so they're often
open when a crash happens.

 It might seem a bit cavalier to recommend that you "trash your Preferences
file" at the first sign of trouble. Usually this isn't a problem; most Mac applications are designed to recreate the preferences file if it's been deleted. If you're
the type who sticks a toe in the shallow end to see how cold the pool is,
though, you can drag a questionable preferences file to the desktop and then
test your application. If the crashing stops, the preferences file might have
been corrupt after all — toss it!

### Corruption in the system

Crashes can causes the contents of RAM or PRAM to become corrupt as well,
requiring a restart in the former case and zapping the PRAM in the latter (see
Chapter 23). So, corruption just happens, and you can usually solve it by
removing the damaged file, restarting something, or zapping something.

The exception is rampant corruption on your Mac — a problem with the hard
disk, a bad hard disk driver, or other trouble that needs to be checked by a
disk doctor program. And corruption can also be caused by something even
more menacing, such as a computer virus. If you notice that more and more
documents are crashing your applications or other corruption-like behavior,
see the sections earlier in this book on dealing with crashes and freezes, and
then check out Chapter 21's coverage of virus protection and disk doctor
programs.

### Recovering from corruption

 In most cases, tossing a corrupt file in the best solution. But what if you really
need the data in that file? If you need to recover the text from a file but trying
to open it in its native application doesn't work, try a text editor instead.
BBEdit Lite (www.barebones.com) is a freeware program that can open nearly
any file, even corrupt ones. After the file is open, you can attempt to recover
the text from the file — just copy and paste it into a new document.

You might also find that you can recover using temporary files and data files
left behind by Microsoft Office (and other) applications. After a major crash,
check the Trash can for a Recovered Items folder; sometimes you'll find
work-in-progress files there. Likewise, you can check your documents folders
for temporary files like Microsoft Word's "Word Work" files. Open them in
Word or BBEdit Lite — they often have useful text.

 Need to recover data from an Excel spreadsheet? If you really need the data and
you're willing to pay for it, try Excel Recovery from www.officerecovery.com.
A free demo can help you determine whether the product is worth your time.

# *Chasing down conflicts*

Conflicts can seem a lot like bugs at first — your application crashes or your Mac freezes, usually when you try to perform a particular task or after a certain amount of time using the program. But conflicts are different from bugs — they usually result not from a programming mistake but from a *testing* mistake. In general, conflicts happen because you have something on your Mac (either a Mac OS extension, a version of the Mac OS, or some other program) that the problematic program wasn't fully tested with.

In this context, when I say *extension,* I also mean control panels and any special files installed in the System Folder. In general, conflicts can be caused by anything that can be turned on and off in the Extensions Manager.

### *Confirming the conflict*

The best way to confirm a conflict is to read about it in the Read Me file or on the software company's Web site. At that point, you can also get their advice on what to do about it. Barring that, though, you have to test for the conflict yourself.

To test, begin by choosing Apple menu ⇨ Control Panels ⇨ Extensions Manager in the Apple menu. The Extensions Manager allows you to select different sets of Mac OS extensions. Set your Mac to Mac OS All and then restart your Mac. Now, open the application and try to duplicate the problem. If the problem recurs, the application either has a bug or a conflict with an Apple Mac OS component.

If the problem doesn't recur, though, you know you have a conflict between your application and a third-party extension. In that case, you need to perform a complete conflict troubleshooting session.

### *Troubleshooting the conflict*

You're gonna love this one. This is probably the least enjoyed, uniquely Mac task in the world of being a Mac guru — troubleshooting a conflict. The problem is, conflict troubleshooting can require hours. In essence, it's a shoot-and-miss game. You disable all extensions and then enable them a few at a time to see which one is the likely culprit. Sounds exciting, eh?

One way to get out of doing this manually is to get your hands on Conflict Catcher from Casady & Greene (www.casadyg.com). Conflict Catcher is the program many know-it-all Mac folks swear by; it automates the conflict troubleshooting process, basically taking over your Mac and testing for conflicts automatically. You might have to sit close to your machine, but at least you can watch the game or read a magazine while the program does its thing. The company offers a downloadable demo, just in case you want to try it out (see Figure 20-2).

**Figure 20-2:**
Conflict
Catcher
automates
conflict
trou-
bleshooting
by taking
over your
Mac and
testing on
its own.

Otherwise, you're in for a sit-down. What you need to do is fairly simple:
Using the Extensions Manager, you turn off most of your extensions. Then
you enable a few, test for the conflict, and keep going depending on what you
find. Here it is in a ...*For Dummies*-o-rama numbered list:

1. **Open the Extensions Manager (choose Apple menu ➪ Control Panels ➪ Extensions Manager). Then in the Extensions Manager window, select Mac *x* OS All from the Selected Set menu.**

   The actual command includes your Mac OS version, such as Mac OS 9 All. This enables only the extensions that Apple shipped with your Mac OS version.

2. **In the Extensions Manager, click Restart. After the restart, launch the program that caused the conflict and test for the error.**

   If the problem doesn't recur, you might have identified a conflict.

   If you're getting a *different* error after restarting, it might be because you've disabled an extension that's required for the application to work correctly. Look into that, re-enable any extensions that belong to that application, and then test again.

3. **In the Extensions Manager (you have to open it again), choose View ⇨ As Folders. Click the little triangle (called a *disclosure triangle*) next to Extensions so that you're viewing all the extensions (in alphabetical order).**

4. **Click to place a check mark next to the first three or four extensions and then click the Restart button again.**

5. **When Extensions Manager asks you to create and name a new set of extensions, do so.**

   Call it Test Set or something similar.

6. **After the Mac starts up, test again for the conflict. If it doesn't occur, return to Step 4 and keep adding extensions.**

7. **After you note the conflict, re-disable the last batch of extensions. Enable the first extension in that batch and then restart and test.**

   At this point, you're trying to isolate the particular extension that's causing the problem. Enable each, one at a time, until the conflict occurs again. Now you know at least one of the problem extensions!

8. **In Extensions Manager, choose Mac OS All from the Selected Set list.**

9. **Place a check mark next to the extension you've identified as a problem. When asked to create another extension set, call it Test Set 2 or something similar.**

10. **Restart and test for a conflict.**

    Here's the kicker. If the conflict recurs, you've isolated the conflicting extension. If the conflict *doesn't* recur, this extension is conflicting with a second extension and you have to keep testing.

11. **If the conflict recurs, jump down to the "Resolving the conflict" section and take care of the problem. If the conflict doesn't recur, move on to the next step.**

12. **Add three more extensions to Test Set 2 and restart.**

    Basically, you'll move through Steps 4, 5, and 6 again, this time testing against the Mac OS All set *plus* the extension you've already identified as a problem. You keep doing this until you hit the conflict, in which case you'll be at Step 7. When you reproduce the conflict, move on to Step 8, this time enabling Mac OS All and *both* trouble extensions. Restart and test. If the conflict happens, you've found your *two* conflicting extensions.

Three-way conflicts are rare but possible. (One extension conflicts when two others are present.) If you get all the way through this testing and you seem to have a problem with more than two extensions, you can enable the Mac OS All set, the two problem extensions and then keep testing. (Frankly, though, I'd recommend getting Conflict Catcher to help you sort this one out.)

## *Resolving the conflict*

After you've found the evil extensions that ruined your day, you're ready to move forward and destroy them (or turn them forever from evil with your charms). First, you need to give them a time-out in the corner; disable the problem extensions in the Extensions Manager. After you do that, though, you can take some steps to try and solve the problem — especially because you probably need the extensions if they were in your System Folder in the first place:

- **Gather information and check for updates.** Check the Read Me file and the online site for the makers of the extension that's causing your trouble. (They might have an update that solves the problem immediately.) If you don't see anything on their site, report the conflict to the proper authorities. You might also check popular Mac troubleshooting sites to see whether anyone else is aware of the problem.

- **Check for corruption.** It's possible that the extension is causing a conflict because it's corrupt. If you can, replace the extension with a fresh version from an installation disk or CD. You should also try all the standbys: Rebuild the desktop, defragment the drive, and run a disk doctor program. If the conflicting control panel or application has a preferences file, try trashing it.

- **Change the load order.** Conflicts between two (or more) extensions can sometimes be solved by changing the *load order*. Extensions load alphabetically, so you can get Extension B to load before Extension A by altering its name. To get an extension to load earlier in the process, put a space as the first character in its name. To get an extension to load near the end of the process, put a bullet (Option+8) as the first character in its name.

  In some cases, this trick will work where there's only one problem extension; it might just want to be loaded earlier in the startup process. Try a space in front of its name and see whether that helps.

- **Increase memory allocation.** A few items in the Extensions and Control Panel folders allow you to change their memory allocation; if they're a few years old, they might not be set correctly for the latest version of the Mac OS. Select the item's icon and then use the File ➪ Get Info command (in later Mac OS versions, select Memory from the pop-up menu in the Get Info window).

- **Replace the software.** If the problem is a third-party extension and you can't get an update, you might look around for an alternative. Try www.download.com and www.macdownload.com for shareware and demo items that might do the trick.

✔ **Manage the conflict.** In Extensions Manager or Conflict Catcher, you can create different extension sets for different circumstances. If you *must* have an extension for a particular application (say, a high-end animation program) but it conflicts with other extensions you use for other things (such as basic word processing), create a few different Extension Sets and switch between them (see Figure 20-3). This is a pain because you have to restart each time, but it beats not being able to use the application at all.

**Figure 20-3:**
If neces-
sary, you
can create
different
extension
sets and
activate
them when
you need to
work with a
particular
application.

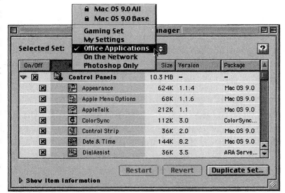

✔ **Live without it.** If you can't replace the extension or work around it, your best plan it to get it off your Mac. Drag it to a folder somewhere outside the System Folder or put it in the Trash and try to forget about it. You had good times, but they didn't work out.

# Chapter 21

# Maintaining Your Mac's Files

*F*or many Mac users, their data is more important than the actual computer. If you fit this category — or, frankly, if you simply don't want to ever have to re-enter Quicken data or reconstruct your address book from memory — adhering to some regular maintenance schedule for your Mac is probably the best thing you can do for it. Because many crashes and failures result from file corruption, a plan of attack to prevent corruption should also help keep the disk doctors away.

# A Regular Routine

Whether it's building your pectorals or memorizing all the dialog on the Andy Griffith Show, true dedication requires a routine. The same is true of your Mac. Although Macs are supposed to be user-friendly, happy, quiet, earthy machines, that doesn't mean they don't occasionally need to do some brushing and flossing to keep from being a yuck-mouth.

Here's the plan. On a regular basis, you perform a few innocuous, unassuming, easy-to-conjure tasks. In exchange, your Mac will run faster and crash less and you're likely to encounter fewer errors. Is it worth the trade-off? You bet your Barcalounger.

## The daily stuff

To keep you Mac fit and trim, the daily regimen isn't too strict. The most important considerations are to turn your Mac off properly and restart it occasionally. Of course, that would be easier to read in bullet form:

✔ **Turn your Mac off properly.** Don't just pull the plug or toss a switch on your power strip. (Likewise, I recommend that you avoid plugging your desktop Mac into an outlet that's controlled by a wall switch. You're bound to throw the switch at the wrong moment.) Instead, choose Special ⇨ Shut Down to turn off your Mac. (Or press the Power key on your keyboard and select Shut Down by clicking it or by simply pressing Return.)

You should have a good surge protector for any Mac. The best types offer more than just extra outlets: They offer legitimate surge protection and an indicator that a surge has taken place. They should also protect your modem line. The best protectors offer insurance or a high-dollar warranty.

✔ **Restart occasionally.** If you leave your Mac on for long stretches (days or weeks) and you open and close many applications over that time, you might end up with *fragmented memory*, which can lead to errors or inefficient behavior. It's best to restart your Mac fairly regularly — daily isn't a bad idea, especially after you've opened and closed numerous applications or after a long Internet surfing session.

## Semiweekly

You should take care of a few tasks somewhere between daily and weekly. First, you should regularly check the amount of disk space left on your Mac's hard disk (or disks). If your startup disk gets very low on disk space, you might begin to encounter errors; your Mac uses the disk for a number of temporary files, preferences files, and so forth. You should do what you can to keep at least 10% of your disk free for such files.

Second, you should maintain your files (create archives of files you don't need anymore and delete unneeded email and attachments), even if you aren't yet low on disk space. A clean disk is a happy disk.

Third, you should back up your files every day, every few days, or once a week, depending on how important your data is. I discuss creating a backup plan a little later in this chapter. In the meantime, simply continue to repeat the mantra "I will back up." (This mantra might even help distract you if you're trying to lose weight, quit smoking, or stop barking like a dog in the middle of crowded theaters.)

## Weekly

Weekly tasks are important for maintaining healthy disks and files — if you perform these regularly, you might see a 16 percent improvement compared to patients who chew regular gum. I get into some of these weekly tasks in more detail later in the chapter, but for now, more bullets:

✔ **Check for viruses.** If you have a good virus-checking program (and, by the end of this chapter, you will), you can probably set it up to check for viruses automatically. Do that. Although there aren't nearly as many viruses for the Macintosh are there are for Microsoft Windows computers, a few malicious ones are out there. You want to be protected, especially if you're in a high-risk group, which includes anyone who uses a LAN, diskettes from others, the Internet, or an online service.

✔ **Check for Mac OS updates.** If you have Mac OS 9 or higher, you can automate the process of checking for Mac OS system software updates. The Software Update control panel will head out on the Internet weekly and check Apple's servers for updated Mac OS components (see Figure 21-1). If you don't have Mac OS 9, you might want to check every few weeks at Apple's software library (http://asu.info.apple.com/) for relevant upgrades for your Mac.

✔ **Check your disks.** Every week, you should also run Disk First Aid, Apple's built-in disk maintenance program. Disk First Aid can fix small problems with your disks and files and alert you to problems that need to be fixed by industrial-strength disk doctors such as Norton Utilities or MicroMat's TechTool Pro. By default, Disk First Aid (in Mac OS 8.5 or higher) is set to turn on automatically after an improper restart. You can change this behavior using the Shut Down Warning option in the General Controls control panel. (See the section "Disk Doctors Observed" later in this chapter for more on disk doctor applications.)

**Figure 21-1:** In Mac OS 9 or higher, use Software Update to automatically check Apple's servers for software updates.

# Monthly

Between weekly tasks and semi-annual tasks come monthly tasks. (Go look at a calendar if you don't believe me.) Without further ado — for once — here's some stuff you should do on a monthly basis:

- ✔ **Rebuild the desktop.** The desktop database is a file (or a group of files, depending on your Mac OS version) that keeps track of where data is stored on your disks. The more saving you do, the more this file gets changed. Eventually, corruption and the occasional error can begin to creep in. To keep from affecting performance or data integrity, you should rebuild the desktop every month or so. You have two ways to do that. You can hold down the ⌘ and Option keys as your Mac starts up (hold them down until you see a dialog box asking whether you want to rebuild the desktop). You can also use the TechTool Freeware utility, discussed in Chapter 24.

- ✔ **Update applications and virus definitions.** This can be an important one. Applications are often updated to make them work better with new Mac OS versions and to quash bugs. Virus definitions are updated monthly to keep your virus software up-to-date with the latest viruses, trojan horses, and worms that have been identified by the crack antiviral staffs at the various centers for computing disease control. You can head directly to the manufacturer's Web sites to search for upgrades, or you can make it easy on yourself and visit sites such as `www.version tracker.com/` or `www.softwatcher.com/mac/` on the Web.

# Every three months

Now we're getting serious. Over the long haul, just working with your Mac can cause it to slow down and encounter more errors. The more files you open and save and open and save, the more your disk can become fragmented, which slows things down. Likewise, cleaning up the clutter of files that no longer have a purpose can lead to more disk space and, in some cases, less trouble. The bullets, please:

- ✔ **Defragment your disk.** When possible, your Mac writes data sequentially to your hard disk. After weeks of deleting files and writing new ones, it becomes increasingly difficult for entire files to be written sequentially. Instead, they're copied into available spaces on the disk, even if it means breaking up the files into smaller pieces and cataloguing them all. When this *fragmentation* of files occurs, reading the files takes longer and the possibility of errors grows great. The solution is to *defragment*, which can be accomplished with a disk doctor program (see "Disk Doctors Observed" later in this chapter).

Want to defragment like the pros do? After a complete backup of everything on your hard disk, you erase (or *reformat*) your hard disk, and then copy everything back onto the drive from your backup. Doing so writes everything to the disk sequentially, giving you a fresh start. Plus, you'll have a full backup, just in case you encounter problems in the process.

✔ **Spring cleaning.** After you become familiar with your System Folder, you find that some programs place items in there that you'd prefer not to worry about and uninstalled applications can leave files on your system that you don't need. By cleaning out your System Folder (and uninstalling unneeded applications or utilities), you can keep your system slim and trim. For help, try Aladdin System's (www.aladdinsys.com) Spring Cleaning software, which walks you through the cleaning process.

✔ **Create an archive.** Along with combing through files in your System Folder, it's a good idea to sift through your documents, email, and downloads every once in a while to make sure you're not loading up your hard disk with junk. Move files you don't work with any more (it might help to use Find File or Sherlock in the Mac OS to find which files haven't been modified in the past few months) to a removable disk that you can use as an archive. That clears up space on your disk and causes your Mac to track fewer files, helping the Finder open folders and access files more quickly.

## Long term

You should reserve a few tasks for even longer terms than three months — perhaps twice a year for a major Mac OS version installation and every two years (or so) for a complete overhaul. Here are some bulleted hints:

✔ **Every six months.** About twice a year, you should perform some major Mac OS maintenance, including any free Mac OS updaters (such as those that take you from Mac OS 9.0 to Mac OS 9.1). To perform such an update, you ideally start up from a CD-ROM, update the hard disk driver (if appropriate for your Mac), and install the update. Likewise, you might find it useful to update your Mac's firmware, if you have an iMac or a Power Macintosh G3, G4, or later. (See Chapter 22 for more on Mac OS and firmware updates.)

✔ **Every two years.** After you've had your Mac up and running for a year or two, a serious overhaul might breathe a little new life into it. In this case, you do a full backup and then use Drive Setup to reformat your hard disk, update the hard disk drivers, and perhaps even do some low-level testing on the disk. You can then reinstall the Mac OS (perhaps even a new version), reinstall any driver software you need for your peripherals, and reinstall your applications and any updates to those applications. Finally, you can return your documents to the disk from your backup disk(s). By the time you're finished, you have a refreshed system that should be cleanly installed with only the drivers and applications you still find necessary and useful. Other stuff will be gone, where it can no longer do harm.

# Automate Your Backups for Good Living

Not backing up your hard drive is like not wearing pants in a snake pit. It's like juggling knives without proper training. It's like testing a vacuum cleaner with your necktie.

To back up properly, you need a good, high-capacity removable drive (see Chapters 11 and 17). Then, you should get yourself some good backup software. Working with most removable drives, backup software automates the backup process so that your important files are stored on some secondary media, other than you hard disk, at regular intervals. If you schedule the backup with software, all you have to do is remember to swap the disk every so often.

## What should you back up?

Even with a 250MB Zip, backing up a 2GB, 6GB, or 30GB hard drive could take a while. If your removable isn't the largest capacity drive on the block, you could consider skipping some files when you back up.

You probably don't need to back up your applications (assuming you have the legal installation disks or CDs around somewhere), although you should back up any updates to those applications that you've installed and any applications you've downloaded from the Internet. You might also get away with not backing up your System Folder because you can always reinstall the Mac OS in a crisis. (You should back up your Preferences folder and any extensions or control panels you've added to your Mac.)

It'd be nice if you could back up the whole hard disk, but that's not always possible. If you're stuck trying to fit your backup on smaller media, you can limit your backups to the following:

✔ **Documents.** These are most important because you wouldn't have saved your documents in the first place if you could easily remember them word-for-word and really wanted to retype them. Creating documents is why you own your Mac, so back them up.

✔ **Upgrades and updates.** If you download drivers and updates for your Mac from the Internet, you should back them up, too. You can either drag them to a special removable disk you've created for storing updates or put them all in a special folder that can be backed up automatically.

- **Internet bookmarks.** Are you a Web junkie? Then you probably like the bookmarks in your Web browser. Back them up — you usually find them inside your browser's folder (Explorer for Internet Explorer; Netscape for Netscape products) in the Preferences folder inside your Mac's System Folder.

- **Email and address books.** Email is the modern paper trail (as Microsoft executives well know). If you keep all yours so that you can find phone numbers, recall past requests, or simply root through to find the answer to an "I told you so. . . ." you should back up your email for safekeeping. Oh, and back up your email address book, too, if you haven't yet memorized all your friends and colleagues e-mail addresses.

- **Preferences.** Your Mac will still work with new Preferences files, but it might be nice to have them on hand if you experience drive trouble.

- **Saved games.** You just reached the point where you're about to rescue the friendly dragon from the evil prince. You don't want to have to start over again from level one, do you?

## Funny words associated with backups

Before you set up your backup plan, let's start by defining some important terms. The world of file backups has three important concepts: rotation, incremental backups, and archiving. In the following, you look at each:

- **Rotation.** To give yourself the best chance of recovering important files, rotate your backup media (usually disks). Even if you back up diligently for a full year, if you use only one disk and that disk is bad, the backup schedule didn't do you any good. You need to get your hands of a few disks and plan to rotate among them.

- **Archive.** Another important part of any backup scheme is creating an occasional archive. This is a full backup session stored to one or more disks, which you then store away from your computer — off-site, preferably, in a safe deposit box or even a fireproof safe. This gives you at least a decent chance of recovering your data in case something catastrophic happens to or near your Mac. Likewise, it gives you something to fall back on if your subsequent backup media becomes corrupt or, even worse, infected with a virus.

- **Incremental backup.** This is a happy term that refers to backups that take less time to create. An incremental backup is performed by analyzing the files that are already backed up and comparing them to files that have been changed since the last backup session. Only the changes are written to the backup disk. This is most easily accomplished with backup software that automates pretty much the entire process.

With these terms under your belt, you're ready to create a backup plan.

## A simple plan

If you're performing backup functions for an organization or a business, consider backing up every night or every other night, rotating between many different disks, and testing regularly. For a home or home-office scenario, I can recommend something a little less strenuous. It also offers a little more room for error, but it's a good start. Here's the rotation:

1. **Start with two fresh disks. On the first week, create a full backup on the first disk.**

2. **On the same day of the second week, use the second disk and create a full backup.**

3. **After you've created the first two disks, use the incremental backup feature in your backup software to create incremental backups during the next few sessions. Rotate between the two disks, each alternating week.**

4. **After the sixth week's backup, drop the first disk out of the rotation and store it as an archive.**

    Do this every six weeks to create an archive of data and to keep your disks fresh so that they're less likely to fail.

5. **Open up a new disk and use it on the next week (the seventh week) to create a full backup.**

6. **Rotate between the two until the twelfth week, at which point you'll drop out the disk (it was originally the second disk you used) as another archive.**

By observing this schedule, you always have one backup that's less than a week old, one backup that's less than two weeks old, and an archive that's less than six weeks old. In case of failure, you're likely to lose very little data.

As mentioned, software can help make this strategy (or a stricter one, if you'd like to back up every day or every few days) easier to keep up with. Retrospect and Retrospect Express (shown in Figure 21-2) from Dantz Corporation (www.dantz.com) are popular options that tell you which disk to use and which to archive, after you've told it your desired schedule. It's also affordable at around $50.

# Check Your Mac for Viruses

A computer *virus* is a program, malicious or not, designed to replicate itself. Many of them attach themselves to other programs and then leap into your Mac's file system where they attempt to wreak havoc. Some infect files just to be annoying; others try to destroy data or erase your disks. In any case, having a virus infect your files is bad news.

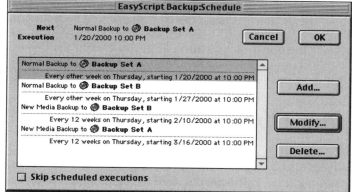

**Figure 21-2:**
Retrospect
Express
helps
schedule
your
backups.

The best way to avoid viruses is to inoculate again them — buy and use Norton Antivirus (www.norton.com) or Virex (www.drsolomon.com). Install them and run them frequently to catch any little buggers and then make sure your virus definitions are updated regularly.

Beyond that, you can take a few additional steps:

✔ **Note virus-like behavior.** Signs of infection include automated behavior that you haven't authorized, disk spins for long durations without explanation, or a launched program that doesn't appear until after a long delay. Other signs are when the Mac restarts after a program is launched or a disk is inserted, files or folders that disappear, or file sizes, dates, or other details that change automatically. If any of these things occur, shut down your Mac until you have virus software available. Then, start up and immediately check your disk with the virus software.

✔ **Note odd behavior from Microsoft Office documents.** Microsoft Word and Excel documents can get special viruses that are among the most common reported by Mac users. Such behavior includes documents that save themselves as templates, disappearing menu commands, and self-activating macros. If you encounter them, shut down Word or Excel and run a virus detector. You might have to toss out the documents. Be prepared to warn your colleagues — many of these viruses (called *macro viruses*) are cross-platform, so they infect both Windows and Mac users of Microsoft applications.

✔ **Avoid unannounced email attachments.** You should open and launch email attachments only from people who are authorized to send them to you — and attachments even from those people should be *expected*. If you get an unexpected attachment, don't open it until you confirm that it's genuine — even trusted email friends can get a virus that causes their email program to attempt to replicate the virus by sending it, as an attachment, to people in their address book.

✔ **Turn off CD-ROM AutoPlay.** A vicious Mac-only virus works through QuickTime on newer Macs. Open the QuickTime Settings control, select AutoPlay from the menu, and turn off the Enable CD-ROM AutoPlay option. (You don't have to turn off the Enable Audio CD AutoPlay option.) This will keep you safe from that particular virus attack.

# Disk Doctors Observed

Every Mac owner should have a disk doctor program of some sort. I know it comes as a shock — you'd think a disk doctor program would be built into the Mac OS, but it isn't. The best utilities for maintaining your files — and fixing any files when they crop up — will cost you a little extra.

In general, all these utilities offer the capability to defragment a hard disk, rebuild the hard disk's desktop database after a major error, and attempt to recover damaged folders and files. In varying degrees, they also benefit from being installed before problems strike, so that they can perform periodic checks and monitor your Mac while it's running.

Three major contenders battle it out in the Mac market:

✔ **TechTool Pro** (www.micromat.com) is an overall diagnostic utility that checks not just your hard disk but also RAM, ROM, the processor, video, and many more components. It's a great utility for the troubleshooter and upgrader and also includes hard disk and file recovery tools.

✔ **Norton Utilities** (www.norton.com) focuses on disk and file recovery. Tools include the Disk Doctor, FileSaver, Volume Recover, Unerase, and SpeedDisk. Some of these are best run before trouble strikes, so that Norton can monitor the disk and create recover scenarios.

✔ **Disk Express Pro** and **Disk Warrior** (www.alsoft.com) are separate programs from Alsoft that complement each other nicely. Basically one-trick ponies, Disk Express Pro defragments and optimizes your disk and Disk Warrior guards against disk corruption and can help recover from a catastrophic disk error or crash.

In my completely subjective opinion, all three have value. TechTool Pro is the most complete solution. Norton Utilities has file and disk recovery, er, covered. Norton's tools have more depth than its competitors when it comes to taking care of files and disks. Alsoft's tools, however, are very good at what they do and can, on occasion, fix and recover problems that both Norton and TechTool Pro can't.

# Chapter 22

# Installing, Reinstalling, and Updating the Mac OS

. . . . . . . . . . . . . . . . . . . . . . . . . . . . . . . . . . . . . . . . . . . . . . .

*In This Chapter*

▶ Determining your reinstall strategy

▶ Installing and reinstalling the Mac OS

▶ Firmer considerations

. . . . . . . . . . . . . . . . . . . . . . . . . . . . . . . . . . . . . . . . . . . . . . .

*R*einstalling the Mac OS should be a solution of last resort — something akin to gnawing off your thumb to escape a pair of handcuffs. If you haven't fully troubleshoot-ed (troubleshot?) your Mac, you might not solve the problem by reinstalling the Mac OS — you might just give it more fresh meat to consume. (This is getting gross.)

So, before you jump in and reinstall the Mac OS, let's make sure you're not doing it for all the wrong reasons. Then we'll look at some of the right reasons for reinstalling and how to go about it.

## The Reinstall Decision

Reinstalling the Mac OS won't cure the common cold or even alleviate the symptoms: runny nose, hacking cough, high fever. Aside from that, a few actual computer problems will also fail to respond to a Mac OS reinstallation. Here's a look at some of those:

> ✔ **Trouble with your file system or hard disk.** Problems that need to be looked over by Disk First Aid or a disk doctor program won't be fixed by reinstalling the Mac OS. The Mac OS will be installed on the same file system, and you'll encounter the same problems.

✔ **Virus infection.** Viruses can attack all sorts of files on your Mac — documents, applications, and utilities — not just the Mac OS. Plus, some viruses attack the desktop database or the *boot sector* on the disk, so they can survive even if you format the drive! You have to get rid of a virus using a virus detector before a reinstall will help.

✔ **Most hardware issues.** If you're having trouble with SCSI, FireWire, USB, networking, serial devices, or other hardware, reinstalling the Mac OS rarely helps. Instead, you need to troubleshoot the device itself or, at best, reinstall the device's software drivers.

✔ **System-folder conflicts.** It might seem to make sense, but reinstalling the Mac OS won't help with most System Folder conflicts. The reason is simple — two Apple extensions (the type that a reinstall would replace) rarely have conflicts. Instead, the conflict is probably with a third-party extension or application, and the problem would likely recur after a reinstallation.

Although some of these issues might be fixed by a *clean install* of the Mac OS (where a brand new System Folder is created and none of the third-party extensions, fonts, or preferences you've had in the past are retained), you still haven't succeeded in finding the problem. After working with the new System Folder for a while (or after you reinstall the problematic driver or extension while trying to get something else to work), you might encounter the trouble again.

That said, a few good reasons to reinstall do exist. If you've successfully identified a troubleshooting problem and the solution is to reformat your hard disk, that's a great time to reinstall. Likewise, if you've traced a conflict to a corrupt Mac OS extension or one of the major system files, such as the System file or the Finder file, those are also good reasons to reinstall. And, if you'd just like to upgrade to a whole new Mac OS version, a reinstallation or a clean install might be the best solution.

# (Re)installing the Mac OS

After you've decided to move forward with a Mac OS installation, you need to decide which type of installation to perform. Then you need to take a few precautionary steps. Although reinstalling isn't likely to do major damage, you do need to make some decisions and preparations. After your preparations are complete, you can move on to the installation process.

# Types of installations

What type of installation will you perform? You have two basic types, which I call over and clean. An *over* installation installs Mac OS files over existing Mac OS files; this is most effective when you're upgrading to a new version of the Mac OS. A *clean* installation creates a new System Folder, which is more effective for fixing trouble.

Most of the time you can simply upgrade over your existing System Folder, as long as you're not having trouble with it. If you're upgrading from Mac OS 8.1 to Mac OS 9, for instance, the installer is smart enough to install the new Mac OS without affecting your third-party extensions, your preferences, and other files like that. After you complete the installation (and if all goes well), your Mac starts right up and runs just as it had, except it has the new Mac OS running.

Although this approach is usually best for new installs or upgrades, it can be used to replace corrupted or problematic Mac OS files of the same version but *only* if you have removed those files from the existing System Folder. (For instance, if a disk doctor program tells you there's a problem with a file in the System Folder, you can move the problem file to the Trash or to a folder on your desktop and then reinstall the Mac OS to get a clean copy of that file installed.) If the problem file remains in the System Folder, however, the Mac OS installer generally won't replace it.

If you choose to perform a clean installation, you get a brand-spanking-new System Folder, but it won't include all your old preferences, third-party extensions, and anything else (such as fonts and application-specific stuff put there by Apple or Microsoft). Instead, you have to drag that stuff over manually.

You can get programs to help you move items from your old System Folder to the new one you create with a clean install. Try Clean Install Assistant (www.marcmoini.com) or Mac OS Installer Helper, available from popular download libraries such as www.macdownload.com.

# Preinstallation due diligence

Reinstalling the Mac OS could take a few hours; after that, it might take a few weeks before you've completely upgraded and updated everything you need for normal operation. So, it's a good idea to take the following steps before a reinstallation or upgrade of the Mac OS:

- ✔ **Back up.** You should not only back up your documents, preferences, important email, and Internet favorites, but also, if possible, create a mirror of your System Folder (assuming it's in working order). With a good System Folder on CD-R or disk, you can drag it back to your startup disk and get back to where you were just in case you have trouble with your new installation.

✔ **Find or download good drivers.** If you're having trouble with your current System Folder, it's more likely to be a problem with your third-party drivers than with the Mac OS itself. It's best to completely reinstall your important drivers — printer, scanner, modem, and removable media — along with the Mac OS. If you're not performing a clean install, you might still want your drivers on hand in case of a problem.

✔ **Fix the disk.** Installing the Mac OS on an error-ridden disk won't help much. With your documents and other files backed up, perform an intense disk doctor session before going ahead with the reinstallation. This guarantees optimal performance.

✔ **Have alternative startup CDs ready.** Although everything *should* go well, you occasionally encounter an error after reinstallation or a half-finished installation that won't allow your Mac to start up from its hard disk. So, you want to have at least two startup options available: The Mac OS installation CD and the original CD that came with your Mac (especially if your computer is a Macintosh clone) are good choices. You might also want a disk doctor CD handy for starting up your Mac in an emergency. If you don't have a CD-ROM drive, you can use Mac OS 8.1 or lower to create a startup diskette for your Mac.

✔ **Have all your instructions printed, a backup computer available, or both.** If you need to hop on the Web for troubleshooting advice from Apple's Support site, you might have trouble if your Mac has a failed installation on its disk or is otherwise incapacitated.

✔ **Turn off Energy Saver features.** Before your installation, it's a good idea to make sure your Mac won't try to spin down the hard disk or go to sleep in the middle of the procedure. Open the Energy Saver control panel and slide the Sleep slider (and any others that are active under the Show Details option) over to Never.

## *Performing the installation or reinstallation*

To begin the installation, follow these steps:

1. **Restart your Mac with the Mac OS CD-ROM in your CD-ROM drive.**

   (Or restart from your system diskettes if you have an older version of the Mac OS and your Mac doesn't have a CD-ROM drive.)

   Your Mac should start up from the CD's System Folder. If it doesn't, restart and hold down the C key immediately after hearing the system chime.

**2. When the Finder appears, double-click the Mac OS Install icon.**

The Install application launches and the screen displays an introduction that outlines the steps for the installation process.

**3. Click Continue to move to the next screen.**

**4. Choose the hard disk on which you want to install the Mac OS.**

The installer analyzes that drive to determine what Mac OS version is currently installed on the Mac and whether or not enough disk space is available for the installation, as shown in Figure 22-1.

**Figure 22-1:**
The installer lets you know whether it thinks you have enough disk space to move on.

**5. If you think a clean installation is the right idea, click the Options button.**

A dialog box appears, where you can place a check mark next to the Perform Clean Installation option. Click OK after you've made your choice.

**6. Whether or not you chose a clean installation, click Select to move to the next screen.**

If the installer detects that you already have this version of the Mac OS installed (for instance, you're trying to run the Mac OS 9 installer and you have Mac OS 9 installed on the selected disk), it asks whether you want to Reinstall or Add/Remove.

**7. If you get the screen asking whether you want to Reinstall or Add/Remove, make your selection (or click Cancel if you need to select a different disk).**

If you choose Add/Remove, move down to the section "Custom Add/Remove."

8. **If you see a screen asking you to read the Important Information document, read it to see whether it might affect you and then click Continue.**

   This document is the same as the Read Me file on your Mac OS installation CD — it reveals any known incompatibilities or problems with this version of the Mac OS.

9. **Read the License agreement thoroughly to make sure Apple hasn't slipped in that ". . . and your first-born child" language that they had briefly in the mid-1980s (I'm kidding) and then click Continue.**

10. **When the small alert box appears, click Agree to move on or Disagree to return to the intro screen of the installer.**

    If you've agreed with the license, the Installation screen appears. If you plan to perform an *easy installation*, which installs the Mac OS components and applications that Apple recommends for your Mac, move down to Step 12.

    On some older Mac OS versions, you might see *custom installation* controls that enable you to turn on (place check marks next to) the installers you'd like to run. On newer installations, the default is an easy installation; you can see custom controls by clicking the Customize button. If you do click Customize, you see a list of the different software technologies that can be installed (see Figure 22-2).

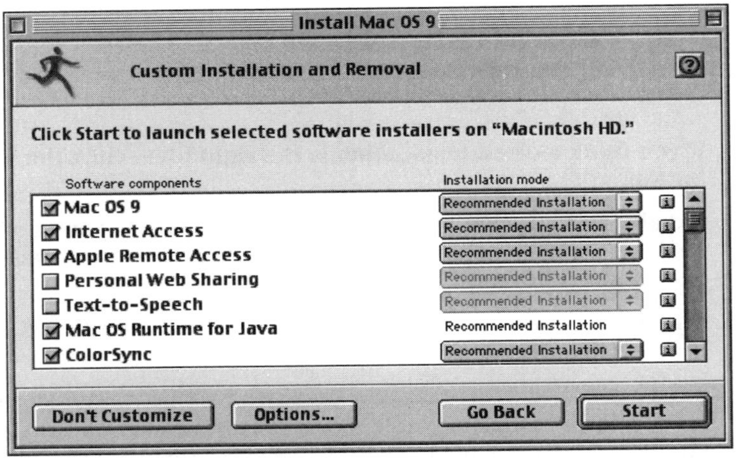

**Figure 22-2:**
Choosing the Customize button allows you to select the individual technologies you'd like to install.

11. **If you're a controlling sort, you can select which technologies to install at this point by clicking to place (or remove) a check mark next to each. You can customize each installer even further, if you like, by pulling down the Installation mode menu in that installer's row.**

If you choose Customized Installation from the Installation mode menu, you see another screen that lets you place check marks to install or avoid specific portions of the installer (see Figure 22-3). Also, note the disclosure triangles, which allow you to get very nit-picky about the files you're going to install.

**Figure 22-3:**
You can customize the installation by choosing components within each installer.

The bottom of the Installation screen offers an Options button, too, which you can use to determine whether the installer will attempt to update the hard disk drivers. If you think, for some reason, that the installer shouldn't attempt this (for instance, you have a Mac OS clone machine and it has its own hard disk drivers), make sure this option isn't selected by removing the check mark next to that option. (You might also have an option to create an installation report; check or uncheck this according to your desires.)

12. **Whether you're performing an easy installation or a custom installation, click the Start button when you've made all your choices. You're ready to install.**

    The installer checks your hard disk using Disk First Aid's technology. If all goes well, the installation proceeds. (If it doesn't you might need to quit the installer and run a disk doctor before you can install the Mac OS.) The installer works through the rest of its installers until it has installed everything (or encounters an error).

13. **At the end, click Continue to install more things or Restart to begin your Mac using the new system software.**

## The Finder quickie install

If you're having a major error with the Finder (especially at startup), the problem might be a corrupt Finder or System file. If that's your suspicion, you can perform a quickie install to get things running again. Here's how: Start up from a Mac OS CD. When the Finder appears, open your hard disk's System Folder and move the System file, the Finder, and the System Resources file (if one exists) to the Trash.

Now, run the Mac OS installer. Choose Reinstall when asked. On the Installation screen, click Start. After just a few moments of installation, you should be able to restart your Mac from the hard disk; if the Finder or System files really were corrupt, you might have solved the problem!

## *Custom Add/Remove*

One option we skipped over is the Mac OS Installer's (as well as many application installer programs') capability to selectively add or remove items to an existing Mac OS installation. You do that by selecting Add/Remove after you've selected a disk through the Select Destination screen. (Note that you can add/remove items only from the currently installed Mac OS installer; that is, you must have Mac OS 9 installed to remove items using the Mac OS 9 installation CD.)

Selecting Add/Remove takes you to the Custom Installation and Removal screen. Here you can select the installers you want to work with and then, from the Installation Mode list, select whether you want to perform a Customized Installation or a Customized Removal. A Customized Installation works as described in the section "Performing the installation or reinstallation" (use Figure 22-3 as a reference).

With a Customized Removal, you place a check mark next to the items you want to *remove* from the current installation (see Figure 22-4). Then you click OK in the dialog box and click Start in the Installation window. The installation process begins as it normally would, except this time it removes things.

This generally works well; your only admonishment is to have some idea of what, exactly, you're trying to remove. If you remove items that your applications or other programs depend on, you might create instability down the road.

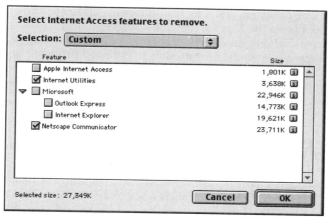

**Figure 22-4:**
With a
Customized
Removal,
you remove
Mac OS
components
from the
current
System
Folder.

## Installation errors

Most of the time, you won't encounter errors installing the Mac OS if you've taken the time to run a disk doctor utility and you start up from the installation CD. If you do encounter trouble, though, it might come in these familiar shapes and sizes:

- ✔ **Unable to quit all applications.** The installer needs to quit all other applications — even the Finder — to install properly and safely. If it can't do that, you need to restart your Mac with only Mac OS extensions enabled. You should also start up from the installation CD, if you can.

- ✔ **Disk write errors.** If the installer stops or complains about a disk *write* error (or a disk full error), you need to quit the installer and check the drive to make sure it has enough free disk space. If you do have enough disk space but still get errors, you might need to quit the installer and run a disk doctor program to diagnose and defragment the drive. If you continue to get errors, you might need to back up your important files and use Drive Setup to test for physical errors on the disk. If you find some, a reformat and a new disk driver might be in order. (See Chapter 24 for more on Drive Setup.)

- ✔ **Disk read errors.** If the installer reports trouble *reading* data from the CD, you should first check the About this Computer command in the Apple menu to make sure you have plenty of RAM available for the installer. You might want to restart from the CD. If RAM isn't the problem, the installation CD might be damaged.

✔ **Crashes or other errors.** If a crash happens, make sure you read the Read Me file on the Mac OS installation CD carefully to see whether anything is said about your particular Mac model. Also, read any error messages carefully — some Mac models might need firmware updates or even a service call to work with newer Mac OS versions. You should also start your Mac from the installation CD if possible. (If not, hold down the Shift key while starting up to turn off extensions.

# *Firmware: Keep Mac from Going Soft*

Newer Mac models have another element you be update for best performance and bug fixing: *firmware*. This is a set of instructions kept in a flashable ROM — a chip on the logic board that can be periodically updated by special software.

Firmware updates are often necessary to get iMac, Power Macintosh G3 and G4 models, and other new Macs up-to-speed for working with newer Mac OS versions and other Apple technologies. They're also updated periodically when Apple finds a new bug that needs to be quashed.

You can find firmware updates in a number of different places. They often come on installation CDs and occasionally on the installation CDs included with peripherals, if they're needed for the hardware to work correctly. Otherwise, you're likely to come across them using the Software Update feature in Mac OS 9 or by visiting Apple's support site at `www.apple.com/support/` on the Web.

After you obtain the update, you're likely to find that it's in the form of a *disk image*. Follow these steps:

1. **Double-click the updater file.**

   A disk icon appears on your desktop.

2. **Double-click the disk icon.**

   A window appears that includes the updater and a Read Me file.

3. **Read that file carefully before proceeding.**

   You launch the installer just like a regular Mac OS installer. This software acts a bit differently, though. First, it checks to make sure you need the update.

4. **If you don't need the update, you see a message telling you that your firmware is up to date. Click OK to return to the Finder.**

5. **If you do need the update, the update takes place and then you see a Shut Down button. Click it and your Mac shuts down.**

6. **Start your Mac back up.**

   In many cases, you need to hold down the Programmer's button on the front (Power Macintosh) or side (iMac) of your computer as you press the Power button on the computer or keyboard. After the tone, release the Programmer's button.

   You then see a progress bar, indicating that the firmware update is taking place.

7. **If the update succeeds, you see a message telling you so; click OK. If the update fails, you need to start again by launching the Firmware Updater application.**

# Part V
# The Part of Tens

The 5th Wave     By Rich Tennant

"Come here, quick! I've got a new iMac trick!"

## In this part . . .

Sure, they look like silly top ten lists, but these chapters pack quite a wallop. Turn here first for answers to the most frequent problems that attack Macs, whether you have an older Mac or one of its new, colorful brethren. You'll find that some answers cover topics not covered elsewhere in the book; whereas others lead you back into the heart of the text for more explanation. Plus, if you're going to get serious about being a doctor of Macintology, you need to turn here to find out about the latest diagnostic tools at your disposal.

# Chapter 23

# Ten Problems and How to Fix Them

*H*aving trouble? Sure, some Mac problems can be really wacky, requiring thousands of people-hours to track down and destroy. Most of the time, though, you encounter one of the ten most common problems, as outlined in this chapter. (The eleventh problem — application crashes and freezes — has its own whole chapter in Chapter 20.) Here, you get the quick fixes and easy solutions to Mac startup- and hardware-related issues.

## Your Mac Doesn't Turn On

If your Mac is turned off and you press the Power key or button, it should turn on, right? When it doesn't, things can get frustrating fast. Don't panic, though. (At least, not yet.) Instead, take a few steps to try and narrow down the problem:

- **Check the monitor.** If your Mac has a separate monitor, make sure you're not confusing an unplugged or turned off monitor for a Mac that isn't starting up. If you hear tones or hear the Mac's hard disk spinning, you should make sure the monitor is connected and getting power.

- **Check the power cable.** Make sure the power cable is plugged into the Mac and into your surge protector or a wall outlet. If you have a surge protector, check to make sure it's working and that its fuse hasn't been tripped because of a surge. If everything is plugged in, test to make sure the Mac's power cable is working; you might be able to swap cables with your monitor or printer. You might also want to test the Mac at another AC outlet in another room, just to make sure it's not a problem with the local circuit. (Or you can plug a lamp into the same outlet, for instance, to test. And don't forget to make sure the wall socket isn't controlled by a wall switch.)

- **Press all the reset buttons you can find.** Check your manual if you're not sure where the reset buttons are on your Mac. (Resetting the iMac is discussed specifically in Chapter 19.) You might have more than one power switch or reset button on your Mac; you might even have a reset button on the logic board, inside your Mac.

- **Undo what you just did.** If you've just installed RAM or an upgrade card, check it again and either reseat the upgrade (to make sure it's installed properly) or uninstall it completely and test to make sure your Mac can start up.

- **Test the keyboard.** Make sure your keyboard and mouse are connected, especially if you're trying to use the keyboard power key to start up the Mac. Unplug and replug your input devices.

- **Change the PRAM battery.** The PRAM battery is discussed later in the section "The Date and Time Get Wacky." If this battery is dead or dying, it might affect your ability to start up your Mac.

Most of the time, your Mac will turn on, lights will blink, and the power supply's fan (if it has one) will begin spinning, even if you're having some other catastrophic problem. If that's not the case (if you can't get the Mac to turn on at all), the problem might be with the power supply. If that's the case, you probably need to take your Mac in for service.

Is your Mac starting up but waiting for a few minutes before the Mac OS loads? If it's a newer, colorful Power Macintosh or iMac, your Startup Disk control panel might be accidentally set to a Network Disk. If that's the case, the Mac will search for two minutes or so before defaulting to a local disk for startup, after which it should start normally. Change the setting in the Startup Disk control panel if you'd like things to go a bit more quickly.

# You See the Sad Mac or Hear Death Chimes

If your Mac gets power but immediately decides that it's fundamentally unhappy, you hear strange chimes or see an unhappy (or dead, with *xs* for eyes) Mac on the screen. In that case, you have to take some steps to get it to load the Mac OS and move on.

## Death chimes

What are *death chimes?* If your Mac starts up and gets power but then chimes four or eight times or makes a sound like the Twilight Zone theme, a car crashing, or breaking glass, you've just heard death chimes.

If you hear a weird sound (not a series of tones), something went wrong when the Mac tried to start up — most likely it's whatever you just changed (RAM, expansion card, hard drive, and so on).

If the sounds are a series of tones, they might mean something more specific. Four tones, according to Apple, means something might be wrong with the hard drive. If you were recently messing with the drive, go back and make sure your SCSI ID, termination, and other settings are correct. (Or troubleshoot IDE, if that's the type of drive you have.)

If you didn't just change the drive, try booting from a Mac OS CD, diskette, or a Zip disk (or other removable disk) and then troubleshoot with a disk doctor program.

If you hear eight tones, that often indicates a memory problem. Check to make sure your memory is properly installed, especially if you were recently changing memory or if your Mac has been moved or dropped — memory might have been dislodged.

If you can't get past the tones, it's time to take the Mac in for service.

If you have an iMac or a blue Power Macintosh G3 or G4, the startup sounds have changed somewhat. See the section on beep codes in Chapter 25 for more details.

## Sad Mac

By Sad Mac, I mean this: The Mac powers up and gives the standard startup chord, but then a sad Mac face appears on the screen instead of a happy one.

Aside from knowing, in general, that your Mac isn't happy, seeing the Sad Mac icon might also give you an indication of the problem. The first thing to note is exactly *when* the Sad Mac icon appears:

 ✔ **Soon after startup.** When a Mac starts up, it self-tests the logic board components, ROM, ports, and system RAM. An early Sad Mac suggests a hardware or configuration problem.

 ✔ **After the Happy Mac or Welcome screens.** This is almost certainly a software problem. Troubleshoot for a conflict or Mac OS installation problem and look into the tips regarding a blinking question mark later in this chapter.

On many Mac models, the Sad Mac icon is generally accompanied by an error code. Sometimes the code includes an error number that you can use to track down the problem. The error number is in the following format:

```
xxxxyyyy
zzzzzzzz
```

Focus on the last four numbers of the first line (represented by *yyyy*). Table 23-1 offers a look at the codes and their meaning.

### Table 23-1    Common Sad Mac Codes and Their Meanings

| If the yyyy Code Number Is . . . | The Trouble Might Be . . . |
|---|---|
| 0001 | The Macintosh ROM |
| 0002, 0003, 0004, 0005 | A RAM module is bad or incorrectly installed |
| 0008 | An ADB port or device is bad and might need service |
| 000A | An expansion card or slot is bad and might need service |
| 000B | The SCSI controller needs repair |
| 000E | A memory module might be bad or the logic board might have a problem |
| 000F | Software problem |

If you're lucky, the problem is with a RAM module or an upgrade card that needs to be reseated; just open up the Mac and reinstall the problematic item. If you're getting a software error, try restarting from a Mac OS CD (or a disk doctor CD) and test the drive with a disk doctor program. If none of that works, you might need to get the Mac serviced.

# You See the Blinking X

If your Mac starts up and you see a small blinking X icon, it just means that the floppy in your floppy drive doesn't have a valid System Folder; you probably didn't mean to leave a floppy in the drive. It should be ejected automatically and your Mac will start up from the hard disk.

If you *did* want to start up from the diskette, the System Folder might not be valid. Try reinstalling it or use a disk doctor program to check the floppy. (If the floppy doesn't eject, you should be able to eject it with a straightened paper clip; look for a small eject hole near the drive opening.)

# You See the Blinking ?

If the Mac starts up and you hear the normal chime but then see a blinking ?, it means the Mac is having trouble finding a valid System Folder. Sometimes this will right itself after the Mac has a chance to check all available drives. If it persists, however, you need to figure out an alternative and get your Mac started up.

If your Mac shows the blinking ? but eventually manages to start up from the main hard disk, you probably have another disk configured as the startup disk in the Startup Disk control panel. Open the Startup Disk control panel and choose the correct disk for future restarts.

## Why the ? icon appears

The ? icon appears and persists because the Mac can't find a System Folder anywhere on an attached drive. Usually, you see the ? icon after something has changed: You've installed something, moved something around on the hard drive, or experienced a crash or other problem that affected the startup drive or your System Folder. If your system got hit by a power surge, for instance, or if you have did some spring cleaning your hard drive, installed a new drive, or had a bad crash, it might have triggered this response from the Mac.

Here are some of the typical causes for a blinking ? icon:

- **The Mac OS system software is missing or damaged.** This might be a result of corruption, an error, or a hardware problem with the drive.

- **Parameter RAM is corrupted.** The Mac stores the startup disk location in PRAM (described in the section "You Have Other Startup Problems: Zap PRAM"). If PRAM becomes corrupted, the Mac might have trouble finding the startup disk.

✔ **There is a SCSI problem.** If there's a SCSI conflict (a drive has the wrong ID or isn't properly terminated), the startup disk might not be easily found. This can be true even if the SCSI device is an external one.

✔ **The drive is misconfigured.** The driver software for the hard disk might be incorrect or corrupt or an IDE drive might not be properly configured as a master or slave, depending on its needs.

Performa and Power Macintosh models with IDE drives can experience problems with Drive Setup versions before Drive Setup 1.3.1. Upgrade to 1.3.1 or a later version to solve this problem. (You can get the update from `asu.info.apple.com` on the Web.) With the latest Drive Setup installed and launched, select Functions ➪ Update Driver.

✔ **The drive is damaged.** If the drive has failed or is encountering major disk structure problems (such as a damaged directory database), you see a ? icon because the System Folder on that drive is damaged or lost.

## What to do when the ? icon appears

After waiting to make sure that the ? icon doesn't resolve itself (because its Startup Disk control panel is misconfigured), move on to the next steps you can take to attempt to recover when your Mac can't find a startup disk. Here are some ideas:

✔ **Zap PRAM.** See the discussion in the section "You Have Other Startup Problems: Zap PRAM." This is where the startup disk location is stored; corruption in PRAM could be causing the problem.

✔ **Boot from another drive.** Restart or reset the Mac and hold down the ⌘+Option+Shift+Delete keys to bypass the internal drive. This might cause another System Folder to load on another of your drives. (In fact, if you happen to know the SCSI ID # of the drive you want to use, press the corresponding number key in addition to the preceding series of keys — that's five total!)

✔ **Boot from a CD-ROM.** Place a Mac OS CD-ROM in the CD-ROM drive and hold down the C key after the Mac restarts until you see evidence of the Mac OS booting. (If this works, move to the next section, "Check the drive.")

✔ **Check the SCSI chain.** If you can't boot from a CD, something might be misconfigured on your SCSI chain. Check the ID and termination settings of your internal and external drives; see Chapters 4, 11, and 17 for more.

### Check the drive

After you've started up from a CD or other external drive, you want to check your startup disk to see whether with the disk or the System Folder has a problem. First, you need to determine whether your disk icon appears on the desktop.

If you get to the desktop and the Finder ask you whether you'd like to erase (format) your internal hard disk, just say no! This indicates directory corruption, but it will be more difficult to recover completely if you format the drive.

If you get to the Finder and you can't find the icon for your disk, you have one of three problems:

- ✔ **Drive misconfiguration.** First, the drive might be misconfigured with a bad SCSI ID, an incorrect termination setting, a master/slave misconfiguration, or a bad hard disk driver. Troubleshoot these issues, especially if you've recently changed them (added a drive, added a device, or upgraded the hard disk drivers).

- ✔ **File damage.** If the disk's catalog database is heavily damaged, it might keep the drive from appearing on the desktop. A disk doctor program might help revive it, especially a disk doctor designed to recover damaged file systems, such as Alsoft's DiskWarrior (www.alsoft.com).

- ✔ **Physical problems.** In this case, the hard disk might be installed incorrectly (check the cable connections, making sure they're connected and not bent or frayed) or damaged (or other internal components might be damaged). Troubleshoot the drive and interface card, if you have one installed. Otherwise, the drive might need service.

### Test and bless the System Folder

If you get to the desktop and you do see the disk icon, things aren't all bad. You have either damage to the file system in general or a problem specific to the System Folder. In either case, you should probably run a disk doctor program first, to check the entire drive. After testing and fixing, you might be able to restart and begin working again.

If the Mac still can't start up from that drive, you can test to make sure that the System Folder is properly *blessed*. (If a System Folder is blessed, that simply means the Mac OS recognizes it as valid and capable of starting up the Mac.)

You can't have more than one blessed System Folder at once; if the unblessed folder is on the same disk volume as another blessed System Folder, that's your problem right there. See the sidebar on unblessing a System Folder.

Here's how to test the System Folder:

1. **Double-click the icon for the problematic disk.**

2. **Find System Folder and examine it.**

   If the icon has a small Macintosh icon as part of the folder icon, that System Folder is blessed (see Figure 23-1). If it isn't blessed, keep troubleshooting. If it's blessed, try restarting your Mac to see whether the Mac will start up properly.

3. **Open the System Folder and locate the file called System.**

   If it doesn't appear in the folder, use the Mac's Find or Sherlock command to locate the System file. If you still can't find System, you should reinstall the Mac OS (see Chapter 22).

4. **Double-click the System file.**

   If it doesn't open correctly, perform a clean install (or a replacement installation) of the Mac OS. Both are described in Chapter 22.

If the System file opens correctly, you should be able to re-bless the System Folder without installing anything additional. (You can go ahead and close the file.) Here's how to re-bless an otherwise working System Folder:

1. **Drag and drop the System file to the Mac's desktop.**

2. **Close the System Folder.**

3. **Reopen the System Folder and drag the System file back into the folder.**

4. **Close the System Folder again.**

Take a look at the System Folder's icon now. Does it show the little Mac as part of its icon? If so, the folder has been successfully re-blessed. (If not, you can try restarting, but there's likely a more serious corruption problem requiring a disk fix session or a clean install of the Mac OS.) Restart your Mac to see whether the System Folder takes hold and the Mac can restart from the drive. If it does, you should still run some check-up maintenance on the drive, as discussed in Chapter 21. If the Mac still doesn't start up properly, try a clean reinstall (or a replacement installation) as outlined in Chapter 22.

---

### Unblessing a System Folder

Having two active System Folders on a single startup disk can confuse the Mac. In this case, you should unbless one of the System Folders to avoid any further sibling rivalry.

To unbless one of the System Folders, drag the System and Finder files from that System Folder to another folder. (I like to use the Fonts subfolder within that same System Folder. Don't use the Extensions or Control Panels folder because the System Folder might remain blessed.) You should also rename the unblessed System Folder "Previous System Folder" or something similar.

---

# You Have Other Startup Problems: Zap PRAM

Parameter RAM is a small bit of RAM that can maintain a small amount of data even when the Mac is turned off, thanks to a special battery on the logic board. This RAM is used to store basic settings — startup drive locations, preferences, network settings, and the like. When PRAM gets corrupted, any number of things can happen; that's why zapping PRAM is a popular "magic" fix for various Mac ailments. Fortunately, zapping it doesn't hurt much — you might have to reset your clock, set your AppleTalk settings, and check a few other control panels.

To zap PRAM, hold down ⌘+Option+P+R immediately after you've heard your Mac's startup chime. If you're successful, you hear another startup chime; keep holding the keys down. After at least two more startup chimes (you can wait longer, if you like), release the keys and allow the Mac to startup. You see some differences: screen resolutions might change, the desktop might be rearranged slightly, or the clock might be set wrong. But you might also mysteriously fix your startup (or other) problems.

You can also use Micromat's TechTool freeware (see Chapter 24) to zap PRAM from software. The advantage is that it fully zaps PRAM and can save the contents, just in case you want to restore PRAM.

# The Date and Time Get Wacky

If your clock is suddenly wrong or your calendar is set to an odd year — 1904, 1956, 1980 — you might be having trouble with your PRAM battery. PRAM, discussed in the preceding section, requires a battery to maintain its stored settings. When the battery dies (usually after 2 to 5 years), the settings are no longer saved. The loss of other PRAM settings would also be symptoms of a dead battery.

The solution is to replace the battery. On most Mac models, you can do it yourself — open up the Mac and you see the battery on the logic board. You should be able to get a replacement from any Mac dealer.

# Icons and Aliases Get Dull

If your icons suddenly become generic looking or your aliases stop working, you might be having trouble with the desktop database. The solution is to rebuild the desktop. You can do that in one of two ways. You can launch Micromat's TechTool freeware and use the Rebuild Desktop command. Or start up the Mac and hold down ⌘+Option until the desktop appears and you get a message asking whether you want to rebuild the desktop.

# Out of Memory Errors Abound

If you're getting *Out of memory* errors when running programs, you might need to reconfigure your applications, run fewer applications, restart the Mac, or in chronic cases, install more RAM. In many cases, these errors occur because you have too many applications open in the background or you need to allocate more RAM for an individual application (see Chapter 15.) If you've recently updated your Mac OS version or applications, the best solution might be adding RAM — for Mac OS 9 and above, at least 64MB is recommended. See Chapter 15 for more on installing RAM.

# You Can't Eject or Alter a Disk

Have a disk on your desktop that you can't seem to get rid of? If you've tried dragging it to the desktop or using the File ➪ Put Away command in the Finder but it refused to go, it might be because you have File Sharing turned on. The Mac doesn't want to eject the disk while a network user might be trying to access it. So, turn off File Sharing and you can eject the disk.

If you can't change the name of a disk, it might also be because File Sharing is turned on. If you can't change the name of a *folder* on that disk, it might be that the Sharing settings for the disk are set so that you can't alter it. Select the disk and choose File ➪ Get Info in the Finder and then choose Sharing. If the Can't Move, Rename or Delete this Item option is checked, the folder is locked. You have to unlock the folder to rename or otherwise change it.

Finally, don't forget that you can't change anything about a CD-ROM, including the CD's name or folder names, and you can't delete any files from the CD-ROM.

# You Have Trouble with Microsoft Documents

Microsoft Office 4.2 or higher includes an interesting feature called Visual Basic for Applications, which allows users to add to documents and document templates their own *macros* — small programs that can be run from Word and Excel. Unfortunately, these macros can be used for evil as well as good — viruses have been written in Visual Basic for Applications.

If you have trouble opening, closing, saving, printing, or otherwise accessing documents in Word or Excel, a macro virus could be the problem. This is especially true if your documents are being saved as templates, if any menu commands disappear, or if you notice any sort of automatic behavior.

The solution is to immediately stop using the suspect documents and the Microsoft application until you've fixed the problem. Run a virus detection program (see Chapter 21) and head to Microsoft's Mac Office Web site (www.microsoft.com/macoffice/) for other fixes.

Need to get to work right away? Most viruses that attack Word do so through the Normal template. Quit Word, open the Templates folder (inside the Word folder) and drag the Normal template to the Trash. Restart Word but don't use any existing files. (Any or all of them might be infected; you need to run your virus detection software to find out.) You can, however, use Word to create new files in the interim.

# Chapter 24

# Ten Utilities for Snooping around Your Mac

*I*n this chapter, I briefly touch on some great, time-honored utilities that you should consider putting in your Mac troubleshooting toolbelt. Most of these are free downloads or low-cost *shareware* programs — programs you can download and use for a certain amount of time before you're required to pay for them if you find them useful.

Most any Mac utility can be found at `www.download.com` or `www.macdownload.com`. In addition, many software authors offer downloads directly from their own Web sites. Just point your browser in one of those directions and do a quick search to find most of these tools. Other tools (especially those from Apple) are included with the Mac OS or can be custom installed from the Mac OS CD, if necessary.

# TechTool Freeware

www.micromat.com

MicroMat, makers of TechTool Pro, offer a freeware version called just TechTool (or sometimes, TechTool freeware) with limited but very useful capabilities. TechTool allows you to fully zap PRAM and completely rebuild the desktop database from within an application instead of holding down keys at startup. The advantages are threefold.

First, there's no hit-or-miss with the timing of your keystrokes. Second, TechTool uses the most effective means possible to clear out PRAM and the desktop database so that no residual corruption can remain. Third, you can save the contents of either before doing the deeds, giving you an extra out in case some damage occurs.

Beyond those capabilities, TechTool can also do some basic diagnostic work on your Mac by estimating system file damage, performing routine floppy disk cleaning and creating detailed reports on your Mac's innards.

# Apple System Profiler

asu.info.apple.com

The Apple System Profiler, included (in increasingly newer versions) with Mac OS 7.6 and higher, offers a bevy of interesting facts about your Mac, including what hardware is connected, the amount and type(s) of memory installed, and how external devices are attached. Although its primary function is to help Apple technicians learn what they need to know to help you troubleshoot your system, it has the additional advantage of being great for troubleshooting upgrades and fixes.

If you're installing RAM, a hard disk, a SCSI device, or external items such as serial, FireWire, USB, or even networked devices, you can use the Apple System Profiler to check your progress and see whether the Mac is recognizing your additions. You can even quickly check the version number of drivers, the SCSI IDs assigned to devices, and much more.

Note that version 2.1.2 is available for download from Apple and is recommended for anyone running Mac OS 7.6 through 8.5. (A newer version is included with Mac OS 8.6 and 9.)

# Disk First Aid

asu.info.apple.com

If you're having any type of disk trouble — or if you just want to participate in a little preventative health care for your Mac's hard disks and other storage media — Disk First Aid is a good little partner to get to know. Fire up Disk First Aid at least monthly and have it look over your disks to catch any directory structure errors before they get out of hand. If Disk First Aid can fix the problem, it will. If it can't, at least you know it's time to pull out a commercial disk doctor program and get serious.

If you have Mac OS 8.1, consider updating to Disk First Aid 8.2, which can be downloaded from Apple. Newer versions of Disk First Aid are included with Mac OS 8.5 and higher.

# Drive Setup

asu.info.apple.com

Drive Setup is Apple's all-in-one drive formatting utility, designed to work with all Apple-branded hard drives (including those that are original equipment in Macs, even if they have another company's name on them). If you need to format, test, or partition your Apple hard drive and then back up your data completely, fire up Drive Setup.

You need a disk driver and proper formatting to use a disk at all. But why partition a disk? Two reasons. First, partitioning creates multiple *volumes*, each of which gets a disk icon on your desktop, even though you might have only one physical hard drive. You might find it useful to have more than one disk icon on your desktop for managing your files — you could have disk icons for documents, applications, and the Mac OS, for instance, each of which you can back up, erase, or share over a network separately.

Second, you can partition a Mac OS Standard formatted drive so that it uses available space more efficiently. Mac OS Standard disks begin to waste a considerable amount of space when they get over 1GB or 2GB; partitioning into smaller volumes can help minimize this waste. If you have Mac OS 8.1 or higher installed, though, the more efficient Mac OS Extended format is recommended.

Drive Setup has the additional perk of being able to format and install driver software for nearly any IDE drive made. So, if you've replaced your existing IDE drive (or, in a few cases, added one), you can use Drive Setup to install a drive and initialize it for its inaugural use. (If you replace your Apple SCSI hard drive with a new one, Apple recommends that you use a third-party formatting utility. That said, Drive Setup will work for many of them.)

If you use Mac OS 7.6 through 8.6, you can download an upgrade to Drive Setup 1.7.3. It fixes issues with older drivers; Apple recommends that you run Drive Setup 1.7.3 and update your hard disk drivers whenever you install or reinstall one of these OS versions. (Mac OS 9 and higher include even newer versions.)

## Disk Copy

asu.info.apple.com

Apple's Disk Copy utility enables you to create and mount *disk images*, or special files that act like removable disks. Disk Copy is how Apple distributes updates to the Mac OS and other downloadable updates. But you can use it, too, to create an image of any disk that you'd like to turn into a file.

What's the advantage? Here's one: Consider the iMac and Power Macintosh G3/G4, which don't include floppy drives. If you have floppy disks that you need to access, you can use an older Mac and Disk Copy to create images of those floppies. Then burn them on a CD, copy them to a Zip, or put them on the network. After they're copied to the iMac or G3/G4, double-clicking them launches the image and mounts it as if it were a disk that's been installed in an external drive. Plus, you can compress the disk image file itself, making it useful for archiving and sending the image across the Internet!

The latest version of Disk Copy is generally available from Apple's Web site; version 6.3.3 works with System 7.0.1 or later.

## Super Save

www.kamprath.net/claireware/

I swear by Super Save, a great little control panel that does two things for your Mac. First, it adds an auto-save capability to many applications that include such a command, allowing you to automatically save documents in a word processor or a similar application every few minutes, according to an option you set. Second, you can set Super Save to record *every* keystroke you type in certain applications, giving you another option if you have a system crash or your documents get corrupted. If you've lost data, you can open the

Super Save text document and recover your actual keystrokes. Recovery can be a bit messy — because the software records every typo, backspace, and other odd characters — but it's a nice last-ditch way to recover items you've typed.

This is shareware, with an asking price of $10. Like many shareware offerings, it's a great price for a nice little helper.

# Conflict Catcher

www.casadyg.com

Although not shareware or freeware, Conflict Catcher is the sort of ally you'd like to have on your hard disk if you ever need to troubleshoot an extension conflict. Plus, Conflict Catcher helps you manage your extensions using far more sophisticated tools than those offered by the Mac OS Extension Manager. It's a bit costly (currently around $80), but if you're a serious power troubleshooter, you need this one in your arsenal. (See Chapter 20 for more details on Conflict Catcher.) You can download a limited demo version of Conflict Catcher from their Web site.

# Extension Overload

www.extensionoverload.com

Extension Overload, a substitute for the Extensions Manager, digs into your System Folder, allowing you to manage your extensions and control panels (turning them on and off). Its real strength, though, is the database of information it has about 2400 extensions and control panels, detailing known conflicts, tips for optimization, and other helpful advice. Plus, you can search its database for information on other extensions and control panels that aren't currently installed on your Mac, look up error codes for their specific meanings, and create detailed reports of the startup items that are installed on your Mac. The program is shareware; registration is $20 for a single license.

# ramBunctious

www.clarkwoodsoftware/rambunctious/

If you're getting serious about using a RAM disk, ramBunctious is another good add-on. This one offers more flexibility than Apple's built-in RAM disk feature, including support for more than one RAM disk and the capability to automatically save contents to the hard disk at regular intervals. You can also save multiple RAM disk images and switch between them as desired. The software is fully AppleScriptable, allowing you to mount and eject RAM disks using AppleScript commands. The ramBunctious shareware is $12 and the downloadable version is full-featured.

# GURU

www.newerram.com

GURU is a freeware utility from NewerRam that might help to sell their RAM upgrades, but it's still a great resource for anyone interested in how and why to upgrade their Mac's RAM. The software includes specifications for nearly every Mac model and most Mac OS clones, including diagrams that show how to optimize RAM installation. You'll find other tidbits, too, such as information on VRAM upgrades and even the occasional factoid about other expansion options.

# Chapter 25

# Ten Special iMac and Power Mac G3 and G4 Fixes

*T*he iMac, the blue Power Macintosh G3, and the Power Macintosh G4 are slightly different beasts from earlier Mac models, thanks to their unique logic board designs and their support for the latest Apple technologies. In this chapter, take a look at some of the special upgrading issues you'll encounter with the latest, most colorful Macs.

## Firmware Updates

Not only do iMac and colorful Power Macs offer only USB and FireWire upgrading, but they also share some logic board design issues. These machines are designed using the Unified Motherboard Architecture (UMA), an approach that offers some logic board advances as well as time-to-market advantages for Apple.

For users, UMA manifests in the unique upgrading for these Macs. The logic board and other internal components can be upgraded through *firmware* updates, which can alter fundamental instructions for various components such as the CD or DVD drive, the USB controller, or the operation of the Mac in general.

You'll find numerous updates for the iMac and Power Macintosh G3 and G4 that change everything from modem behavior to the video card and the spinning of the CD-ROM drive. Check each machine's page on the Apple Support site (www.apple.com/support/) to see what updates are available and appropriate for your Mac.

# Telling Newer Macs Apart

For marketing reasons, Apple has tended over the past few years to name their computers the same thing, even in subsequent revisions. When you're trying to troubleshoot and get answers, it's incredibly important to know exactly which iMac or Power Mac model you're talking about. Table 25-1 shows the names that Apple uses in its Tech Info Library (til.info.apple.com) when referring to those machines.

| Table 25-1 | Tech Info Names for Newer Macs | |
|---|---|---|
| *Tech Info Name* | *Other Names for That Model* | *Significance* |
| iMac | iMac 233, 266, 333 | Offers Rage II or Rage Pro graphics, single-channel USB bus |
| iMac (slot-loading) | iMac 350, iMac DV, iMac DV SE | Rage 128 graphics, FireWire and DVD (DV models), dual-channel USB bus, Ultra ATA drive |
| Power Macintosh G3 or Power Macintosh G3 (platinum) | Beige G3 | Built-in video, internal and external SCSI connectors |
| Power Macintosh G3 (blue and white) | Blue G3s | ATI Rage 128 graphics, one USB bus, Ultra ATA drive |
| Power Macintosh G4 (PCI) | Yosemite G4 | (Based on G3 logic board), PCI graphics card, Ultra ATA drive |
| Power Macintosh G4 (AGP) | Sawtooth G4 | 2x AGP graphics port; dual-channel USB, ATA/66 drive |

# Beep Codes

The original iMac, the Power Macintosh G3, and the Power Macintosh G4 (PCI Graphics) offer beep codes at startup time that differ from earlier Mac models. These codes alert you to a component that failed the startup test. Table 25-2 shows the beep codes and meanings.

| Table 25-2 | Beep Codes and Their Meanings |
|---|---|
| *Number of Beeps* | *Meaning* |
| One | RAM not installed correctly or not detected |
| Two | RAM type not supported |
| Three | None of the RAM banks passed the memory test |
| Four | Boot ROM failed test |
| Five | Boot sector of boot ROM failed test |

The Power Macintosh G4 and slot-loading iMac offer similar beep codes, except five beeps mean the processor is unusable. If you hear one beep or three beeps (the RAM beep codes), try reseating your RAM modules. If you hear two beeps, replace the RAM with a compatible type. If you hear beep codes after installing a processor upgrade, you should troubleshoot it, too. Otherwise, you might have to take your machine to an authorized service center.

Apple notes a special problem with some Power Macintosh G3 and G4 models. If you get a beep-tone error when starting up with an external, powered USB device connected to the Mac, try disconnecting the USB device and restarting. If you don't get the same beep-tone error, your Mac might have shipped with a faulty batch of RAM. (If you *do* get the beep tone, it's indicating some other problem.) Apple recommends taking your Mac to an authorized service center to see whether the RAM needs to be replaced; in the meantime, the Mac should start up fine if you unplug the powered USB device.

# Mac Won't Restart

If you're having trouble getting a USB-based Mac to restart (it shuts down instead), you might have a problem with an external USB device. Remove all USB devices and then add them one by one, restarting each time. When it shuts down instead of restarting, you've identified the problem device. Make sure you have all Apple USB-related firmware updates and contact the device manufacturer to see whether they have updated drivers or instructions.

# Noisy CDs and Stuck Screens

The earlier iMac models exhibited two behaviors that worried users: The CD sometimes seemed violently noisy and the screen sometimes froze for up to ten seconds. Both were related to the CD mechanism and both were addressed by an iMac CD Update (currently iMac CD Update 2.0), a firmware updater that's downloadable from Apple's Support site.

# Disc Gets Stuck

Having trouble with a CD or a DVD? Assuming that you've dragged the disc's icon to the Trash and it didn't pop out, you can look to a manual solution.

If you need to manually eject a disk from a G3 or a G4, use a fingernail to get the CD or DVD door to open from the top. With the door open, you should see a small hole underneath the tray on the drive (probably close to the eject button). After trying the eject button, straighten a paper clip and stick it in that hole until the tray pops out.

On the iMac, look for a small paper clip hole on the far-right side of the drive in both models. That hole can also accept a straightened paper clip to eject a stuck disc.

 If the Mac is powered off, don't attempt to eject the CD or DVD manually. Instead, power on the Mac and press the eject button on the drive immediately after startup. (On a slot-loading iMac, hold down the mouse button after startup until the disc ejects.)

# Adjusting the Monitor

Many newer Macs (and all iMacs) use software controls to adjust the Mac's screen image and other settings. Open the Monitors & Sound or Monitors control panel and look for a Geometry option. There you can set various characteristics about the screen.

The Power Macintosh G3 has a known issue that causes it to report incorrect screen resolutions when attached to certain monitors. To see all available resolutions in the control strip, hold down the Control button while accessing the resolution control strip module.

# DVD Synchronization

iMac DV and Power Macintosh G4 models use software to play back DVD video, and that software tends to tax the processor. If you have problems with the audio-video synchronization on your iMac (or any DVD-equipped Mac), you should take a few steps. First, make sure you've installed any DVD updates issued by Apple. Then you should avoid running other applications (or other automatic behavior) on your Mac while a DVD video is being shown. You should also turn off virtual memory (see Chapter 15), if you can.

Chapter 20 discusses creating different sets of extensions for different applications; you might consider a minimal extension set and no startup items running in the background for best DVD movie playback.

# Speed Up Your G4

The PowerPC G4 gets most of its speedup from a new set of instructions, called the Velocity Engine (or AltiVec), which improves the speeds at which many multimedia tasks are accomplished. The trick is, software must be updated to take advantage of the Velocity Engine. Although Mac OS X is written to take full advantage of it, Mac OS 9 and its progeny rely on software patches for your applications to really show the speed. If you have Adobe PhotoShop or a similar high-end application, look for special updaters from the respective companies.

# Select a Startup Disk

All colorful Macs have been designed with *NetBoot* in mind, meaning they're capable of starting up and getting all the necessary Mac OS code from a network connection. This can also be a cause of a major slowdown for iMac, Power Macintosh G3, and Power Macintosh G4 machines.

If your Mac is set to boot from a network volume in the Startup Disk control panel (or in some cases, if it isn't specifically set to your main startup disk), your Mac might be delayed at startup. It can take two minutes or more before the Mac will stop looking for a network startup volume and start up from the internal drive or a CD. If you notice that your Mac seems frozen at startup, wait a few minutes to make sure it doesn't eventually start up. If it does, you know that Startup Disk is set incorrectly; open the control panel and select your internal disk.

If you want to specify the drive to use for starting up your Power Macintosh G4 or slot-loading iMac, just hold down the Option key after hearing the startup tone. You'll see the new Startup Manager, where you can choose the icon associated with the drive you'd like to use to start up the Mac.

# Index

# WWW.DUMMIES.COM

## Discover Dummies Online!

The Dummies Web Site is your fun and friendly online resource for the latest information about *For Dummies®* books and your favorite topics. The Web site is the place to communicate with us, exchange ideas with other *For Dummies* readers, chat with authors, and have fun!

## Ten Fun and Useful Things You Can Do at www.dummies.com

1. Win free *For Dummies* books and more!
2. Register your book and be entered in a prize drawing.
3. Meet your favorite authors through the IDG Books Worldwide Author Chat Series.
4. Exchange helpful information with other *For Dummies* readers.
5. Discover other great *For Dummies* books you must have!
6. Purchase Dummieswear® exclusively from our Web site.
7. Buy *For Dummies* books online.
8. Talk to us. Make comments, ask questions, get answers!
9. Download free software.
10. Find additional useful resources from authors.

Link directly to these ten fun and useful things at **http://www.dummies.com/10useful**

For other technology titles from IDG Books Worldwide, go to
www.idgbooks.com

Not on the Web yet? It's easy to get started with *Dummies 101®: The Internet For Windows® 98* or *The Internet For Dummies®* at local retailers everywhere.

Find other *For Dummies* books on these topics:

Business • Career • Databases • Food & Beverage • Games • Gardening • Graphics • Hardware
Health & Fitness • Internet and the World Wide Web • Networking • Office Suites
Operating Systems • Personal Finance • Pets • Programming • Recreation • Sports
Spreadsheets • Teacher Resources • Test Prep • Word Processing

# IDG BOOKS WORLDWIDE BOOK REGISTRATION

**Register This Book and Win!**

## We want to hear from you!

Visit **http://my2cents.dummies.com** to register this book and tell us how you liked it!

- ✔ Get entered in our monthly prize giveaway.

- ✔ Give us feedback about this book — tell us what you like best, what you like least, or maybe what you'd like to ask the author and us to change!

- ✔ Let us know any other *For Dummies*® topics that interest you.

Your feedback helps us determine what books to publish, tells us what coverage to add as we revise our books, and lets us know whether we're meeting your needs as a *For Dummies* reader. You're our most valuable resource, and what you have to say is important to us!

Not on the Web yet? It's easy to get started with *Dummies 101*®: *The Internet For Windows*® *98* or *The Internet For Dummies*® at local retailers everywhere.

Or let us know what you think by sending us a letter at the following address:

*For Dummies* Book Registration
Dummies Press
10475 Crosspoint Blvd.
Indianapolis, IN 46256

**...FOR DUMMIES™**

**BESTSELLING BOOK SERIES**